RENEWALS 458-4574
DATE DUE

WITHDRAWN
UTSA LIBRARIES

The Making of Global City Regions

Johns Hopkins Studies in Globalization

Christopher Chase-Dunn, *Series Editor*

Consulting editors: Volker Bornschier, Christine Gailey, Walter L. Goldfrank, Su-Hoon Lee, William R. Thompson, Immanuel Wallerstein, and David Wilkinson

The Making of Global City Regions
Johannesburg, Mumbai/Bombay, São Paulo, and Shanghai

Edited by Klaus Segbers
*With the assistance of Simon Raiser
and Krister Volkmann*

The Johns Hopkins University Press
Baltimore

© 2007 The Johns Hopkins University Press
All rights reserved. Published 2007
Printed in the United States of America on acid-free paper
9 8 7 6 5 4 3 2 1

The Johns Hopkins University Press
2715 North Charles Street
Baltimore, Maryland 21218-4363
www.press.jhu.edu

Library of Congress Cataloging-in-Publication Data

The making of global city regions : Johannesburg, Mumbai/
Bombay, São Paulo, and Shanghai / edited by Klaus Segbers,
with the assistance of Simon Raiser and Krister Volkmann.
 p. cm. — (Johns Hopkins studies in globalization)
 Includes bibliographical references and index.
 ISBN-13: 978-0-8018-8515-0 (hardcover : alk. paper)
 ISBN-10: 0-8018-8515-9 (hardcover : alk. paper)
 1. Cities and towns—Case studies. 2. Globalization.
I. Segbers, Klaus. II. Raiser, Simon. III. Volkmann, Krister.
HT151.M346 2007
307.76—dc22   2006019752

A catalog record for this book is available from the British Library.

Contents

List of Figures and Tables   vii
Acknowledgments   ix

1. Introduction: Global Politics and the Making of Global City Regions   1
   Klaus Segbers

2. City Regions between Their Legacies and the Global Context   27
   Johannesburg: (South) Africa's Aspirant Global City   32
   Alan Mabin
   Mumbai: The Mega-City of a Poor Country   64
   Sujata Patel
   São Paulo: The Metropolis of an Elite Society   85
   Csaba Deák and Sueli Schiffer
   Shanghai: The Evolution of China's Future Global City   113
   Weiping Wu

3. Who Runs the City? The "Makers" of Global City Regions   135
   Politics of Transformation: Defining the City Strategy in Johannesburg   139
   Susan Parnell
   Formal and Informal Structures of Power in Mumbai   168
   Jim Masselos

Legitimating Power Structures in São Paulo   186
Sueli Schiffer and Csaba Deák

From "State-Owned" to "City Inc.": The Case of Shanghai   207
Fulong Wu

4. Contested Future: Discourses and Images in City Regions   233

   The Discourse of Governance in Post-Apartheid Johannesburg   237
   Robert A. Beauregard and Richard Tomlinson

   Versions of a Postcolonial Metropolis: Competing Discourses on Bombay's Image   258
   Ranjit Hoskote

   Two Cities in One: Diverse Images of São Paulo   279
   Pedro Jacobi

   Shaping Perceptions of Shanghai: Discourses, Images, and Visions   295
   Zhongxin Sun

5. Comments by Senior Officials   317

   Johannesburg   319
   Roland Hunter

   Mumbai/Bombay   323
   Vidyadhar K. Phatak

   São Paulo   329
   Jorge Wilheim

   Shanghai   335
   Zhu Linchu

6. Conclusion: Challenges Ahead for the Southern Contenders   339
   Simon Raiser and Krister Volkmann

List of Contributors   357
Index   361

Figures and Tables

Figures

Global network connectivity of African cities   14
Global network connectivity of South Asian cities   14
Global network connectivity of South American cities   15
Global network connectivity of East Asian cities   15
The changing local government boundaries of Johannesburg   41
Mumbai Metropolitan Region   67
Urbanization at the core of Mercosul   86
The overall structure of São Paulo   87
Main directions of the *bandeiras*, São Paulo   89
The main road and Metro structure of São Paulo   94
A Metro network for São Paulo   95
The thirty-nine boroughs of legal São Paulo Metropolitan Region   105
The Latin crescent in Mercosul   109
Shanghai metropolitan area   117
Brazil: metropolitan regions. Share of spending on public services in household income (1996–2002)   191
GDP per capita in comparison to nation   342

Tables

Incoming and outgoing airport cargo and passengers, 2002/3   17
Size and population in the four selected city regions, 2001–3   28
Summary statistics for the City of Johannesburg   43
Occupational distribution of employment by sector, Johannesburg 1996   46

Poor housing in Johannesburg   47
Economic output by sectors   51
Government spending as share of GNP, 1880–1985:
   Selected countries   99
Greater São Paulo, 1992–2002: Length of traffic bottlenecks in rush
   hours   102
Income distribution in São Paulo state, Brazil, and selected countries,
   1999   104
Built floor space by building type in São Paulo municipality, 1985,
   1990, 1995, and 2000   107
Key indicators of Metropolitan Shanghai, 1990–2001   118
Share of Shanghai in the nation, 1990–2001   118
Phases of the City Development Strategy process in
   Johannesburg   144
Selected content items in Joburg 2030 changed by the Mayoral
   Committee   158
Political supporters and shifting focus within the Joburg CDS   160
Growth of foreign capital and direct investment in Shanghai,
   1980–2001   218
The source of foreign direct investment in Shanghai, 2001   219
The distribution of foreign direct investment by economic sectors,
   2001   220
The number of households relocated and property floor space
   demolished, 1995–2001   227

Acknowledgments

This book is the product of a research project that was conducted at the Freie Universitaet Berlin and funded by Volkswagenstiftung (Volkswagen Foundation).

I am grateful to everyone who helped to make this book possible. I thank, first of all, my two colleagues, Simon Raiser and Krister Volkmann, who did more for the project than anyone else, and, of course, Peter Haegel, with whom I developed the initial idea of the project. For a short period of time, we also benefited from the input of Kristina Pezzei as a research fellow.

There were many student assistants whose contributions were valuable beyond their immediate tasks: above all, Christina Cathey Schuetz, who provided background information for the countries involved, wrote most of the texts for the project homepage, and expertly coordinated the project conference in Berlin in the summer of 2003.

Melanie Fasche prepared a helpful Powerpoint-project introduction. She, Cosima Strasser, and Mundo Yang helped us with the searching, generation, and compilation of relevant data on the city regions (a sometimes daunting challenge, in light of the lack of data for some of the city regions). Christina Cathey Schuetz and Johannes von Weizsaecker took care of the language editing. Bartosz Penczek designed the project homepage and was an indispensable assistant for technology-related questions. Jens Giersdorf and Cosima Strasser assisted in the search for literature. Gregor Herse compiled some of the maps. Julia Leininger did a great job as editor. Tobias Wegenast and Conny Beyer were involved in different phases of the project, as were Eva Bretschneider and Henry Rauscher.

For valuable comments on draft versions of the papers, I am most grateful to Anne Haila (University of Helsinki) and Frank Eckardt (Weimar University).

We are obliged to many people for their enlightening guidance and for their stimulating, sometimes puzzling insights into the functioning of the respective city regions:

In Johannesburg: Jerry Maryobone, who guided us through Soweto and Alexandra; Carmel Joseph, knowledge specialist at the Visitors and Resource Centre of the City of Johannesburg, who organized high-level meetings with the following city officials: Roland Hunter (executive director: finance), Vinod Singh (project manager: Joburg 2030), Anthony Still (Joburg Water), David van Niekerk (Corporate Planning Unit), Kubeshni Govender (director of the Visitors and Resource Centre), John A. Singh (specialist for Municipal International Relations), Prem Govender (Contract Management Unit), and Elwyn Pelser (Joburg Metropolitan Police Department); and Johannes Dietrich, foreign correspondent, who shared with us his valuable impressions about the city.

In Mumbai/Bombay: Lajwanti D'souza, chief reporter of the newspaper *Mid-Day*, for guiding us patiently and sensitively through a chaotic city; Rahul Mehrotra, the executive director of the Urban Design Research Institute, for very instructive meetings and additional material on Bombay; Ilija Trojanow, a freelance journalist, who provided us with valuable insights into the current discourses in the city, including a fascinating (and disturbing) meeting with a group of young Mederesse Koran students; S. S. Bhandare, chief executive officer of Bombay First; Rahul Srivastava and Shekhar Krishnan from PUKAR (Partners for Urban Knowledge Action and Research); and the Maharashtra Economic Development Council.

In São Paulo: Jorge Wilheim, director of the Municipal Urban Planning Department, for a good discussion and an excursion to the city center; Christiane Henkel, foreign correspondent, for interesting perspectives; Argelina Cheibub Figueiredo, director of the Center of Metropolitan Studies (CEM), for important contacts; Professors Regina Meyer and Martha Grostein, faculty for Urban Studies and Architecture (FAU) at the University of São Paulo, for sharing their views; EMPLASA, the planning institution for the São Paulo Metropolitan Region, which provided us with material, data, and the opportunity for extensive discussions; and Antonio José Zagatto, executive of *Viva o Centro*, an organization for the revitalization of the city center of São Paulo.

In Shanghai: Allie Yang, who organized a large part of our meetings and without whose translations we would have gotten lost in the city; Gerald Chungu, interior design architect, who vividly shared his multifaceted impressions of the city; Professor Bao Zhongao, East China University of Science and Technology, who was so kind to take us to the countryside; Knut Dethlefsen, from the Friedrich Ebert Foundation; Fons Tuinstra, from the Dutch News Agency Shanghai, and Janis Vougioukas, foreign correspondent, for their amazing insights; Bernd Reitmeier, deputy chief representative of the Delegation of German Industry and Commerce Shanghai, for his encouraging comments and data suggestions; Professors Zhou Minkai and Yang Ye, East China Normal University, for sharing their profound knowledge; and Professor Gang Zeng, East China Normal University, for providing many contacts.

In Hong Kong: Professor Leslie Lu, Deputy Head Department of Architecture, University of Hong Kong, and Professor Stephen Lau, Associate Dean, Department of Architecture, University of Hong Kong, and Oliver Mueller, foreign correspondent, for interesting insights into the competition between Shanghai and Hong Kong.

In addition, I would like to thank the respective program coordinators of the Goethe Institutes, the German Cultural Institutes in foreign countries, in Shanghai, Johannesburg, and São Paulo for their help in organizing public project presentations: Andreas Schiekofer, Nikolai Petersen, and Joachim Bernauer.

Students of a seminar at Free University Berlin, held in the summer of 2003, gave us the background for project-related discussions. Some good ideas for the publication stem from these sessions.

Finally, thanks to Peter Taylor for providing important data on the cities from the Globalization and World Cities (GaWC) network.

The Making of Global City Regions

1 | Introduction
Global Politics and the Making of Global City Regions
Klaus Segbers

Thus far, projects and books on (global) city regions, especially on city regions in the south, have been rare.[1] This book seeks to fill the gap. It also attempts to portray the strategies of city region elites who have to cope with two processes simultaneously: globalization and the ongoing devolution of the state. Both trends present challenges as well as opportunities. The book analyzes several questions with respect to four selected city regions: Johannesburg, Mumbai/Bombay,[2] São Paulo, and Shanghai. This enables the reader to look at the same question from four different regional perspectives. The same set of cities will be revisited from different scientific angles, reflecting the existing contradictions and disjunctures of any city. Thus the analytical structure of this volume allows a much broader approach to the selected cities than can be found in previously existing literature.

When they are compared to each another, the concrete problem-solving strategies of the city regions are as diverse as the city regions themselves. After all, their elites must come to terms with different local legacies, resources, and national contexts. However, the four cases presented here all share the goals of reaching beyond the status quo, improving their present condition, and thus coping with changing realities. The growing importance of the global level at the expense of the national level is not just being experienced, accepted, or denied. City regions are endeavoring to shape their own future and are succeeding in doing so, at least to some extent.

While it is obvious that many factors influence city regions and the countries in which they are located, the city regions share one characteristic: not one of them functions as a unitary actor. Different groups of actors are simultaneously trying to exert control over the developments affecting their respective city regions.

In addition to an introduction and a conclusion, the book offers four chapters, each comprising four essays. Chapters 2, 3, and 4 provide a general introduction to the city regions, analytical sketches of the relevant actors involved in city development, and essays on dominant and competing discourses in the four cities that consider how to encourage further urban development. In chapter 5, there are four essays that include brief comments by senior officials from the four city regions, which provide interesting additional perspectives from inside city administration.

In this introduction, I begin by offering a framework for the following, more detailed essays. I situate the studies first within the context of substantial change currently occurring in global politics (a field formerly referred to as international relations). Second, I identify global cities, or city regions, as a suitable field for analysis within this framework and then point out the rationale behind selecting the four regions explored in this book. Finally, I outline the basic research task and briefly discuss some of the findings (a more in-depth summary of which is contained in the conclusion).

How to Situate City Regions in the Global Political Architecture

The Traditional Structure of World Politics

We are living in a time of a quickly changing configuration of world politics. So it may be useful to look back briefly at the traditional landscape of international relations. For more than 300 years, this landscape was dominated by nation-states and by their governments and leaders. For most of the time, these units acted in and through coalitions, trying to balance power. For half a century after World War II, this model of shifting coalitions was replaced by a stable bipolar macrostructure. Both these configurations now appear to be more or less redundant, and instead we are experiencing the rapid development of a multilevel and multiactor global landscape whose underlying concepts we are yet to comprehend fully.

After the end of the Thirty Years' War (1648), a new concept of foreign affairs, a new concert of powers, and new rules for the international game were established. Concepts like sovereignty and territoriality were embraced. The modern nation-state appeared as the main agent for developing national economies, protecting citizens against intruders and businesses against foreign competitors, providing public goods, and enforcing homogeneous cultural spaces. This configuration was rather effective and has had a devoted following ever since. Collecting taxes, standardizing educational systems, and organizing armed forces became the main internal function of governments. This so-called Westphalian system prevailed for many centuries, and some believe—mistakenly—that it is alive even today.

At the end of World War II a new macrostructure evolved in which two major powers dominated the world. Both defended their respective blocs and were centered on two poles. The first part of the world, led by the United States, was driven by basically market-regulated mechanisms, was organized in formal democracies, and generated increasing wealth for the "developed" parts of the world. The second was a group of states led by the USSR, driven by an extensive growth model, organized in formal one-party systems, reproducing itself by administrative markets and all-encompassing bargaining mechanisms, and creating basic social services on a rather low level.

This period was characterized by a binary code, notwithstanding attempts to defect from this logic by some elites and countries in the "Third World" and by political movements in the heartland of the two blocs.

This international macrostructure was surprisingly stable, though many participants and observers of the Cold War perceived it as rather dangerous and risky. From the perspective of game theory, the relative higher stability of bipolar games can be explained.[3] In addition to the stability-enhancing bipolar structure itself, the growing role of international institutions also increased certainty and predictability, at least to a certain extent. Organizations and regimes like the Bretton Woods system with the World Bank and the International Monetary Fund (IMF), the United Nations and its Security Council, the mechanisms of the Conference for Security and Co-operation in Europe and the Organization for Security and Co-operation in Europe, arms control and trade regimes, and, more recently, norms for preserving the environment and supporting human rights all contributed to a growing texture of global politics, even though a system of predictable and reliable all-encompassing stability was never achieved.

The New Context of Global Politics

Westphalian and Cold War language still dominates most private and public discourses on world politics. Media coverage of global politics is saturated with reports on the activities of diplomats, and "foreign policy" language is still *en vogue*. States are seen as the prevalent actors, defending sovereignty and territory. Yet this type of language is no longer linked to a context it can sufficiently and productively describe. The macrostructure has changed too significantly. The Cold War system with its dominant binary code is in a process of deep transformation and has, to some degree, already been overcome. The Westphalian system is, for the most part, history.

The changing role of states has been subject to debate in international relations. States have traditionally been the main "unit of analysis." By questioning their dominant role in world politics, many theoretical approaches lose their foundation. Thus, it is not surprising that some researchers continue to view the state as the most relevant actor in international relations (e.g., Hirst and Thompson 1996; Waltz 2001).[4]

However, this introduction and most contributions to this book maintain that states and governments no longer dominate most processes of global politics (for similar arguments, see Robinson 1998; Strange 1996; Ohmae 1995; Taylor 1996). Governments still may be in charge, at least formally, but they obviously are not in control. Interactions in the global landscape today may be described rather in terms of flows of capital, communications, entertainment, goods, services and people rather than in terms of organized exchanges (see Appadurai 1997; Castells 1996). One can hardly describe national governments as being suited to control these multifaceted flows effectively. The black-boxed container states are still around, and their traditional representatives engage in all kinds of negotiations. But the containers themselves have lost many or most of their attributes.

Neither this book nor this introduction addresses the dynamics and effects of globalization separately because there is already sufficient literature on this subject (e.g., Albrow 1996; Scholte 2000; Baylis and Smith 2001; Held et al. 1999; Dicken 2003). In our understanding, globalization is a highly contested concept with many connotations and meanings. For the purpose of this book we understand globalization as a process fueled by the worldwide interplay of increasingly dense flows in capital and communications, driven by new technologies. These flows connect (and disconnect) countries, societies, cities, firms, and individuals. While perceptions and interpretations of these trends differ, as well as capabilities to cope with them, it is becoming ever more difficult, if not impossible, to opt out. Globalization apparently is all-encompassing.

Furthermore, the currency of politics has changed. Military power still matters sometimes, as was demonstrated recently by the U.S.-led campaign against Iraq in 2003 and Western measures against Yugoslavia in the 1990s. Yet this is hardly the only, or most adequate and appropriate, tool by which main players can achieve their goals in global times. The same examples, especially Iraq in 2004, reveal the limits of traditional hard power and "preemptive thinking."

First, transnational capital flows are often more relevant than national budgets. Second, new cultural images and discourses are challenging traditional national cultures. Strategies of access and denial as well as of inclusion and exclusion are thereby becoming as important as guarding national borders. In this environment, a revised cartography of global politics, power, and access is urgently needed, as new methods for spreading influence and dominating the knots of networks are emerging rapidly. Influencing nodes and hubs of flows, cascades of power tools, and new centralities of patchworks is nowadays at least as important as conquering the capitals of states and controlling natural resources. Stalin's dismissive question in which he demanded to know how many divisions the pope has made now seems outdated. What matters is influence in and over rating agencies, content producers, and images.

The following list compiles five characteristic attributes of global politics within the new international and transnational context:

1. There are many more relevant actors in global politics than at any time before. These actors have ties to the state, the market, and society. The main political cleavages are public versus private, and state versus nonstate. States continue to play an important role as regulators and the addressees of public expectations. Yet this role is diminishing and changing. State actors interact and at times compete with a multitude of supranational and nonstate actors, such as international organizations, international regimes, transnational corporations, nongovernmental organizations, regional players (supra- and substate), city regions, cities, the media, domestic structures and interests, and powerful individuals who are active in the realm of global politics.
2. Today's game of global politics is a multilevel game. Individual acts, in-

teractions between actors, and various types of flow occur and have effects on different levels simultaneously, including global, supranational, international, transnational, national, regional, local (like city regions), and societal levels, as well as at the level of individuals.
3. While the playground of world politics is becoming much more colorful, the relative strength of different groups of players is shifting, depending on the game as well as on the hard and soft resources available to the players. The decisive power currencies are much more diverse than the concept of the military as the mere core of hard power. Asymmetries between those very diverse actors are sometimes extreme—the relation between Al Qaeda und the United States or between Falun Gong and the Chinese authorities are only two examples.
4. Clearly delineated boundaries between the domestic and the external spheres of politics no longer exist. The global environment sometimes impacts domestic constellations significantly. In turn, domestic structures and coalitions produce significant changes in the transnational landscape. Today, formerly sophisticated-sounding concepts like the second image reversed (Gourevitch 1978), two-level games (Putnam 1988), and the internationalization of domestic politics look outdated. The problem does not so much lie with linkages between the domestic and international spheres as it does with disappearing markers between the two realms.
5. The nature of interactions is increasingly difficult to monitor, control, and govern. Diplomats may talk a lot, but their effect on capital markets is limited, to say the least. The impact of satellites transmitting content into different cultural settings can hardly be predicted and is also difficult to regulate. On the whole, capital and content flows are difficult to organize and cannot be regulated effectively, at least not by traditional instruments and strategies inherited from the Westphalian and Cold War settings. This inability means that the very concept of regulation and control is in crisis. Regulation requires a clear understanding of the relevant players' interests and resources, effective monitoring mechanisms, sufficient funding, tools for shaping the behavior of the actors involved, incentives inducing relevant actors to accept the foreseen governance mechanisms, and more. But, above all, regulation requires an overall conception of what should be regulated in what manner. These circumstances limit governance capability not only for countries but also for cities.

Today's reality consists of a patchwork of coexisting and competing norms, tools, and governance systems. As such, the term *governance* is in crisis. The time is ripe to think about concepts more appropriate to the early twenty-first century and then to build on metaphors of moderating and navigating. To moderate processes is not to try to change the direction of these processes, but to influence their intensity and the tempo of their development. To navigate trends and currents is even less of an engineering concept. Rather, when navigating, one tries to move within the confines or between the currents of existing processes whose sources and intensity are beyond one's own control.

Global City Regions as Actors in the New Global Context

When analyzing global city regions as new actors in global politics, it may be important to recall that world cities already existed in the late medieval and early modern period, long before the signing of the Treaty of Westphalia (Friedrichs 1995; Tilly and Brockmans 1994). Examples include the commercial centers of northern Italy and the Low Countries, as well as some cities of the Hanseatic League. These cosmopolitan metropolises spurred the exchange of goods, people, and cultures from different parts of the world. For a long time, they enjoyed a high degree of autonomy. Eventually, however, the cities had to acknowledge the reality of growing state power. Once incorporated into the state structure, cities were granted privileges and freedoms in order to stimulate their economic performance and the production of taxable wealth. The strong bargaining power they achieved against the central state led to various conflicts between the urban elites and the state leaders who strived for centralizing their authority. Without going further into detail, understanding the historically important role of cities in the process of state formation is a prerequisite for the analysis of the new role of cities.[5]

Although the general mechanisms and dynamics of globalization have been analyzed rather extensively in the field of international relations, the study of the effects of globalization has concentrated mostly on states and, to some extent, enterprises. Here we see an embedded form of stagnation in political science, where the Westphalian Order of organized politics in and among territorial states seems to be basically unquestioned.[6]

While political science is still struggling to grasp the new context and to come up with new concepts and terms to describe and explain them adequately, some neighboring disciplines such as geography and sociology recently have demonstrated that the dynamics of globalization tend to crystallize not only in states but in specific city regions as well (see Knox and Taylor 1995; Sassen 1991; Short and Kim 1999; Scott 2001a). These are views and findings that this book tries to take up and to expand. Metropolitan areas function as the centers and gateways of global business, culture, and social relations. Common sense tells us that global flows need to originate, be channeled, and arrive somewhere. Under the model presented by geographers and sociologists, city regions are the nodes and hubs of these flows. They constitute an "extended archipelago or mosaic of large city-regions," which are "now beginning to function as the spatial foundations of the new world system" (Scott 2001b, 1).

Beyond that, for at least two reasons city regions are an increasingly important political sphere in their own right. First, many central state governments are overburdened with a growing task load and rising expectations. In response (though not always voluntarily), they opt to devolve political authority and responsibilities to substate levels (McCarney 1996). When state elites realize that they are not living up to expectations, they tend to shift tasks downward, in particular those tasks related to the provision of basic services and security. Second, regions, and city regions in particular, are rapidly becoming sites of self-induced and self-centered economic activities, innovation, and growth independent from the national economic environment. City regions are nodes in network societies, and thus constitute central junctions to different types of flow. They belong to the most relevant "new centralities" in the post-etatist global configuration (Castells 1996; Storper 1997; Cooke and Morgan 1998; Sassen 1994).

Consequently, as cities and city regions are becoming new centers and are affecting the lives of more and more people, the issue of increasingly independent city region developments has led to a growing volume of research devoted to the interplay between urban development and governance. This growing interest in cities, certainly very welcome from a researcher's point of view, raises serious questions with regard to the location and the possibilities of politics under conditions of contemporary globalization. This is the classic problem of "level of analysis under new conditions." Instead of looking at neatly separated layers of institutions and decision makers, we now must address a diverse set of political actors and institutions composing a patchwork of politics rather than clear-cut hierarchies of places, actors, and institutions.

In the framework of this book, the authors broaden our horizons by shifting attention from the nation-state level downward. City regions and cities are the meaningful units incorporated into patchwork politics. These units, city regions, are not simply smaller states. Rather, these new city regions usually consist of a plurality of interdependent actors and polities. They are connected to the macroregions, to their states, and to each other. They have to market, sell, and place themselves in a competitive environment. These circumstances can no longer be described using the notion of *government*. We have to develop and make operational the concept of *governance* on the level of city regions such as those described in this book. The outstanding importance of cities as nodal points of a worldwide network was already recognized by Peter Hall (1966). Since then, most of the research conducted on cities or city regions has focused primarily on the world's leading financial and economic centers (i.e., New York, London, Tokyo, and Frankfurt) and their role in a network of globally connected cities (e.g., Friedmann 1986; Sassen 1991; 2002). Comparative research on the changing role of larger cities in the developing world, however, is considerably less advanced, despite the fact that urban growth rates in these cities are much higher than in the cities of the north.

For the purpose of this study we have considered several of the classic definitions of globally connected cities.[7] In my view, none of them are really applicable to the city regions selected for this publication. Although the four city regions are embedded in a global network of cities (Castells 1996; Taylor 2004), none is part of the upper level of the global city hierarchy. Indeed, rather than being the top strategic sites *in* the global economy (Sassen 1991), they function as gateways *to* the global economy for their country and/or the surrounding region. Thus, they connect their societies and sometimes even their subcontinents with the global economy and act as sites of economic, social, and political innovation. Economic actors, for their part, approach these city regions as a point of entry for new and even potential markets.

So it is in this context that we finally can situate the city regions. They serve as subnational units of interaction and they have a transnational outreach. Increasingly, researchers treat them as significant units of analysis, viewing them as the "conspicuous geographical manifestation of contemporary trans-state processes" (Taylor 2000, 6). The new, enhanced role of city regions is both an outcome of global changes (i.e., globalization) and of weak performance at the nation-state level, in particular the distribution crisis in traditional welfare states (Whitfield 2001). The first aspect is related to the fact that city regions form a group of units in the new macrostructure of global politics. As they increase in size, they usually retain more flexibility than states. They are more exposed to flows, better able to adapt to a changing environment (at least in theory), and better equipped to position themselves as a node or hub. The second aspect points to the ongoing demise of the state (Taylor 1995). Whether we opt for a political science perspective where states were starting points for centuries, or an economic one with firms as the traditional entities—in reality cities and city regions increasingly are being turned into central units of political and economic activity and, consequently, of analysis (Sassen 2002, 21–23).

At the same time, the increase in city region autonomy also is enhanced by developments in the respective national and (subnational) regional contexts. Currently, almost all states face structural problems linked to strained national budgets, which as a rule lead to a reduction in the capacity to redistribute resources to regions and cities. As a result, cities feel the need to develop their particular profile in order to attract transnational capital and firms, which ultimately should help them prosper. Establishing favorable conditions for specialized services and for leisure and entertainment for various social strata (including globalizing elites) are sine qua non conditions for winning over transnational firms (Sassen 2002).

Obviously, city regions also are actors. They act within the framework of the global economy, but they (or, more precisely, city administrations along with commercial and societal actors) also influence and shape their environment. City regions impact their respective contexts and, sometimes, the global macrostructure as well. For potential investors, it is easier (and, in the case of parallel negotiations, also more profitable) to negotiate directly with city administrations. On the future world map, city regions may become what nation-states once were: central units of political action. As some predict, a new core of "top city regions" may emerge, including some city regions from the south (Taylor 2004, 105–6). Yet rather than displacing national governments, they constitute a class by themselves, increasingly independent of the national context, bypassing their governments when pursuing placement strategies in the new global configuration.[8]

This last aspect is exactly what the authors are interested in. How are city regions in the Southern Hemisphere acting under conditions of globalization? What do they do and what can they do to promote themselves to the status of global city regions? How do they *make* their territories competitive in their regional and, possibly, in the global context?

As mentioned before, city regions cannot opt out of the global context unless their administrations accept the risk of marginalization. In the south global flows will be more influential than in the north in developing potentially powerful nodes and hubs of the post-Westphalian world. In this sphere, competing bodies of law are being established, producing ambivalence, but also enabling diverging and competing city-law spaces.[9] Here flows of capital, goods, and services are being created, attracted, and channeled. Content flows of information and entertainment are circulated, producing powerful new images—such as images of future cities—and simultaneously endangering old ones. Globally meandering flows are increasingly being processed and, partly, organized by territorial nodes and hubs—namely, the most dynamic cities and city regions of the south.

These tendencies give rise to new research questions. Researchers seek to explain city images that are relevant nationally, on a supranational regional basis, and finally at the global level.

The most important of these questions addressed in this book are:

1. How do relevant actors in southern city regions, which are important at least at the regional level, organize their cities' development, and how do they go about trying to promote their city regions to the status of global city regions?
2. How do these city regions frame their discourses?

One of the main findings of the book is that there are basically two functions of these discourses, namely, to mobilize the city internally and to create an identity for the city vis-à-vis the outside world, which it can use in competition with other cities.

The chapters of this volume focus on how the dominant elites in four carefully selected city regions are trying to cope with a situation that was brought about by three sets of factors. The first of these is their cities' past and the path dependencies that constrain and enable current strategies to cope with the global. Obviously, specific political legacies are significant in this respect (apartheid in South Africa, the caste system in India, narrow and often personalized elite rule in Brazil, and so-called communism in China). Institutional features of the past may also still have an impact.

The second set of factors concerns the relationship between a given city and the national context. In this respect it is important to study the shifting division of labor between national capitals and local governments, as well as resource-distribution and governance patterns.

The third set of factors originates in the global context. The global context is the playground where decisive rules and trends are born and which subsequently influence the options of regional elites. The emerging global context threatens to exclude nonadapters and promises to include successful modernizers.

One important theoretical point should be mentioned here. In many instances, city regions, like nation-states, are treated as unitary actors. Although it is still possible to treat both states and city regions as unitary actors, this approach has probably never been sufficient and, in the more recent debates, has become increasingly obsolete. Hence, one should take care not to transfer implicitly the biased realist approach of states to cities.

Most of these questions actually have been addressed by some authors with respect to the better-known city regions of the OECD world; however, they have thus far been virtually ignored with respect to the Southern Hemisphere.[10] This book attempts to remedy this perceived deficit.

The Sample: Selecting Four City Regions

Four cities or city regions have been chosen for the project whose results we are presenting here: Johannesburg (South Africa), Mumbai/Bombay (India), São Paolo (Brazil), and Shanghai (China). So far, these cities and regions have not been at the center of academic analytical interest. We hope that by focusing on them we can provide fresh insights for the field of global city research, and possibly even for neighboring disciplines.

The four places selected do not (yet) play major roles in the emerging global economy. Nonetheless, they hold "dominant positions at the regional level or within very large countries such as China and India" (Gugler 2004, 7) and serve as economic gateways for their respective macroregions.

Although most metropolitan regions of the developing world are not (yet) global nodes and command centers, they are home to increasingly globally oriented economic sectors and social groups, which are at least partially becoming or seeking to become detached from their past and their national fate. The metropolitan regions of the developing world thus are developing their own identities independent from the national level. The globally oriented sectors and groups are establishing themselves as a driving force for creating city region hubs. They have started to make their places global (Parnreiter 1999). In the old Wallersteinian terminology, however, all four of the city regions selected here nonetheless should be designated as (still) belonging to the semiperiphery (Wallerstein 1979).

Although it can be debated whether the four selected city regions are global cities following Sassen's understanding (Sassen 1991; 1994; 2002), from the regional perspective they all are characterized by high levels of global linkages.[11] The city regions are located in four countries on different continents. While there are relevant differences between them, it was possible to control relatively many factors shaping their performances. This is important to ensure comparability. We maintain that the city regions selected here do not belong to the OECD world; they all are located in countries that were opened up to the global economy and liberalized internally in the 1990s; none is a national capital; all four places experienced massive urbanization over the past decades; all four cities are important regional hubs; at the same time, all of them have to cope with enormous social disparities; and, finally, they all underwent political decentralization in recent years.

The starting point of the studies collected in this book is the phenomenon of effective decentralization. At the same time, this phenomenon—intentional or not—needs to be explained. The devolution of power and competence is a broad tendency in both the OECD and non-OECD parts of the globe. Flows of capital, content, and people often are attracted and processed by city regions rather than by states. States are ever less able to fulfill their traditional interventionist, regulatory, and redistributional functions (Parnreiter 1999; see also Amen 2002). State power, while certainly still an important factor (especially in China), is gradually eroding, leading to a "'release' of cities towards a more global destiny" (Derudder et al. 2003).

We define the global integration and connectedness of the selected city regions, besides other factors, with reference to the presence of globally active specialized services,[12] the capacity to function as a hub and node in the respective world region, and the city region's current ability to attract foreign direct investment.[13] Four charts give insight into the degree of connectedness of these city regions.[14] They show that Johannesburg (Africa), Mumbai/Bombay (South Asia), and São Paulo (South America) are the best-connected places in their respective regions, so it should be obvious why we chose them. As for Shanghai, one cannot say the same. Other cities in East Asia are more connected, such as Hong Kong and

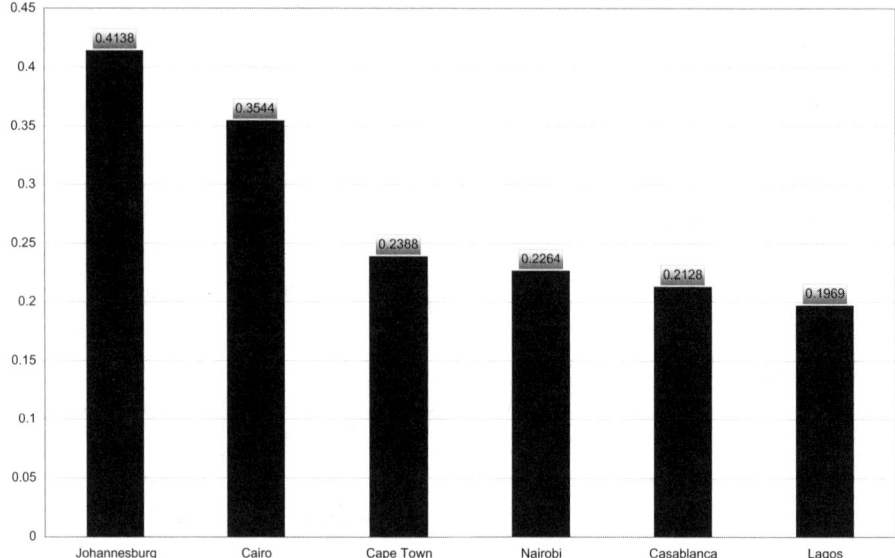
Global network connectivity of African cities.

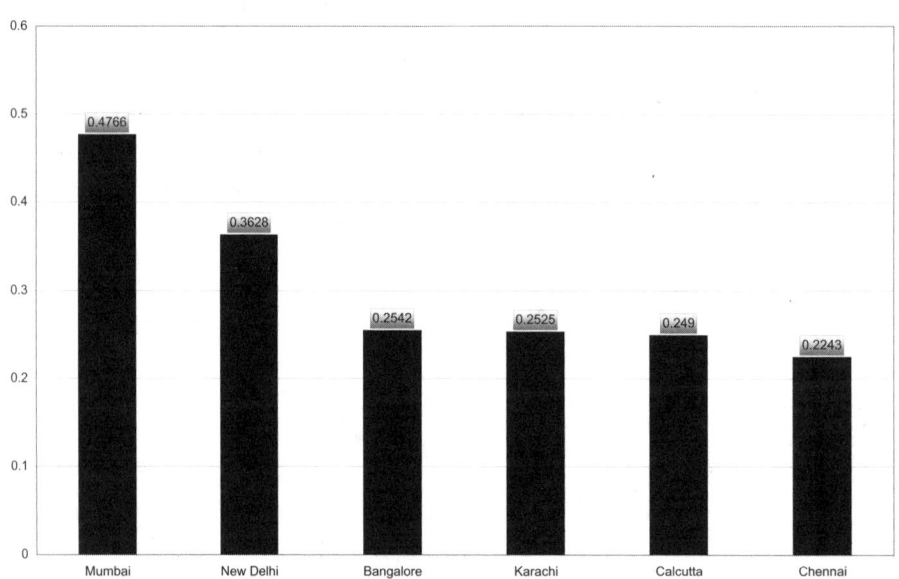
Global network connectivity of South Asian cities.

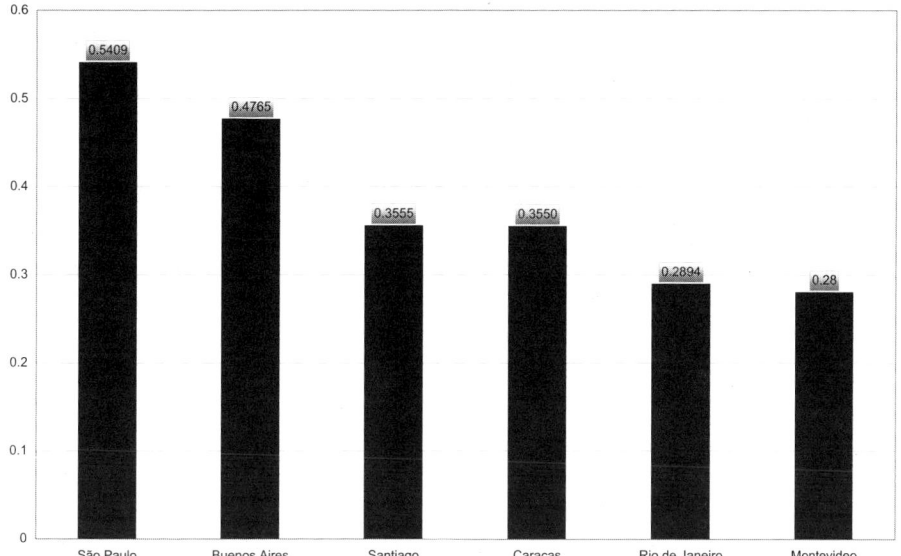

Global network connectivity of South American cities.

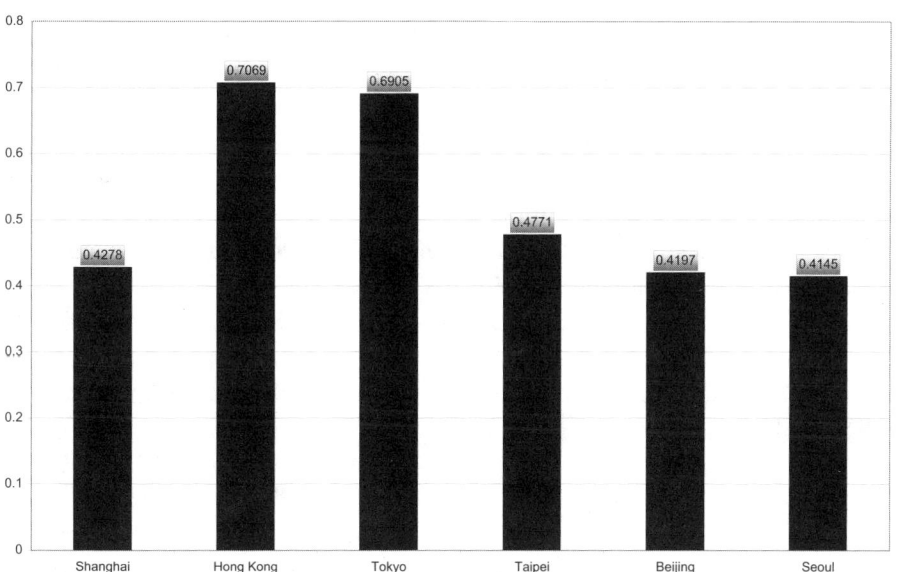

Global network connectivity of East Asian cities.

Tokyo. Yet Tokyo was not qualified for our sample because it is a capital and belongs to the OECD world, and Hong Kong is a special case because of its Commonwealth legacy. Compared to other cities like Taipei and Beijing, Shanghai certainly is the most dynamic one.

Shanghai still has a way to go before it reaches the top of the global hierarchy. However, the data show that the city has the largest growth rates in the region, underlining its rising importance. GDP has risen from 60,133 million USD (purchasing power parity) in 1990 to 288,175 million USD in 2002, an increase of 479% as compared to 346% for the whole of China.[15] Arguably it is only a question of time before Shanghai takes over as the leading city in China.

Air passenger and cargo flows are often taken as another indicator for measuring the city's status as a hub in the global network economy (Smith and Timberlake 2002; Witlox, Vereecken, and Derudder 2004). The respective figures, as tabulated for the airports in the four selected city regions, further underline their dominant role.[16] Although the four airports do not belong to the twenty-five largest airports in the world, they nevertheless serve as the major transportation hubs for their world region (Shanghai seems destined to become China's major airport).

Finally, the stock exchanges in the selected city regions are among the most relevant in their larger regional neighborhoods. They are even the most important securities and derivative markets of their continental regions in terms of market capitalization, share trading, and capital raised. All exchanges are members of the World Federation of Stock Exchanges (WFSE).[17] The corporate offices of the two Indian stock exchanges are both based in Mumbai/Bombay, the only other, considerably smaller South Asian WFSE exchange being in Colombo. Johannesburg is the only African exchange listed as a member of WFSE. In South America, there are three additional exchanges besides São Paulo, but São Paulo is the most important with respect to the three listed criteria. Within China, Shanghai and Shenzen are the most recently admitted members of WFSE. However, Shanghai's market capitalization is roughly double that of Shenzen.[18]

There is one more aspect worth mentioning. Why are we interested in city regions and not just the cities themselves? Cities are increasingly extending beyond their actual municipal boundaries. Former core cities already have expanded beyond their city limits. Investors and citizens, producers and customers are increasingly transgressing old boundaries. Hence, a global city region is "any metropolitan area or any contiguous

Incoming and Outgoing Airport Cargo and Passengers, 2002/3

Cargo in metric tons		Passengers	
African Airports			
Johannesburg	273,256	Johannesburg	13,151,668
Nairobi	177,203	Cairo	8,151,788
Casablanca	44,515	Cape Town	5,193,573
Lagos	39,070	Lagos	3,370,401
Cairo	NA	Casablanca	3,359,445
Cape Town	NA	Nairobi	3,183,710
South Asian airports			
Mumbai	327,795	Mumbai	12,430,363
New Delhi	289,739	New Delhi	9,563,896
Chennai	141,530	Chennai	4,150,604
Colombo	122,694	Colombo	3,028,345
Bangalore	82,943	Bangalore	3,089,646
South American airports			
São Paulo	413,533	São Paulo	12,164,644
Santiago	268,696	Buenos Aires	8,986,161
Buenos Aires	173,750	Brasilia	7,028,827
Campinas	149,638	Santiago	5,546,680
Lima	146,483	Rio de Janeiro	5,272,506
Rio de Janeiro	119,627	Caracas	5,263,355
East Asian airports			
Hong Kong	2,582,744	Seoul	36,544,947
Seoul	2,007,675	Hong Kong	27,238,000
Taipei	1,427,142	Beijing	23,456,631
Shanghai*	1,229,045	Shanghai	22,758,863
Beijing	628,989	Taipei	15,573,700
Guangzhou	537,753	Guangzhou	14,185,234

Source: Airports Council International, *Worldwide Airport Traffic Report 2004* (Geneva, 2004).
Note: Figures on cargo illustrate loaded and unloaded freight and mail in metric tons from July 2002 to June 2003. Figures on passengers show total passengers enplaned and deplaned from July 2002 to June 2003. Passengers in transit are counted once. Cargo data for Cairo and Cape Town not available; for Shanghai, cargo in 2001 was 804,465 metric tons.

set of metropolitan areas together with a surrounding hinterland of variable extent—itself a locus of scattered urban settlements—whose internal economic and political affairs are bound up in intricate ways in intensifying and far-flung extra-national relationships" (Scott 2001b, 2).

We can observe this tendency in all four selected city regions. The cities are growing beyond set administrative boundaries. Subsequently, it is becoming increasingly difficult to distinguish the actual city from the surrounding region. However, while economic activities do not stop at administrative boundaries, in terms of political organization many city regions lack an administrative structure at the metropolitan level. The institutions created on the metropolitan level are mostly mere planning agencies with very limited funds and no actual political power. This is especially true in São Paulo and Mumbai/ Bombay. So should we analyze the city proper or the city and its surrounding region? In terms of administrative structure and accessible data, it would make more sense to focus on the city. Yet in terms of analyzing the political, economic, and societal transformations, we ought to focus on the city region.

The time period to be covered by the contributions in this volume is from the early 1990s to the first years of the twenty-first century. We consider this to be a period during which Brazil, India, China, and South Africa underwent significant transformations. First, they all underwent political decentralization. Second, they were opening up to the global economy during this time.

Structure of the Book

The entire research project was realized in cooperation with local partners in the respective city regions. The questions raised call for a transdisciplinary approach. Thus, we incorporate different academic backgrounds, such as political science, urban studies, economics, sociology, and geography. Most of these disciplines have treated cities as objects of academic interest for a long time.

We begin our examination in chapter 2, which addresses the basics of our four cities. The contributions provide a general, as well as a more focused, context of the city regions' development since the early 1990s. Alan Mabin traces the evolution of Johannesburg in the turbulent post-apartheid 1990s. Sujata Patel provides the framework for events in Mumbai/Bombay over the past fifteen years. Csaba Deák and Sueli Schiffer contextualize São Paulo's development in Brazil since the early 1990s.

Weiping Wu looks at Shanghai's leap from an old-style industrial city straight into the global age.

Chapter 3 looks into the actors relevant for making the city regions more competitive. Cities are no more unitary than states are. In order to understand the behavior of a city's administration and its other relevant actors, one must analyze its underlying power structures. This involves studying the existing formal and informal arrangements between public authorities, civic associations, and business interests. It is important to define as closely as possible who actually sets the agenda and makes relevant decisions. Also, changing relationships between the public and private sectors require greater scrutiny. Susan Parnell analyzes the hegemonic forces of city strategy development in Johannesburg. Jim Masselos focuses on formal and informal power structures in Mumbai/Bombay. In their second essay, Sueli Schiffer and Csaba Deák aim at deconstructing the often behind-the-scenes activities of São Paulo's elite groups. Fulong Wu traces the evolution of moving actors in Shanghai from state bureaucracies toward a "City Inc."

Chapter 4 is devoted to the discourses organized and taking place in the four regions. The city regions are engaged in "place marketing and promotion" to varying degrees. Most of them try to sell themselves "with assertions of [their] own competitive place advantage" (Ward 1998, 1). These organized visions aim not only at global investors but also at the local population—consumers, human capital, civil-society groups, and the electorate. Robert A. Beauregard and Richard Tomlinson describe and analyze the official discourse of city administration of post-apartheid Johannesburg, which aims at making Johannesburg the world-class city of Africa. Ranjit Hoskote from Mumbai/Bombay presents competing versions of a postcolonial metropolis. Pedro Jacobi looks into distinct images of and visions for São Paulo. Zhongxin Sun connects the historical Shanghai metaphors with the avant-gardist rhetoric of today's Shanghai.

The role of discourses in the process of raising a city's status and establishing it as a global node was one of the more unexpected, even surprising findings of the project presented here. This observation is, of course, not only true for Third World cities. In general, places are presented as combinations of factors that may attract investors, human capital, and tourists. As one author in this volume put it, "[s]pace is turned into place through acts of discursive representation." These discourses and visions "include whole sets of ideas, concepts, and practices" (Short 1999, 39).

Most authors touch upon issues such as the probusiness attitude of cities, good labor relations, low labor costs, adequate infrastructure, technological advantages, educational excellence, and historical, leisure, and life-style-related advantages. It is particularly interesting to look at slogans currently promoted by city administrations. Catchwords like gateway, twenty-first century, partnership, adventure, and the like are combined with images of the respective locations.[19]

The last group of essays in chapter 5 may be the most unexpected. We asked well-known practitioners in the four city regions, who themselves are (or were) involved in developing their cities, to offer brief comments on the project results. Roland Hunter, executive director general for finance and economic development of the City of Johannesburg, addresses the Johannesburg essays. Vidyadhar K. Phatak, former principal chief of the Town and Country Planning Division of Mumbai Metropolitan Region Development Authority, offers his views on the Mumbai/Bombay studies. Jorge Wilheim, the director of the Municipal Planning Department of São Paulo and former deputy director of HABITAT II, comments on the São Paulo essays. Zhu Linchu, the deputy director general of the Development Research Center of Shanghai, provides his evaluation of the Shanghai contributions. The reader may find in this book at least the core of a discussion on city development often called for elsewhere.

In chapter 6, my colleagues Simon Raiser and Krister Volkmann conclude the volume. Here they take up the difficult task of summing up the findings of the preceding essays.

Finally, this introduction should not be silent on difficulties encountered in organizing the project. It was harder than anticipated to come up with reasonably comparable objects for research. City boundaries are often not broad enough to include the relevant observations and links. In some cases, like in Mumbai/Bombay, data for the metropolitan regions are not sufficient or nonexistent. Recurring administrative restructuring in Johannesburg resulted in data that was confusing and sometimes of little help. In our attempts to determine what exactly is the relevant level of analysis (cities or city regions), we had to reluctantly accept some ambivalence.

Findings

Although a comparative study survey such as this is always presented with heterogeneous conditions and diversities, I think that the studies can provide new and relevant insights into these four southern city regions. Among the findings that are certainly not homogeneous are those involving the movers and shapers, who can be found inside and outside the administrative structure. Both formal and informal players may be decisive in shaping the city region's profile and developing promotional formulas. Thus, we see how important it is to decode the relevant actors in city regions. Another important result (and future field for analysis and debate) is the role of mission discourses for getting cities to move forward, both externally and internally.

Beyond that, the findings differ as much as the city regions themselves.[20] Some of the cities presented and analyzed are apparently well on their way to becoming global city regions. Others move more slowly, like Mumbai/Bombay. Nonetheless, all of them are already highly relevant regional hubs. Yet differences in the process of making a global city are visible, and they remain strong. The contributions of this book show that the selected city regions are situated in a similar context of current globalization but nevertheless vary in the ways in which they address the making of a global city region. Local traditions and specifics are influencing the priorities that each city region establishes.

The recent development of Shanghai is quite impressive. Here we witness the strongest orientation toward a deliberate strategy of catching up with city centers in the OECD world. Johannesburg, too, has developed a very ambitious strategy to become the world-class city of Africa. The city administrations of São Paulo and Mumbai/Bombay, however, have experienced more difficulties in developing a coherent marketing strategy for the metropolitan region.[21]

There is one particular aspect in which the findings of this project do not confirm a hypothesis suggested by Gugler. States and civil or popular movements cannot be discounted, but neither of them can be considered as particularly "strong" (Gugler 2004, 2, 10–11). First, the authority of the state is declining in all four cases, although in China the Communist Party continues to dominate the agenda-setting process. Second, popular movements in the four city regions have not appeared to be exerting significant influence on the key decision makers. However, in many instances they step in where state activity is inadequate and form networks to make demands on officials or to resist government and/or business action.[22]

Many cities (not only) in the developing world face similar dilemmas: while confronted with increasing socioeconomic fragmentation, most cities massively engage in place marketing and promotion to enhance their economic competitiveness. The cases presented in this book may offer useful insights for further research into the making of global city regions and thus add to the knowledge on city regions in developing countries.

Will the four city regions become—or are they already—southern contenders competing with their OECD counterparts, the northern global cities? While this notion may seem somewhat farfetched today, I would not dismiss it when looking to the future. Many of the cities playing in the traditional premier league do not betray much dynamism and (positive) development any more. They are caught in complex bargaining situations, often blocked by veto players, vested interests, rent seekers, and welfare institutions designed for preglobalization societies, which are neither competitive nor sustainable today. These "old" cities and their national environments obviously need more incentives to regain vitality and again become centers of inspiration and development. Making this happen is perhaps the hidden and unintended consequence of turning the vibrant southern contenders presented in this book into globalizing city regions.

Notes

1. *South* is meant to indicate here "belonging to the non-OECD world."

2. Bombay was officially renamed Mumbai in 1995. Still, the name Bombay is popular among parts of the population. To avoid political bias, we decided to name this city Mumbai/Bombay.

3. Bipolar structures are more stable than hegemonic ones. These, in turn, are more stable than three-actor games. Basically, the more actors involved, the less stable a configuration becomes, all other factors being equal.

4. However, even proponents of research into states and state power increasingly concede that there is a need to diversify the view of the state with regard to variability in its form and its capacities to govern. Thus, the state is increasingly seen as merely one institutional order among others (Jessop 2001).

5. For an illustrative overview on the historical role of towns and cities in the process of state formation, see Tilly and Brockmans 1994.

6. See Krasner 1999 and Ruggie 1993 for discussions of the Westphalian Order; Agnew 1994, Robinson 1998, and Taylor 1996 for critiques of embedded statism.

7. Some of the classic definitions and terms are *world city* (Hall 1966; Friedmann 1986; Knox and Taylor 1995), *informational city* (Castells 1989), *global city* (Sassen 1991; 1994), and *global city region* (Scott 2001a).

Introduction   23

8. Of course, next to their growing role as nodes in the global arena, these four city regions remain key actors in their respective national city systems. It therefore would be an interesting question to analyze the implications of this dual role. However, this question goes beyond the focus of this volume and should be subject to further research.

9. It is a fascinating question if and to what extent cities can build alliances with each other to avoid the typical collective action problems one would expect under the conditions described. A new research project on this question is being prepared currently.

10. Peter Taylor's new book *World City Network* (2004) presents a global approach and is a rare exception.

11. Most of the data on the four city regions is derived from the research group Globalization and World Cities (GaWC) at Loughborough University. Peter Taylor and his colleagues have done an admirable job in providing comprehensive data on global linkages between world cities. For the most recent findings, see Taylor 2004.

12. This factor (as suggested by Sassen 1991) cannot be shown in detail for the selected cases due to a lack of data.

13. For different options of defining and clustering city regions, see the overview of GaWC, in Beaverstock, Smith, and Taylor 1999. Our intention to include foreign direct investment had to be given up because—with the exception of Shanghai—no sufficient and hard data for the other cities was available.

14. The index cited was established by Taylor, Catalano, and Walker (2002). It rates the Global Network Connectivity of office networks of 100 global service firms in the fields of accounting, advertising, banking/finance, insurance, law, and management consultancy. The offices were studied in terms of their size and function within the firm's regional and global network. The joint service value of a city's offices was then used to compute the ranking of the city relative to the highest city connectivity possible (London), resulting in a scale from 0 to 1.

15. Shanghai Municipal Statistics Bureau 2003; World Bank 2003.

16. Smith and Timberlake (2002; 1998; 1995) have published several pioneering articles on the network of world cities based on airline passenger flows. Their analyses depict clear patterns of dominance among world cities. Witlox, Vereecken, and Derudder (2004), who provide a more comprehensive dataset on passenger transport flows, reveal similar patterns of dominance among the cities with the largest number of incoming and outgoing passengers.

17. The WFSE is a private international organization and its fifty-four member exchanges account for more than 97% of world stock market capitalization. Mumbai/Bombay and Shanghai were accepted as members in 2002.

18. www.world-exchanges.org/.

19. For more details, see the interesting lists and explanations in Short 1999, 48–49.

20. This finding resembles the first of the results outlined in Gugler 2004.

21. For more details, see the conclusion in chapter 6.

22. For a detailed account on the role of the civil society in the selected city regions, see Raiser and Volkmann 2005.

References

Agnew, J. 1994. The Territorial Trap: The Geographical Assumptions of International Relations Theory. *Review of International Political Economy* 1, no. 1: 53–80.

Albrow, M. 1996. *The Global Age: State and Society beyond Modernity.* Cambridge: Polity Press.

Amen, M. M. 2002. Cities in the Global Economy: A Place for Tampa Bay? Paper presented at the International Studies Association annual meeting, New Orleans, 26 March.

Appadurai, A. 1997. *Modernity at Large: Cultural Dimensions of Globalization.* Minneapolis: University of Minnesota Press.

Baylis, J., and S. Smith (eds.). 2001. *The Globalization of World Politics.* 2d. Oxford: Oxford University Press.

Beaverstock, J. V., R. G. Smith, and P. J. Taylor. 1999. A Roster of World Cities. Globalization and World Cities Study Group and Network. *Cities* 16, no. 6: 445–58.

Castells, M. 1989. *The Informational City: Information, Technology, Economic Restructuring and the Urban-Regional Process.* Oxford: Oxford University Press.

———. 1996. *The Rise of the Network Society. The Information Age: Economy, Society and Culture.* Vol. 1. Malden: Blackwell.

Cooke, P., and K. Morgan. 1998. *The Associational Economy: Firms, Regions, and Innovation.* Oxford: Oxford University Press.

Derudder, B., P. J. Taylor, F. Witlox, and G. Catalano. 2003. Beyond Friedmann's World City Hypothesis: Twenty-Two Urban Arenas across the World. *Mitteilungen der Österreichischen Geographischen Gesellschaft* 145: 35–55.

Dicken, P. 2003. *Global Shift: Reshaping the Global Economic Map in the 21st Century.* 4th ed. London: Sage.

Friedmann, J. 1986. The World City Hypotheses. *Development and Change* 17, no. 1: 69–83.

Friedrichs, C. R. 1995. *The Early Modern City: 1450–1750.* London: Longman.

Gourevitch, P. 1978. The Second Image Reversed: The International Sources of Domestic Politics. *International Organization* 32, no. 4: 881–912.

Gugler, J. 2004. Introduction. In J. Gugler (ed.), *World Cities beyond the West: Globalization, Development and Inequality.* Cambridge: Cambridge University Press. Available at www.sociology.uconn.edu/faculty/gugler/worldcities.htm (accessed 23 June 2006).

Hall, P. 1966. *The World Cities.* London: Weidenfeld and Nicholson.

Held, D., A. McGrew, D. Goldblatt, and J. Perraton (eds.). 1999. *Global Transformations: Politics, Economics, Culture.* Stanford: Stanford University Press.

Hirst, P., and G. Thompson. 1996. *Globalization in Question: The International Economy, and the Possibilities of Governance.* Cambridge: Polity Press.
Jessop, B. 2001. Bringing the State Back in (Yet Again): Reviews, Revisions, Rejections, and Redirections. *International Review of Sociology* 11, no. 2: 149–73.
Knox, P. L., and P. J. Taylor (eds.). 1995. *World Cities in a World-System.* Cambridge: Cambridge University Press.
Krasner, S. D. 1999. *Sovereignty: Organized Hypocrisy.* Princeton, N.J.: Princeton University Press.
McCarney, P. L. (ed.). 1996. *Cities and Governance: New Directions in Latin America, Asia and Africa.* Toronto: University of Toronto.
Ohmae, K. 1995. *The End of the Nation State.* New York: Free Press.
Parnreiter, C. 1999. Globalisierung, Binnenmigration und Megastädte der "Dritten Welt"—Theoretische Reflexionen. In K. Husa and H. Wohlschlaegl (eds.), *Megastaedte der Dritten Welt im Globalisierungsprozess. Mexiko City, Jakarta, Bombay. Vergleichende Fallstudien in ausgewählten Kulturkreisen,* 17–58. Vienna: Institut für Geographie der Universität Wien.
Putnam, R. D. 1988. Diplomacy and Domestics Politics: The Logic of Two-Level Games. *International Organization* 42, no. 3: 427–60.
Raiser, S., and K. Volkmann (eds.). 2005. Bringing the Citizens In: Civil Society in Globalizing Cities of the South. *Working Paper Series of the Osteuropa-Institut,* Freie Universität Berlin, no. 54.
Robinson, W. I. 1998. Beyond Nation-State Paradigms: Globalization, Sociology, and the Challenge of Transnational Studies. *Sociological Forum* 13, no. 4: 561–94.
Ruggie, J. G. 1993. Territoriality and Beyond: Problematizing Modernity in International Relations. *International Organization* 47, no. 1: 139–74.
Sassen, S. 1991. *The Global City.* Princeton, N.J.: Princeton University Press.
———. 1994. *Cities in a World Economy.* Thousand Oaks, Calif.: Sage.
——— (ed.). 2002. *Global Networks, Linked Cities.* New York: Routledge.
Scholte, J. A. 2000. *Globalization: A Critical Introduction.* Houndmills, Basingstoke: Macmillan Press.
Scott, A. J. 2001a. Globalization and the Rise of City-Regions. *European Planning Studies* 9, no. 7: 813–26.
———. 2001b. Introduction. In A. J. Scott (ed.), *Global City-Regions: Trends, Theory, Policy,* 1–9. Oxford: Oxford University Press.
Shanghai Municipal Statistics Bureau. 2003. *Shanghai Statistical Yearbook 2003.* Beijing: China Statistics Press.
Short, J. R. 1999. Urban Imagineers: Boosterism and the Representation of Cities. In A. E. Jonas and D. Wilson (eds.), *The Urban Growth Machine: Critical Perspectives Two Decades Later,* 37–54. Albany: State University of New York Press.
Short, J. R., and Y.-H. Kim. 1999. *Globalization and the City.* New York: Addison Wesley Longman.
Smith, D. A., and M. Timberlake. 1995. Conceptualising and Mapping the Structure of the World's City System. *Urban Studies* 32, no. 2: 287–302.

———. 1998. Cities and the Spatial Articulation of the World-Economy through Air Travel. In S. Bunker and P. Ciccantell (eds.), *Space and Transport and the World-System*, 213–40. Westport, Conn.: Greenwood Press.

———. 2002. Hierarchies of Dominance among World Cities: A Network Approach. In S. Sassen (ed.), *Global Networks, Linked Cities*, 117–41. New York: Routledge.

Storper, M. 1997. *The Regional World: Territorial Development in a Global Economy.* New York: Guilford Press.

Strange, S. 1996. *The Retreat of the State: The Diffusion of Power in the World Economy.* Cambridge: Cambridge University Press.

Taylor, P. J. 1995. World Cities and Territorial States: The Rise and Fall of Their Mutuality. In P. L. Knox and P. J. Taylor (eds.), *World Cities in a World System*, 48–62. Cambridge: Cambridge University Press.

———. 1996. Embedded Statism and the Social Sciences: Opening Up New Spaces. *Environment and Planning A* 28: 1917–28.

———. 2000. World Cities and Territorial States under Conditions of Contemporary Globalization. *Political Geography* 19, no. 1: 5–32.

———. 2004. *World City Network: A Global Urban Analysis.* New York: Routledge.

Taylor, P. J., G. Catalano, and D. R. F. Walker. 2002. Measurement of the World City Network. *Urban Studies* 39, no. 13: 2367–76.

Tilly, C., and W. Brockmans (eds.). 1994. *Cities and the Rise of State in Europe.* Boulder: Westview Press.

Wallerstein, I. 1979. *The Capitalist World-Economy.* Cambridge: Cambridge University Press.

Waltz, K. 2001. *Man, the State, and War: A Theoretical Analysis.* Rev. ed. New York: Columbia University Press.

Ward, S. V. 1998. *Selling Places: The Marketing and Promotion of Towns and Cities, 1850–2000.* New York: Routledge.

Whitfield, D. 2001. *Public Services or Corporate Welfare: Rethinking the Nation State in the Global Economy.* London: Westview Press.

Witlox, F., L. Vereecken, and B. Derudder. 2004. Mapping the Global Network Economy on the Basis of Air Passenger Transport Flows. *GaWC Research Bulletin*, no. 157. Available at www.lboro.ac.uk/gawc/rb/rb157.html.

World Bank. 2003. *World Development Indicators 2003.* Washington, D.C.: World Bank.

2 | City Regions between Their Legacies and the Global Context

The four city regions to be analyzed in the following essays—Johannesburg, Mumbai/Bombay, São Paulo, and Shanghai—all underwent profound changes over the past ten to fifteen years due to globalization. The city regions are situated in countries that do not belong to the Organization for Economic Cooperation and Development (OECD) and that recently opened up their economies to the world market. This liberalization triggered the far-reaching transformation of various economic sectors and also of labor markets. Like many other cities in the world, the four city regions have seen a rampant deindustrialization and spatial relocation of industries from the confines of the city to the wider region, followed by a gradual shift in the cities toward a business- and service-oriented economy. As such, they function increasingly as regional hubs for global financial and economic flows, thereby linking their world region to the global market. The process of deindustrialization in turn has produced high unemployment and increasing socioeconomic fragmentation. As a result, more and more people are forced to earn their living in the informal sectors of the economy.

To meet the challenges posed by these new economic realities, the city administrations of the four city regions have had to redesign their policy agendas. While all four cities are in some ways preparing themselves for deepened integration into global networks, they are faced with the dilemma whether to place more emphasis on the promotion of economic growth and global competitiveness or, alternatively, on the needs of the poorer population, which is largely sidelined by the global resource flows. The cities' varying responses to this complex dilemma must be seen in light of their different economic positions and historical legacies. As will

Size and Population in the Four Selected City Regions, 2001–3

	Area (sq. km.)	Population	Population Density (persons/sq. km.)
City of Johannesburg[a]	2,300	3,226,000	1,403
Mumbai Metropolitan Region[b]	4,355	18,893,000	4,338
Greater Mumbai	468	11,914,000	27,715
São Paulo Metropolitan Region[c]	8,051	18,100,000	2,248
Municipality of São Paulo	1,509	10,489,000	6,951
Shanghai[d]	6,340	13,271,000	2,104

[a]Statistics of South Africa: Census 2001, www.statssa.gov.za/census01 (accessed 15 June 2004).
[b]Census of India 2001, www.censusindia.net (accessed 14 June 2004); Mumbai Metropolitan Regional Development Authority, www.mmrdamumbai.org (accessed 14 June 2004).
[c]Instituto Brasileiro de Geografia e Estatística (IBGE), http://www.ibge.gov.br; Fundação Sistema Estadual de Auálise de Dados (SEADE), www.seade.gov.br (accessed 15 June 2004).
[d]Shanghai Municipal Statistics Bureau, *Shanghai Statistical Yearbook 2003* (Shanghai: China Statistics Press, 2003).

be shown in the following contributions, each city is characterized by local peculiarities that require specific responses. Hence, the authors illuminate the respective local contexts of Johannesburg, Mumbai/Bombay, São Paulo, and Shanghai in which the making of a global city takes place.

Various stories, approaches, and cultures mingle in Johannesburg, which is known by a number of other names: Joburg, Jozi, Gauteng, and Egoli, reflecting the fact that English is only a minority language in the city. Founded as a gold-mining town, it soon became the commercial center of South Africa toward the end of the nineteenth century. Massive industrial growth took place from the 1930s to 1950s. Today, Johannesburg is the heart of an urbanized region of 9 million people stretching across great parts of Gauteng province. Because the region serves as the key point of global economic contact for South Africa and the wider region, it facilitates the exchange of enormous wealth. Despite this, the vast majority of the black population still lives in poverty, prompting the assertion that apartheid is still omnipresent ten years after the first free elections. In this context, Alan Mabin describes the existence of three cities in one: the wealthy and mostly white suburban city in the north, the poverty-ridden former black townships in the south, and the historical town of Johannesburg, which was deserted by white business after the end of the apartheid regime and is now mostly occupied by small black businesses. This resilient socioeconomic polarization partly explains the ongoing political wrangling over agenda setting in urban development. Yet despite strong resistance, the city administration, led by the African National Congress, lately shifted its emphasis from the redistribution of existing wealth toward the promotion of economic growth and competitiveness.

As for Mumbai/Bombay, Sujata Patel describes a complex and contradictory relationship with the global economy. The city hosts the best and the worst of India. It is the economic powerhouse of India, also showing excellence in the arts and fashion. A large part of the population, however, remains employed under archaic and onerous working conditions. In her portrayal of Bombay, which now carries the official name Mumbai (derived from Marathi language), Patel identifies three phases in its history. As a port city in the global colonial system, it witnessed an initial boom around 1870 with the rise of the cotton and subsequent textile industry. Later, trading profits were invested in other, capital-intensive industries. During the second phase, in independent India, modern Bombay emerged as a major manufacturing city catering mainly to national markets. These years were marked by exceptionally high migration from rural areas. In the early 1980s, Bombay experienced the decline of its textile industry, which was exacerbated by a long strike. The third phase of global Bombay/Mumbai started with the liberalization policies of the Indian government in the early 1990s. This phase is characterized by the growing importance of the service sector, by a spatial reorganization spreading into outer regions, and by a sharp increase of informal employment. Despite the far-reaching changes in each phase of history, extreme socioeconomic contrasts have prevailed. Half of the population still lives in slums today. Patel concludes that fragmented governance structures and lack of political will have so far prevented determined solutions. Instead, the city's political landscape is shaped by regional identity politics.

São Paulo is equally a city of extremes. The largest agglomeration in South America, it owes its initial growth to the coffee production in the area. Rapid industrialization in the early twentieth century and the growth of the home market during the Brazilian economic miracle of the 1970s made São Paulo the economic heart of Brazil. According to Csaba Deák and Sueli Schiffer, its development is strongly intertwined with the economic and social development of Brazil as a whole. They describe a specifically Brazilian (or Latin American) process that they call "hindered accumulation," under which only a part of the surplus of production is reinvested in the local economy, while a greater part is sent overseas. The dominance of a small elite prevents real development and keeps the country captive in its dependence on economic core countries. These highly unequal societal structures date back to colonial times and have not developed into the bourgeois structures known in the European countries. The result is a deliberate fragmentation of urban space with islands of great wealth surrounded by areas with extreme poverty and very precarious infrastructure. With the rise of neoliberal ideology, earlier comprehensive development planning has made room for strategic planning. This, according to Deák and Schiffer, comes close to nonplanning. Some recent projects of the current city administration are moving in the right direction, but only a radical change in the historical Brazilian pattern of development would enable substantial improvements in infrastructure and services.

Weiping Wu illustrates the unique position that Shanghai holds in contemporary China. The city advanced to a premier position already in the mid-nineteenth century after its port was opened as a result of the Opium War. After 1949 it lost its supreme status and went through thirty years of neglect by the Chinese central government. When economic reforms finally reached Shanghai in the late 1980s, roughly a decade later than in China's southern cities, it set out to catch up in its development. Consequently, the urban economy is rapidly shifting from traditional industries to the service sector. However, this profound transformation has been made possible only by the strong backing of the central government, which wants Shanghai to become *the* global city of China. Global players quickly realized the importance of Shanghai as a new gateway to the huge Chinese market. As a result, the city has received an enormous inflow of foreign investment. To accommodate the needs of these new actors and to relink itself to the outside world, Shanghai has invested heavily in its infrastructure—from a gigantic container port to broadband telecommunications to the creation of the Luijazui financial district in the new development area Pudong, which is designed to become *the* center of global finance. Thus far, measures have dealt mainly with building and modernizing "hardware." A careful look reveals that there is a lack of entrepreneurship, skills, and creativity, that is, of the "software" needed to make the city thrive. At the same time, the population is aging rapidly, increasing the need for migratory inflow. According to Wu, openness, entrepreneurial drive, and a tolerant culture will be key factors for the successful development of Shanghai as a global city region.

The making of a global city region in these four urban areas takes place in the common context of globalization. This has set in motion similar trends, which influence current urban and regional development in powerful ways. Most notable of these is the development of districts with privileged access to global networks next to districts that are only precariously serviced and rely mainly on informal structures. At the same time, the four city regions are characterized by a unique local context, which derives from long-standing cultural specifics as well as more recent history, including apartheid, military rule, and a socialist state-economy. Adapting the general trends to the local context of each city region may turn out to be decisive for the making of global city regions.

Simon Raiser and Krister Volkmann

Johannesburg
(South) Africa's Aspirant Global City
Alan Mabin

Johannesburg is alive. For good or evil, things happen there. From its restless vitality spring the excitements and the movements of South Africa. Johannesburg is ardent and urgent. It spurs men to ideas, to action, to competition. There is electricity in its atmosphere.
—Sarah Gertrude Millin

Johannesburg has long been Africa's most developed city.
—AbdouMaliq Simone

Introducing Johannesburg

Johannesburg is the name conferred by a nineteenth-century republic in 1886 upon an original triangle of a few square kilometers—which even then did not actually encompass everything in the growing and unruly urban place.[1] It is the name moreover accepted by the present, democratically elected, city government, in contrast to several other metropolitan areas in South Africa.[2] There is, thus, an official definition of a large metropolitan space today. But less officially, seldom is the full title spoken—indicating that definition, description, and understanding of the city can be elusive. For many decades the common name has been Joburg, the title now used on local government documents (e.g., City of Johannesburg 2002). This is "a city now widely known by young hip South Africans as *Jozi*" (Nuttall 2006). Often the city is called Gauteng, place of gold, now the name of the post-1994 province to which the city is central. Obviously, defining geography is tricky. At least as often now, one hears Egoli, the Xhosa and Zulu equivalent. And very often local names are used by citizens—"I'm a Sowetan," or "I'm from Sandton."

This chapter is in English, perhaps the most known language of the city, and one that certainly connects it to the anglo globe in a way that is not entirely shared by São Paulo and Shanghai, but is something more like Mumbai perhaps. It is useful to remember that English is the first language of a minority in the city and the country. In fact, there is a lack of published material that approaches the city from outside the perspective of anglophone academics or writers. Joburg has only one daily paper of reasonable circulation in anything other than English—and the exception is in Afrikaans, not—say like Durban—in Zulu. The impression created in the English-language representation of the city may be partial, or perhaps false.

The chapter proceeds by reviewing some of the existing literature on the city and then, in turn, briefly examining facets of the city's nature—its history, geography, sociology, economy, government, and politics. It is an introduction, and more detail will be found in the other chapters on the city in this collection. It seeks to contextualize, and then to pose, the question of linkages between globalization and governance in Johannesburg. But by no means does it provide answers.

Literature and the City of Johannesburg

This essay is one among many texts to introduce the city. Johannesburg was the subject of a number of important works in an earlier period, before the international response to apartheid removed the city from global consciousness and turned it into merely an exceptional case of urban oppression. For example, Redcliffe-Maud wrote of the significance of the Johannesburg model of local government in a widely read study in the 1930s (Redcliffe-Maud 1937). From the mid-fifties onward, however, the kind of energy that in other parts of the world went into explorations of local political machines and urban development was devoted, in Johannesburg, to detailed work in a number of traditions mostly concerned with opposition to apartheid. There is no muckraking tradition of the type that gave Americans and Canadians important if controversial critiques: no "Johannesburg Inc." to match, for example, Donald Gutstein's (1975) portrayal of a city of the same age in *Vancouver Ltd*. There has not yet been a Rutheiser (1996) to examine business or local government-based promotion of the city.

Fortunately the city has been blessed with some fabulous fiction and poetry—some of it collected in Ricci (1986) and in Holland and Roberts (2002). As with many cities, a better introduction can often be gained through fiction than nonfiction. While most of the published material is in English, there are more women and black fiction writers and poets than analysts and academics. Yet the literature mostly addresses bits of life in the city. There is little that allows us to grasp the city as a whole from diverse perspectives.

Descriptive and travel writing on Johannesburg, too, often gives us elements that are missing from local material. From one among many examples, Christine Routier Le Diraison (2001) passed comments on the city that are rare internally, partly because of her attempt to place Sandton's peculiar features in a much wider context for her French readers. Nat Nakasa (1986) explained why she could, perhaps, do so when he wrote

> People who have the best time in Johannesburg are the visitors. People who stay in town for a month or two and then fly out to their homes across the seas, with memories as their only link with Johannesburg ... they ask crucial questions without getting emotionally involved with the town's preoccupations. ... I have often tried to put myself in this position, to approach Johannesburg with the attitude of a disengaged visitor. Unfortunately for me, I cannot succeed in doing this. I am a part of Johannesburg.

By contrast, the perspective here is from within, but still mostly for those without. In some ways this same view is taken in a recent trilingual text, authored by an architect who has taken a harsh line on city administrators since she resigned from city administration in 1997. The title of this cross between critique and coffee-table book (lavishly illustrated with photographs, and with less than 18,000 words of text) is *Johannesburg: One City Colliding Worlds* (Bremner 2004). Such a theme is familiar but not necessarily helpful in understanding Johannesburg. The limits of a cultural conflict view are revealed in another recent text in the illustrated genre, an article titled "Africa's City of Hope and Fear" in the *National Geographic* (Godwin 2004). The photographer for the latter piece claims in a footnote to the article that the city was "the most dangerous, difficult shoot of a lifetime," evoking a depressing theme that peppers much media coverage of the city: can Johannesburg "help save Africa ... or will [it] simply be overwhelmed by the needy and desperate. A woeful harbinger of the chaos to come?" (Godwin 2004, 77). Such are the tones of many of the most widely sold and circulated readings of the city. As in most cities, making sense of it all is an elusive quest. For Joburg, Monty Narsoo captures the difficulty: "[S]omehow, somewhere, there is sense in all this, but I'm still grasping for it" (Narsoo 2004, 174). The present chapter introduces a number of contributions that do attempt from scholarly perspectives to make some sense of Joburg in the globalizing world of the early twenty-first century. A backdrop is provided by recent contributions to what has been a surprisingly thin academic literature on the city.

This material includes several new volumes on Johannesburg that have fundamentally altered the existing academic literature on the city, at least by beginning to fill the gap. Four significant publications can be mentioned, one collectively written by three scholars, a second being a collection of articles, the third a research study conducted by a local think tank, and last the city government's own strategic analysis and program, which contains an important analysis of economic change. These works all take a "whole city" view, which is in line with the approach in this book.

Beall, Crankshaw, and Parnell (2002) deliver the most coherent of these works, although even here there are profound gaps and disjunctures. They cover a wide range of issues in economic, social, and policy contexts and also illustrate their work with cases of life in various sections of the city. They argue that Johannesburg is far from being alone in many of its features and suggest, following Parnell and Mabin (1995), that while racial issues are "unequivocally important," there are other important issues of social differentiation, polarization, exclusion, and inequality that require a different approach to that of much previous work (see Parnell and Mabin 1995, 45).

The collection edited by Tomlinson et al. (2003) draws on work presented to the Urban Futures conference of 2000 (on which see Mabin 2001). Like almost all collections, it is uneven but it contains several important essays. Most interestingly, the editors are perhaps more constantly aware of questions of governance than the book noted previously. One of them, Xolela Mangcu (the only black South African author in the volume), suggests that the city has seen a shift in the past decade from "left-wing to right-wing modernism" (2003, 288). And the volume also contains an intriguing essay on governmentality in Johannesburg by Graeme Gotz and AbdouMaliq Simone that reports the experience of a part of city government, frustrated in its attempts to "improve" the inner city, that ultimately began to find success through "respect[ing] and confirm[ing] multiple existing urban identifications in the process of elaborating new ones more appropriate to the exploitation of fluid . . . opportunities" (2003, 146). Here we are reminded of the need to explore changing governance through far more than a single lens.

In their research report, Ann Bernstein and Jeff McCarthy examine Johannesburg as the most global city in Africa. This report is close to the topic of the present chapter and provides an excellent analysis of the city. It argues that Johannesburg is an "increasingly unlikely member of a global network of world cities" (2002, 123). However, it does not really extend our understanding of how and why governance may be shifting in response to global changes, being more focused upon apparent failures on the part of governments at all scales (local, provincial, and national) to provide an environment conducive to more successful competition in the global economy. Whether its proposals respond adequately to the strategic program proposed by the city government under the title *Joburg 2030* (City of Johannesburg 2002) is a different question that need not concern us here.

In the latter volume, one finds a report with an extensive if partial analysis of the issues facing the city, which arrives at the conclusion that two key social issues have to be addressed if the city is to provide a space for serious levels of investment and economic growth. Those issues are skills, on one hand, and crime, on the other. Neither is fully within the range of powers formally available to the city government, but along with a range of issues considered at two lower levels of import, Joburg 2030 provides a fascinating insight into the thinking of those at the center of local political power—and a powerful analysis too.

Along with a number of shorter works in a range of journals, there is thus emerging a new literature on the city, which begins to provide some sense of possibilities. But the published literature still lacks contributions that might address a large number of important topics. Among those are a historical account of the role of local government and its impact (but see Tomlinson 2003); an analysis of the Johannesburg economy in more depth and insight (but see both Monitor 2000 and Solomon and Chen 1998); more attention to urban culture and its relationships to political and economic life (but see Mbembe and Nuttall 2006); and examination of the relationships between power (political and economic) in Johannesburg and power in the country, the continent, and the world (but see Chipkin 2004). So the challenge for this chapter is to provide an account addressing governance in globalizing Johannesburg while these lacunae exist.

The chapter undertakes this task by sketching in turn the history, geography, sociology, economy, and government of Johannesburg. On that basis, it then turns to situating Johannesburg in the present and future global context; and in the national and continental context.

A Sketch of the History of the City

Like other South African cities, Johannesburg is perhaps best known for its history of racial segregation. This is a city that has been polarized from the start. At various times, different regimes—usually operating at a scale much wider than the city itself—have deepened residential segregation and contributed to social dislocation and fragmentation. At the same time the economy of the city has both partially integrated the population, the spaces and the life of the city, and contributed to dividing the city.

Charles van Onselen (1982) wrote the most important account of Johannesburg's history. His essay on the political economy of the city from its beginnings to the First World War gave us an important understanding of the power of the mining and financial interests whose descendants, much altered, still straddle the city. His seven stories of diversity, conflict, and outcomes remain essential to understanding the creation of urban life. Van Onselen would be the first to point to the huge gaps that remain in knowledge of the city's history. One of those gaps concerns its government.

Local government in Johannesburg was a tiny thing until British colonialism arrived after Britain's victory in the Anglo-Boer War. Reconstruction after the war had enormously important results for the city, some of them physical. Perhaps the crowds of citizens who enjoy the environs of the city's largest park (in Emmarentia) on weekends need not be aware that the main water feature was built as a direct postwar reconstruction project, though some may now be more aware that Newtown, which present city government promotes as a cultural precinct, was the site of the first major urban renewal (i.e., destruction and forced removal) project in the city's history—again a direct result of postwar reconstruction (cf. Mabin and Smit 1997). From the present perspective, more significant is the institutional reconstruction that resulted, including the creation of the new city council (symbolized physically by the erection of the Edwardian city hall, ostentatiously facing the largest public building of the previous defeated regime, the republican post office, now sadly dilapidated). The new city government formed part of the creation of local government in much of the then-Transvaal colony under the influence of a group of young British civil servants, who attempted to plant on the African highveld some of the ideas that they and their colleagues were attempting to develop in Britain at the same time (Parnell and Mabin 1995).

Johannesburg's was never a purely mining economy. From the start the elite—which in any event in some respects transferred its location from Kimberley, the earlier mining and financial center—was more a financial than a mining elite, whose interests spread rapidly into land and a range of other activities. The growth of the economy in this peculiar inland area, hundreds of kilometers from the sea with no navigable water at hand, led to industrial development within the first few decades. As the city became the largest commercial center in the subcontinent, with the largest labor market and the largest concentration of wealth, the imbrication of ethnicities, identities, and activities proceeded to create something undeniably urban yet different from previous urban forms in the region.

The creation of a university around 1920 illustrates the interlocking power of the local elite, in which power in local government, finance, commerce, and industry was intimately connected across a relatively small grouping. This linking was still evident seventy years later (Taylor 1989). The conglomeration essentially controlled by this elite attracted huge migration and diversity—in the midst of which extraordinary and on occasion exceedingly violent conflict occurred. Parts of the city were bombed by the air force during a general strike in 1922. Then, perhaps as now, the establishment of authority in Johannesburg and political power in the city were vitally national in scope, and not really local at all—and at the same time, local economic power did not translate at all points easily into national political power.

The majority white population of Johannesburg, mostly of British origin, in many though not all respects reflected the type of population found in many other settler cities of the British Empire, from Melbourne to Vancouver. That was the global context in which many white minds were formed—again symbolically supported by imitations of the Kensington Gardens Peter Pan and Wendy statues in Joubert Park, with a Douglas Fir flagpole presented by the city of Vancouver not far away. What was close in Africa were the centers of mining and of British settler colonialism; Johannesburg's practical cousin in São Paulo was far more remote in the Joburg white mind than Sydney, the latter city of course being 60% more remote in distance—even though among some middle minority sectors of the population one could find those with family connections in the former. For all of these people, Joburg was not just a place of passage—it was a terminus, a home. And, increasingly, that was true for many in the black population too, as the growth of Marabi culture illustrated in the thirties or the Sophiatown-centered culture of the fifties (Dikobe 1973).

From the thirties to the fifties, Johannesburg's survival amid depression and war created the foundation for massive industrial growth (Freund 1989). But, in addition, the city became firmly the center of much national political life—particularly among those excluded from formal electoral politics. Nelson Mandela and Walter Sisulu lived in Joburg and revolutionized the African National Congress (ANC) from here. Yet the arrival of full apartheid government in 1948 created a profound shock. A certain uneasiness in relations between Johannesburg politics and between Johannesburg business and national government remained persistent. After the economic shock associated with the police killings of protestors at Sharpeville in 1960, rapid growth returned: now the plans of the fifties for freeways could begin to be realized, as indeed they were by the 1970s.

That decade saw the rise of the black voice—in trade unions and in the Soweto revolt of 1976—leading to the highly charged times of the 1980s. In part this was simply a result of the shift to a large African majority in a city that, before the Second World War, had a white majority, and the diverse employment changes to which reference will be made shortly. In addition, the rise of unemployment and the informal sector (previously displaced via controls on urbanward migration) from the late seventies created a very different social environment. Gradually, also, a shift in accumulation appeared at the edges of the economy. The best illustration runs in the form of taxis, that is, minibus transport, operated on or over the edge of regulation, while the economy of drugs and crime remains hidden. Certainly Johannesburg became a much less regulated city.

With the unbanning of political organizations such as the ANC and the Communist Party and the beginnings of negotiation toward democracy in 1990, the city commenced a period of regaining its global connections, which had been attenuated during the long decades of apartheid. A series of events represent that increased global prominence—the rugby world cup of 1995, the African football cup of nations in 1998, the World Summit on Sustainable Development in 2002, the cricket world cup in 2003, and the football World Cup scheduled for 2010. These events parallel a general freeing-up of markets and massively increased interaction with the wider world, as foreign arrivals at Johannesburg International Airport have multiplied many times over in the course of a decade.

A Sketch of the Geography and Sociology of the City

Johannesburg is the center of a large, varied, and often diffuse urban region with a population of about 9 million people in which boundaries are always arbitrary. Its area can be defined as a result in variable ways. Inside its current municipal boundaries, the city has a population of more than 3 million. There are several sources of difficulty in defining the population, among them the usual problem in large and complex urban areas: are we interested in the official city or in the larger urban area, and in the latter case, where does it end? Johannesburg presents a particularly difficult case for geographical definition, as demarcation boards discovered after the end of apartheid in 1994 and again with further reform of local government in 1999 (Mabin 1999a). Although the map of municipal boundaries has been revolutionized since 1994, and both separate "townships" and suburban municipalities merged into one metropolitan authority, the current city boundaries cover by no means the entire city region. Visitors arriving by air land at Johannesburg International Airport, which is more than ten kilometers from the eastern boundary of the city, and approach Johannesburg through a completely urbanized area beyond that boundary. The continuous urban area around the old city center stretches for more than fifty kilometers to the east, for more than thirty kilometers to the west, and for more than sixty kilometers to the southwest, and in the north there is scarcely a break between it and Pretoria, the national capital with its center sixty kilometers from Johannesburg—and, in turn, stretching dozens of kilometers further. The present province of Gauteng includes most of this area as well as some more rural territory.

The reasons for the particular separations of Johannesburg as a municipal area from its surroundings have been diverse but, more than anything else, can be claimed to relate to political considerations of diverse types over many decades. The most important official frontier is that to the east. There one finds a vast mining, industrial, residential, and commercial area developed along several axes, dating back as long as Johannesburg itself. For most of its history the area has been known in general as the East Rand, a geographical abbreviation of the common term Witwatersrand, the name by which the gold mining belt and its urban surrounds running through Johannesburg has historically been known. It has since the beginning of the twentieth century had many different municipalities, all much smaller than that of Johannesburg. But in many respects it is part of the greater urban area, in much the same way that Santo André, São Bernardo, São Caetano, and Diadema could not be contemplated as functionally separate from São Paulo. Only since 2000 has the East Rand had a metropolitan government, called Ekurhuleni, equal in status to that created at the same time for Johannesburg, and with a pop-

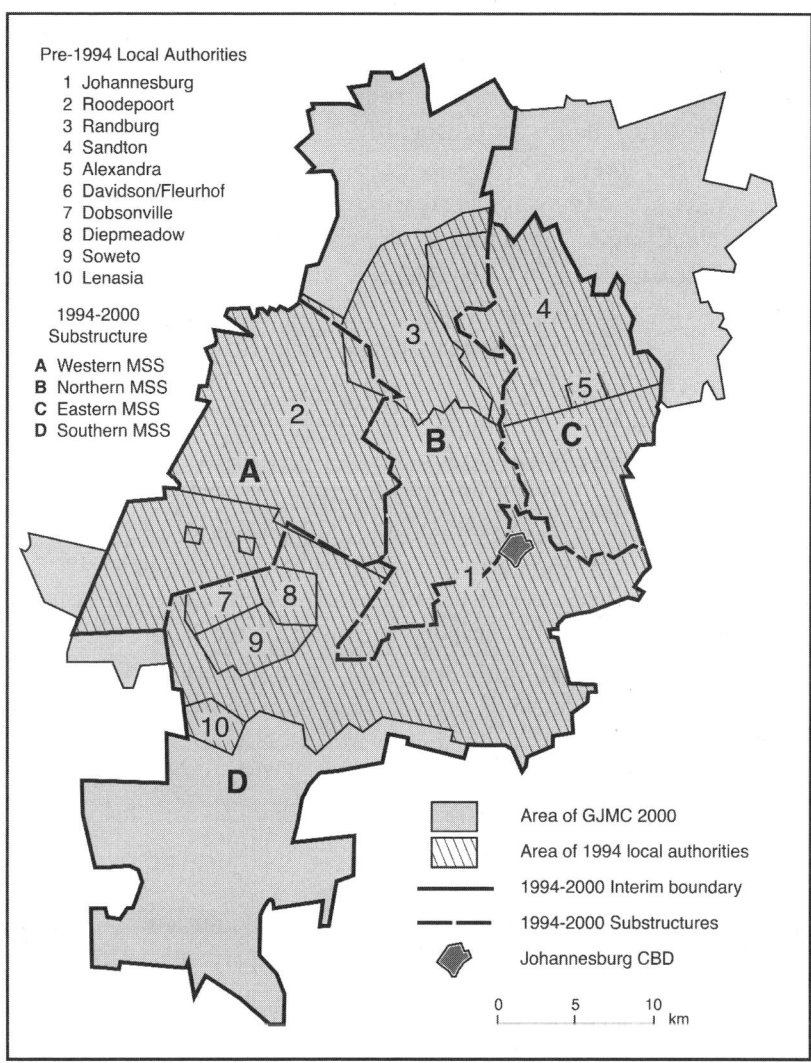

The changing local government boundaries of Johannesburg. CBD = central business district; GJMC = Greater Johannesburg Metropolitan Council; MSS = Metropolitan Sub-Structure.

ulation of 2.5 million. The line between the two is not entirely arbitrary, though it often cuts through areas indistinguishable on either side of the boundary and is crossed by massive daily commuting. But the history of that line is subtle, relating to an old politics of restricting Johannesburg as a city long ruled by opposition parties under apartheid (Mabin 1996).

More recently the greater opportunities offered by continued separation from Johannesburg may have been significant for local politicians to the east: had Johannesburg been extended in the 1999–2000 reforms to include the Ekurhuleni area, it would have contained two-thirds of the population of Gauteng province, perhaps placing provincial government in doubt (as in relationships between large city government and state, province, and region government elsewhere). This chapter generally speaks of Johannesburg as being the place within the current boundaries of Johannesburg as fixed in 1999. However, that does not solve the data difficulty, since there is no easy assemblage of data from existing censuses and other series to match the new boundaries. Still less does it allow us to think through all of the components that constitute the broader urban region with Johannesburg at its heart.

A second difficulty in defining and counting the population of Johannesburg (and South African cities in general) relates to the large and continuous circular migration that makes enumeration particularly difficult in a country such as South Africa. Is a person counted in Johannesburg or in the Nebo district of Limpopo province, or the Nqutu district of KwaZulu-Natal, where she or he may have family and another home? We simply do not know how well the census has yet been able to address this problem, since there is an inclination to inflate numbers for the distribution of finance and no absolute clarity about counting the exact status quo at a fixed time as opposed to a more fluid idea of where people live.

In addition there are many uncertainties relating to census accuracy. These are not uncommon, and very serious attempts have been made by StatsSA, a national agency, to improve the census. But enormous estimated corrections were required to the first post-apartheid census (1996) and the results of the next one (2001) reveal similar problems—for example, the precipitous fall in reported average household size between the two censuses raises many questions. Thus we must be satisfied with estimates and projections.

Like Shanghai but for different reasons, Johannesburg has been restricted in its past growth by policy and practice of urban containment, in this case racially motivated. But whether or not the effects of those practices persist at this point is hard to say, since there has been enormous in-migration—particularly in the period before 1960, and again after about 1980, tapering off in the more recent period. The city has grown enormously since the 1950s, but clearly not to the extent of creating a megacity on the scale of São Paulo, Mumbai, or Shanghai. On the other hand,

Summary Statistics for the City of Johannesburg

Population 1996	2,639,110
Population 2000	3,225,812
Five-year population growth 1996–2001	22.23%
Employment 1996	954,600
Employment 2001	1,085,500
Unemployed 2001	647,000
Unemployment rate 2001	37%
Daily commuters into city	800,000
Gross value added 2002[a]	15,564,000,000
Annual growth in value added 1996–2002	4.2%

Source: South African Cities Network 2004.
[a] In U.S. dollars, assuming one dollar equals 6.5 rand.

it could be argued that the entire continuous polycentric urban region to which Johannesburg is central, and including Pretoria to the north and Ekurhuleni to the east, with a population likely to exceed 15 million within fifteen years, is indeed in the process of becoming a "mega-urban region" equivalent to some of the larger world cities (South African Cities Network 2004, 167).

A simple (but not entirely simplistic!) way of thinking about the geography of the city was penned for a play performed in an inner-city theater: "There are three cities in Johannesburg: the suburban city, the township city and then the Town of Johannesburg itself. Joburg town gave birth to our metropolis. It is here where South Africa concretely manifests: Sangomas [traditional healers] compete for space with wholesalers, mining houses and banks compete with taxi ranks. But what happens after sunset?" (Levin 2002).

The other two types of areas are, very broadly speaking, the immense northern suburbs meaning mostly low-density sections, with a smaller parallel to the south, and the "townships," which include a variety of different living patterns but in general are equated with former mostly public housing and segregated black areas at considerable distances from the city center (among them everything from Ivory Park and Alexandra in the north to Soweto and Orange Farm in the south). The southern cone, stretching from Soweto to Orange Farm, contains 53% of the population.

A panoply of legislation extended the long-standing segregation of residence in Johannesburg in the 1950s and 1960s (Parnell and Pirie 1991). Though never absolutely fully applied, the consequence was the growth of residential areas of two main types: those almost exclusively inhabited by the victims of apartheid (black, colored, and Indian), and those almost exclusively owned and rented by whites, but with a substantial population of others, mostly domestic workers or in some cases illegal residents.

These segregation measures operated in tandem with town planning, meaning a system of public control of land use in the city. While the subdivision of land was subject to control from the early years of the twentieth century, only in the thirties was a type of zoning introduced. Both systems probably reinforced the racial segregation of the city but were perhaps less important in such outcomes, given the general degree of segregation in the society and other powerful legal instruments wielded by various state agencies (Mabin and Smit 1997).

The type of zoning applied tended toward the development of monofunctional areas in the city. In later years, selective use of town-planning provisions allowed the old Johannesburg municipality to encourage and to manage the transformation of several residential districts to commercial and office areas. It did so in part in order to fend off the challenge of then existing suburban municipalities, such as Randburg and Sandton, which in typical style attempted to attract business investment. From the eighties onward, there was a general decline in the effectiveness of zoning: not only did city authorities begin to favor mixed use over monofunctionality, but the capacity of city government to enforce land use regulation declined. During the transition period of the 1990s, that problem was particularly acute.

As apartheid declined during the 1980s, there was substantial change in many of the former white areas, with some parts becoming mostly black (Morris 1999; Beall, Crankshaw, and Parnell 2002). Residential change after apartheid was in some respects comparable to that in Harare, Zimbabwe, after independence in 1980, with the departure of whites from some areas and, in particular, the beginning of a movement of black and other formerly excluded groups to affordable areas with proximity to townships that were more familiar (Cummings 1993). These changes related very strongly to a changing racial division of labor (Beall, Crankshaw, and Parnell 2002). The upper echelons of work drew dramatically increasing numbers of black people from the 1970s until today. These changes have occurred in a context of declining manufacturing employment, rapidly increasing labor force participation on the part of women, and a general concentration of employment in services, commerce, and finance. Poorly educated workers find themselves increasingly excluded, a development in common with many other cities. Johannesburg concentrates a very large middle class as well as an unusually large elite, which owns and controls much of southern African business. The 1996 census suggested that a quarter of million residents work in professional, high-tech, and senior managerial positions, and in addition many more enter the city each day from neighboring areas, Tshwane and Ekurhuleni included (Bernstein and McCarthy 2002, 29).

It also has a substantial working class, but not one as organized or as clearly demarcated as in some of the surrounding areas—like Ekurhuleni. And it has an increasing marginal population—formally unemployed, often engaged in informal activities, which are concentrated in the townships and inner city. Some of the faster-growing areas of informal settlement lie within the city boundary, and others are in adjacent areas. Especially in the working class and more marginal populations, strong patterns of circular migration of varying periodicity link the city to many areas both near and far with substantial consequences for the city—for example, in whether households choose to invest in their city property, or in other parts of South Africa and beyond. An increasingly distant series of places is embroiled in similar patterns. These facets of social life make Johannesburg somewhat different from São Paulo, and in some respects more akin to Mumbai, or even Shanghai.

At least as important to the spatial organization of the city, centrality in the city has fragmented over time, not only due to a diffuse social centrality flowing from enforced residential segregation, but also due to the periodic development of new business centers, at distances from the original center. Here Johannesburg is very similar to São Paulo; these newer centers have challenged and complicated the issue of centrality in the city. Whereas in São Paulo one might speak of the progressive development of areas around Avenida Paulista, Avenida Faria Lima, and Avenida Berrini, Johannesburg has newer centers at Rosebank, Sandton, and Fourways. It is Sandton that captures most attention and most investment, with most international companies locating their offices there, and with the significant move of the Johannesburg Stock Exchange (now called the JSE Securities Exchange) to Sandton in the very recent past. The recomposition of patterns of work, with many more smaller offices dispersed

Occupational Distribution of Employment, Percent by Sector, Johannesburg 1996

				Service Sector		
Occupational Category	Mining	Manufacturing	Commerce	Financial Real Estate, Business Services	Community, Social, Personal Services	Total Service Sector
Managers, professionals, technicians	29	21	21	43	30	32
Clerks, service and sales workers	14	13	43	45	15	34
Craft, trades workers	31	41	16	3	6	8
Plant and machine operators	14	15	4	2	2	3
Unskilled manual workers	12	9	16	6	47	23
Total	100	100	100	100	100	100

Source: Beall, Crankshaw, and Parnell 2002, table 3.2 based on 1996 Census.

through former residential areas and along major roads previously protected by land use regulation, has revolutionized the distribution of employment.

This set of movements and associated shifts in the status of residential addresses has challenged the long-standing basic geography of the city, leading Keith Beavon to suggest that the northern suburbs are becoming "a neo-apartheid city" with new forms of exclusion through property prices (Beavon 2000) and, I would add, the labor market. Thus a perceptive commentator on politics and governance in South Africa, Hein Marais (2000), has noted that "Suburbanisation in Johannesburg is not just a temporary kink, a kind of collective tic in the face of change. It entails a massive relocation of material and political power toward specific city zones, where the middle classes recongregate and regroup." Younger populations see the new forms as normal, including those who seek quiet and security through the large number of gated communities of diverse types that have developed particularly in the northern suburbs of Johannesburg (Bremner 1999; Jurgens and Gnad 2000; Beall, Crankshaw, and Parnell 2002, chap. 10; Jurgens, Gnad, and Bahr 2003; Mabin and Harrison 2006; Bremner 2004). Many residents, including many foreigners working for periods in the city, consider these spaces to be "a normal environment, like it should be" (a comment from a well-known golfer who lives in a security estate, quoted in Burdett 2001, 21). To some extent these shifts are a response to crime, violence, and insecurity, for which Johannesburg is apparently infamous (Bremner 1999). But, in reality, such pathologies are concentrated in the townships and often relate to domestic situations (Palmary, Rauch, and Simpson 2003).

Johannesburg thus presents "geographies of exclusion" in the words of a French scholar (Guillaume 2002). A crucial component of this pattern is the presence of substantial populations in very poor accommodation, "which reinforce an impression of stark class inequalities" (Bernstein and McCarthy 2002, 23). Areas that might be called *favelas* in Brazil are very significant, and in the townships (and some former white sections) there are many poorly built extensions or "back yard shacks"; however, illegal subdivision and occupation are scarce and, since poor people often find accommodation through the assistance of others (Gilbert et al. 1997), there are remarkably few absolutely homeless people on the streets.

While a significant proportion of the population lives in poor housing, most of the housing environment in Johannesburg is of better quality than those numbers might otherwise suggest. A large part of the recently built housing stock has been subsidized by the government and built by private developers for some of the poorest sections of the population, and although located in peripheral areas, these new additions to the housing stock allow a degree of connection to urban services and use of modern appliances that is rare in comparison to poorer cities in the region.

Poor Housing in Johannesburg	
Shack settlements: households	155,000
Backyard shacks: households	57,000
Homeless street people	4,500

Source: South African Cities Network 2004; City of Johannesburg Web site, www.joburg.org.

In the context of the present study, the extent to which these patterns are a result of globalization is significant. It can certainly be concluded that the strong move toward tertiary employment in Johannesburg has exercised an enormous impact on the populations that are socially and geographically disadvantaged (Benit 2001, 234–37; Beall, Crankshaw, and Parnell 2002). But whether this is a consequence of globalization is not demonstrated, and indeed not substantially developed by recent authors (Beall, Crankshaw, and Parnell 2002, 22–24). And its implications for governance are yet to be tested.

A key question for the city, then, is whether these social exclusions and spatial fragmentations can be overcome. In the heady excitement of the immediate post-apartheid period, many felt positive on this subject. In particular, the geography of the apartheid city seemed a target for democratic rearrangement. But experience has demonstrated, over the past decade, that denting the geographies of exclusion through policy and planning is very difficult indeed. For example, a well-known optimistic project to link Soweto into the fabric of the city, called Bara Link, has made little headway. As a Dutch commentator observed, "So far there isn't much to see of Bara Link. On the other hand, free enterprise is creating one complex after another in the northern periphery of the metropolis" (De Meulder 1998). The evidence suggests that new investment, particularly globally sourced and connected investment, goes to spaces in the north of the city, the suburban or edge city. In other words, the neo-apartheid geographies of exclusion, involving both the heritage of racial division and the workings of property and labor markets, are also a product of increasing global connection. In addressing the problems of the city, herein lies a spatial challenge for governance in the present period. Municipal government has thus far responded hardly at all to this change, except to turn to trumpeting the receptivity of the new, suburban environments to global corporations.

A Sketch of the Urban Region Economy

Johannesburg is historically a mining center, and an industrial city, but today its economy is that of a financial and business services center, with a diverse commercial economy as well as a changing industrial economy. It is the key point of global economic contact for South Africa and a wider region. There have been significant changes in this role since 1990, with increasing flows through Johannesburg. Under changing national regulation, some of the largest South African companies, mostly based in Johannesburg, have registered and listed abroad. As yet no studies appear to measure what the effects of those direct forms of globalization may be having on the city economy, but it is reasonable to infer that the direct effects include some loss of income to the city, while the indirect effects—if these shifts actually encourage general economic growth—may be the inverse.

It could be asserted that Johannesburg exists in a pattern of competition with other cities (from Lagos to Cape Town) on cultural, ideological, political, and economic grounds. Such competition introduces potential strains into the future of Johannesburg. The city government is larger than most South African provinces in financial terms, and although it is politically closely aligned to the dominant party nationally, a key source of potential instability in coming decades will be in its relationship with other spheres of government, both provincial and national, as well as with its large neighbors (the cities of Tshwane [Pretoria] and Ekhuruleni [East Rand]).

Johannesburg's gross geographic product may be estimated at approximately 15.5 billion USD in 2002. This constitutes 16.4% of the gross national product as against the city's 7.2% share of national population. The average annual growth rate over the past decade has been rising from the region of 2% per annum to more than 4%, while that of the country averaged 1.8% per annum. Employment growth has averaged only 1% per annum while unemployment has risen between 1996 and 2001 from 27% to 37% (South African Cities Network 2004).

There is an enormous concentration of business in Johannesburg. There are approximately 290,000 formal sector business enterprises that employ about 840,000 people (on some estimates: up to 950,000 on others). Some 74% of national corporate head offices are in the city, using much of the approximately 6.52 million square meters of office space available—which in turn represents 55% of the total office space in the country. Among the companies based in Johannesburg are most South African and international banks operating in the country, with approximately 70% of banks headquartered here. As illustrations of the concentration of certain business service sectors in the city, 45% of travel agencies are in the city, and there are 580 accountancy firms representing 40% of the national capacity. The JSE Securities Exchange is eleven times larger than the next largest exchange in Africa (Bernstein and McCarthy 2002) and is effectively the only such exchange in the country. At the end of 2002 it ranked twentieth in the world measured by market capitalization of shares of domestic companies, being roughly equivalent in size to those of Mumbai, São Paulo, Singapore, and Helsinki, among others.

The growth of business services has entailed a rapid increase in small enterprises run by former employees of large companies. This change has altered the employment geography of the city as much as anything else. With the continued shift toward the financial and servicing sectors, the structural changes in Johannesburg have made it South Africa's "quintessential professional, private sector city" (Bernstein and McCarthy 2002, 19).

From the first, Johannesburg has been a site of international organizations, particularly corporations, and media. It remains overwhelmingly the main site of foreign business in the country and wider region, although of course foreign companies are engaged in production in many other parts of the country (the automobile industry is scarcely represented in the city); and some multinationals in particular sectors have preferred other cities for their South African headquarters (such as oil companies in Cape Town). But banks, financial services, business services more generally, and a large range of international companies are to be found in Johannesburg. It is also the site of most foreign media representation. In each of these aspects there has been substantial change in the post-apartheid period, with significant growth of foreign representation. It appears that after a period of stagnation the urban economy is again expanding rapidly, though with some particular weaknesses. Employment growth is found in the tourism, technology, and retail sectors.

Like most other countries of the global south, a large part of the local economy (especially in terms of human scale) is generally thought of as informal in Johannesburg. According to data gathered by the city, the informal sector is growing very rapidly—between 1996 and 1999 employment in the informal sector rose from 9.6% to 16% of total employment (City of Johannesburg 2002, 26).

Whether or not one would wish to argue that the presence of such large-scale informality means that there are two separate circuits of the urban economy, there would appear to be little direct integration between formal and informal. A key challenge for the future is to find the means of intervening in the informal economy in order to raise productivity and income levels toward those of the formal economy (Mhone 2003).

In addition to the contrasting growth of informal activity on one hand and the development of more and more sophisticated financial and other

Economic Output by Sectors

Sector	Proportion of Total Formal Employment, %	Employment Annual Growth Rate, %	Contribution to City Gross Geographic Product	GGP Annual Growth Rate
Finance and business services	22.6	4.1	31.7	1.0
Trade	18.7	6.0	20.7	0.6
Manufacturing	19.8	−2.7	15.1	3.7
Community and social services	17.8	−0.3	12.4	0.7
Transport and communication	6.2	−2.0	8.3	5.6
Public administration and defense	4.5	−0.3	1.7	0.7
Construction	7.6	2.1	3.9	4.5
Other	2.4	0.9	5.7	0.9

Source: Monitor 2000, 21.

services on the other, a further change in the Johannesburg economy involves growth in the culture, tourism, and technology sectors. It has been claimed that Johannesburg, from the later 1990s, was becoming a creative city through these shifts (Dirsuweit 1999).

The connection with global business and broader society is particularly striking in Johannesburg. But that connection involves, directly, only a minority symbolized by the mingling of business tourists and local high-income people in the most expensive shopping centers in the northern suburbs. Yet there are other forms of connection with economies (and social life) in other parts of the world. Particularly notable in this regard are the patterns of movement between Johannesburg and much of the rest of the African continent. Traders from Mali sell wares in marketplaces and purchase commodities in Johannesburg to take to markets in west Africa. There are increasingly complex social economies that, in addition to those long tying much of southern Africa to Johannesburg, now begin to integrate spaces especially in cities from Kampala to Dakar. These are new patterns, altering long-established colonial forms of north-south interaction and offering both challenges and opportunities to government in Johannesburg.

A Sketch of City Government and Politics

South Africa has fundamentally been a unitary state since 1910 when its present area was established from a number of previous colonial territories. Constitutional negotiation in 1991–93 produced three levels of government, national, provincial, and local, each of which began a first process of (re)organization during the term of the first democratic government, led by Nelson Mandela, from 1994 to 1999. The major activities of provincial governments were defined as education, health, and aspects of transport and welfare, as well as rather vague notions of provincial development and stronger ideas of managing local government. Local government itself continued previous, apartheid-era, activities, albeit within transitional structures that brought together previously divided black and white areas. This interim arrangement began to change, however, with the adoption of the 1997 constitution, which set out a much greater degree of equality in the relations between the three spheres (not levels) of government. Provincial and national power to intervene in local government was restricted. This somewhat different new approach was reflected in the White Paper on Local Government in 1998 (South Africa 1998), which saw municipalities as much more than the mere "hands and feet" of the center. The new approach was cemented by the local government elections of 2000, which saw Johannesburg emerge as a unified metropolitan council led by an executive mayor (the first being Amos Masondo, who moved from a provincial cabinet position to take the central role in the city).

While the city certainly enjoys substantial formal autonomy, its position is greatly affected by national and regional power. In the first place, the party in power in Johannesburg is also in power nationally, and has a distinct agenda for the reshaping of South African society. Political decision making in the city is subordinate to that agenda. While it is hard to point to direct national interference in local affairs, a distinct direction of city politics is yet to emerge. Even the new national association of the largest cities, known as the South African Cities Network, in which there is some potential for setting a specific metropolitan agenda, was born from the national ministry of local government affairs.

Second, the city experienced a serious financial crisis during the late nineties (Beall, Crankshaw, and Parnell 2002). A consequence has been that Johannesburg's capital expenditure budget has been severely limited and the city has been dependent on other scales of government for major new projects. The key example here is the provincial operation known as Blue IQ, an agency of the provincial premier's office, which has significant capital funds available and has several major projects in Johannesburg as well as other parts of the province of Gauteng. Thus the city finds itself to some extent tied to a wider agenda, whether or not that is the desire of its politicians and senior officials. Yet the financial picture is changing. In future electoral terms, it may be that the city leadership will find itself increasingly at odds with other spheres of government as it seeks to pursue its strategic agenda—which, as noted later, points to an increasing separation of Johannesburg as a world-class African city from much of the rest of its country and wider region.

Meanwhile, however, local government in South Africa has historically been, and remains, concerned primarily with the delivery of urban services to residents and businesses—water, electricity, waste disposal, road building and maintenance, and so on. It has almost always had only limited health, safety, and policing functions, and has no responsibility for education, which of course looms large in the politics of local government in many other countries. In South Africa, the latter is primarily a provincial activity, with substantial national involvement.

Johannesburg's major elected council goes back to the beginning of the twentieth century; while originally it was a ratepayer elected body, which meant essentially a white male electorate, it became a white universal franchise body during the course of the century.

The main financial basis of local government is twofold: property taxes, in Johannesburg historically charged on land values alone, called "rates" in the English tradition; and charges for services, particularly electricity delivered by the city. The fragmentation of the city in the long era of segregation and apartheid implies an extremely complex history.

The initial period of reform of local government after apartheid was based not on a locally agreed system of governance but on a nationally negotiated deal, cut in 1993 before the first democratic elections. Prior to that, there had been a significant period of negotiation in Johannesburg between the former white-elected councils that covered a large part of the area, and the civic association movement based in the townships (Swilling and Boya 1997; Mabin 1999a). In late 1994 and 1995 urgent work was done by a provincial demarcation board to redraw the map of Johannesburg in order to create a space of local government not defined in large part by race. For complex reasons (Mabin 1999a) the process resulted in the erasing of not only the boundaries dividing black and white local authorities, with their own shorter and longer histories, but also the independent suburban municipalities such as Randburg and Sandton that had been created in the 1960s.

An interim body consisting of representatives of the old regimes and the opposition—that is, various parties to the national negotiation process—ran most of the area of the current city. The first semidemocratic elections were held in 1995. They produced councils for four subareas of the city (as well as for certain areas then still outside the current boundaries, such as Midrand) as well as a metropolitan council—the latter intended by many to be a strong body, but which faced many initial difficulties, among them questions of the division of powers between the four local bodies and the metro. After a further five years and a nationally decided process once more, new boundaries were drawn up for local government across the country and Johannesburg was expanded, the local councils were abolished, and a single metropolitan council was elected in 2000.

This constitutional account, however, provides only the backdrop for a period that brought three types of radical changes in urban governance in the city. One aspect was corporatism after a period of turmoil in government. From the end of the 1980s there had been a paralysis of local government in the Johannesburg area, brought about by a massive boycott of public housing rentals and service charge payments in the townships (Swilling and Boya 1997). But the constitutional changes did not provide a satisfactory revival of local government, since Johannesburg found itself in a continuing fiscal crisis (Beall, Crankshaw, and Parnell 2002). One result was the involvement of provincial government and powerful forces in the ruling party, the ANC, in a new form of management for the city, which among other things brought the local councils under the heel of the metropolitan central offices. However, what was most significant was that these new politics permitted the beginnings of a corporatist approach to the city's institutions. A program known as iGoli 2002 was developed and resulted very rapidly in the corporatization of most major aspects of the city's public business, including electricity, water, roads, and lands. Some units were fully privatized (gas, the old city airport). In consequence, the functioning of several large and significant former departments of city government became registered companies, with a single shareholder (the City of Johannesburg) and with executives responsible not to the city council but to the appointed boards of directors. Services were effectively outsourced to private entities, some owned by the city. Many staff members were retrenched or laid off, resulting in a large strike and protest actions, which were defused by national political intervention. But that intervention was consistent with the new institutional approach in the city.

These moves were warmly welcomed by established businesses in the city. Such opinion was reflected in South Africa's major financial weekly, *Financial Mail*, which wrote that the appointment of the city manager who planned these moves involved "probably the most radical change in style of government since the ANC came to power in 1994" (cited in Beall, Crankshaw, and Parnell 2002, 98). The consequence was certainly that the city government entered a period of consolidation with more stable institutions and strategies.

A second radical change affected strategy and policy at the general level. When the ANC came to power in Johannesburg in 1994, its program essentially assumed that the city was wealthy enough to accomplish greatly improved services in townships through redistributing expenditure from the former white areas. That proved to be unworkable. However, the ANC remained at least rhetorically committed to the constituency that had elected it—mostly poor and black and living in the townships. It was for a time unable to make a break toward a new strategic approach, but during a period of rule largely by a city manager and a nominated committee rather than by the five (four local, one metro) councils, the ground was prepared for a shift from the emphasis on redistribution to a new growth focus as the means to acquire the resources to ameliorate conditions of life in the city. This shift was symbolized by the frequent use of the phrase, "world-class city" to describe what the city manager and others apparently wanted Johannesburg to become.

As the corporatization process began, the city also commenced a program intended to develop a new strategic plan, with the goal of contributing to economic growth very much in mind. That process, known as iGoli 2010, looked toward a decade-long strategy. The process was based on a new approach to governance, which is a third arena of radical change in the city's recent history. The basis was the creation of an iGoli 2010 partnership, involving social movements, business leaders, and politicians. These constituencies met frequently in a forum that commissioned a series of research reports from a large international consulting firm with offices in Johannesburg, the Monitor Group. Particularly important was the inclusion of business leaders in the forum, since in the previous few years of democratic government, local government and business leaders had found it very difficult to find a means of discussion.[3] In the end, however, it was not the forum that found a strategy. The local government elections of 2000 intervened, and the election of a new slate of councillors together with the appointment of new officials, particularly in the financial portfolios, created an opportunity for key individuals to develop a new strategic vision and program for the city. They put the period over which poverty might be eliminated in the city at a generation, thirty years. On the basis of the forum's research and new work conducted by a carefully selected individual consultant, a report was produced and promoted by these key individuals to the most significant councillors and a few others. A process of retreats and workshops resulted in this new strategy being adopted by the council early in 2002. The varied meanings of this appearance of participation are explored by Parnell in her essay in this collection.

Adoption of the *Joburg 2030* strategy by the Council (City of Johannesburg 2002) demonstrated that the trappings of new consultative governance provided an opportunity for a tactics of spreading a new set of ideas, informed by much discussion but shaped by a few individuals, then essentially agreed to in an essentially top-down manner. This policy puts economic growth at the center of the city's goals. It finds that investment is inversely proportional to crime, and thus makes dealing with violence and crime one of two key elements in helping to foster growth (the other being skills development). This strategy clearly illuminates the shift from redistribution to growth as the basic philosophy of those in power. And the experience shows that governance has altered significantly in the city. Certainly this has happened in a period of rapidly increasing global linkage. However, that does not necessarily mean that the radical shifts in governance (constitutionally, institutionally, strategically, and in terms of government-citizen relations) are closely connected to globalization.

The political situation in Johannesburg is vital to examining the question whether recent changes in the city are related to globalization. Johannesburg is a large city experiencing change of all kinds—economic, political, social, and geographic and with respect to its position in the world—changes that create extraordinary opportunities and also anxieties. The society in which the city exists happens to be one of the world's more unequal, from income and wealth perspectives. There is a history of division, much but not all of it imposed in pursuit of an apartheid policy until less than a decade ago. In this context it is not surprising that radically different views exist on the means, both individual and collective, of addressing the problems that confront citizens.

The Johannesburg City Council has more than 200 seats, half of which are elected on a ward basis and half on a party list, proportional representation basis. In 2004 the ANC held about 60% of the seats. For the most part, formal council politics are dominated by the ANC—harried by its opposition, most prominently the Democratic Alliance (DA) inside the council—and by groups both in and just outside the tent on the left of the core ANC in extracouncil politics. The latter are mostly concerned with organizing the allegedly forgotten constituencies of poorer people who face inadequate water, sanitation, energy, transport and housing delivery (Bond 2004). They conspicuously avoid the violence and crime issues that probably affect poorer groups more severely than anyone else in the city. On the other side, the DA is apparently more conservative than the ANC as well as noticeably whiter, and at least appears to campaign on behalf of constituencies that have substantial property to protect from crime. Both nationally and locally the DA is vociferous in its criticism of the alleged failure of government institutions to protect citizens from crime and violence.

The ANC and DA, to some extent, compete for the high ground in the struggle to situate Johannesburg as a global city. Both have moved to emphasize, among other things, stability and security as key elements in this supposed status. In this context the issue of retrofitting gates and fences to enclose residential areas (creating effectively gated communities) is a highly contradictory issue for governance (Mabin and Harrison 2006). The cleavages around city policy for handling gating of communities illustrates the unexpected tensions of Johannesburg politics. Thus one finds ANC supporters in some neighborhoods strongly in favor of access restriction. One also finds DA supporting residents campaigning against the closure of their suburbs. One hears the (ANC) executive anxiously calling for access restriction in industrial areas to protect factories from crime. Because of the nonalignment of these fractures with normal political division, the access restriction issue has become exceedingly difficult for the ANC to handle in the Johannesburg council. And because of the fragility of its opponents, no other large or formal grouping has been able to use the issue as a stick with which to beat those in power.

Like liberation movements around the world, the ANC is a broad church and is certainly not purely a party of the disadvantaged. Indeed, its prominent members are very much among the (new) elite of South African society—and, just like bourgeois citizens in other parts of the world, their concerns include safety and security for themselves, their property, and their investments. But the ANC is also the party of liberty in South Africa, and privatization of public space must be anathema to many of its supporters. Managing this tension presents a challenge symbolic of many more.

It could readily be argued in this context that the key constituency in urban politics in the city is the rising black middle class. Some have suggested that this constituency has been neglected in governance (W. James 1997 cited in Bernstein and McCarthy 2002: 30). However, the recent evidence in Johannesburg circumstantially suggests the opposite. The policies adopted by the city, in line with national government, are essentially similar to those pursued by foreign governments under Thatcher, Reagan, Chirac, or local government under Giuliani (contemplate the security issue), and implicitly favor the middle classes. In the political culture of the ruling party, it is probable that those who dominate the present discourse are drawn from the same classes, with a cloak of black economic empowerment as a highly significant feature of advancing the interests of a powerful political (but not economically dominant) black elite.

Thus in this context the question is posed, how much of any or all of change in the city's governance can be explained by global connection and change? In the specifically Johannesburg context, the answer might be that the influence of global organizations and experience on a small number of strategically placed individuals combined with some (but not clearly determined) effects of global economic and political change have had an enormous impact. Where these relationships, effects, and trajectories will lead in the future is even less clear.

An interesting contribution to this debate has been made by two French scholars, who suggest that globalization is "instrumentalized" by those in power as a means of rationalizing the types of urban interventions that are emerging. Benit and Gervais-Lambony (2004) argue that a politics of the *double vitrine* has developed: the public pronouncements of city authorities promote investment in the newer, globally connected spaces of finance and business as the public "shop window," while the mounting poverty and exclusion characteristic of large sections of the townships and some inner-city areas is hidden away, to a considerable extent, in the "back room of the shop." In other words, rather than suggesting that processes of globalization are responsible directly for changes in the economy, geography, and governance of the city, they suggest that the rhetoric of globalization allows those in power to explain and justify particular approaches to development, which actually entrench at least spatial forms of inequality. In this analysis, governance becomes a process of promoting development in the shop window and managing poverty in the back shop.

Johannesburg presents any analysis of present urban change in large cities with intriguing problems. Is the city evidencing increasing private-sector dominance or is that a superficial understanding of city change? Is Johannesburg likely to become increasingly divergent from South African trends?

For those who accept that "world cities are fundamentally different from other kinds of cities [and that] their essential roles are to provide 'homes' for national and international corporate and financial management" (Bernstein and McCarthy 2002, 70), the role of urban governance in such contexts is clear. Yet governance is also about contest, and about resolving contradictions. Indeed, governance concerns relationships and not simply management.

Thus the particular form of change linked to global change in Johannesburg's governance is both toward more democratic practice and, at the same time, toward a more business-friendly and generally global system of governance. In this way it seems an archetypal case—just what one would expect to find in a sense.

Conclusion

This essay is positioned within a discourse that argues that Johannesburg is a prism through which to view the world (Mabin 1999b; Mbembe and Nuttall 2006), but in order to do so, much work is needed. There are limits to the application of this perspective—many Western appearances to the contrary, Johannesburg is not a Western city: "Just another western city. Yes, but not quite. The difference, it seemed to me, was simply that here, nearly always now, was the threat of Africa bursting up through the tarmac and alienation of the littered western streets" (Robbins 1987, 154).

By the same token, it is quite distinct from Asian cities (compare Lee Boon Thon 1995), whatever similarities of positioning occur in the era of globalization. It is indeed an *African* city and may, for that reason, reveal some peculiarities—some of which are in cultural realms little explored in this chapter (e.g., Ashforth 2000). There is much more to be done in order to understand and project the directions of change in governance in the African city, and Johannesburg is no exception.

Notes

1. Thus excluded were some of the more important mining camps, such as Ferreirastown.
2. Ethekwini for Durban, Nelson Mandela for Port Elizabeth, Tshwane for Pretoria.
3. Interviews with business sector individuals, conducted by Alan Mabin, January 2002.

References

Ashforth, A. 2000. *Madumo: A Man Bewitched*. Chicago: University of Chicago Press.
Badal, S. 2000. Slaughter in a smart suburb. *Financial Times*, 12–13 August, Weekend supplement.
Beall, J., O. Crankshaw, and S. Parnell (eds.). 2002. *Uniting a Divided City: Governance and Social Exclusion in Johannesburg*. London: Earthscan.
Beavon, K. 2000. Northern Johannesburg: Part of the "Rainbow" or Neo-apartheid City in the Making? *Mots Pluriels Revue électronique de Lettres à caractère international*. www.arts.uwa.edu.au/MotsPluriels/MP1300kb.html.
Benit, C. 2001. La fragmentation urbaine à Johannesburg: Recomposition des pouvoirs locaux, mobilités de travail et dynamiques résidentielles dans la ville post-apartheid. Doctoral thesis, Université de Poitiers.
Benit, C., and P. Gervais-Lambony. 2004. La mondialisation comme instrument politique local dans les métropoles sud-africaines Johannesburg et Ekhuruleni: les "pauvres" face aux "vitrines." *Annales de Géographie*, no. 633.
Bernstein, A., and J. McCarthy. 2002. *Johannesburg: Africa's World City? A Challenge to Action*. Johannesburg: Centre for Development and Enterprise.
Bond, P. 2004. *Talk Left, Walk Right: South Africa's Frustrated Global Reforms*. New York: International Specialized Book Service.
Bremner, L. 1999. Crime and the Emerging Landscape of Post-Apartheid Johannesburg. In H. Judin and I. Vladislovic (eds.), *Blank _____ Architecture, Apartheid and After*, 48–63. Rotterdam: Netherlands Architectural Institute.
———. 2004. *Johannesburg: One City Colliding Worlds*. Johannesburg: STE Publishers.
Burdett, S. 2001. Security Estates: Under the Boom and over the Rainbow. *UpFront* (Comair British Airways), October, p. 21.
Chipkin, I. 2004. L'objet sublime du nationalisme: Le nationalisme et la démocratie en Afrique du Sud. Doctoral thesis, École Normale Superieure, Cachan.

City of Johannesburg. 2002. *Joburg 2030.* Johannesburg: City of Johannesburg.

Cummings, S. 1993. Post Colonial Urban Residential Change in Harare, a Case Study. In L. Zinyama, D. Tevera, and S. Cummings (eds.), *Harare: The Growth and Problems of the City,* 153–76. Harare: University of Zimbabwe.

De Meulder, B. 1998. South African Cities in the Maelstrom of Post-Apartheid. *Archis* 12: 38–49.

Dikobe, M. 1973. *The Marabi Dance.* London: Heinemann.

Dirsuweit, T. 1999. From Fortress City to Creative City, Developing Culture and Information-Based Sectors in the Regeneration and Reconstruction of the Greater Johannesburg Area. *Urban Forum* 10, no. 2: 183–213.

Freund, W. 1989. The Economy of the Witwatersrand in the Thirties. In A. Mabin (ed.), *Organisation and Economic Change,* 78–119. Johannesburg: Ravan.

Gilbert, A., A. Mabin, M. McCarthy, and V. Watson. 1997. Low-Income Rental Housing: Are South African Cities Different? *Environment and Urbanisation* 9, no. 1: 133–47.

Godwin, P. 2004. Africa's City of Hope, City of Fear. *National Geographic* 205, no. 4: 58–77.

Goga, S. 2003. Property Investors in Johannesburg. In R. Tomlinson, R. Beauregard, L. Bremner, and X. Mangcu (eds.), *Emerging Johannesburg: Perspectives on the Post-Apartheid City,* 71–82. New York: Routledge.

Gotz, G., and A. Simone. 2003. On Belonging and Becoming in African Cities. In R. Tomlinson, R. Beauregard, L. Bremner, and X. Mangcu (eds.), *Emerging Johannesburg: Perspectives on the Post-Apartheid City,* 123–154. New York: Routledge.

Guillaume, P. 2002. *Johannesburg: Géographies de l'exclusion.* Paris: Karthala.

Gutstein, D. 1975. *Vancouver Ltd.* Toronto: Lorimer.

Holland, H., and A. Roberts. 2002. *From Joburg to Jozi: Stories about Africa's Infamous City.* Johannesburg: Penguin.

Judin, H., and I. Vladislovic (eds.). 1999. *Blank _____ Architecture, Apartheid and After.* Rotterdam: Netherlands Architectural Institute.

Jurgens, U., and M. Gnad. 2000. Gated Communities in Südafrika; Untersuchungen im Großraum Johannesburg. *Erdkunde* 54: 198–207.

Jurgens, U., M. Gnad, and J. Bahr. 2003. New Forms of Class and Racial Segregation: Ghettos or Ethnic Enclaves? In R. Tomlinson, R. Beauregard, L. Bremner, and X. Mangcu (eds.), *Emerging Johannesburg: Perspectives on the Post-Apartheid City,* 56–70. New York: Routledge.

Lee Boon Thon. 1995. Challenges of Super-Induced Development: The Mega Urban Region of Kuala Lumpur-Klang Valley. In T. G. McGee and I. Robinson (eds.), *The Mega-Urban Regions of Southeast Asia: Urbanization in Asia,* 315–27. Seattle: University of Washington Press.

Levin, A. 2002. *Composer's Note in Programme for Sauer St Musical.* Johannesburg: Wits Theatre.

Mabin, A. 1996. Conceptualising, Making and Governing the Witwatersrand. Paper presented at Africa's Urban Past conference, SOAS, London, June.

———. 1999a. From Hard Top to Soft Serve: Demarcation of Metropolitan Government in Johannesburg for the 1995 Elections. In R. Cameron (ed.), *A Tale of Three Cities: The Democratisation of South African Local Government*, 159–200. Pretoria: Van Schaik.

———. 1999b. The Urban World through a South African Prism. In R. Beauregard and S. Body-Gendrot (eds.), *The Urban Moment*, 141–52. Los Angeles: Sage.

———. 2001. Contested Urban Futures—Report on a Global Gathering in Johannesburg, 2000. *International Journal of Urban and Regional Research* 25, no. 1: 180–84.

Mabin, A., and P. Harrison. 2006. Security and Space: Managing Contradictions of Access Restriction in Johannesburg. *Environment and Planning B*: 3–20.

Mabin, A., and D. Smit. 1997. Reconstructing South Africa's Cities? The Making of Urban Planning, 1900–2000. *Planning Perspectives* 12, no. 2: 193–223.

Mangcu, X. 2003. Johannesburg in Flight from Itself: Political Culture Shapes Urban Discourse. In R. Tomlinson, Beauregard, L. Bremner, and X. Mangcu (eds.), *Emerging Johannesburg: Perspectives on the Post-Apartheid City*, 281–91. New York: Routledge.

Marais, H. 2000. *Urban Politics Paper*. Commissioned by Isandla Institute Lekgotla, Johannesburg, 9 July 2000.

Mbembe, A., and S. Nuttall (eds.). 2006. Writing the Global City from Johannesburg. Special issue. *Public Culture*.

Mhone, G. 2003. Democratisation, Economic Liberalisation and the Quest for Sustainable Development in South Africa. In G. Mhone and O. Edigheji (eds.), *Governance in the New South Africa: The Challenge of Globalization*, 18–68. Cape Town: University of Cape Town Press.

Millin, S. 1926. *The South Africans*. London: Constable.

Monitor. 2000. *The Johannesburg Economy*. Report for the iGoli 2010 Partnership. Johannesburg: Monitor Group.

Morris, A. 1999. *Bleakness and Light: Inner City Transition in Hillbrow, Johannesburg*. Johannesburg: Witwatersrand University Press.

Nakasa, N. 1986. Johannesburg, Johannesburg. Reprinted in D. Ricci (ed.), *Reef of Time, Johannesburg in Writing*, 232–42. Johannesburg: Ad Donker.

Narsoo, M. 2004. Ruminations on Seven Sojourns. In E. Pieterse and F. Meintjies (eds.), *Voices of the Transition: The Politics, Poetics and Practices of Social Change in South Africa*, 163–74. Johannesburg: Heinemann.

Nuttall, S. 2006. Stylizing the Self: The Y Generation in Rosebank, Johannesburg. In A. Mbembe, and S. Nuttall (eds.), Writing the Global City from Johannesburg. Special issue. *Public Culture*.

Palmary, I., J. Rauch, and G. Simpson. 2003. Violent Crime in Johannesburg. In R. Tomlinson, R. Beauregard, L. Bremner, and X. Mangcu (eds.), *Emerging Johannesburg: Perspectives on the Post-Apartheid City*, 101–22. New York: Routledge.

Parnell, S. 2006. Financescapes. In A. Mbembe and S. Nuttall (eds.), Writing the Global City from Johannesburg. Special issue. *Public Culture*.

Parnell, S., and A. Mabin. 1995. Rethinking Urban South Africa. *Journal of Southern African Studies* 21, no. 1: 39–61.

Parnell, S., and G. Pirie. 1991. Johannesburg. In A. Lemon (ed.), *Homes Apart: South Africa's Segregated Cities*, 129–45. Cape Town: David Philip.

Pieterse, E., and F. Meintjies (eds.). 2004. *Voices of the Transition: The Politics, Poetics and Practices of Social Change in South Africa*. Johannesburg: Heinemann.

Redcliffe-Maud, J. 1937. *Johannesburg and the Art of Self-Government*. London: Esson.

Ricci, D. (ed.). 1986. *Reef of Time, Johannesburg in Writing*. Johannesburg: Ad Donker.

Robbins, D. 1987. *Wasteland*. Johannesburg: Lowry Publishers.

Routier Le Diraison, C. 2001. *Changement de siècle à Johannesburg*. Paris: Editions de l'Aube.

Rutheiser, C. 1996. *Imagineering Atlanta: The Politics of Place in the City of Dreams*. London: Verso.

Simone, A. 2000. Going South: African Immigrants in Johannesburg. In S. Nuttall and C. Michael (eds.), *Senses of Culture: South African Culture Studies*, 426–42. Cape Town: Oxford University Press.

Solomon D., and K.-J. Chen. 1998. Economy of Johannesburg-Gauteng. Report commissioned by Centre for Development and Enterprise, Johannesburg.

South Africa. 1998. *White Paper on Local Government*. Pretoria: Department of Constitutional Development. www.local.gov.za.

South African Cities Network. 2004. *State of the Cities Report 2004*. Johannesburg: SACN.

Swilling, M., and L. Boya. 1997. Local Government in Transition. In P. Fitzgerald, B. Munslow, and A. McLennan (eds.), *Managing Sustainable Development*, 165–91. Cape Town: Oxford University Press.

Taylor, R. 1989. University of the Witwatersrand Ltd.: Big Business Connections and Influence on the University Council. *Perspectives in Education* 10, no. 2: 71 76.

Tomlinson, R. 2003. Ten Years in the Making: A History of Metropolitan Government in Johannesburg. *Urban Forum* 10, no. 1: 1–40.

Tomlinson R., R. Beauregard, L. Bremner, and X. Mangcu (eds.). 2003. *Emerging Johannesburg: Perspectives on the Post-Apartheid City*. New York: Routledge.

van Onselen, C. 1982. *New Babylon, New Nineveh: Studies in the Social and Economic History of the Witwatersrand, 1886–1914*. Johannesburg: Ravan.

Mumbai
The Mega-City of a Poor Country
Sujata Patel

Bombay, now renamed Mumbai,[1] was the first Indian city to experience economic, technological, and social change associated with the growth of capitalism in India. By the mid-twentieth century it was considered India's most modern city (Thorner 1995). Once a colonial city, it has been and is home to many migrant communities that settled and found creative expression there. Bombay has nurtured modern India's literary and artistic articulation and today is home to the largest film industry in the world. Additionally, in view of its range of manufacturing, finance, and service activities, some commentators would also like it to be coined a global city. Whether Bombay can carry this label is open to dispute, though one of the city's leading historians suggests that it incorporates many characteristics of a postmodern city.

If the city hosts the best of India in terms of art, style, and finance, it is also a place where a large portion of the population lives on the margins of existence. Bombay, whether we call it modern, postmodern, or global evokes images of decline—of infrastructure, manufacturing, and law and order.[2] With more than 50% of its inhabitants living in slums or shanties where they have little access to water and sanitation, the name Bombay also conjures up the worst that contemporary urban India represents. The city has been associated with the seamier side of life, including crime, gang warfare, drugs, and prostitution.[3] In 1992–93 Bombay witnessed post-Independence India's worst communal (religious) riots, the scars of which it still has not overcome (Sharma 2000; Punwani 2003). Its politics is controlled by an urbanization that has chauvinist and fascist ideologies (Patel 2003).

This essay introduces Bombay and traces three phases of its life as it emerged as India's modern metropolis and later as a mega-city: first it was a port city, then a manufacturing city, and lately it has molded itself to the new economies promoted through globalization. I argue that it is important to understand and assess the different roles played by local, regional, national, and global processes in fashioning the urbanity of the city. Bombay emerged from being a peripheral city within a global-colonial system in the early twentieth century to take the lead from the forties onward as a city promoting national markets. Later, after the collapse of its manufacturing base in the eighties (the textile industry), it came to be linked to the global system through its financial, telecommunications, and media service sectors. During the same period, it came to be integrated in regional politics. Today, Bombay is the capital of the province Maharashtra state.

Although processes of globalization have been embraced by Bombay, the city has not been able to define and incorporate its economy into the fold. Large parts of the city continue to employ archaic and preglobal technology. This unevenness in internal structure manifests itself in the way inequalities are structured in the city. These inequalities reveal the lack of organic connection between old and new economies and are not representative of the features of the fully developed global economy. In this context the city's political landscape is defined by identity politics in the form of regionalism. Hence the thesis of the existence of a global city region does not seem to define Bombay's growth and contemporary structure.

As I narrate the three phases of the life of the city, I assess the way the economy, political institutions, and democratic aspirations structure the city. I argue that Bombay's economy and governance structures have a complex and contradictory relationship with the emerging contemporary national regional and global processes and ideologies. This complexity is related to history, the way in which inequalities in the city have arisen, and the policies implemented by the Indian nation-state and the state of Maharashtra.

Before I proceed, there is a need for two clarifications. The first concerns definitions of Bombay. Bombay is geographically defined in three different ways. In its earlier history the name was coterminous with the island city.[4] Later on, planners conceived of the city as an urban agglomeration called Bombay Metropolitan Region, now known as Mumbai Metropolitan Region. It covers an area of 4,355 square kilometers and includes seven municipal corporations, thirteen municipal councils, and a number of villages, with a total population of 18 million. In this essay I discuss the third entity, called Greater Bombay. It is a city of fewer than 12 million (according to the 2001 census), with its own municipal corporation called the Municipal Corporation of Greater Mumbai (MCGM). It covers an area of 437.71 square kilometers.[5]

Scott's (2001, 814) argument that global city regions emerge as "contiguous local government areas club together to form spatial coalitions in search of an effective basis from which to deal with both the threats and opportunities of globalization" does not seem to describe Bombay. Although the Mumbai Metropolitan Regional Development Authority (MMRDA)[6] is empowered to coordinate a number of projects such as the Mumbai Urban Infrastructure Project, the Mumbai Urban Transport Project, and the Backbay Reclamation area, municipalities under the Mumbai Metropolitan Region neither form one political body nor consolidate into a spatial coalition capable of leading an economically viable global city region. Thus, though the planners have subscribed to the importance of the metropolitan region, for all practical purposes including economic,[7] political, and administrative[8] reasons, it is Greater Bombay that remains the key unit of analysis.[9]

The second clarification relates to the nature of governance and management of Greater Bombay. The city's management is divided among three political bodies, these being the Municipal Corporation of Greater Bombay, the state of Maharashtra, and the government of India. The suburban railways, for instance, are part of the rail network run by the Railway Board of the Indian Railways. They are managed by cabinet ministers in the Government of India. An autonomous public sector corporation, MTNL, manages Bombay's telephone services (it also handles Delhi's telephones).

The state of Maharashtra, on the other hand, is in charge of the general policy on economic development of cities, including that of Greater Bombay, as well as land policy, housing for the poor, and slum redevelopment programs. It also controls and manages law and order in the city through the cabinet minister in charge of the Home Department. Additionally, the state government has set up autonomous public-sector corporations, such as the Maharashtra Housing and Area Development Authority (MHADA), which construct houses in Bombay and other cities. Though autonomous, the authority's chair is appointed by the state government.

Lastly, the MCGM manages the supply of water, organizes sanitation and sewage management, and the public health system together with pri-

Mumbai Metropolitan Region.

mary education, public street lighting, fire fighting services, urban forestry, and environmental ecology. Though the corporation organizes and manages most of these services, some others are in the hands of the private sector or in partnership with the private sector. While the MCGM-owned Bombay Electric Supply and Transport Company (BEST) supplies electricity to the island city drawing on power supplied by Tata Power, BSES (a Reliance company) supplies electricity to the rest of the Greater Bombay region and to some areas outside it.

On all key issues pertaining to the city—economic development, land and housing, and law and order—the state government has a decided voice.[10] With a significant portion of the state's per capita income coming from Bombay, this city has become a center of political rivalries between state-level parties, within ruling state parties, and between individuals as the city's population is mobilized to realize these goals. The influence of the state government and state political parties has increased over time, especially after the seventies, when regional parties became key political players in India. In the first two decades after Independence the

Congress Party ran the entire country. Its decline in the late sixties and later demise led to the ascendancy of regional (state politics) over national politics, especially in the context of cities administered by the provinces. Regional politics and regional issues have become the rallying points for the populace of Indian cities, with the local being filtered through a regional lens. The way politics is articulated in Maharashtra determines the way Bombay's issues of governance are being settled (or nor settled).

A Historical Overview

From a Port Town to a Modern Manufacturing City

Even in the late eighteenth century Bombay was primarily a marine supply point that, unlike Calcutta and Madras, had few linkages with the hinterland. Bombay's early development was dependent on imperialist interests. Specific economic factors spurred its growth. Up to the early nineteenth century Britain used Calcutta as its main port. Bombay became significant with the development of foreign shipping, which exploited Bombay's closer location to Europe. An initial boom and increase of wealth followed the extension of the railway line to cotton-growing areas in the hinterland of Bombay, and also were the result of a rise in world cotton prices due to shortages caused by the American Civil War and the opening of Suez Canal in 1869.

The establishment of a British base in the city lured migrants from the north, mainly Parsee and Gujarati traders, who were the indigenous partners and collaborators of imperialist business interests. Bombay also attracted distress migration resulting from famines and floods. Displaced peasants, agricultural workers, and artisans migrated to Bombay to become workers in the port and other transport facilities. Soon the city became a center for the export of cotton brought in from the hinterland, and it developed from an entrepôt to a manufacturing city. Indians channeled the profits from trading into setting up mills. This encouraged another wave of migration, namely that of millworkers. By the end of nineteenth century Bombay had grown to a population of little less than 800,000 (Patel 2003).

The interwar period was an important moment in the city's growth. Colonial ties loosened and the textile industry developed a domestic market. This labor-intensive industry attracted its highest work participant rate (Morris 1965). Profits doubled and then trebled. While a part of these were reinvested in the textile industry, a significant portion went into the emerging capital-intensive industries of food processing, pharmaceuticals and drugs, and small and medium engineering. The development of manufacturing did not completely reverse the service orientation of the city. Some of the surplus was also invested in promoting the various arts—theater, dance, painting, and cinema. Thus, while the city began as port city, over time it developed extensive links into the hinterland and to imperialist interests. It also became the headquarters of financial and corporate houses as well as the stock market (Chandavarkar 1994).

Civil Society as an Agent of Change

In spite of attempts by the colonial state to control the formation of a strong middle class and organized workers, the interwar period saw the growth of the nationalist movement that forged political and cultural links between the indigenous multilingual elites. This was also the time when various social welfare agencies started forging links and building alliances with the city's underclass. By the end of the thirties, a radical working-class movement with a communist ideology emerged, independent of the prior-named initiatives and in spite of a concentrated effort to prevent this from happening by European and Indian textile owners.[11]

The development of a vibrant civil society was the harbinger of an independent Indian nation-state. These changes had profound repercussions on the economy and spatial structures of Bombay. In the two decades from the forties onward, the economy of the city changed radically. A city that combined industrial and commercial activities in its physical heartland had been reshaped into a commercial and service center surrounded by restructured industrial production dispersed to ever more remote locations. This was also the time when the city experienced enormously high migration rates. Between 1941 and 1971 two-thirds of the city's residents had been born outside the city (Patel 1995). This spurt made Bombay a haven for migrants of all kinds, upper castes and deprived castes from Maharashtra, now from the backward regions, as well as from other regional groups, including the Punjab as well as the other northern, eastern, and southern states. When the partition occurred, migrants from Sindh and what is now Pakistan flooded the city.

Decline of the Textile Industry and Restructuring of Labor

Though by now the municipal government had created a measure of services, migrant groups of all kinds had to resort to their own resources in order to manage not only their housing but the mobility of their own communities—hence, the expansion of the city space into various settlements. This expansion included both deprived housing colonies (later called slums) and colonies mainly consisting of regional groups such as Sindhis and Punjabis, who settled in Khar or the eastern suburbs. Other examples of such settlements are the south Indian settlements in the northeast suburbs such as Chembur and Mulund and the new Gujarati migrant colonies in Vile Parle (West) and Ghatkopar. The poor living conditions and ethnic diversity of the labor market together with the relocation of industries resulted in a weakening of the bargaining power of organized and unorganized labor (Patel 2003).

In the early twentieth century Bombay's economy was organically connected to the fate of the textile industry. Yet this relationship started to disintegrate rapidly after Independence, when autarky policies promoted a new range of import-substitution manufacturing units in the city. In this phase the Indian government embarked on a massive industrialization program and began investing in the emerging capital-intensive industries of food processing, petrochemicals, and engineering, to the neglect of the consumer goods industry, including textiles. The profits that accrued through the boom in the textile industry during the interwar period were reinvested in capital-intensive industries. A small but important capital-intensive sector developed and slowly cut the city's umbilical link with the textile industry (Harris 1995).

Modern Bombay: State Policy and Spatial Restructuring

Sassen (1991) has argued that deindustrialization and spatial deconcentration is a special feature of modern capitalism. In the case of Bombay this process happened in the context of a national policy to develop small-scale industrialization and decentralized units in industrial estates spread over hinterland and rural areas. The encouragement of restructuring was also a factor contributing to concerns about the governability of overgrown cities. From the seventies onward, the state set up metropolitan bodies (such as the Mumbai Metropolitan Region) to encourage decongestion and the spread of industrialization beyond big cities. During this period New Bombay, a twin city of Bombay, was planned as a magnet to assist in the deconcentration and decentralization of Bombay.

As a large number of textile mills closed, there were changes affecting where, by whom, and on what terms cloth and yarn were produced. Given the symbolic value of the textile industry, however, a nonviable sector was kept in existence by state policy. As a result, the industry became divided and differentiated in terms of a backward sector, a modern profitable sector with expanding investment and production, and a growing small-scale sector, often producing under subcontract to larger units. The latter became characteristic of the entire spectrum of Mumbai industry.

These changes reflected on the structure of the labor force. Until the seventies manufacturing represented 40% of employment, with textiles still accounting for almost half of that amount, though the number was slowly declining (Patel 1995) The wave of sustained economic growth in the post-Independence period came to an end in the mid-sixties. Industrial growth on an all-India basis averaged 7.7% per annum from 1951 to 1965, but slumped to an average of 3.6% per annum from 1965 to 1975 (Patel 2003).

The process of differentiation in the textile industry was heightened in and through the textile strike of 1982–83, which occurred in the context of the slowdown of industrial production, the decentralization of the textile industry, and the shift of interests of capital and the state toward capital-intensive industry. During and after the strike, the power-loom sector began to grow particularly rapidly when millowners sent yarn to places like Bhiwandi and Malegaon (towns outside Bombay) for weaving. The strike saw the mass retrenchment of workers—more than 100,000 were displaced and several mills were closed. There was a simultaneous transfer of mill functions into the unorganized sector. The unorganized work force began to expand as retrenched millworkers began to sink into the unemployed or underemployed categories (Chhachhi and Kurian 1982).

This segmentation was reinforced through spatial relocation of various decentralized units of industries within the city. Much of the shift from formal-sector production to production in the informal and small-scale sector was part of a process of specialization. At one end, those industries were relocated from Bombay in which the particular demands of their process of production made improvements in labor productivity difficult to achieve. Industries like footwear and garment manufacturing required large amounts of semiskilled labor and thus lent themselves to unskilled, fragmented, and dispersed operations in order to maximize profits by reducing the overall costs of production. Costs reduced included the cost of paying and controlling labor, real estate, government subsidies, and congested services and infrastructure. Expansion into new labor markets also brought down the price of labor (Sherlock 1996).

Global Mumbai

The New Markets

The subsidiaries of capital-intensive, consumer-goods-based multinational companies in India, like Hindustan Lever Limited and Bata, have often established a manufacturing base for domestic consumption in Mumbai. Yet even here the production of high-volume, low-value goods was moved out of the city, much of it carried out by subcontractors. At the same time, high-value production was kept in the city because of the higher incidence of skilled labor. This process is not one of deindustrialization but a spatial reorganization, combined with an ever-increasing territorial expansion of the effective economic boundaries of the city.

The central (southern) areas of the city became less important as manufacturing centers and production moved out into the suburbs and to satellite centers such as Thane, Kalyan, and Navi Mumbai (these areas are outside Greater Bombay but within the Mumbai Metropolitan Region). Other production moved still further to nearby cities such as Pune and Nasik. With this shift, the older precincts, in and around the island city have become increasingly devoted to Mumbai's burgeoning service industries, including finance, tourism, retailing, and entertainment.[12] The only exception to this rule is the maintenance of a few old textile mills. Mumbai is becoming like most cities in the developing world, one based on services and the flow of information with dispersed manufacturing located in specialized areas (Banerjee-Guha 1996). This development was encouraged when the Maharashtra Regional and Town Planning Act was amended in 1966 to allow for any private company registered under the Companies Act of 1956 to function as a Special Planning Authority (SPA) with the approval of the state government. This legislative step opened the way for private-sector and international finance to participate more actively in the governance of the region and the shaping of a global market.

The restructuring of production in Mumbai had profound effects on the labor market and the bargaining power of workers in the city. For labor, the important element was the breakdown of large workplaces such as textile mills, and the growth of small-scale units in both the service and manufacturing sectors as well as a rapid growth of employment in casual positions and the informal sector. This lowered the ability of most workers to improve their living and working conditions or even to defend their existing standard of living. Nevertheless, smaller numbers of workers benefited from the growth of specialized services and manufacturing. The reality for most workers however, was insecure employment in small, often unregulated and informal units in spatially dispersed locations.[13]

Thus, despite its capitalist modernity, Bombay did not replicate a pyramidal form, the classic stratification system associated with other cities in the First World. There the continued growth of labor-intensive manufacturing together with the establishment of working-class movements led to the increase in real wages and other benefits for the workers.[14]

These economic changes were happening as regions were being reorganized into linguistic states (provinces) by the Government of India starting in the mid-fifties (brought to fruition in case of Maharashtra in 1960). This reframed the city's politics. Henceforth the politics of the region defined the city's politics rather than its own localized interests. Additionally, there was a shift in focus of the city's business elite from the city to the country. These differing and contradictory trends led to new political alliances. Language substituted locality-based class interests to become a key issue for identity formation in the city. Issues of local governance were thereby displaced with the politics of region.

Restructuring of the Economy

During the course of Bombay's uneven economic development, as it evolved from a port town to a modern manufacturing city, the city's industries changed their orientation from labor-intensive to capital-intensive production. This shift emerged as a response to the policies of the nation-state. Paradoxically, the decline in manufacturing took place when the city's population was increasing and demanding more jobs, housing, and services. The decline was accompanied by two political developments: the fragmentation in trade-union movements on the one hand and the growth of the sons-of-soil movement on the other hand (Patel 2003). From the late sixties to early eighties the city was caught up in coping with economic and political challenges. In that moment the city's economy, which was already service-oriented, was pulled into the new global economy as the Indian nation-state initiated export-led growth in the eighties and adopted liberalization policies in the early nineties.[15] Bombay was the first city to take advantage of this opportunity.

The new global economy reorganized Bombay's economy, which was facing a generalized crisis. It gave it a new direction with both positive and negative effects. In the early 1990s, Bombay saw a globalization-related increase in jobs associated with producer services. By 1994 Bombay handled 41% of domestic air traffic. Its airport handled 75% of the country's imports and 64% of its exports. Employment in financial and business services increased by 43% between the 1970s and 1980s. Bombay collected 25% of the country's income tax revenues and 60% of custom revenues. Its banks controlled 12% of national deposits and a quarter of the country's outstanding credits. The number of new issues listed on the Bombay stock exchange grew from 203 in 1991–92 to 694 in 1993–94, and the amount of fresh capital in old and new companies increased from 54 billion to 213 billion rupees between these years (Harris 1995; Deshpande 1996).

The growth of the financial sector and the trade in stocks and bonds as well as the participation of international financial groups in Bombay's stock exchange led to ancillary developments, such as the increase of investments in the communications industry, real estate, and the expansion of other services including life-style maintenance. This trend was significant in the mid-nineties, after Bombay became the hub of the telecommunications industry. The total number of employed persons in the financial sector increased at 2.66% per annum between 1992 and 1997 (Fact Book on Mumbai 2000, 22). This led to a marked growth in businesses producing goods related to information technology, banking, insurance, and other financial services and also to travel, tourism, and the hotel trade. Also, there was an expansion of related service industries, specifically the film and music industries.

In July 1994 the runaway success of the film *Hum Aapke Hain Kaun* (Who Am I of Yours?) established the importance of the overseas market for Indian movies. A quarter of the revenues of this film came from overseas. Given the synergistic relationship between the film and the audio industry, globalization of the film industry led to a boom in the audiocassette industry. As a result, many Bombay-based audio companies are today increasing their film production. With an average of 140 Bollywood releases and exports per year, the economics of the film and audio industry radically changed. These changes in turn gave a further fillip to those service industries already experiencing an upward swing—travel, tourism, and the hotel trade as well as advertising, cable, and television (Fact Book on Mumbai 2000, 46–47).

Structure of the Labor Force in the 1990s

The increase of the service sector together with the expansion of economic activities led to the growth of a new class, which is linked to the world of international finance and producer services. The decline in the manufacturing sector, however, now supported through globalization, led to a rise in unemployment. Between 1981 and 1996, unemployment more than doubled. This intensified inequities, escalating economic and social distance between the new upper class and workers, most of whom now survive in the nonorganized sector of the city. As mentioned, this decline in manufacturing ran parallel both with a drop in the numbers of the organized working class in the city and with the weakening of the influence of the trade unions (Fact Book on Mumbai 2000, 22).

In 1976, 27% of the city's organized labor force found employment in the textile industry. By 1991 the figure had decreased to 12.5%. In absolute terms, employment in the textile industry fell from 600,000 in 1981 to 400,000 in 1991. Statistics reveal that over the same period there was growth in unregistered units with downgraded technology. A substantial part of manufacturing was also contracted out to increase the so-called informalized processes of manufacturing. Thus, it is no surprise that the tertiary sector increased from 39% in 1951 to 60% in 1991, while formal employment in the private sector declined.[16]

With little possibility of finding other factory jobs, retrenched textile workers found themselves forced to survive by associating with informalized modes of manufacturing and service occupations. In 1981 the informal sector or nonwage employment would not have exceeded more than a quarter of the work force (Deshpande and Deshpande 1991). The same authors make a second estimate using data culled from the Establishment Census. The total number of persons employed in the informal sector increased to 27% in 1970 and 33% in 1980. If self-employed without premises are added to the picture, the percentage further increases to 35%. On the basis of a third estimate, calculated from the Employment Market Information Programme, the Deshpandes assert that those employed in the informal sector constituted 49% in 1971 and 55% in 1981. Current figures confirm this trend. One estimate, computed from the Employment Market Information, states that there was an increase of workers in the informal sector from 49% in 1961 to 65.6% 1991. Another estimate suggests an increase of units employing less than ten workers from 27.4% in 1970 to 46.3% in 1991 (Fact Book on Mumbai 2000, 20).

Deshpande and Deshpande (2003) have argued that there has been a very slight increase in the income of workers and a slight reduction of poverty. On the basis of computations from an expenditure survey conducted in 1958–59 and later in 1981–82, they argued that the average family income increased by 0.88 % per annum, though income per member decreased by 0.78% in the twenty-three years. They also show that the real wages of factory workers increased only by 2.68% during the period 1975–77 to 1985–87.

Even if income and earnings have risen, basic conditions of work and the living environment have not changed for many of Bombay's citizens. Most commentators, including Swaminathan (2003), now suggest that the issue of deprivation and poverty should be evaluated not only in context of income and earnings, but also in terms of access to land and housing, health and education, environment and population density, and the occupations of inhabitants. In Bombay today, whether in manufacturing or in services, the employment of a large majority of workers is unregulated with respect to wages, working conditions, security of tenure or rights to health care, and retirement pay. Most workers in this mode of activity not only use their own labor but also their residence and infrastructure (e.g., electricity and water) for the manufacture of goods and services. Access to housing therefore is critical for gaining employment.[17]

Poverty, Space, and Deprivation

Bombay is now a city of extreme contrasts. More than half of the city's population of fewer than 12 million inhabitants lives in slums and on pavements or under bridges and near railway tracks. A large number of them do not have legal tenure over the land that they occupy. In 1971 the slum population was about 1.25 million. Data collected in 1985 suggest that they constituted more than half of the city's population, though they occupied only 2,525 of its 43,000 hectares of land. Today, more than a decade later, 6% of Bombay's land houses more than 50% of its population. Another 12,000 hectares out of 43,000 is used for private residential housing. The 1985 data indicate that there were 10,000 hectares of vacant land in possession of private builders, and about ninety landlords owned 55% of this vacant land (Patel 2003).[18]

Two factors, the concentration of ownership and the price of property, reinforce inequities in land and housing. These also make for fictitious scarcity, speculation, and capital accumulation through rent. Prices in south Bombay, on and around Marine Drive, were twenty-seven times higher than in the northern Bombay suburb of Bhayander. In 1993–94 real-estate prices in south Bombay were higher than in downtown Tokyo and Manhattan. The provision of services has gone hand in hand with class determinants. Adequate to better services are thus made available to residents of housing colonies and upper-class apartment blocks. Spatial concentration of commercial areas and upper-class residential areas has led to the concentration of transport networks, which has resulted in the rich being subsidized by the poor in this matter (Patel 2003).

Land has always been a marketable commodity in Bombay, and it has been the private-public collaboration that has created a superfluous scarcity. This gave an opportunity for the private sector to hike up prices of built apartment blocks. Most of these slums are built on encroached land of private landlords (50%), state government land (25%), and municipal corporation land, and the rest on central government land. Additionally, nearly 1 million live on pavements and 2 million live in old rundown building structures known as *chawls* (Patel 2003).

Living quarters in slums are overcrowded and lacking in proper ventilation.[19] Given the extremely skewed distribution of space, it is possible to find many different strata of income groups living in slums and utilizing various building materials locally available, including saris and other cloth. In some slums, as Swaminathan (2003) shows, the space available is four feet by five feet—just enough to seat four to five members of a household. Even access to sanitation remains unequal. Again, Swaminathan draws our attention to a survey noting that in 174 of the 619 documented slums, there were no public toilets. The city also produces large amounts of waste, including 5,000 tons of garbage. There is no adequate provision to biodegrade this garbage. Many slums have reported high morbidity rates. Furthermore, a number of surveys indicate that half or less than half of Bombay's slum dwellers fall below the poverty line. This fact, together with the ones mentioned previously, exemplifies the deprivation suffered by the city's slum dwellers.

Over time we can discern two kinds of responses from government. First, an attempt to improve and upgrade services for slums and thereby develop a policy on improvement. Second, a desire to relocate slum dwellers in permanent structures. Early in 1954 an amendment was introduced in the Bombay Municipal Act to make this possible. However, there was no political will to implement this project.

In 1956 the central government approved the Slum Clearance Plan, and Bombay was one of the six pilot cities covered under this scheme. It took the state government another seven years to pass the Maharashtra State Slum Improvement Act to ensure prompt action under the central government plan. However, it was only in 1972 that the government created a Slum Improvement Board to implement the scheme. As central assistance had dried up by then, the state government decided to finance the scheme through its own budget. In 1976 the state made its first census enumeration and found that the city had 1,680 slum settlements with a total population of 2.8 million. The population of slum dwellers had more than doubled by 1986.[20]

In the decade between 1976 and 1986, the government's policy was to ensure that no further migrants entered the city. The government employed the police to evict slum dwellers until 1985. The Supreme Court then ruled that pavement dwellers had as much right to the city as those living in middle- and upper-middle-class housing. Following this decision, government resorted to its earlier policy of improving slums. This time it managed to get 530 million rupees from the World Bank for a slum upgrading program, whereby it attempted to draw in the community to upgrade the living conditions of the population. Despite the outside financing, only 22,000 households were covered by this scheme in the period up to eight years until 1993 (Das 2003).

In 1991 the government mooted a public-private partnership orientation for the first time by announcing the Slum Redevelopment Scheme. This remained a scheme on paper. A new policy was initiated by the Shiv Sena–Bharatiya Janata Party (BJP) government to improve the stock of housing through a new Slum Rehabilitation Scheme (actually a new version of the old scheme). Again the government wanted private-public partnerships to redevelop slums and gave incentives to private developers through cross-subsidization and floor space index bonuses to provide housing for the poor. Sufficient data are not yet available, but one assessment of the projects completed has shown that, in most cases, slum dwellers shifted out from the buildings and areas set aside for them and middle-class families have moved in (Das 2003).

The lack of legal tenure has made the issue of the right to land and physical space a critical one. A large part of the population's struggles focuses on the attempt to obtain and then maintain a space to live and then to attain a modicum of amenities. It would not be an exaggeration to state that a majority of the workers and laborers live a life on the margins both figuratively and metaphorically. This situation has evoked a culture of deprivation. Being part of the informalized modes of manufacturing or services means having an unsteady, unprotected, and unregulated work life. Neither work nor access to housing integrates these individuals into a rhythm of organized discipline. Instability together with cultural and economic deprivation rules their lives.

Data from the 1991 census suggests that more than 50% of migrants settled in the city within the past twenty years (Das 2003). Though they have broken the bonds of community life defined by the villages they come from, they have also not become part of the urban industrial culture. Their life has become restricted both culturally and geographically in overcrowded areas. In this context, the need for affirmation for the "village community" gets translated into an affiliation of the members of the small slum community, the slums being organized in terms of clusters of regional, ethnic, and religious groups. Identification with the microscopic local dominates consciousness. This is the context in the city for the growth of identity movements such as the Shiv Sena—a political movement with chauvinist and fascist tendencies. In the late sixties and seventies it put forward the so-called sons-of-soil politics, from the eighties onward it mobilized the population in terms of religious identity (Hansen 2001; Eckert 2003).

The slum population is presently treated as a ready-made constituency for garnering votes. Politicians allow new settlements to arise and then protest against an increase of the city's population, suggesting a cutoff date for legalizing slums. Whenever there has been a protest against eviction, politicians have legalized illegal settlements. This has guaranteed rights of stay for people, but not better housing or better services. There have been two cutoff dates thus far: 1986 and 1995.

Conclusion

In this essay, I argued that historical processes, the governance structure of the federal Indian state, and the way in which production process and inequalities structured the city explain Bombay's limited integration to global markets. Because of its history and the way it represents the contradictory strands of the global economy, Bombay presents an interesting case for studying the specific form that globalization takes in India.

Several factors make Bombay apt to accept new global economies: first, Bombay's growth as a colonial city, with its transition from a manufacturing-oriented to an export market and the attraction of financial and corporate headquarters; second, the development of a national market for its products after Independence, together with the growth of a media and film industry and a multiethnic entrepreneurial group. And yet the synergy developed by the globalization process did not engulf the city's entire economy.

Commentators have suggested that the program of structural adjustment and liberalization in India led to contradictory outcomes (Corbridge and Harriss 2000). On the one hand, partial convertibility and the entrance of foreign firms increased equity participation, expanded the stock market, and changed the nature of manufacturing, making it more service-oriented and related to global markets. On the other hand, in the absence of the political will to increase direct taxes on higher income groups or cut wasteful expenditure, there was a heavy cut in welfare expenditures, such as those for water supply and health. There was also a reduction in subsidies for basic needs and amenities such as food and electricity. Additionally, as a result of privatization, public-sector corporations, most of them located in big cities, were reorganized. Unemployment increased and so have inequalities, despite the expansion of the nonorganized economy. The latter gained further impetus due to the service orientation of the new economies.

In this essay I explored the decline of manufacturing and the growth of service industries as well as locational issues and the reurbanization of space. I related them to new forms of marginalization and inequalities in the context of the political processes. I argued that the economic and political features have to be understood in the way the local, regional, and national political processes have interfaced with the global processes to restructure the economy of cities, such as Mumbai. More particularly, it is not the external economy that has oriented the city to globalization, but the national policy of the government and the way political processes have organized the democratic aspirations of the populace. In this city, globalization is distinctly different from globalization elsewhere.

Notes

1. The name Bombay can trace its genesis to a modest *quinta* (manor house) built by a Portuguese physician and botanist who leased the Bombaim Island from the then Portuguese regime in the mid-sixteenth century. It was a corruption of the island's indigenous name Mumbai, drawn from its patron goddess, Mumbadevi. Bombay and Mumbai are used interchangeably in this essay.

2. For instance, Hindi films such as *Bombay, Chakra, Dharavi,* and *Satya,* to name a few, represent Bombay in these terms.

3. This statement is to be seen in context with other urban cities in India and not other cities in the world.

4. The British obtained the seven islands given to Catherine as dowry on her marriage.

5. Bombay municipality used to govern the island city, covering 67.67 square

kilometers till 1950 when the limits of the city were extended to include eastern and western suburbs, adding 187.46 square kilometers, and giving rise to Greater Bombay. The process of suburbanization was accelerated in 1957 as the administrative limits of Bombay were extended further with the addition of another 174.76 square kilometers. For planning purposes, an even larger metropolitan region administered by the Mumbai Metropolitan Regional Development Authority (MMRDA) was established in 1965.

6. MMRDA was initially a central government's gesture to the World Bank while the bank was considering a loan for the Urban Transport Project. Since its constitution as a local authority in 1975, there has been little to no clarity of roles and functions. Internal strife, lack of adequate representation in its board of particular departments such as the Industries and Environment, as well as its political tension with the Municipal Corporation of Greater Mumbai has rendered it more in line with an agency under the Urban Development Department than an economically commanding nodal body. It is true that MMRDA is entitled to coordinate a number of projects such as Mumbai Urban Infrastructure Project, Mumbai Urban Transport Project, and the Backbay Reclamation area. Yet municipalities in the Mumbai Metropolitan Region do not constitute one geographic jurisdiction nor do they consolidate into "definite political entities" (Scott 2001) and spatial coalitions capable of leading an economically viable global city region.

7. For instance, Greater Bombay's economic share is more significant in terms of income, proportion of net domestic product, employment, and foreign direct investment. According to the regional plan of 1996–2011, in 1973 the growth rate of regional income for Greater Bombay was 63% compared to 61% for the Bombay Metropolitan Region and 45% for Maharashtra state as a whole. Per capita income displayed a similar trend with 45% for Greater Bombay, 38% for the Bombay Metropolitan Region, and 33% for Maharashtra. The share of the net domestic product of Greater Bombay in that of the Mumbai Metropolitan Region has been constant at 65% over the period 1993–99. The total employment in the Mumbai region was found to be 3.55 million in 1998 compared to 3.22 in 1990, while in Greater Bombay, it has been increasing albeit slowly, from a total of 1.53 million in 1971 to 2.63 million in 1998. Over the period 1991–98, out of 2005 foreign collaborations in Maharashtra, 674 were located in Bombay. In absolute numbers out of 22,215 crores of rupees, 6,539 crores went to Bombay (Ghorpade 2005).

8. The governance of Mumbai is in the hands of the Municipal Corporation of Greater Mumbai. The corporation has an elected body of 227 members.

9. Henceforth, all further references to Bombay or Mumbai imply the political area called Greater Bombay/Mumbai.

10. The state government appoints the municipal commissioner in all cities, and thus there is a history of conflicts between the commissioner and the corporators. For Bombay, see Thakkar 1995.

11. For a contemporary interpretation of the working-class movement in Bombay and its discourse in the early twentieth century, see Chandavarkar (1994; 1998).

12. In 1961 the island city (that is south Bombay) housed 66.7% of the city's population. In 1991 this was reduced to 32% (Patel 2004).

13. Between 1961 and 1980, 32,000 laborers employed in the textile industry had been displaced, due to modernization (Sherlock 1996).

14. Bombay's experience runs parallel to other cities in the case of displacement of women workers from manufacturing. This displacement started in 1891, and by mid-twentieth century there were hardly any women workers left in the industry.

15. See Corbridge and Harriss (2000) for an overview of changes in India's economic policies and its hesitant adoption of liberalization.

16. The work participation rate of males has decreased substantially from 57.7% in 1971 to 54.3% in 1991. Consequently there has been a feminization of the economy with an increase of the work participation rates from 7.7% in 1971 to 10.5% in 1991. Also private employment dominated public employment in 1961 and 1971. It lagged behind in 1981 but declined by 2.4%—and thus employed fewer people than the public-sector employment in 1991 and 1996. See Fact-Book on Mumbai 2000, 21, table 26.

17. For instance, in the Dharavi slum of central Bombay, there are 400 leather processing units. The air and water pollution that these units generate determine the conditions of living of the people there. See Sharma 2000.

18. Recent data not available.

19. In 1991, 72.9% of households lived in one room. See Fact-Book on Mumbai 2000, 85, table 133.

20. The workers of textile mills were provided with housing and have not experienced—unless displaced—this form of deprivation.

References

Banerjee-Guha, S. 1996. Dividing Space and Labour: Spatial Dynamics of Multinational Corporations. *Economic and Political Weekly* 31, no. 8: L21–L24.

Chandavarkar, R. 1994. *The Origins of Industrial Capitalism in India: Business Strategies and the Working Classes in Bombay, 1900–1940.* Cambridge: Cambridge University Press.

———. 1998. *Imperial Power and Popular Politics: Class, Resistance and the State in India, 1850–1950.* Cambridge: Cambridge University Press.

Chhachhi, A., and P. Kurian. 1982. New Phase in Textile Unionism? *Economic and Political Weekly* 17, no. 8: 267–72.

Corbridge S., and J. Harriss. 2000. *Reinventing India: Liberalisation, Nationalism and Popular Democracy.* Delhi: Oxford University Press.

Das, P. K. 2003. Slums: The Continuing Struggle for Housing. In S. Patel and J. Masselos (eds.), *Bombay and Mumbai: The City in Transition*, 207–34. Delhi: Oxford University Press.

Deshpande, L. 1996. Impact of Globalisation on Mumbai. Paper presented at

UNU-Unesco Workshop on Globalisation and Mega City Development in Pacific Asia, Tokyo, October.

Deshpande, S., and L. Deshpande. 1991. *Problems of Urbanization and Growth of Large Cities in Developing Countries: A Case Study of Bombay*. Population and Labour Policies Programme. Working Paper no. 177. International Labour Organization, Geneva.

———. 2003. Work, Wages and Well-Being: 1950s and 1990s. In S. Patel and J. Masselos (eds.), *Bombay and Mumbai: The City in Transition*, 53–80. Delhi: Oxford University Press.

Eckert, J. M. 2003. *The Charisma of Direct Action: Power, Politics and the Shiv Sena*. New Delhi: Oxford University Press.

Fact-Book on Mumbai. 2000. Mumbai: Bombay First.

Ghorpade, K. R. 2005. Mumbai: Economic Restructuring by Default. In K. Segbers, S. Raiser, and K. Volkmann (eds.), *Public Problems—Private Solutions? Globalizing Cities in the South*, 35–50. Aldershot: Ashgate Publishing.

Hansen, T. B. 2001. *Urban Violence in Bombay: Identity Politics, "Mumbai" and the Post Colonial City*. Delhi: Permanent Black.

Harris N. 1995. Bombay in the Global Economy. In S. Patel and A. Thorner (eds.), *Bombay: Metaphor for Modern India*, 47–63. Bombay: Oxford University Press.

Morris, M. D. 1965. *The Emergence of an Industrial Labour Force in India: A Study of the Bombay Cotton Mills, 1854–1947*. Berkeley: University of California Press.

Narayanan, H. 2003. In Search of Shelter: The Politics of the Implementation of the Urban Land (Ceiling and Regulation) Act of 1976 in Greater Mumbai. In S. Patel and J. Masselos (eds.), *Bombay and Mumbai: The City in Transition*, 183–206. Delhi: Oxford University Press:

Patel, S. 1995. Bombay's Urban Predicament. In S. Patel and A. Thorner (eds.), *Bombay: Metaphor for Modern India*, xiii–xxxv. Bombay: Oxford University Press.

———. 2003. Bombay and Mumbai: Identities, Politics and Populism. In S. Patel and J. Masselos (eds.), *Bombay and Mumbai: The City in Transition*, 3–30. Delhi: Oxford University Press.

———. 2004. Bombay/Mumbai: Globalization, Inequalities and Politics. In J. Gugler (ed.), *World Cities beyond the West: Globalisation Development, and Inequalities*, 328–47. Cambridge: Cambridge University Press.

Punwani, J. 2003. "My Area, Your Area": How Riots Changed the City. In S. Patel and J. Masselos (eds.), *Bombay and Mumbai: The City in Transition*, 235–66. Delhi: Oxford University Press.

Sassen, S. 1991. *The Global City: New York, London., Tokyo*. Princeton, N.J.: Princeton University Press.

Scott. A. J. 2001. Globalization and the Rise of City-Regions. *European Planning Studies* 9, no. 7: 813–26.

Sharma, K. 2000. *Rediscovering Dharavi: Stories from India's Largest Slum*. New Delhi: Penguin Books India.

Sherlock, S. 1996. Class Re-formation in Mumbai: Has Organized Labour Risen to the Challenge? *Economic and Political Weekly* 31, no. 52: L34–L38.

Swaminathan, M. 2003. Aspects of Poverty and Living Standards. In S. Patel and J. Masselos (eds.), *Bombay and Mumbai: The City in Transition*, 81–110. Delhi: Oxford University Press.

Thakkar, U. 1995. The Commissioner and the Corporators: Power Politics at the Municipal Level. In S. Patel, S. and A. Thorner (eds.), *Bombay: Metaphor for Modern India*, 248–67. Delhi: Oxford University Press.

Thorner, A. 1995. Bombay: Diversity and Exchange. In S. Patel and A. Thorner (eds.), *Bombay: Mosaic of Modern Culture*, xiii–xxxv. Delhi: Oxford University Press.

São Paulo
The Metropolis of an Elite Society
Csaba Deák and Sueli Schiffer

São Paulo is the economic heart of Brazil. Thus both its development in general and the specific features of this development are intertwined with the economic and social development of Brazil as a whole. These processes are outlined in this essay from a standpoint at odds with the "new regionalism" theory, suggesting that both the greatness and dynamism of São Paulo and its structural weaknesses are at a time cause and consequence, indeed an organic part, of the country's development. In very concrete terms, and again at odds with the "global cities" or "network societies" approach, the connections of São Paulo with the world economy materialize through the mediation of the nation-state to which it belongs. By the same token, at a more general level, the conflicts ensuing from the line-up of forces in favor and against the implementation of neoliberal policies that dominated São Paulo in the nineties were part and parcel of the same conflicts at work nationwide. Finally, the prospects of future development of these conflicts depend likewise on the way in which they will be fought out in Brazilian society as a whole.

São Paulo Today

São Paulo is the largest urban agglomeration in South America, with a population of 18 million people. It lies at 800 meters above sea level and at 60 kilometers from the coast, at the bank of the Tietê River. The climate is more temperate than in neighboring Rio de Janeiro, which is located on the coast at the same latitude 400 kilometers away. The built area of 200,000 hectares spreads out from the original center in a large octopus shape with a 70-kilometer east-west and 50-kilometer north-south axis.

86   The Making of Global City Regions

Urbanization at the core of Mercosul. A night view of southern Brazil, Paraguay, Uruguay, northern Argentina, and Chile shows the intensity of urbanization in the region. Based on NASA/NOAA image of 2000; country boundaries and city names added by Csaba Deák.

The main mass of urbanization is bordered in the south by two water reservoirs and a steep slope, where the plateau falls to sea level, and in the north by a hill range. Thus, most of the land available for expansion lies in the east and west.

The urban form is radioconcentric, with more radial than tangential elements. High-income groups have traditionally occupied the southwestern sector. As the city grew, the city center started drifting southwest, as though following the high-income population. After several such leaps, new locations of office headquarters today reach out as far as about 15 kilometers from the old center. São Paulo's center today is something like a comet with a tail stretched out toward the southwest.

The southwestern district concentrates most of the economic activities (except manufacturing) and most of the higher-income residential settlements. The district consists of a 15- to 20-kilometer-long equilateral tri-

Legacies and the Global Context   87

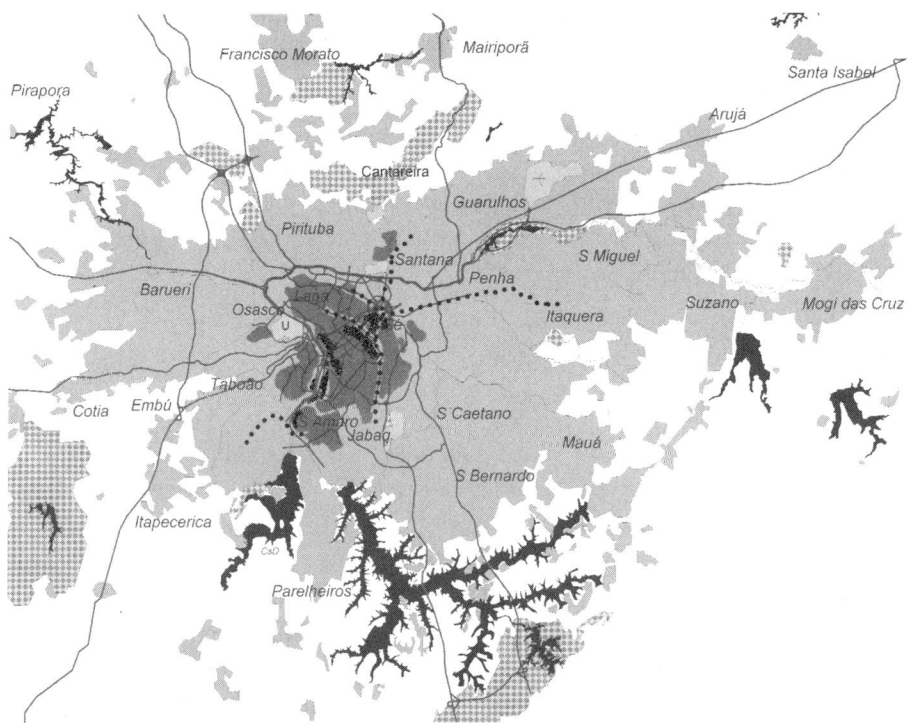

The overall structure of São Paulo. The southwesten sector concentrates most of the economic activities except manufactures (tertiary centers in *dark gray*) and most of the higher income residential settlements (*medium gray*). Drawing by Csaba Deák.

angle with relatively high standard infrastructure, where the quality of the environment is fair, and accessibility is reasonable. The original residential settlements consisted of low-density detached houses that were built up to the 1930s, but high-rise apartment blocks are now being built at rates twice as fast as regular houses, and they already make up one-third of dwellings. The other districts and the outer periphery consist of predominantly middle- and working-class areas. They are home to the bulk of the manufacturing industry, which originally was located along the railways (since 1850) and the newly built motorways (after 1950). Here the infrastructure and environmental conditions are poor to extremely poor.

A relatively new development is the mushrooming of *favelas* since the mid-seventies. These settlements were formed by squatters invading generally public land. Today *favela* dwellers make up about 15% of the urban population of the metropolitan area—some 2.5 million people. These, together with the precarious stock of peripheral half-self-built housing, coexist uneasily with big company headquarters in energy-thirsty glass towers dubbed "intelligent" and with gated high-income residential developments.

The roots of such extreme differences both in the income of its residents and the quality of the environment go back to the origins of São Paulo and Brazilian society itself.

The Economic Heart of Modern Brazil

The Formation of the National Space

São Paulo is the largest South American metropolis, but it is also the youngest. Rio de Janeiro became the capital of the Portuguese colony in 1763 because of its coastal location and proximity to the mining region of Minas Gerais. Buenos Aires, in its turn, became capital of the newborn Vice-Kingdom of the River Plate at about the same time (1776), reflecting its growing economic weight at the expense of Lima. In contrast, up to as late as 1850, São Paulo had been little more than a jumping-off point for the *bandeiras,* the slave and gold-hunting expeditions, as well as military campaigns in the struggle against Spain for control over the southwestern border regions. These helped to forge the confines of present-day Brazil well beyond the westerly Tordesilhas line, but they did not induce the formation of a great city. Thus, up to 1850, São Paulo remained a small borough of scarcely 15,000 people. In 1850 the African slave trade was suspended and the Land Laws were promulgated, which instituted private ownership of land. This development enabled the introduction of wage labor and capitalism in Brazil, about three decades after the declaration of independence (1822). With wage labor and capitalism came industrialization and urbanization and a period of high rates of accumulation and rapid growth, similar to that experienced in England in the eighteenth century. São Paulo was to become the center of this process.

In the early nineteenth century coffee became the main export staple of Brazil. It remained so for a century. Coffee production started in the state of Espírito Santo and soon began migrating southwest, going through Rio de Janeiro, and reaching São Paulo by the middle of the nineteenth century. At this time the institutions of the new country were consolidated after two and half decades of internal wars and early capitalist development. São Paulo, which was then the center of coffee production

Main directions of the *bandeiras*—expeditions of exploration and conquest—from the starting point of São Paulo, which in a century and a half extended Portuguese territory well beyond the originally agreed Tordesilhas line (approximately longitude 49°W) a little to the west of São Paulo. Source: Aroldo Azevedo, *Geografia do Brasil Editora Nacional* (São Paulo: 1958), p. 60.

and also of the Brazilian economy, was to become the center of Brazilian industrialization.

When the world economic crisis of 1929 put an end to the coffee cycle, São Paulo's leading position in the Brazilian economy was already firmly established. A self-imposed policy of curtailing home production notwithstanding, the balance-of-trade constraints ensuing from the coffee crisis nonetheless made it necessary to broaden industrial production and supply the rapidly increasing home market with the bulk of consumer goods. Under the effect of a peculiar and rather baffling stop-and-go policy, an interpretation of which we will return to, a home industry of sizable proportions and some complexity developed gradually, despite the fact that machinery and key industries were systematically kept out of the structure of home production or left in the hands of foreign capital.

Cultural Dynamism: Semana de '22

As a counterpart to São Paulo's economic dynamism, by the early twentieth century São Paulo was also becoming the country's cultural center. An explicit bid for that position was made in 1922 (the centenary year of Independence), when a *paulista* group of artists—painters, poets, writers, and musicians[1]—produced a festival of arts under the name of *Semana de Arte Moderna* (Week of Modern Art) or *Semana de '22*, for short. Soon thereafter it launched a manifesto entitled *Anthropophagi Manifesto* "against all the importers of canned conscience." Laying the foundations of the *movimento modernista* in a declaration against academicism and for a valorization of Brazilian culture and its expression in modern forms, they effectively determined the main directions of artistic production over the next generations. One of the movement's most prestigious literary productions is *Macunaíma*, by Mário de Andrade, the "hero with no character at all."

Macunaíma is a caustic satire of its author's society, but here we invoke it for its references to São Paulo in particular. Its hero enters life in an Indian tribe of the Amazonian jungle and begins life with a long yawn, saying: "Aw, what a laze . . ." The hero spends his youth having an eye mainly for women, including his relatives. Then he sets off on a long odyssey through the Amazonian forest, the description of which is a delicious anthology of folklore. When he eventually arrives in the "city," the city is São Paulo. He writes his impressions back to his people:

> São Paulo is built on seven hills, in the traditional manner of Roma, the city caesarean, "capita" of Latinity which we descend from; and the gracious and unruly lymph of the *Tietê* kisses its feet. . . . The city is most beautiful, and rewarding is its life. All cut by streets smartly narrow, taken by statues and lamp posts of most gracious and exquisite sculpture; all concurring to lessen the space in ways such that in these arteries scarce room is left for people. Thus is obtained the effect of a gathering of numerous gents, the size of which may be augmented at leisure, which is propitious to the elections, this invention of these most astute *mineiros*;[2] at the same time that the councillors are pro-

vided with ample subjects with which to earn their days of honour, with peaks of eloquence wrought in the purest style and sublime labour.

The aforesaid arteries all are recovered by fluttering paper strips and bits and quick-sailing fruit peels; and foremost of the finest dust, indefatigable dancer, spreading around fierce macrobes innumerable, which decimate the population. (de Andrade 1926)[3]

Except for its style, this description of São Paulo is not unlike William Morris's description, half a century earlier: "London and the great commercial cities of Britain as 'mere masses of sordidness, filth, and squalor, embroidered with patches of pompous and vulgar hideousness'" (Ashworth 1954, 171). But what society is this, which builds São Paulo in this manner?

Hindered Accumulation in Brazil

Brazilian society is in sharp contrast to the societies of the countries in the centers of world capitalism. A leading social scientist, Florestan Fernandes, called it an "elite society," as distinct from bourgeois, with an overprivileged ruling class (Fernandes 1972). The material basis of this society is the reproduction of a peculiar modality of accumulation, or development, originated in the colonial status of Brazil before Independence (1822) and reproduced ever since. In this process, the surplus produced by society is divided into two parts: one is reinvested in the expansion of production (and, to this extent, it is expanded reproduction, an accumulation process); the other is constantly creamed off and sent abroad—expatriated—under such titles as profit remittance, service on foreign debt, unfavorable terms of trade, and chronic deficit in services (freight and insurance payments) with no counterpart whatsoever, in such a way that much less is accumulated. Accumulation, since not of all surplus produced, is hence named "hindered accumulation" (Deák 1988). The distinctive features of such an economy are soaring interest rates, no long-term credit or stable currency, denationalization of production (especially in the key branches of industry), and precarious infrastructure. In a bourgeois society (such as obtains in developed countries), these characteristics would be seen as structural weaknesses of the economy. In Brazil they are in fact the main instruments of the continued reproduction of the established status quo.

This peculiar form of economy—and the equally peculiar elite society it sustains—was able to reproduce itself for a century and a half. In the extensive stage of development,[4] rates of growth of production were high and the subdivision of the excess produce—which could be accommodated for the time being, despite the strain on both economy and society—proved feasible.

The elite society develops its peculiar political forms as well. Thus, if democracy is the political form proper to bourgeois society, built on the idea of commonwealth and the concrete equality of citizens before the law, in elite societies it becomes a farce. The overprivileging of the elite completely belies any notion of commonwealth, and equality before the law likewise does not obtain.

Here is how a literary critique refers to the elite as portrayed by the first great Brazilian novelist Machado de Assis:

> [Thus] life in Brazil imposed upon the bourgeois conscience a series of acrobatics which scandalise and irritate common sense. . . . Under such circumstances, an offence is also the norm, and as well as a norm, the norm is also an offence. . . . In this way, the Europeanized sectors of Brazilian society did take part in bourgeois civilization, although in a peculiar, semi-detached way, whereby they invoked it and defied it, alternately and indefinitely. (Schwarz 1979)

This is the logic behind political processes that frequently appear not to make any sense at all. The elite constantly negates any notion of public interest, equality before the law, and many other principles basic to democracy. The elite makes innumerable recklessly ambitious and ridiculously elaborate laws just to break them, thereby asserting its ultimate authority. It can make the law and it can break it the next moment. This behavior is socially accepted as normal.

As to spatial organization, which provides physical support for production, whether nationwide or within urban agglomerations, we have chronically precarious and unevenly distributed infrastructure and fragmentation rather than homogenization of space. This explains the spatial organization in São Paulo as well, which will be discussed further.

Countrywide infrastructure building eloquently illustrates hindered accumulation. In an early period of capitalist development (second half of the nineteenth century), the totality of railways—both tracks and rolling stock—could be imported from England, and were indeed built and operated by British companies. Coffee exports and some increase of foreign debt paid for this installation. Yet during the motor age, when new transportation infrastructure was needed, coffee exports and prices slumped due to the 1929 crisis and failed to recover even after the Second World War. Now it quickly became clear that all cars could not be imported. A powerful motor industry was therefore set up, but entirely made up by subsidiaries of foreign companies. In 1959 the first homemade car—the Volkswagen Beetle—rolled off the assembly line, and other plants soon followed suit. By the seventies the country had become the third largest car maker after the United States and Japan.

Cars and trucks—which were by then becoming the main means of transportation—needed roads. A countrywide network was built in less than thirty years almost from nothing. Its design clearly shows the central position of São Paulo. Now, for the first time, an infrastructure was provided for a unified home market—a condition of capitalist development, which had never been provided by the railways a century earlier, which had consisted of isolated stretches running toward the coast, designed exclusively for the transportation of the export staple, coffee. Catering for the home market gave São Paulo a new role in the national economy: its dynamism henceforth was based on manufacturing rather than on an ephemeral export staple.

By the end of the 1970s and after a decade of exceptionally rapid growth (which had been dubbed the Brazilian economic miracle), Brazil's GDP rose to the seventh rank internationally, with a variegated structure of manufacturing dominated by car production. The share of São Paulo state in the Brazilian manufacturing GDP amounted to more than 42%. Half of this was concentrated in the metropolitan region itself. The increase in production was accompanied by massive urbanization.

The Urban Process with Rapid Growth in São Paulo

In the century between 1870 and 1970, São Paulo grew from a small town of 23,000 people to become a major metropolis of more than 7 million inhabitants. More than 5% yearly demographic growth rates were predominantly based on migration. People came from other parts of the country, notably the northeastern region, but immigration from abroad also had a significant impact. Thus São Paulo became a multiethnic city with more than a million-strong Italian and Portuguese communities, somewhat smaller German and Japanese communities, and more than a dozen lesser groups from Europe and Asia. In this period of rapid growth, other contrasts in the pattern of urbanization also arose.

A generally precarious infrastructure coupled with a concentration of investment in limited areas, which then become "privileged," induced more differentiation than homogeneity into the urban space. The main road network, for example, today is heavily concentrated in the southwestern area of the city. This preferential area of settlement of the elite concentrates most of the investment in virtually any component of infrastructure. Price differentials are high. A clear spatial segregation according to household income is the result in the southwestern sector, as mentioned earlier.

Traditional fragmentation of space leaves many age-old barriers in São Paulo waiting to be transposed to allow better integration of its more isolated portions. Often merely a lack of investment is at fault, as in the foregoing example. In some cases, however, there is deliberate reinforcement of divisions through investment. Such is the case with a controversial monorail line currently being built along the Tamanduetei River, which will buttress an already almost insurmountable barrier formed by the

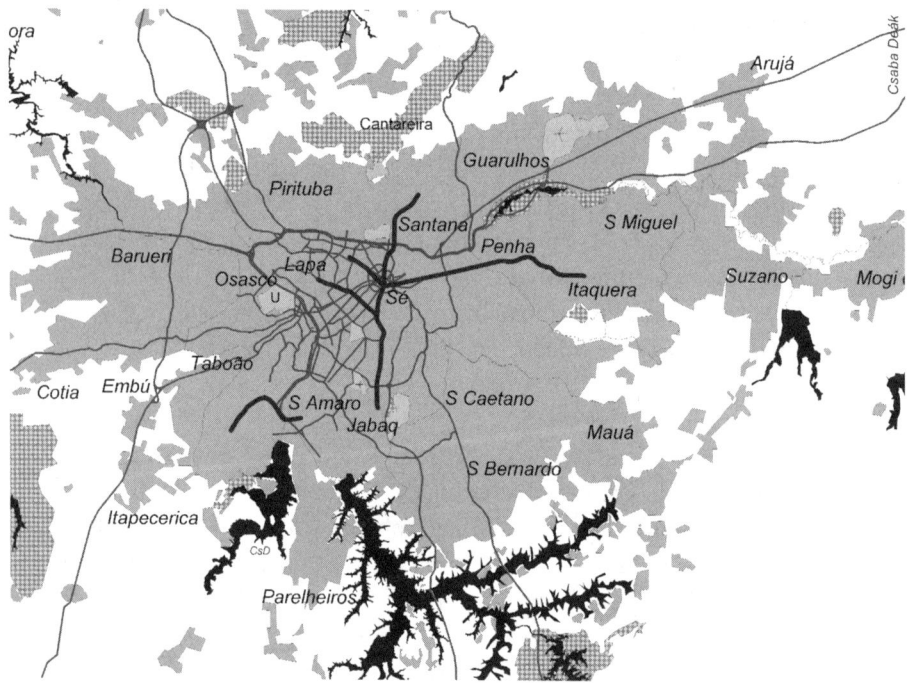

The main road (*light gray lines*) and Metro (*dark gray lines*) structure of São Paulo, where an isolated stretch of recently finished (2002) Metro line in the southwestern periphery is also shown. Built-up area (*shaded*) as in 1997, as opposed to the next figure which shows built-up area in 1987. Drawing by Csaba Deák.

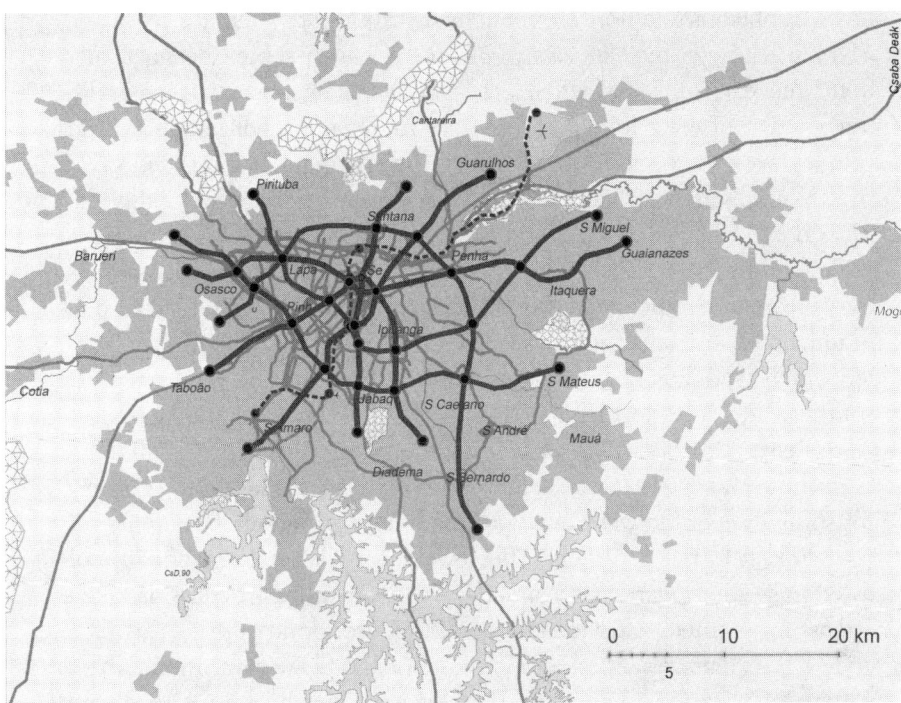

A Metro network for São Paulo. A Metro network more to the scale of São Paulo such as the one pictured here was designed in the late 1980s (about 250 kilometers of track). It would be able to give cohesion back to the metropolitan agglomeration, transpose natural barriers, ensure the center's accessibility, and provide some 8 million daily trips, half of about 16 million demanded on public transport. After a nine-year lull in Metro building, the State Secretariat for Metropolitan Transport has recently (2000) adopted a plan for building a network very similar to the one pictured above in twenty years. Drawing by Csaba Deák.

canal, which is lined by highways on either side and an old railway track. The canal divides the poorly structured but populous eastern zone from the job-rich southwestern sector.

The waste of resources is also a usual practice in spatial organization, as illustrated by the pattern in which the Metro was built. After some years of no new development, work on an isolated stretch in the southwestern periphery suddenly appeared from nowhere (because there was no urban transportation plan). This stretch was useless because it was not connected to the existing network. This is not an isolated incident: it is a method of systematically destroying common sense and the notions of both the obvious and nonsense. Such absurdities of systematic or ad hoc overprivileging of the elite as a whole or of individual members gets lost in the maze of nonsense, whereas every obvious need (such as the building of a decent mass transportation system in a metropolis of 18 million people) needs to be proved by means of scientific reasoning and great rhetorical eloquence. Here we see in actual practice the mentality described by Machado de Assis and discussed by Roberto Schwarz.

One of the main consequences of the acute lack of transport facilities (apart from the tremendous loss of time spent traveling, increased air pollution, noise, and other environmental costs) is the decay of the town center, which gradually became inaccessible to cars and the whole wealthy southwestern sector, which has no access to the center via the Metro.

Infrastructure is similarly scarce in other areas as well. Although there is running water over almost the whole urban area, the pipes go empty for some days of the week during the first longer period of draught—of course, first in the periphery. The sewer network barely covers 70% of dwellings. The slogan "poor country, precarious infrastructure" is taken almost for granted. After the ebbing of the "economic miracle," also the end of the extensive stage of development (and rapid urbanization), a new pattern of urbanization emerged, a stage of consolidation. Growth no longer is rapid and still has failed to lead to an improvement of the urban infrastructure.

Slowdown and Crisis

The Crisis of Hindered Accumulation

By the mid-seventies the stage of extensive accumulation—with high rates of excess produce, part of which was expatriated, while the rest still could be accumulated—came to a halt. The country became predominantly urban, wage labor was generalized, and the expansion of production henceforward became restricted largely to technical progress and an associated increase of labor productivity.

If the process of hindered accumulation was feasible in the extensive stage with rapid growth, it became problematic with the exhaustion of this stage and the concomitant fall of the rate of surplus, by about the mid-1970s. Henceforth either the surplus was to be accumulated—giving rise to unhindered development, raising the level of subsistence of labor, and ultimately leading to the demise of elite society—or it was to be expatriated, thereby annihilating any development or even simple growth. Either way, the reproduction of elite society was checked, having lost its basis in hindered accumulation. There was no choice within the premise for the reproduction of the status quo.

This is the underlying cause of the impasse Brazilian society finds itself in and which it fails to face openly. It materialized first in one "lost decade" (as the eighties were dubbed), to be followed by a second, and now by third, decade of economic stagnation and social disarray.

The Stalemate

Thus the period preceding the nineties was dominated by the crisis of hindered accumulation in the mid-seventies. At first there was a move after the miracle years to defy the rule of imposing a recession after a period of expansion (1974), but soon the Second National Development Plan (II PND) was abandoned (1976) and the hindrances to development were gradually reimposed. Recessive policies drove the Brazilian economy into a nosedive (the 1981–83 slump), followed by a period of stagnation that has lasted for some twenty years now (the two lost decades). Much of what can be told about the urban process in São Paulo is a consequence of this impasse, of which Brazilian society has thus far been unable to find a way out.

São Paulo: Slow Growth and Consolidation

Since the mid-seventies, two major trends made themselves felt in the São Paulo Metropolitan Region. First, its population growth rate fell to an almost vegetative level with a drastic slowdown in rural-urban migration. The size of the population still grew and today has reached 18 million inhabitants, but the growth rate has hovered around 1.5% per annum. The odds are that the metropolitan region will extend little beyond 23 million inhabitants by 2020. Second, São Paulo entered a transition from a predominantly industrial region to a major commercial, financial, and services center. Such trends reflect broader trends at the national level: as a consequence of a drop in the demographic growth rate coupled with an already high level of urbanization (80% in 2000, being 98% in the state of São Paulo), the process of migration from rural to urban areas has slowed down and the times of high rates of urban growth are over. On the other hand, manufacturing started losing its share in GDP nationwide (as it did, indeed, worldwide) at the expense of finance and services.

At slower growth rates and in a stage of consolidation, it became easier, in a way, to discern the distinguishing features of the urban process in São Paulo than at the time of runaway growth. Because São Paulo is the economic center of the Brazilian process of hindered accumulation, the effects of the economic hindrances have always made themselves acutely felt at the level of the metropolitan region both in spatial organization and in their consequences for the urban environment and the subsistence level of the workers. We already mentioned the glaring contrasts apparent at first sight to any newcomer or casual visitor to São Paulo, as well as the underlying causes of those extremes, among them precarious infrastructure, fragmentation of space, and deliberate waste of resources often coupled with offense to reason. In the times of rapid growth, however, the latter was frequently invoked as a reason, or indeed an excuse, for poor urban conditions. It was said that it is impossible to administer and provide infrastructure for a city that doubles its population every ten years.

Although São Paulo does not grow as rapidly any more, there has still been no improvement in the urban conditions. It is true that the eighties were taken by the 1981–84 recession, the conversion from military to civilian government (1984), and an institutional adjustment that culminated in the 1988 Constitution. But before a new pattern of urbanization could mature on the basis of these developments and could be assessed in its own terms, an new wave of ideology changed the pattern of thinking and practicing the urban process. Neoliberalism landed in Brazil by the close of the decade of 1980, though somewhat belatedly in comparison to the developed countries.

São Paulo in the Nineties

The Era of Neoliberalism

During the twentieth century, and especially after World War II, it became clear that the new forms of capitalism that were developing were nothing like the classical capitalism of the industrial revolution or the Victorian age. One important change was that there was now definitely no new room for expansion—the entire world had already been conquered by wage labor and commodity production. This meant that any increase in commodity production could only proceed through an increase of the productivity of labor. This was, in fact, a new stage of capitalism, called the stage of intensive accumulation or, for short, the intensive stage.

Crucial to contemporary capitalism is the significant role of techniques and technical progress, which became the sole source of growth (and, therefore, of profit). As a result, the level of subsistence of workers was greatly increased: more health, more education, more leisure time, and better urban environment. All were necessary to operate the increasingly sophisticated productive processes and provide an equally increasing variety of services in the greatly reduced working day. This was the material basis of the welfare state and its political form, social democracy.

During the welfare state years and the intensive stage of capitalism, there was a manifold increase of state intervention in the economy and a corresponding decrease of commodity production regulated by the market. That was tolerable while there was room for growth, but it became crushing with the decline of the postwar boom in the late sixties. Neoliberalism came as an attempt at restoring the primacy of the commodity form in contemporary capitalism. However, the expansion of the state is a consequence of the development of capitalism and the ever greater complexity of the structure of production. Thus, it is hardly a reversible process. The period covered by the accompanying table, which already includes ten years of Reaganism/Thatcherism, shows no discernible effect on the expansion of the state.[5]

Failing to reduce the presence of the state in the economy, neoliberal policies are in fact a reduction of the welfare state (Gough 1982), and their net result is concentration of capital and income (as shown in Ball et al. 1989, in an early assessment of the two terms of the Thatcher government). In support of its policies, neoliberalism has been producing an increasing body of ideology with a welter of neologisms (globalization, network society, new regionalism, or strategic planning, for a few examples). This has attracted, in its turn, an increasing chorus of criticism (see, e.g., Brenner 2002; Gill 1995; Jessop 1998; Budd 1998).

Government Spending as Share of GNP, 1880–1985:
Selected Countries (%)

Year	Great Britain	Germany	France	Japan	Sweden	United States
1880	10	10	15	11	6	8
1929	24	31	19	19	8	10
1960	32	32	35	18	31	28
1985	48	47	52	33	65	37

Source: World Bank, World Development Report, 1991 (Washington, D.C.).

Neoliberalism in Brazil

The questions related to globalization, the retreat of the state, new regionalism, and ultimately, neoliberalism have, of course, been widely discussed in Brazil and have attracted varying degrees of criticism everywhere except in government circles. These writers are among those most skeptical toward neoliberal ideas (Deák 1994; Schiffer 2002). In their view globalization and its companion terms are at best pseudoconcepts created to present the contemporary features of economy and society as though they were a new stage of capitalism, seeking thereby to present the tenets of neoliberalism as positive and in any case inevitable developments. At worst, the same are simply a cover for regressive policies aimed at implementing those changes which were presented as inevitable.

Thus in the Brazilian elite society neoliberalism as a policy also became dominant just as in developed countries. Yet, in addition to promoting privatization and concentration of capital and income, it acquired an additional meaning: it became a new cover for old *entreguismo*—the handing over of key branches to foreign capital. In addition to the traditional "agricultural vocation," globalization now also is invoked to justify—or present as unavoidable—open-door policies that offer up the home market to unequal competition from abroad. There is always, as before, careful selection of key branches of industry that are targeted to go over to foreign control.

There is, however, a serious mismatch between hindered accumulation and neoliberalism. Neoliberalism is a reaction to social democracy and the welfare state or, more generally, to the consequences of the intensive stage of development. Brazil, however, never entered that stage. This is precisely what causes the stalemate referred to earlier. There is thus no room whatsoever for capital or income concentration, or the dismantling of the welfare state, which are the main results of neoliberal policies in the developed countries. These neoliberal policies, while controversial in these countries, become simply pointless in the Brazilian context. This adds to the disarray caused by the crisis of hindered accumulation in consequence of the impending transition to intensive accumulation. Especially at the political level, the eruption of neoliberalism in the early nineties aborted an embryonic and already problematic social democratic opening.

A concrete outcome of the double stalemate was a host of recessive policies, backed off from time to time as though to let off some steam. These resulted in the two wasted decades mentioned earlier. The statistics for the two decades show no real movement of income distribution, only oscillations and ephemeral distributive effects of monetary stabilizations (1986, 1989, 1994). As for the economy, the oscillation of the classical stop-and-go policy rose to such frequency that it was now dubbed the "chicken flight."

Because home production will soon have to be expanded (as always, in the face of the balance-of-payments constraint), *entreguismo* is intensified. We mentioned already that strategic branches of industry are the first to go. This is vividly illustrated by a few figures: the share of foreign capital in Brazilian industry increased overall (from 36% in 1991 to 54% by 1999), but it increased even more and from an already higher level in the machinery and high-tech industries: from 60% to a crippling 87%.

At the same time surplus expatriation intensified: foreign debt servicing plus the deficit on services amounted to 75 billion USD in 2001 and again in 2002, which is equivalent to about 11–12% of Brazilian GDP (depending on the currency conversion rates). Meanwhile, internal debt skyrocketed. In eight years government revenue was raised by 50% (from 26% to 37% through 1995–2002) just to service this debt, since investment remained stagnant. This resulted in a broad transfer from productive to banking capital.

The nineties thus were a period of virtual stagnation combined with a structural weakening of the economy. The instruments of destructuring and slowing down production were reimposed and as it were, perfected. An overvalued currency (under the guise of monetary stabilization) gave the middle classes a feeling of welfare because of the ease with which it could purchase consumer goods, much of them imported. At the same time, one-third of Brazilian firms went bankrupt and the trade balance slumped, adding to the already heavy foreign debt. Interest rates soared to more than 15% and even 30%—allegedly in order to attract the foreign investment necessary to close the balance-of-payments deficit. This asphyxiated the productive structure as a whole, while the country sent abroad triple the speculative (short-term) capital inflows (the aforementioned 75 billion USD paid out against some 23 billion inflow in 2001). Import taxes declined to negligible levels or even zero, and import goods were exempt even from the value added tax—in a de facto negative stimulus to home industry. It is then no wonder that both unemployment and "informality" rose higher than in the developed countries, and this made itself felt primarily in the great urban agglomerations, which were helpless to do anything about it.

Infrastructure Provision

As mentioned already, the level and quality of infrastructure has always been kept at low levels in the elite society. But even in that context, the 1990s saw a sharp downturn, and investment in infrastructure virtually stalled. At the national level, the most acute cases were power generation (which led to a nationwide shortage and actual blackout in 1999, despite recessive policies that kept production at minimum levels and high idle capacity) as well as telecommunications (which were starved of investment to the point of bankruptcy with an additional and rather more specific purpose: namely, its devalorization and then privatization). Roads, railways, and sanitation also suffered.

Within the São Paulo Metropolitan Region, the worst case was perhaps the halt of an already very slow construction of the Metro. Construction began in the early 1970s, when São Paulo already had 7 million inhabitants, and progressed at an average rate of two kilometers yearly. That was so slow that by 1990, when São Paulo had already grown to an agglomeration of 16 million people, the Metro network was merely forty-five kilometers long, composed of two and a half lines. But then work stopped altogether, just when the construction of the all-important southwestern line was about to begin. Traffic jams increased dramatically, and urban

Length of Traffic Bottlenecks in Rush Hours in Greater São Paulo, 1992–2002 (km.)

Year	Morning	Evening
1992	28	39
1997	65	109
2001	85	116
2002[a]	108	124

Source: Companhia de Engenharia de Tráfego, 1998, 2003. The table shows the effect of traffic restriction in peak hours (one-fifth of all cars forbidden in central area) introduced in 1997. Collected from Csaba Deák at www.usp.br/fau/docentes/depprojeto/c-deak/CD/5bd/1rausp/t-g/06-vias-congest/index.html (accessed 15 June 2006).
[a]Value for 2002 is average in March only.

mobility remained stagnant. Even though the car ownership rate was up 50% from fourteen to twenty cars for every hundred people between 1987 and 1997, the number of daily car trips per capita remained the same (0.6). There was simply no room in the streets for the new cars.

The slowdown in infrastructure building was not, of course, a result of any explicitly stated policy. On the contrary, planning became ever less ambitious to the point of becoming self-effacing. There were, however, indirect reasons, outside the reach of local governments, for more restraint in infrastructure investment during the 1990s. In a letter of agreement to the International Monetary Fund (IMF), Brazil in 1992 agreed to the idea that any investment of the state (meaning any level of government) is deficit spending, having no return whatsoever to be accounted against it. Some years later the federal government enacted a law according to which, although budgets were to be strictly observed and no government body was allowed to overspend, loan contracts did not come under this rule and could be freely spent. Although they, of course, have to be repaid some day, this was invisible to a present-day government, especially a local government. Thus, unbelievably, investment became pure waste and a loan became free money.

Income Distribution

During the stagnation years of the wasted decades, São Paulo followed the Brazilian pattern and per capita income remained barely stagnant. There was no change in household income distribution either. On this score São Paulo is only slightly better off than Brazil, which has one of the most unequal income distributions in the world.

Planning: From Development to Strategic

Development plans saw their heydays in the 1960s and early 1970s, epitomized by the 1968 *Plano Urbanístico Básico,* a long-term, comprehensive plan, with encompassing analysis and propositions for the urban structure as a whole. It was complemented with sectoral plans for infrastructure components. When the slowdown came by the mid-seventies, planning gradually became restricted to sectoral planning. After the 1981–83 recession, it was virtually dying out.

The 1988 Constitution made it compulsory for every municipality except the smallest (fewer than 20,000 inhabitants) to elaborate its plan (*Plano Diretor*). Yet these plans were very different in scope than earlier plans. The first such plan issued in 1990 for the São Paulo municipality

Income Distribution in São Paulo State, Brazil, and Selected Countries, 1999

	Gini Index	10% Poorest	Quintiles of Income, in Increasing Order of Personal Income, %					10% Richest
			1	2	3	4	5	
São Paulo state	0.51	1.6	4.3	7.9	11.6	18.8	57.4	41.2
Brazil	0.57	1.0	3.3	6.4	10.6	17.9	61.8	45.7
South Africa	0.59	1.1	2.9	5.5	9.2	17.7	64.8	45.9
China	0.42	2.2	5.5	9.8	14.9	22.3	47.5	30.9
India	0.30	4.1	9.2	13.0	16.8	21.7	39.3	25.0

Source: Fundação Sustituto Brasileiro de Geografia e Estátitica (IGBE); Fundação Sistema Estadual de Auálise de Dados (SEADE); World Bank (other countries). Collected from Csaba Deák at www.usp.br/fau/docentes/depprojeto/c-deak/CD/5bd/3world/t-3-dReu-5countries/index.html (accessed 15 June 2006).

(for the administrative division of the metropolitan region, see the accompanying map) contained some elements that subsequently became generalized. It called for participation in its elaboration, although nothing really came out of that. It contained very vague directives and already made use, in a pioneering and experimental way, of the instruments of "interlinked operations" (an early form of the later "urban operations" discussed shortly). It also enabled the sale of building rights above a certain floor and up to certain ceiling levels, all of which were fixed by regions of the city.

That was only a start, and while public administration and its governing bodies were being ever more disqualified on account of the standard (neoliberal) charges of inefficiency and centrality, there was a mushrooming of new forms of spatial organization in the framework of various new combinations of public, semipublic, and private associations, such as councils, consortia, associations, nongovernmental organizations, or simply any pressure groups and ad hoc assemblies around strategic projects or urban operations.

"Strategic planning," as it became known, was to become the new form of planning to deal with specific and particular problems of the city, rather than administration on the basis of an overall view of the city or in the name of collective interest. It had at its disposal a number of new instruments, prominent among which were so-called urban operations. These

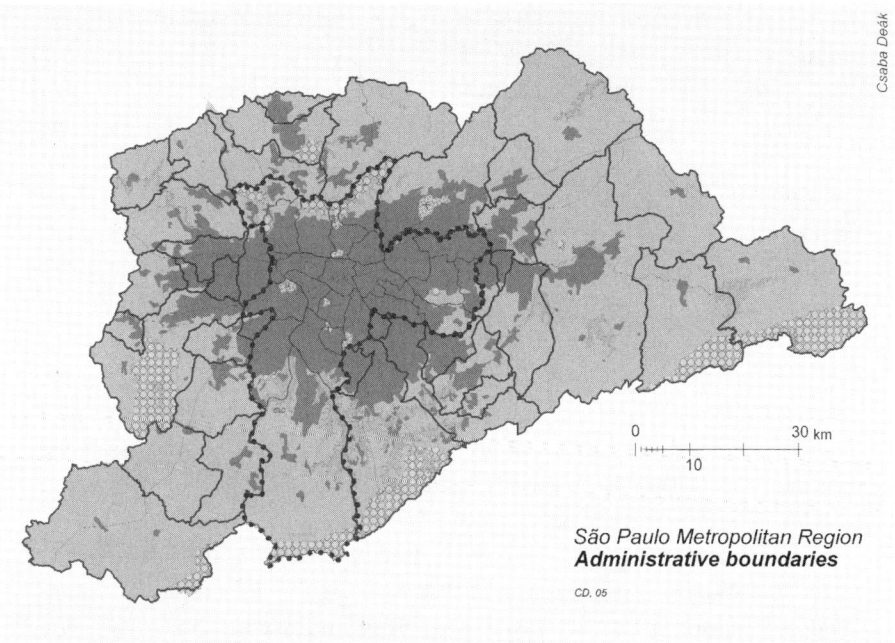

The thirty-nine boroughs of legal São Paulo Metropolitan Region. The map shows the municipal boundaries (*heavier dotted line*) with the city of São Paulo itself, within which regional administrations (sub-prefectures, since 2002) are also shown. Depicted in medium gray is the urban agglomeration proper (built-up area). The already weak legal status of the metropolitan region suffered a further loss after the 1988 Constitution, which increased municipal autonomy. Drawing by Csaba Deák.

were consolidated in a 2001 federal law known as the Statute of the City. They were inspired by France's *Zones d'Aménagement Concerté* and São Paulo's own "interlinked operations."

The rationale is well known: urban operations are to be applied in areas with potential intensification of land use, provided that additional or upgraded infrastructure is implemented. The operation itself consists in the provision of infrastructure through a mix of private and public investment. This should lead to a valorization of real estate in the area. Local government could capture part of this valorization through the sale of building rights. Such practice has been criticized on the grounds that it allows investment-capable groups to attract further investment from the state and get additional concessions in the form of tax rebates or relaxed land use restrictions, further weakening control of the overall urban structure.

Paradigmatic of the new planning is the *Plano Diretor 2001–2010,* also called the strategic municipal plan for São Paulo. It identifies a set of areas, mostly along the main axes of the city, recommended for urban operations (with a view at the upgrading or intensification of land use). The guidelines for land use regulation are limited to a few specific uses, such as (high-income) residential districts, predominantly industrial districts, and a number of environmentally protected zones. In the vein of decentralization and participation, the plan calls for more detailed local plans to be elaborated by the recently created subprefectures. These have experienced varying degrees of difficulty in drawing up local plans, due to a lack of qualified personnel and of a reliable database. In some cases, especially where they happened to contain crucial elements of the overall urban structure, they suffered from a lack of general guidelines concerning those elements (which had been left to be defined in the future by urban operations). It may be hoped that some of the difficulties of decentralized planning will be eased with time and a consolidation of the process, but even then the problem of administrative fragmentation of the metropolitan region as a whole will still remain.

Apart from creating urban operations, the Statute of the City transformed a number of planning concepts into concrete instruments of control, such as the social function of private property in land, a basis for expropriation, zones of social interest facilitating low-income settlements, and a progressive property tax, a powerful means of taxation and encouragement of more efficient land use. However, the precise contours of the use of these instruments have yet to be defined.

Tertiarization and Deindustrialization

One of the most debated trends in the São Paulo Metropolitan Region is the loss of industrial jobs. This has been seen as decentralization toward the hinterland, mainly São Paulo state or Brazil as a whole. Indeed, the share of São Paulo in industrial produce has been falling with respect to both greater regions. An interpretation of this process, however, requires putting it into broader perspective.

One the broadest trends in contemporary capitalism is the fall of the proportion of workers in the manufacturing industry, due to the increase in productivity without a corresponding increase in the size of the markets. Thus, the loss of manufacturing jobs in São Paulo can only partly be

Built Floor Space by Building Type in São Paulo Municipality, 1985, 1990, 1995, and 2000 (million sq. m.)

	1985	1990	1995	2000
Housing	116	122	135	143
Flats	52	68	83	100
Commerce	26	32	46	59
Office building	5	8	28	32
Industry	24	34	34	29
Other	25	38	8	26

Source: Secretaria Municipal de Planejainento (several years), www2.prefeitwa.sp.gov.br/secretarias/planejainento.

ascribed to decentralization. Another factor is tertiarization. As for the latter, again, it is not an effect of some globalization, but simply the local manifestation of a general tendency of world capitalism. This distinction matters, because if the cause is decentralization, São Paulo might fight back and try to reverse the tendency, whereas if it is tertiarization in contemporary capitalism, São Paulo must prepare itself for more tertiarization and restructure its urban policies and, above all, its tax revenues. These are currently based mainly on taxes on industrial products—the value added tax—and less on the taxation of services and real estate (land and built property). Taxation of the latter two must form the bulk of revenue in a tertiary metropolis, and this means that the whole system of taxation along with its information and database needs to be overhauled.

It goes without saying that the prospects for reducing unemployment (currently at 13.6% in São Paulo, which is slightly above the Brazilian average of 12.8%) also depend on the way in which those tendencies with respect to deindustrialization or tertiarization are interpreted.

A Balance

During the nineties, city region administration has been as disrupted as ever (the metropolitan planning entity EMPLASA always had a fragile existence and barely survives today), although there has been a change in form. If the state once was responsible for planning in the name of public interest, even if a good part of this was pure make-believe, it today says that it does less on the equally empty assertion that this is more efficient. The idea of planning (public interest) has been substituted by participation—which can easily be construed as a populist legitimation of the absence, or weakening, of planning.

Also, there was a shift from the public to the private sector, a move to privatization of public services, which is now being reassessed and reconsidered on the basis of frequently disastrous results (as in power generation and telecommunications, but also in transportation and environmental conservation). Hence, at least a strengthening of regulating bodies can be observed, and there even has been talk of the need for a recovery of the capacity of planning, both at the metropolitan as well as the national level.

Finally, there are a number of larger-scale initiatives protesting the precarious situation of infrastructure. For instance, there have been initiatives to resume the construction of the Metro, although voices arguing for cheap solutions, such as exclusive bus lanes, aerial bus or rail tracks, and the like, never die. Similar trends exist in the fields of communications, environment, and public facilities.

Oddly enough, on these scores, the political orientation of the successive mayors of the São Paulo municipality—the Partido dos Trabalhadores (PT) from 1988 to 1992, then two right-wing administrations, then again the PT, and since 2004 a right-wing administration again—seems to make no difference. There were differences concerning specific policies, such as more emphasis on social housing and public transportation by leftist governments and more slum clearance and road building by the right-wing administrations. Yet those measures were of such small a scale and scope that they would not affect the existing trends.

No full account or assessment of these can be given in the space available here, but we may probably construe those trends and signs as an indication that, as so much else, neoliberal policies, having already run most of their course, are not going to last forever either.

The Prospects for São Paulo

The best alternatives and projects, if implemented, would indicate that Brazilian society is finally ready for a far-reaching change to its historic pattern of development. They would make sense only in combination with a national resolve for real development and reversal of the reproduction of the status quo. In fact, this would not be far from the vision of the optimistic scenario of a recent (1994), but also half-forgotten, EMPLASA metropolitan plan—*Plano Metropolitano de Desenvolvimento*

The Latin crescent (*dark gray*) in Mercosul (*medium gray*). It aggregates about half of the population of Mercosul and is home to some half-dozen world cities. Drawing by Csaba Deák on map from Consórcio Brasiliana, *Eixos de desenvolvimento* (Brasília: BNDES, 1999).

Integrado. Public expenditure would be put on a footing consistent with the potential status of São Paulo as world city. Schooling, higher education, and public health levels would be upgraded to ensure the formation a skilled work force needed to keep up with the requirements of technical progress in manufacturing, high-tech infrastructure, and telecommunications; research and development; and a widening range of services and expanding leisure time.

In short, it would mean that some of the development potential of the most developed part of South America, the core of Mercosul, has a good chance of being realized. Brazil, for one, must be one of the few large countries, along with China and India, that possesses ample room for growth not dependent on conjunctures of the world economy or exports but based on the expansion of the home market. It is worth mentioning that the biggest metropolitan agglomerations of the region—São Paulo, Buenos Aires, and Rio de Janeiro—will certainly compete for the status of world city and the position of being the main center of development and prestige within Mercosul. Yet this competition is like a contest between rival football teams where each plays better because it plays the others and gains in skill, experience, and the thrill of the match. In the same way, there is little doubt that, say, Buenos Aires is far more capable of its potential within Mercosul than in Argentina alone, or that both São Paulo and Rio de Janeiro carry more weight due to their proximity to each other—to say nothing of Santiago de Chile, which from its isolation on the other side of the Andes can ascend to become a part of the Latin crescent and, indeed, its outlet to the Pacific. There is certainly room for several world cities in the region—let us recall only that London and Paris are separated merely by 300 kilometers, that is, by less than the distance from São Paulo to Rio.

Just how much of the potential development of these metropolises will materialize will depend crucially on their own development plans, on the development policies of their respective nations, and even on the development and the level of integration of the Mercosul region as a whole.

Notes

1. Di Cavalcanti, Anita Malfatti, Tarsila do Amaral, Victor Brecheret; Oswald de Andrade, Manuel Bandeira, Carlos Drummond de Andrade; Mário de Andrade; and Heitor Villa-Lobos are among the most renowned artists.

2. *Mineiros:* people from the neighboring Minas Gerais state, the second

strongest in the country both in population and economy, an occasional rival of São Paulo.

3. De Andrade (1926). Translation by Csaba Deák.

4. We use the concepts of extensive and intensive stages of development as in Aglietta (1976).

5. This series was discontinued after 1985, but according to another World Bank data series, central government revenue in the OECD countries, as a share of the national product, was up from 19% in 1970 to 30% in 1998 (excluding local government and state enterprises), which suggests that the state continued to expand after 1985, as before, www.worldbank.org/data/wdi2000/pdfs/tab1_5.pdf (accessed 20 July 2001).

References

Aglietta, M. 1976. *A Theory of Capitalist Regulation.* London: New Left Books.

Ashworth, W. 1954. *The Genesis of Modern British Town Planning.* London: Routledge & Kegan Paul.

Ball, M., F. Gray, and L. McDowell. 1989. *The Transformation of Britain: Contemporary Economic and Social Change.* London: Fontana.

Brenner, N. 2002. Decoding the Newest "Metropolitan Regionalism" in the USA: A Critical Overview. *Cities* 19, no. 1: 3–21.

Budd, L. 1998. Territorial Competition and Globalization: Scylla and Charybdis of European Cities. *Urban Studies* 35, no. 4: 663–85.

Deák, C. 1988. The Crisis of Hindered Accumulation in Brazil, BISS 10. Bartlett International Summer School on the Production of the Built Environment, Cidade do México. *Proceedings BISS 10,* 253–59. London.

———. 1994. Globalization or Global Crisis? XIII World Congress of Sociology, RC 21: Regional and Urban Development. Bielefeld, 18–23 July. Revised version in Bartlett International Summer School on the Production of the Built Environment, Glasgow, 1995. *Proceedings BISS 17,* 137–48. London.

de Andrade, M. 1926. *Macunaíma, o herói sem nenhum caráter.* Published in chapters in *Revista de Antropofagia,* 1928. São Paulo.

Fernandes, F. 1972. *Capitalismo dependente e classes sociais na América Latina.* São Paulo: Zahar.

Gill, S. 1993. Neo-liberalism and the Shift toward a US-Centered Transnational Hegemony. In H. Overbeek (ed.), *Restructuring Hegemony in the Global Political Economy: The Rise of Transnational Neo-liberalism in the 1980s,* 246–82. London: Routledge.

———. 1995. Globalisation, Market Civilisation and Disciplinary Neoliberalism. *Millennium* 24, no. 3: 399–423.

Gough, I. 1982. The Crisis of the British Welfare State. In N. Fainstein and S. Fainstain (eds.), *Urban Policy under Capitalism,* 43–64. Urban Affairs Annual Review, vol. 20. Beverly Hills: Sage.

Jessop, B. 1998. The Rise of Governance and the Risks of Failure: The Case of Economic Development. *International Social Science Journal* 155: 29–46.

Schiffer, S. 2002. São Paulo: Articulating a Cross-Border Region. In S. Sassen (ed.), *Global Networks, Linked Cities*, 209–36. London: Routledge.

Schwarz, R. 1979. *Um mestre na periferia do capitalismo*. São Paulo: Duas Cidades.

Shanghai
The Evolution of China's Future Global City
Weiping Wu

Strategically located at the mouth of the Yangtze River and endowed with a prosperous economic hinterland, Shanghai witnessed phenomenal industrialization and commercialization during the first half of the twentieth century. After three decades of disinvestment between 1949 and 1979, the city still managed to contribute a sizable share of the nation's production. The attention devoted to Shanghai since the late 1980s represents in part the increasing attention given to the urban areas in which China's wealth is concentrated. Similar to cities in southern China, Shanghai has acquired greater local autonomy, and its leadership also has undergone marked change.

For several years now, Shanghai has proclaimed its intention of becoming an international metropolis of the twenty-first century. As one ambitious former mayor, Ju Huang, said, "Shanghai of the future must be a metropolis equal to New York or London" (cited in Gamble 2003, 10). Among a handful of globalizing cities in Asia, Shanghai has reasonable long-term prospects. It is also facing competition from an established center—Hong Kong—as well as other aspirants, such as Beijing. Since the mid-1990s, a set of strategic development objectives has been defined and, to a degree, implemented in Shanghai. A key element is to advance in high-tech manufacturing, business services, transport and communications facilities, commercial facilities, and the availability of skills (cited in Chan 2000). This calls for action in a number of areas as well as a variety of ongoing initiatives, such as industrial restructuring, infrastructure building and privatization, housing and land reforms, and cultural regeneration.

Often called the "crucible of modern China," Shanghai has been a popular topic in scholarly literature. Many academic volumes have been devoted to Shanghai's past, chief among which are Murphy (1953), Howe (1981), Wei (1987), Johnson (1995), Goodman (1995), and Lu (1999). Scholars have argued that it was precisely because of the demographic heterodoxy in the early twentieth century that Shanghai rose above a country of vast conservatism and became a great, modern city. After a near silence for more than three decades, the city's recent development is again attracting significant attention. Within the scholarly literature, four book-length publications have offered considerable insight into how Shanghai is navigating its modernization efforts and integrating with the global economy.[1]

This essay is intended to provide an overview of the city and consists of six sections. Following a brief discussion of Shanghai's history and geography, the second section highlights the changing relationship between the city and the nation-state. Next, the essay outlines the existing global and regional linkages and addresses the potential competition between Shanghai and other globalizing cities in East Asia. The fourth and fifth sections assess the key aspects of the socioeconomic and physical transformation the city has undergone in the era of globalization. The essay concludes with a discussion of likely risks and challenges in the current development of Shanghai.

Shanghai in Time and Space

Built along the Huangpu River in the lower Yangtze delta, Shanghai's development has been linked to its history as China's largest seaport. First established as a fishing village in the tenth century, Shanghai became a county seat in 1074. Merchant families from nearby Ningbo (in Zhejiang province) were instrumental in making it an integral part of the coastal trading system, and Shanghai grew steadily to become a regional commercial center. By 1853 it had surpassed Guangzhou (Canton) as China's premier trading city (Yusuf and Wu 1997). Modern industrial development commenced in Shanghai in the late nineteenth century, and cultural activities and modern institutions of higher learning followed shortly. Banking and other producer services began taking root in the early twentieth century.

Shanghai's development since the mid-nineteenth century was closely related to the increasing foreign presence in industry, trade and transport, and a strengthening of commercial links with the outside world. The city was among the earliest treaty ports along the coast and the major waterways after the succession of "unequal treaties" imposed by external powers on China. These treaties gave foreign citizens, primarily from Britain, France, and the United States, rights of extraterritoriality that allowed them to claim exclusive jurisdiction over concession areas within the city. The foreign community even set up its own municipal council in 1854, marking a century of semicolonial rule (Gamble 2003; Pott 1928).

During its golden age in the 1920s, with a local tradition of easy acceptance of outsiders, the city attracted both foreigners and a great variety of migrants from other parts of China. The city also obtained a kind of sophistication with a strong merchant character. Commerce served as the primary motor of society. In effect, Shanghai was regarded as the epicenter of modern China's commercialism and gained the name of Haipai culture (the Shanghai school). Ranked as the seventh largest city in the world in 1936, no Asian city from that period could "match Shanghai's cosmopolitan and sophisticated reputation" (Yeung 1996, 2). It was the "Paris of the East," and the largest recipient of foreign investment in China. In addition, Shanghai boasted the most highly developed urban amenities in Asia outside of Tokyo. The foreign officials who managed the concession areas built electricity networks, sewerage lines, and tramways that were equal to the standard of most European cities. Western influence was particularly visible in Shanghai's architecture and urban space (W. Wu 2004a). The Bund, the famous area along the west bank of the Huangpu River, for instance, housed more than 100 financial institutions in neoclassical and art deco buildings.

After 1949, however, the city experienced more than thirty years of neglect and disinvestment. The antiurban bias and austere official attitude toward cities resulted in limited investment in housing and other urban amenities. Compared to the national urban average and Beijing specifically (a city of comparable size), Shanghai lagged in several important indexes of urban infrastructure, including per capita living space and per capita paved roads (W. Wu 1999a). For the central authorities, Shanghai served as a major pillar of the planned economy. Its manufacturing facilities, among China's most advanced, were crucial for meeting production targets. With its concentration of industrial products, the city became the single biggest source of revenue for the state, providing about 25% in an average year during the latter part of the 1970s. An enormous range of industries, spanning 140 of the 146 listed subsectors, were established (Yusuf and Wu 1997). But with the closing of China's door to the outside world, Shanghai ceased to be a "world city" with diverse functions and was transformed into an industrial workhorse for a command economy. Tightly controlled by the central government, it also ceased to be the financial, trade, and business center. Financial and information functions were transferred to Beijing, the capital city.

Due to its strategic role as an industrial center and revenue contributor, Shanghai was largely bypassed during the early round of reforms since 1979 that occurred primarily in the southeastern provinces. At that time, top officials in Shanghai also were not ardent supporters of the changing national economic policies and did not act as pioneers in launching reforms (Cheung 1996). It was only after the success of reforms in south China that Shanghai finally embarked on a rapid path of modernization in the late 1980s. The attention given to Shanghai represented in part an attempt by the center to promote development in the northern part of the country to balance the rapid advances taking place in the southeastern region. As China continues to open up to the world and undergo market reforms, Shanghai is renewing its cosmopolitan reputation and external linkages.

Today, with a population of more than 16 million and land area of 6,377 square kilometers within the metropolitan area, Shanghai is the biggest of three cities—the two others are Hangzhou and Wuxi—that together constitute the principal urban region in China. With a gross national product (GDP) of 495.1 billion yuan (about 59.7 billion USD) in 2001, it has a per capita income of 37,382 yuan (4,505 USD), a highly diversified industrial base responsible for 5% of national industrial output, and an expanding services sector. The metropolitan area, governed by the Shanghai municipal government—equivalent to a provincial government because of Shanghai's special administrative status—consists of sixteen urban districts (nine of them are located in the central city) and three suburban counties. These nineteen units are then divided into subdistricts (*jiedao*) for urban areas or towns (*zhen*) for rural areas. Between 50,000 to 100,000 residents live in a subdistrict or town. Each subdistrict or town is further divided into a number of neighborhood or village committees, which are the smallest residential administrative units.

Around Shanghai and extending westward along the Yangtze River Valley is one of the two most prosperous economic hinterlands (the other being the Pearl River Delta region) in China, with an urban population of 200 million and a GDP of more than 300 billion USD. Close to half of China's richest small towns are located in this hinterland (Yusuf and Wu

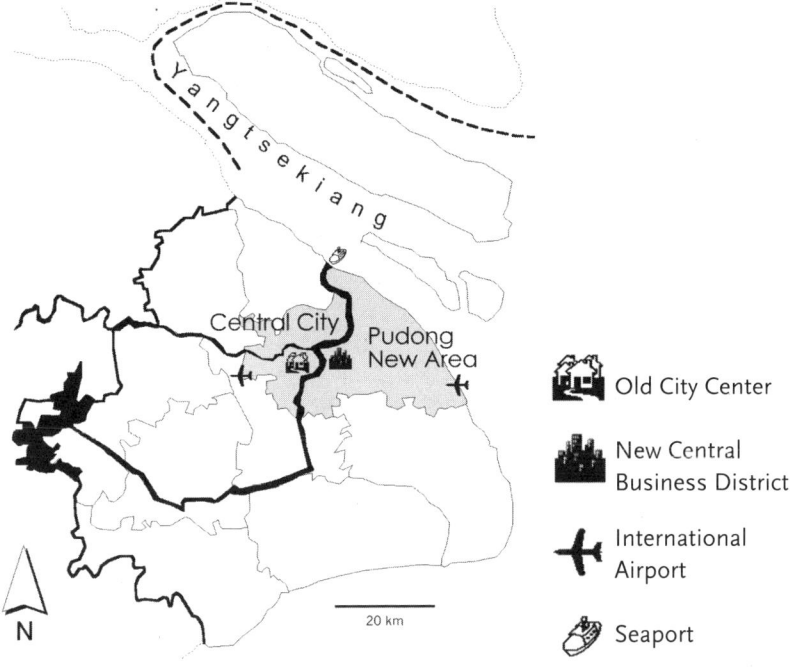

Shanghai metropolitan area.

2002). In 1982 central and municipal governments put together the lower Yangtze Economic Region to coordinate development and began dismantling trade barriers between Shanghai and the neighboring provinces of Jiangsu and Zhejiang. Enterprises in Shanghai have quickly discovered the advantages of moving some production facilities out of the city and entering into subcontracting arrangements with manufacturers in the hinterland. Township and village enterprises in southern Jiangsu and nearby Zhejiang often turn to Shanghai for skills, equipment and markets.

Shanghai in the National Context

In contemporary China, Shanghai has a unique position in economic development and politics. The relations between the central government and Shanghai are a crucial determinant of the city's growth trajectory. To ensure both central control and efficient implementation of national policies, the central government has retained the authority to appoint most

Key Indicators of Metropolitan Shanghai, 1990–2001

	Population[a] (million)	Density (per sq. km.)	GDP (billion yuan)	Per Capita GDP (yuan)
1991	12.87	2,030	89.4	6,955
1996	13.04	2,057	290.2	22,275
2001	13.27	2,093	495.1	37,382

Source: Shanghai Statistical Bureau 2002.
[a]This population figure includes only registered local residents. An estimated 3.2 million temporary migrants, largely from rural China, also reside in Shanghai (in 2000).

Share of Shanghai in the Nation, 1990–2001 (%)

	GDP	GDP in Industry	GDP in Service Sector	Local Revenue	Local Expenditure
1991	4.1	6.4	4.3	5.6	2.5
1996	4.3	4.9	5.9	3.9	4.3
2001	5.2	5.0	7.8	3.8	NA

Source: Shanghai Statistical Bureau 1996–2002; National Statistics Bureau 1999.

provincial leaders, including Shanghai's top officials (Chen 1998; Cheung 1996). On the other hand, Shanghai's economic might has made it an important actor in Chinese politics and influenced how the central government deals with it. Officials from Shanghai have been far more active in national politics than most other provinces. Because of national policy adjustments, the appointment of the city's leadership has undergone marked change during recent years. The appointment first of Jiang Zemin (1985) and then of Zhu Rongji (1987) as mayors of Shanghai put in place leaders with close links to Beijing. The current municipal leaders are generally better-educated, technically trained industrial managers and professionals. More of them are native to the city rather than being outsiders directly appointed by the central government, tilting the balance of power between the center and Shanghai more toward the city (Chen 1998). Unlike those appointed in the prereform era who acted as agents of the central government, these officials have become more active in promoting local interests.

Since the late 1980s, central support and incentives have been particularly strong. In 1990 Deng Xiaoping lent his support to the city by calling for rapid development of the Pudong New Area project on 522 square kilometers of farmland to the east of the city, proposed in the early 1980s by the then mayor of Shanghai Wang Daohan (Yusuf and Wu 2002). Planned for a three-phase development and designed to relieve the spatial pressure on old Shanghai, it contains China's largest free-trade zone, a fully operational export processing zone, a high-technology development zone, and a large number of new residential communities. Formally launched in April 1990, the Pudong project was followed by a number of preferential measures, which, among others, allowed Shanghai to establish a stock market and a number of service industries. Jiang Zemin's appointment as party secretary and Zhu Rongji as premier further strengthened Shanghai's links with the capital and support for its development ambitions. Thus, in 1995, eighteen super-special policies gave preferential status to projects in Pudong, 700 million yuan (approximately 84.5 million USD) in annual loans from the center, and a number of other benefits. Between 1990 and 2000, the central and municipal governments invested a total of 22 billion USD in Pudong (Yatsko 2001).

Fiscal relations with central authorities have improved as well. With the start of economic reforms, the central government introduced a new decentralizing fiscal regime that visualized each provincial entity as a "separate kitchen" for fiscal purposes. This allowed many municipalities to retain higher rates of revenue and to allocate funding more freely. In 1980 a new system of fiscal contract was introduced, which designated separate types of taxes or revenue. Under this arrangement participating provinces and municipalities were allowed to remit a share of revenue and retain all income collected in excess of this share. In exchange for being given a bigger slice of revenue, they also were required to accept responsibility for most items of expenditure (W. Wu 1999b). But Shanghai was largely bypassed during the early fiscal reforms in the late 1970s. Between 1949 and 1980, roughly 86% of Shanghai's revenue was remitted to the central government (Yusuf and Wu 1997).

After several rounds of hard-pressed negotiation, however, Shanghai finally was allowed a higher ratio of revenue retention (about 25%) in 1983 (Lin 1994). The central government eased its tight grip on expenditure decision making, with the result that municipal spending in Shanghai rose moderately between 1980 and 1983 and tripled over the 1983–86 period (Yusuf and Wu 1997). A more favorable fiscal arrangement negotiated by Shanghai with the central government in 1988 gave the city greater autonomy in revenue collection and municipal expenditure. The new terms were broadly similar to those enjoyed by Guangdong since the early 1980s and entailed remitting a fixed annual sum. Shanghai also initiated its own district-level fiscal decentralization in 1990. Typically the formula used has been to allow district finance bureaus to retain revenues collected above a base value. The rationale is that revenue retention encourages greater tax collection, some of which may feed the municipality's budget, while improving the allocation of resources for self-determined expenditure (Shanghai Academy of Social Sciences 1998).

Designated as one of the fourteen coastal open cities in 1984, Shanghai has obtained increased autonomy to manage foreign trade and investment, as well as increased foreign-exchange retention rights over the proceeds from exports. The central government also has granted Shanghai permission to issue stocks and shares and permit trading in the city stocks issued elsewhere in the country (Gamble 2003). Yet, although the Shanghai municipality enjoys substantial fiscal and administrative autonomy, it is subject to the same restrictions as the rest of the country regarding relations with the outside world. The central government formulates the framework to regulate and limit contacts with foreigners, control movement into and out of the country, and regulate Internet traffic (Yusuf and Wu 2002).

Given its industrial depth and tradition, Shanghai continues to be one of China's economic centers, despite some below-average growth in the early reform period prior to the 1990s. Its share of the nation's GDP remains significant (as shown in the preceding table), almost twice that of Beijing, and recently its growth has been among the highest of any city in China. Shanghai accounted for 11.6% of the national industrial output in 1980, and this declined to a still impressive 5.0% in 2001. Its national prominence is increasingly in the service sector, with a steadily growing share reaching 7.8% in 2001. Shanghai's prospect for acquiring the status of regional hub is undoubtedly tied to China's future development. If the Chinese economy can sustain its growth rate, it will rival the United States in a few decades (Yusuf and Wu 2002). And if Shanghai is able to retain its preeminence in the Chinese context, then it is likely to be the East Asian city with the best prospect of becoming a global center.

Preeminence in a national context, however, is only one of several attributes of a regional or global hub. In its path to becoming a world city, Shanghai will undoubtedly face competition from other regional centers. In the East Asia region, Hong Kong and Singapore already lead the way in acquiring global economic functions, particularly with respect to international flights and international airfreight movements (Yusuf and Wu 2002). Hong Kong, in particular, will retain an edge for at least several reasons. It enjoys a more advantageous location at the intersection of Chinese and foreign social networks mediating the flow of capital and is the most centrally located city relative to the other capitals in East and Southeast Asia (Enright, Scott, and Dodwell 1997). If in the future Asia's economic center of gravity shifts more to the southeast and the south, then Hong Kong (as well as Singapore) is better positioned to service emerging demands. Hong Kong's hinterland, the Pearl River Delta Region, also has experienced phenomenal growth rates and has superior transport and communication facilities. Yet this is not to say that the number of global and regional hubs will remain fixed. New regional centers could emerge as East Asia continues to develop and urbanize.

Regional and Global Linkages

Shanghai has followed a path similar to that of other globalizing cities in enhancing its external linkages. The new international airport that opened in September 1999 marks a significant step in the city's long-term goal to become an aviation hub in the Asia and Pacific region. A magnetic levitation high-speed train will connect the airport to the city center and the planned Beijing-Shanghai expressway. Foreign airlines have responded to the city's rising significance as a business center and the growth in airport capacity by increasing the volume of service. Since 1999, several new, nonstop flights have been added, including KLM Royal Dutch Airlines to Amsterdam, Austrian Airlines to Vienna, and China Eastern Airlines to Japan's Fukushima. Shanghai now has nonstop flights reaching most of the world's important urban centers (Yusuf and Wu 2002). By 2001 Shanghai was the fifth busiest container port ahead of Rotterdam, with annual traffic of 6.3 million twenty-foot-equivalent containers. When Yangshan port is completed in a few years, Shanghai will have the capacity to absorb traffic from Southeast Asia that is currently channeled through Hong Kong. At that point, Shanghai could emerge as the third most important port worldwide.[2]

Becoming a major cyber hub is another ambitious undertaking in Shanghai's building of external linkages. A key five-year project has been launched to integrate all the circuits and pipelines for telecom services into one underground broadband pipeline (*China Daily*, 21 December 2000). Upon completion, this project will not only offer a strong backbone for the city's development as an Internet-smart metropolis, it will also improve the aesthetic quality of the environment while reducing the number of accidents caused by open-air circuit poles and lines. Rapidly increasing Internet usage also relates to the export orientation of Shanghai-based enterprises, and the steadily improving quality of the telecom facilities is helping integrate Shanghai with the world economy.

Due to its industrial depth and skilled work force, Shanghai has outpaced other Chinese cities in the race to attract international investment. By 2001 the stock of utilized foreign investment reached 57.5 billion USD, of which about 11.5 billion USD involved technology imports (Shanghai Statistical Bureau 2002). More investors are coming from the United States and Japan, while investment originating in Hong Kong is steadily declining. Shanghai's strategic location and external linkages also lure domestic firms to invest in the city and use it as a springboard to the world market. To appeal to foreign investment and international businesses, several new industrial districts (often called Economic and Technology Development Zones, ETDZ) have been created since 1984. Special regulations comparable to those offered by other coastal provinces have been extended to these districts: tax exemptions for enterprises doing business with foreign companies for a limited duration, tax holidays for new factories set up with foreign investment (e.g., 15% reduction in income tax), and exemption from import-duty for production materials used by these facilities (W. Wu 1999a; F. Wu 2003).

Overseas investment has been instrumental in the building of the city's new subway system, new industrial districts, as well as hotel and other facilities needed to attract large numbers of businesses and tourists (W. Wu 1999b). In particular, the manufacturing sector is attracting more foreign investors. As of July 2000, 254 of the Fortune 500 companies have invested or established offices here (*China Daily*, 18 July 2000), and the chief examples are Alcatel, Volkswagen, General Motors, NEC, DuPont, and IBM. This could be a prelude to the shift of some regional headquarters functions to the city. The largest gains in output value are registered in such rising industries as telecommunications equipment, integrated circuits and computers, biomedical technologies, and new materials (Yusuf and Wu 2002).

Investment in services has been actively promoted since the early 1990s, with the backing of the central government. Foreign insurers have been allowed to operate only in Shanghai, and all foreign banks currently licensed to deal in the domestic currency are in Shanghai's Pudong New

Area.[3] By the end of 2001, twenty-one foreign banks had established their main offices in the city (Yusuf and Wu 2002). International companies also are changing the traditional face of the city's food markets and department stores. Deals jointly financed by funds from Hong Kong and Taiwan are helping Shanghai to rejuvenate its motion picture industry, which gave the city the title of Hollywood of China in the 1930s.

But compared to other global cities, Shanghai remains in a country with significantly less economic openness. The lack of transparency in decision making and the problems of coping with complex local regulations are a serious disincentive for many transnational companies. China also remains largely segregated from international financial markets. By limiting links with the rest of the world, the central government makes it harder for Shanghai to capitalize fully on foreign investment in infrastructure building, international production networking, and the growth of producer services (Yusuf and Wu 2002).

Economic and Social Transformations in an Era of Globalization

While policies determining economic openness are largely decided by the central government, Shanghai's municipal authorities have had a firm hand in determining the timing, pace, and configuration of the city's development since the late 1980s. With increasing local autonomy and a rising cadre of younger technocrats, the new leaderships share in the vision of a market system and the creation of formal institutions. They also have guided the city through industrial restructuring to acquire some of the functions commonly associated with world city status, including finance, transnational corporate headquarter functions, global services, transport, information, and cultural activities (Friedmann 1998; Sassen 1991). This is reflected in the substantial shift in Shanghai's economic structure during the past two decades, as the manufacturing sector was giving away its dominance to the tertiary sector that is now counting for more than half of the municipal GDP. Now municipal authorities are paying closer attention to the development of high-tech products and six manufacturing subsectors—automobiles, electronics and telecommunications equipment, power station equipment, steel, petrochemicals, and home appliances (*Shanghai Star*, 28 May 1999).

More important, in the steady transition from a command to market economy, reforms are occurring in finance, land market and property rights, labor market, and housing provision. Reforming the financial infrastructure has been a priority, as city leaders are increasingly aware of the importance of well-functioning market institutions. Among the financial initiatives, the one with the greatest promise is the setting up of a stock market in December 1990. Initially with shares for domestic investors only, a high proportion of the market's capitalized value was held by governmental agencies. Starting in January 1992 the issue of a million B class shares (worth 100 million USD), for overseas investors, was a significant step toward the broadening of the financial market. Since 1990, ten exchanges also have been opened for securities, metals, coal, farm production materials and equipment, chemicals, grain and edible oil, motor vehicles, building materials, and technology.

Some drastic reform measures in the financial sector followed (Yusuf and Wu 1997). For instance, the Shanghai foreign-exchange swap market removed the ceiling for exchange quota to allow free trading of foreign currency by individuals. Another major step in 1994 pushed various state-owned specialized banks into becoming commercial banks through the pursuit of "risk-related management." Credit co-ops in both urban and rural areas are currently being turned into cooperative banks to help spur the growth of the local economy. Moreover, Shanghai's Lujiazui central business district now contains foreign banks conducting local currency business, from which they are barred in the rest of the country.

The introduction of market-guided prices into municipal operation is most significant in the area of urban land management. Before 1988 urban land was owned almost entirely by municipal governments, and cities could not lease or sell the use right of land. But the implementation of a series of new national regulations set forth drastic reforms that aimed to allow the right of land use to be transferred, leased, rented, and mortgaged. Land reform has been a gradual process in Shanghai, as in many other Chinese cities. Given the city's population density, its relative prosperity, and burgeoning commercial development, real estate is now extremely valuable and has become an important component of the urban economy. Yet the results of land reform are at best a dual land market or coexistence of leased and administrative land (F. Wu 2003; Zhu 2000). A limited amount of land is allocated through compensatory leasing and acquired at market prices primarily by foreign investors and commercial developers. On the other hand, the values of most land leasing are largely determined by public authorities and not through competitive and transparent auctions. With the lack of formal, standardized land transaction procedures, government subsidies are still common in land allocation.

Measures to ensure an adequate supply of entrepreneurship, skills, and labor is another challenge as state enterprises move away from the practice of providing the work force with tenured employment and guaranteed pensions along with health, housing, and other benefits. The foremost task is relocating workers displaced by the large-scale closure and divestiture of state enterprises, which is particularly difficult for middle-aged workers close to retirement in the city's core industries like textiles. Labor use in these enterprises is highly compartmentalized, with workers trained in a narrow specialization. Therefore, the retraining of workers, either for reassignment within their enterprises in response to production shifts or in order to facilitate employment after closure, greatly influences internal and external labor mobility. For the moment, the city has opted for the absorption of surplus workers in low-skill service operations where job prospects have multiplied and retraining is minimal. Specifically, these workers find employment in retail, repair and maintenance works, grounds maintenance, household services, and cleaning services.

Shanghai's workers command a wider range of skills compared to workers in other industrial cities in China, but the share of professional and technical personnel lags far behind key global centers. To address this educational gap, measures have been taken to attract new, young talent into the city. Enrollment for local students in universities and colleges, as well as in vocational schools, increased substantially. Municipal bureaus also have relaxed restrictions on enterprises in hiring personnel with college or graduate education from other parts of China by allowing them to revise quotas for urban household registration. In particular, welcome is extended to students who are returning from overseas, either temporarily or permanently, to open new businesses. The first formal step took place in 2002, when Shanghai granted sixty professionals from elsewhere in China and abroad the official registration to live in the city and engage in business.[4]

In meeting labor force needs in Shanghai, temporary migration (without change of household registration) has become an alternative to permanent migration (with household registration change). About 3 million temporary migrants and transients, largely permitted by relaxed migration policies, are now working and living in metropolitan Shanghai. Without urban household registration, temporary migrants have virtually no access to free education, subsidized housing, and pensions. Most migrants are restricted to nonstate jobs undesirable to the local population, such as in construction, domestic services, factory and farm labor, and retail trade. Due to the heavy presence of migrants in small-scale trades and services, they also are contributing to the formation of an urban informal sector. Largely excluded from the mainstream urban housing system, migrants tend to live in overcrowded housing with few amenities and rudimentary conditions. While some migrants show signs of adjustment to urban life, others may have no choice but to become the first of an emerging group of poor in the city.

The housing situation of migrants is particularly troublesome as recent urban housing reforms have overlooked their needs. Housing, long a form of social welfare, has ceased to be provided either by the municipal government or state-owned work units. A new approach relies on market mechanisms, in which new commodity housing is developed and sold by real-estate companies. Sitting tenants of public housing can choose to buy out the property rights of the units and have the option to trade them on a secondary market. More recently, low-rent public housing has become available to benefit urbanites with the lowest income and smallest living space. Yet a local urban household registration continues to be an important qualification for accessing several types of urban housing, particularly those that are more affordable (W. Wu 2004b). Even when migrants are able to purchase commodity housing, they are not eligible for bank mortgage loans.

Given the persistence of China's migration trends over the past two decades, migrants will assert their influence on Shanghai's spatial structure. Increasing migrant concentration may aggravate existing residential differentiation, as most migrant housing is in much worse conditions than local housing. This compounds substantial changes in the spatial structure that resulted from increasing socioeconomic differentiation. In the city's central core, some residential areas with extreme dilapidation and high density have been left out of commercial redevelopment because of the high costs associated with resettlement (F. Wu 2002). As a result of such selective real-estate development, there are many instances of awkward juxtaposition of flashy, high-rise commercial buildings and dilapidated, pre-1949 dwellings. In the urban periphery, on the other hand, there is an increasing juxtaposition of rural towns, resettlement housing for central-city residents, and new commodity housing projects. Specifically, inner suburban areas immediately outside of the central city are accommodating a large number of local residents as well as migrants. The use of real-estate business as the key to the rebuilding of the increasingly depressed domestic market (seen in the late 1990s) also has led to overbuilding of commercial real estate and luxury residences.

Building the Hardware of Modernization

Shanghai's determination to renew itself can best be seen in its effort to overhaul the city's aging infrastructure. Unmet demand is shrinking as Shanghai makes progress in virtually every infrastructure service. Improvements are particularly rapid in road construction, park expansion, and wastewater treatment. Numerous large infrastructure projects have been completed, such as three bridges and two tunnels across the Huangpu River, an inner ring road, elevated north-south and east-west throughways, and two new subway lines. The first phase of a new light rail system is operational. Municipal authorities recently unveiled a twenty-year blueprint for the construction of eleven subway lines, seven light rail lines, and three suburban railways (Yusuf and Wu 2002). To remove itself from the list of heavily polluted cities by the World Health Organization, Shanghai has invested in a new combined wastewater collection system, solid waste and night soil management, and environment-friendly diesel engines for buses and, by moving the collection point further upstream, has increased the supply of potable water from the Huangpu River (World Bank 1994).

Investment in infrastructure services has increased steadily, with a greater emphasis on city streets, sewerage systems, and other municipal works. The infrastructure sector now receives the level of attention from the municipal government it deserves and accounts for about one-tenth of total capital investment. Much of the success in renewing infrastructure can be attributed to a comprehensive program of resource mobilization and expenditure management (Yusuf and Wu 1997). As a part of the reform to unify financial and administrative responsibilities for municipal bureaus, the Shanghai Urban Construction Investment and Development Company was formed in 1992 to mobilize, allocate, and manage funds for urban construction. To the extent feasible, municipal service departments have been given full responsibility for planning, investment, operations, and maintenance. Some infrastructure services also are in the process of privatization, such as the waste disposal business, as a company from neighboring Jiangsu Province has won the contract to collect garbage for the city (Yusuf and Wu 2002).

Substantial progress has been made in raising the supply of better-quality housing since the early 1990s through heavy investment (increasing from 4.3 billion yuan in 1990 to 46.7 billion in 2001; Shanghai Statistical Bureau 2002). The objective is to raise the per capita living space from 11 square meters currently to 23 square meters.[5] About 3.6 million square meters of endangered structures and shanty apartments are being replaced, mostly in the old central city. The accessibility of housing to the average family is on the rise as a result of reforms (W. Wu 1999a). By early 2001, officials estimate that about 60% of all families had bought their own homes, either from their employers or from private developers ("Windows of Opportunity," *Far Eastern Economic Review*, 3 May 2001).

Since the late 1980s, an accelerated process of urban development and reconstruction has been underway, thanks to investment from both the central government and foreign investors. The transformation of urban space embodies both preservation and creation. One of the first items on the agenda is to revive and restore the mile-long Bund, along which about 250 buildings have recently been designated as historic. The wide waterfront area also has been designated a Historical Protection Zone, and a special agency has been helping relocate government departments in the historic buildings (Balderstone, Qian, and Zhang 2002; Streshinsky 2000).

Some central, previously residential areas are increasingly under pressure for redevelopment, largely for commercial and office uses. At the heart of Shanghai's new development is a set of commercial cores scattered throughout the city. Each of these cores, including Nanjing Road, Huaihai Road, Hongqiao, Xujiahui, the Passenger Rail Station (Tianmu Road), and Sichuan Road, has become increasingly commercial in character, with shops and offices displacing residential and industrial space (Gaubatz 1999). In a particular effort to rejuvenate the city's commercial prominence, Shanghai is in search of the defining commercial street, an emblematic boulevard that boasts the best in fashion, food, and culture (*Far Eastern Economic Review*, 13 September 2001). After studying the celebrated French thoroughfare Champs Elysées, London's Oxford Street, and Tokyo's Ginza, municipal authorities are now redeveloping a core running three kilometers along a fully pedestrianized Nanjing Road and connecting to the Bund.

A new central business district has been constructed in Pudong, which can accommodate a variety of business activities and, most importantly, financial and business services that are the backbone of other major world cities. The building of Lujiazui—an area of 1.7 square kilometers on the east bank of the Huangpu River—has been guided by the long-term ambitions of the city and facilitated by an international consultative planning process in which experts from France, Britain, Italy, and Japan participated (Olds 1997). The sleek, ultramodern new skyline emerging from this district bears a remarkable resemblance to that of Hong Kong. A host of financial institutions, corporate headquarters, and commercial and cultural activities are being housed there, including the Shanghai Stock Exchange and more than forty foreign banks—the only area in the country where foreign banks are allowed by the central government to conduct regular business operations in local currency.

Becoming an international cultural center is also a future vision—a continuation of the city's legendary cosmopolitan reputation. In a manner typical of socialist cities, Shanghai's cultural renaissance begins with the building of big buildings and organization of big events (W. Wu 2004a). Compared to an annual amount of 1 billion yuan (about 121 million USD) during 1990–95, annual investment in cultural infrastructure has doubled between 1996 and 2000 (Yin 2000). Today the city boasts a new art gallery, an elegant museum for antiquities, a luminous 150 million USD grand theater, a new expansive convention center, and one of the largest libraries in the world (Yin 2000; "Art Rivalry," *Time International*, 10 April 2000). The new Shanghai museum is now considered the finest museum of Chinese art in the world. Every major school of Chinese art is shown with style and clarity (Yatsko 2001). The new grand theater has put Shanghai on the international cultural map, making it more likely that world-class troupes will perform here.

In another bold attempt to promote the heritage industry, overseas developers and architects have helped create a large-scale shopping, eating, and entertainment complex in the center of the former French concession, named Xintiandi (New Heaven and Earth). It features a multitude of upscale retail, entertainment, cultural, recreational, commercial, and residential facilities in restored Shikumen houses (a unique old form of residential architecture found only in Shanghai) as well as new buildings, catering to both the locals and tourists. Similar to the preservation of the Bund, this project really has less to do with restoring the buildings than it has to do with becoming a new tourist attraction. It is motivated more by the vision of a new Shanghai to rival the old (Abbas 2000). This project, together with the Lujiazui central business district, also shows the prominent role of the so-called Global Intelligence Corps (elite architectural firms) in the remaking of Shanghai (Olds 1997).

Although Pudong and the other development zones have been more successful than past efforts aimed at creating satellite towns, the central city area still houses a sizable proportion of Shanghai's industrial base. To solve problems associated with fragmented industrial land use, municipal authorities have recently relied on relocating factories in the central city to new urban districts. Between 1991 and 1998, about 12,000 work units as well as 400,000 households were moved from downtown to the city's outskirts (*Shanghai Daily*, 1 September 2000). This process of industrial relocation, albeit slow and with mixed results, has freed up a significant amount of space in the central city. But industrial fragmentation remains at the metropolitan level, aggravated by the chaotic location of rural and township enterprises across suburban areas. About 27% of the land in the metro area is currently for industrial use, a level much higher than the average for other large Chinese cities (about 15%) and comparable cities elsewhere in the world. This may be largely attributable to the fact that nearly 44% of Shanghai's industrial land use is scattered and not in concentrated forms such as industrial parks (Xiong and Zong 2000).

Challenges and Prospects

The modernization program Shanghai has embarked on is not without costs and challenges. Recent reforms have allowed housing to become a commodity and to be developed with both domestic and global capital, giving rise to a variety of residential spaces and increasing differentiation. Central-city residential neighborhoods face mounting pressure for commercial/office development and many residents are being relocated to outlying housing complexes. As a result, the downtown spatial fabric is changing rapidly. Even a fledgling artistic community covering several blocks of old warehouse space, now home for artists and gallery owners, is being torn down to make way for high-rise apartments (W. Wu 2004a). Clearly, more traditional neighborhoods may be displaced by the city's redevelopment plans and vision for a modern city.

The rapidly aging population presents Shanghai with a difficult challenge. Those over age sixty-five accounted for 12.5% of the total population in 1996 and 13.3% in 1998 and, if current trends continue, are expected to account for 26% in the year 2020 (*Shanghai Star*, 5 June 1998).

Shanghai now ranks uppermost among Chinese cities in aging population, about twenty years ahead of the national trend. It is perhaps the only city in China that is witnessing a phenomenon similar to that occurring in countries with substantially higher income levels. A growing number of retirees will demand better pensions, housing, and medical benefits.

The projected decline in the city's work force can be offset by an increasing volume of migrant workers, as is the case elsewhere in the world. Accommodating migrants and attracting those with the required skills are likely to be a long-term issue facing municipal authorities. This will require a change in the provision of adequate housing as well as services. To sustain, let alone improve, the quality of its work force while preventing social stratification and urban poverty, Shanghai will have to tackle the laws governing migration. Housing reform, for instance, can help improve migrants' quality of life and prevent slum formation. Specifically, migrants can be allowed to participate in the secondary housing market, where apartments are more affordable. Migrants also need greater access to jobs and educational facilities previously open to local residents only.

In contrast to the substantial investment in cultural venues and infrastructure services, less has been done in the way of supporting creative talent. Shanghai, as a result, is still a long distance away from reasserting its cultural prominence. Censorship further dampens the climate for artistic creativity and causes the loss of artistic talent (W. Wu 2004a). Public funding for cultural activities is decreasing at the same time as new, grandiose venues are being built. Diversity also may be eroding as early migrants have become assimilated into the local culture, and the new generation of urbanites is no longer tolerant of the millions of recent migrants.

All of these problems point to the importance of openness as Shanghai strives to become a regional or even global hub. Existing world cities draw upon a range of economic, geographical, and institutional strengths, but in addition they rely upon the energies released by openness (Landes 1998; Yusuf and Wu 2002). This openness will help lead to a spirit of inquiry, fruitfulness of research, entrepreneurial drive, the growth of trade, speedy financial innovation, and cultural resurgence. These outcomes will likely put Shanghai back on the map of the world's great cities.

Notes

1. Yeung and Sung (1996) focuses on the physical and socioeconomic transformation across a wide range of topics, drawing on the expertise of researchers based primarily in Hong Kong. There is a strong positive sentiment among the contributors, indicating that Shanghai seems to be on its way to an economic and cultural resurgence. Yusuf and Wu (1997) looks at the interplay between geography, size, and industrial structure that determines the industrial vigor of three cities—Shanghai, Guangzhou, and Tianjin. Specifically it explores the salient features of Shanghai's recent development and reforms to enhance its industrial strength, by employing concepts of agglomeration, neighborhood effects, factor supplies, and urban life cycle. More of a journalistic account, Yatsko (2001) explores key aspects of contemporary Shanghai—from finance, foreign businesses, and state enterprise reform to cultural and social change. It also exposes the down sides, such as the world of shady stock speculators and distraught laid-off workers. Gamble (2003) presents an evocative series of ethnographic perspectives of the city's shifting sociological landscape in the reform period. It builds upward from street-level perspectives and stresses ways in which the lives of Shanghai residents are implicated with wider historical, political, and economic phenomena.

2. See "Shanghai Sets Date for Deep Water Port Project," *Financial Times*, 1 March 2002.

3. See "Pudong Rises to the Task," *Far Eastern Economic Review*, 2 November 2000.

4. See "Economist Intelligence Unit," *Business China*, 24 June 2002.

5. See "A Room of One's to Own," *Business China*, Economist Intelligence Unit, 7 May 2001.

References

Abbas, A. 2000. Cosmopolitan Description: Shanghai and Hong Kong. *Public Culture* 12, no. 3: 769–86.

Balderstone, S., F. Qian, and B. Zhang. 2002. Shanghai Reincarnated. In W. S. Logan (ed.), *The Disappearing "Asian City": Protecting Asia's Urban Heritage in a Globalizing World,* 21–34. New York: Oxford University Press.

Chan, R. C. K. 2000. Shanghai: Development Strategy and Planning Implications. In M. K. Ng (ed.), *Proceedings of International Conference on Re-inventing Global Cities,* 168–83. Hong Kong: Center of Urban Planning and Environmental Management, University of Hong Kong.

Chen, S. 1998. Leadership Change in Shanghai: Toward the Dominance of Party Technocrats. *Asian Survey* 38, no. 7: 671–88.

Cheung, P. 1996. The Political Context of Shanghai's Economic Development. In Y. Yeung and Y. Sung (eds.), *Shanghai: Transformation and Modernization under China's Open Door Policy,* 49–92. Hong Kong: Chinese University Press.

Enright, M. J., Edith E. Scott, and D. Dodwell. 1997. *The Hong Kong Advantage.* Oxford: Oxford University Press.
Friedmann, J. 1998. World City Futures: The Role of Urban and Regional Policies in the Asia Pacific Region. In Y. M. Yeung (ed.), *Urban Development in Asia: Retrospect and Prospect,* 25–54. Hong Kong: Chinese University of Hong Kong Press.
Gamble, J. 2003. *Shanghai in Transition: Changing Perspectives and Social Contours of a Chinese Metropolis.* London: Routledge Curzon.
Gaubatz, P. 1999. China's Urban Transformation: Patterns and Processes of Morphological Change in Beijing, Shanghai and Guangzhou. *Urban Studies* 36, no. 9: 1495–1521.
Goodman, B. 1995. *Native Place, City and Nation: Regional Networks and Identities in Shanghai, 1853–1937.* Berkeley: University of California Press.
Howe, Ch. (ed.). 1981. *Shanghai: Revolution and Development in an Asian Metropolis.* Cambridge: Cambridge University Press.
Johnson, L. C. 1995. *Shanghai: From Market Town to Treaty Port, 1074–1858.* Stanford, Calif.: Stanford University Press.
Landes, D. S. 1998. *The Wealth and Poverty of Nations.* New York: W. W. Norton.
Lin, Z. 1994. Reform and Shanghai: Changing Central-Local Fiscal Relations. In Jia Hao and Lin Zhimin (eds.), *Changing Central-Local Relations in China: Reform and State Capacity,* 239–60. Boulder, Colo.: Westview Press.
Lu, H. 1999. *Beyond the Neon Lights: Everyday Shanghai in the Early Twentieth Century.* Berkeley: University of California Press.
Murphy, R. 1953. *Shanghai: Key to Modern China.* Cambridge, Mass.: Harvard University Press.
Olds, K. 1997. Globalizing Shanghai: The "Global Intelligence Corps" and the Building of Pudong. *Cities: The International Journal for Urban Policy and Planning* 14, no. 2 : 109–23.
Pott, F. L. H. 1928. *A Short History of Shanghai.* Shanghai: Kelly and Walsh.
Sassen, S. 1991. *The Global City: New York, London, Tokyo.* Princeton, N.J.: Princeton University Press.
Shanghai Academy of Social Sciences. 1998. *Shanghai Economic Yearbook.* Shanghai: Shanghai Academy of Social Sciences Press.
Shanghai Statistical Bureau. 1996–2002. *Statistical Yearbook of Shanghai.* Beijing: China Statistics Press.
Streshinsky, S. 2000. Shanghai Sees the Light. *Preservation* (September–October): 34–43.
Wei, B. P. 1987. *Shanghai: Crucible of Modern China.* Oxford: Oxford University Press.
World Bank. 1994. *China: Shanghai Environment Project.* Washington, D.C.: World Bank.
Wu, F. 2002. Real Estate Development and the Transformation of Urban Space in Chinese Transitional Economy: With Special Reference to Shanghai. In J. R.

Logan (ed.), *Globalization, Market Reform, and the New Chinese City*, 151–66. New York: Blackwell.

———. 2003. Globalization, Place Promotion and Urban Development in Shanghai. *Journal of Urban Affairs* 25, no. 1: 55–78.

Wu, W. 1999a. City Profile: Shanghai. *Cities: The International Journal of Urban Policy and Planning* 16, no. 3: 207–16.

———. 1999b. Reforming China's Institutional Environment for Urban Infrastructure Provision. *Urban Studies* 36, no. 13: 2263–82.

———. 2004a. Cultural Strategies in Shanghai: Regenerating Cosmopolitanism in an Era of Globalization. *Progress in Planning* 61, no. 3 (2004): 159–80.

———. 2004b. Sources of Migrant Housing Disadvantage in Urban China. *Environment and Planning A*.

Xiong, L., and L. Zong. 2000. Shanghaishi gongye yongdi de xiaolu yu buju [The Efficiency and Pattern of Shanghai's Industrial Land Use]. *Chengshi Guihua Huikan* [Urban Planning Forum] 126: 22–29.

Yatsko, Pamela. 2001. *New Shanghai*. New York: John Wiley and Sons.

Yeung, Y. 1996. Introduction. In Y. Yeung and Y. Sung (eds.), *Shanghai: Transformation and Modernization under China's Open Policy*, 1–23. Hong Kong: Chinese University Press.

Yeung, Y., and Y. Sung (eds.). 1996. *Shanghai: Transformation and Modernization under China's Open Policy*. Hong Kong: Chinese University Press.

Yin, J. (ed.). 2000. *A Report of Cultural Development in Shanghai 2000*. Shanghai: Shanghai Academy of Social Sciences Press.

Yusuf, S., and W. Wu. 1997. *The Dynamics of Urban Growth in Three Chinese Cities*. New York: Oxford University Press for the World Bank.

———. 2002. Pathways to a World City: Shanghai Rising in an Era of Globalization. *Urban Studies* 39, no. 7: 1213–40.

Zheng, Z. 1999. *One Hundred Years of Shanghai*, Shanghai: Xuelin Press.

Zhu, J. 2000. Urban Physical Development in Transition to Market: The Case of China as a Transitional Economy. *Urban Affairs Review* 36, no. 2: 178–96.

3 | Who Runs the City?
The "Makers" of Global City Regions

The topic of the book implies that there are certain "makers" who act to transform a city region into a globalized city region. Whereas the previous chapter drew a picture of the general transformation processes in the 1990s in Johannesburg, Mumbai/Bombay, São Paulo, and Shanghai, we will now look more specifically at the actors who determine the development of the city regions. The authors of the following contributions examine the role and influence of government institutions at the local, regional, and national levels, and also of ruling parties, national elites, foreign investors, donor agencies, civic associations, and informal traditional leaders.

The experiences from the four city regions reveal a complex interplay of actors at the global, national, and local level. It turns out that no single actor runs any of the four cities, but that different interests need to pull in the same direction in order to make a global city region. This observation leads to the question about the capacity of local government to actively shape the development of a city region. Whose contribution and whose participation is necessary for the successful integration of a region into the global economy? What is in the power of the state and where is the involvement of private actors needed? What forms of governance need to be installed to satisfy the demands of the various actors? The four studies reveal very different answers to those questions.

When talking about the makers of a global city region, the underlying structures of power inevitably also must be addressed. These determine whose interests are considered and whose are excluded in the transformation process. However, the sources of power in cities of the global periphery are still poorly understood, not least because of the increasing fragmentation and diffusion of decision-making processes. Urban governance today includes the involvement of public, semipublic, and private actors with varying degrees of power and authority. At the same time, the line between formal and informal spheres of power is increasingly blurred, making it even more difficult to disentangle the complex power structures at work.

In post-apartheid Johannesburg, the restructuring of the power base has been a central issue. As Susan Parnell points out in her contribution, old structures of modernist governance prevail alongside innovations aimed at increasing the participation of formerly marginalized citizens. In her study of the City Development Strategy, which was formulated in the recent past to bring Johannesburg on the way to becoming the world-class city in Africa, she arrives at interesting findings: whether actors in city politics gain or lose influence depends very much on whether they participate in the right forums of negotiation. In Johannesburg, the introduction of a wide array of participatory processes has obscured the real arenas of power and thus may have divided and dissipated the influence of marginalized groups. Furthermore, most formal and informal institutions are controlled by the African National Congress (ANC). Though the party includes heterogeneous groups, this means that a great part of decision making takes place behind closed doors.

An overview of the key actors in Mumbai turns out to be more diffuse. In fact, power structures of all kinds increasingly overlap in the city context. The power of city government is constricted through higher levels of government. While the central government holds extensive financial and political powers, the state of Maharashtra administers many urban affairs through its parastatal and functionally divided agencies. Party competition on and between different political levels further complicates the formulation of a coherent strategy for the city. The contribution by Jim Masselos focuses on the interplay of formal and informal actors, which seems to be of particular importance in Mumbai. The city appears as a colorful patchwork of socioculturally determined localities with specific informal and traditional leaders. Surprisingly, though, Masselos concludes that these seemingly anarchic and fragmented local patterns of power are linked to each other, which is conducive to the construction of a strong urban identity.

In the case of São Paulo, a clear party domination like that in Johannesburg is not evident. Formal partnerships between the public sector and private capital, social organizations, or nongovernmental organizations have been encouraged by the ruling party, the Partido dos Trabalhadores. However, the introduction of these new mechanisms in the decision-making process does not represent a real shift in the Brazilian socioeconomic development. In their scrutinizing analysis, Sueli Schiffer and Csaba Deák unmask the structures of an elite society, which still pulls the strings behind the new governance facade and thereby controls the development of the city and the entire country. According to Schiffer and Deák, the elite strives to uphold the socioeconomic status quo, which reinforces the structural inequalities within the society to its personal advantage. In São Paulo it uses the new legal instruments provided by the novel Statute of the City to sustain a fragmented structure that weakens the state. Although the new tools were designed to strengthen the influence of social organizations, they equally offer new opportunities for the established real-estate sector. The political reforms introduced by the Partido dos Trabalhadores do not yet reach far enough to curtail the power of the old elite, which dates back to colonial times.

Shanghai presents the most ambitious model of making a global city region. Fulong Wu speaks of a reterritorialization of the state, where the state reorganizes itself at the local level in the form of a gigantic corporation. This wording reflects the intricate entanglement of the public and the private spheres. State actors and institutions transform themselves according to the logic of the market, while business leaders gain influence in city development matters. Wu views this as a local response to globalization, which enables local politicians to promote the economic development of their territory. Making Shanghai a global city is an active strategy of the city administration as well as the Chinese central government, which is keen to retain control of the overall development. Nevertheless, the Shanghai case also suggests that there is a shift to the private sector, increasing the influence of investors, the real-estate sector, and generally those who command purchasing power, as well as a shift to smaller levels of governance: from central to municipal government and further down to city districts and "communities"—the Chinese variant of urban neighborhoods.

Summing up, Mumbai turns out to be the most difficult case of the four city regions for locating and identifying the relevant actors. By contrast, the local authorities in Shanghai obviously succeed in asserting their leadership in steering local development. In São Paulo the real power structures of a self-interested and status-quo-oriented elite are hidden behind official institutions. In Johannesburg the African National

Congress can be identified as the key power base, yet the existence of different forums for negotiation makes it difficult to identify the relevance of the competing platforms. The number of such forums of negotiation, the number of actors, and the convergence or divergence of their interests appear to be the most important determinants for the process of "making" a global city region. The case of Shanghai demonstrates that few relevant actors can effectively work in a common direction under the leadership of a still powerful Communist Party that integrates the different structures at the local level. However, this happens at the expense of a greater participation of ordinary citizens in the decision-making process.

Simon Raiser and Krister Volkmann

Politics of Transformation
Defining the City Strategy in Johannesburg
Susan Parnell

Who shapes the strategic direction of any city is a question of politics and power. The problem is that we have a poorly developed understanding of the sources of power within cities of the global periphery. The post-apartheid city of Johannesburg, also known as Joburg, is an interesting case in this regard. Since the introduction of democracy in 1994, the formal urban political landscape has been transformed from a racist and exclusionary local government to democratically elected municipal councils. The city itself now articulates aspirations to be a world-class center. Achieving this goal (alongside other policy imperatives such as redistribution and nonracialism) has necessitated fundamental shifts in the practice of city government. Old systems of modernist governance now exist alongside innovations aimed at making the state more participatory and flexible. Remarkably, the vast majority of South Africans voted in the two democratic local elections, though it is true that a small but growing proportion of the population live without direct or indirect engagement with the state (Simone 2002; Gotz and Simone 2002). In this middle-income country, government is the major agent of development. It therefore remains the focus of political exchange, even where there is oppositionary or protest politics. Yet, despite massive institutional and technical shifts within the organs of the state,[1] the focus of post-apartheid urban scholarship remains on the relationship between the state and weakened civil society (Chipkin 2003).[2] Much less is known of the internal structures and politics of power within the local government system. There is in South Africa, like elsewhere in the south, an uncomfortable silence around the role of the postmodern state itself in urban reconstruction and development.[3] Pieterse argues that this failure to confront the shortcomings of post-apartheid urban politics means a lost opportunity for articulating a radical democracy where opportunities for "antagonistic engagement are institutionally embedded" (2003, 2).

This essay begins to address the complex question of who runs the most powerful city in sub-Saharan Africa through an exploration of the diversification of the formal political systems in Joburg since the democratic transition. More than anywhere else on the African continent, Joburg has a carefully assembled popular and academic narrative of the disparate actors that transformed the city at the close of the twentieth century.[4] Also, thanks to several published accounts of institutional change in the city, we have a fairly clear picture of the new political sites, forums, and arenas that were created to facilitate the building of a nonracial and democratic city. What is still unclear is how effectively those in the anti-apartheid opposition, who became agents of transformation and are now the drivers of reconstruction, have managed to utilize these developmental platforms within the municipality to establish a self-sustaining power base in the newly created systems of city governance (Beall, Crankshaw, and Parnell 2002; Shubane and Shaw 1993). We are equally vague on how urban elites have managed to use, circumvent, or appropriate the newly established channels of influence within the democratic municipal governance regime. In other words, it is not clear whose interests dominate in the running of the city of Joburg.

Given the plethora of writing about South Africa's "miracle negotiation," it is odd that the analysis of the transitional democratic state is so weak. At the city scale, our lack of insight is even more obvious. Curiously little has been written about the African National Congress (ANC) as an urban ruling party[5] or of the role of business in governance, and there is no clear understanding of the post-apartheid elite and its role in metropolitan government.[6] There has been some, but not enough, academic reflection on the efficacy and impacts of the technical transformations of city governance regimes, especially the now ubiquitous participatory forums (Watson 2002). The most deafening silence relates to the formative role of expert urban consultants. As a result, our understanding of who holds power in South African cities is crude, dated, and generally ill-informed, even in a relatively well-researched city like Joburg.[7]

Ambiguity over who controls cities is not peculiar to Joburg. In general we know very little about the operation of power in cities where there has been a dramatic shift or upheaval. As much of the urban world is undergoing profound change, either because of war, HIV/AIDS, globalization, or regime change, or simply because of the dramatic impacts of urbanization and urban growth, this seems to be something of an academic lacuna. Whereas there is a sophisticated literature dedicated to uncovering the dynamics of global political regimes in stable Western democracies, the intellectual project is rarely extended to unraveling the proliferation of formal and informal structures within unstable and/or undercapacitated city and national governments. Yet it is in these often very large and complex cities at the global economic periphery that new systems of urban governance are being forged out of the dynamic process of city development.

In this essay I grapple with the issue of sites of political representation and engagement within the city and use it as a device for revealing the power of the diverse actors in urban management. I take Johannesburg's City Development Strategy (CDS) process as a reference point for reflecting on the operation of urban power under conditions of massive transformation. The Johannesburg CDS is a multi-stakeholder, medium-term planning framework that lays out Johannesburg's vision of becoming a global city in Africa. Its elements are the texts that provide the basis for much of the recent literature on Johannesburg, which discusses the viability or desirability of making or maintaining the vision of global city status. I, however, am using the CDS in a different way. First, I am concerned with the elements of the strategic planning process and not its outcome. Second, I am interested in how the different actors or interests in the processes come to position themselves within the vision of an African world-class city, which the Joburg CDS espouses (Bernstein and McCarthy 2002). In this regard the process is a useful proxy for city governance more generally.

What makes the study of power in transitional Joburg interesting to a wider audience is the following. Not only does the city lie at the heart of the world's poorest region, but during the past two decades South Africa has undergone massive social and political transformation. This shift in the systems of city governance was informed, at least in part, by global discourses. As a city in transition Joburg is therefore subject to influences and pressures from global, national, and local interests. Set against diverse writings about the sources of power in the city, the key questions I raise in this essay are who shapes the strategic management of Joburg as a (global) city and through what forums or sites is this power assumed and articulated?

Institutional Opportunities for Engaging in City Governance in Joburg

In a city like Johannesburg, the processes for negotiating power are being contested and changed. Not only are there the competing platforms of opposition politics, electoral democracy, civic participatory forums, lobbying, and advocacy, but the formal structures of the state are in transition too. On the one hand the city is an autonomous sphere of government and an economic unit that interacts directly with global markets. On the other hand, what happens in Johannesburg is not simply a product of municipal policy, but also a reflection of national and provincial government action, private-sector interests, and civil society interests. In the context of rapid political, economic, and demographic transition the problem of each of the constituencies finding the right place to speak and be heard is compounded by changes in the institutional structures of government. In the case of Joburg, as in many other cities, new and additional forums have been incorporated into or alongside traditional municipal practice. Paradoxically, the Joburg case suggests that the proliferation of processes and structures aimed at enhancing participatory engagement may have overloaded the system that is already weak due to stresses associated with democratic transition. As a result, it is unclear where citizens should make their voices heard since it is unclear which are the key decision-making forums. In other words, it is not obvious where the city is run from, or who runs the city.

One thing, however, is clear: power in Joburg has shifted. In practice apartheid may not yet be dead, but the primary goals of post-apartheid urban reconstruction are evident—to unite the city under one tax base, to integrate the city spatially, and to overcome the legacy of unequal development. Achieving the reconstruction goal began with the introduction of a universal franchise and a change in the ruling party. It also involved a fundamental reinvention of the structures and systems of local government.[8] The introduction of a model of "developmental local government" sought consciously to break with previous models of electoral city government by introducing the principles of participation and parallel representation of civil society in negotiating forums that overlapped with the traditional roles of councillors (Parnell and Pieterse 2001). Our interest is in what has actually changed in how (and from where) Joburg is run, and what this means for the locus of power in the city today.[9]

Evidence that things have changed can be seen in the postdemocracy fervor of spending to reduce poverty. Yet the outcomes of participatory processes that called for redress and redistribution soon hit the hard reality of fiscal constraints in Joburg.[10] Such was the impact of the 1997 fiscal crisis in Johannesburg that the fundamental assumptions of the city were reassessed, largely through a series of three processes that are now referred to collectively as the City Development Strategy. In October 1997 the central government, anticipating that Johannesburg was heading for a large budget deficit, imposed a new system of externally regulated financial administration on the city. Under the watchful eye of the national Department of Finance and under the direct stewardship of the Provincial Departments of Local Government and Housing, the council had a financial "super executive" running its financial affairs. Through a Committee of Ten (subsequently fifteen and renamed the Transformation Lekgotla),[11] the financial powers of the metropolitan and local councils were abrogated and a financial restructuring plan was put in place. During this period the first element of the CDS, iGoli 2002 (GJMC 1999) was formulated as the mechanism for getting the city out of its financial crisis. Phase 2 of the CDS, or iGoli 2010, involved a medium-term planning process that was largely dependent on outside (political and official) contributions from consultants or stakeholders (GJMC 2001). The failure of the 2010 process to define a new strategy and the coming to power of a new mayor heralded the final phase of the CDS, know as Vision 2030. This final phase emerged from a document authored within the city, which was then placed out for public comment. These three phases underpinned the CDS process that now provides a blue print for Joburg's future (Table 3.1.1).

Competing Sites of Negotiation within the CDS Process

There are clear changes in political direction evident as a result of the CDS process, but our concern in this essay is with process, not its outcome, and so I want to explore the different forums of governance that emerged within the phases of the CDS. Although the post-1994 period is characterized by greater democracy, accountability, and participation, the ability and obligations of the council in defining a direction for the city were highly circumscribed by external realities. Within a fluid institutional environment, the post-apartheid identity of Joburg as a global city was negotiated, largely through the CDS process. However, it would be an error to overstate the autonomy of the local authority in shaping the city's future. Johannesburg's CDS is constrained not only by global realities, but also by its intergovernmental position, its finances, and the highly un-

Phases of the City Development Strategy Process in Johannesburg

	Phase 1 of the CDS: iGoli 2002 (October 1997–2000)	Phase 2 of the CDS: iGoli 2010 (research and forum process 2000)	Phase 3 of the CDS: 2030 Vision (launched February 2002)
Key documents	iGoli 2002 + Metropolitan Spatial Development Framework + the annual Integrated Development Plan (known in Johannesburg as The City Development Plan)	iGoli 2010 + The Monitor Reports + World Bank SMME and firm surveys + Inner City Economic Development Strategy funded by the UMP[a]	Joburg 2030—The City Development Strategy
Context	Fiscal crisis and interim local government structure	Consolidation of metropolitan structure in final phase of interim local government	Post-apartheid metropolitan government in place
Objectives	• Three-year revenue-led budget, credit control • Institutional rationalization: creation of metropolitan structure • Privatization and other restructuring	• Data gathering • Linked focus on economic growth, competitiveness, and basic needs	• An African world-class city • Economic growth: increased GDP through skills development and crime reduction

Institutional strategy drivers	Provincial and national government, lenders who make up the iGoli 2002 Emergency Committee, and the associated international technical advice team under guidance of the World Bank	Transitional Metropolitan Council, stakeholders, and external consultants	City Managers Office, endorsed by Mayoral Committee
Participatory process	• Elected councillors • Represented not elected appointments on Emergency Committee • Council negotiations with municipal unions • Appointment of 2010 Steering Committee	• Elected councillors • Extensive process of consultation through a stakeholders forum, focus groups, and city summit	• Elected councillors • To be announced, proposed to include forums of all stakeholders and a people's assembly

Source: Monitor Group 2001; City of Johannesburg Council 2001; City of Johannesburg 2001.
Note: SMME = Small, medium, and micro enterprises; UMP = Urban Management Programme.
[a]Further surveys conducted by the World Bank on services and a study on social exclusion funded by British Department for International Development were done after the Monitor Reports were not included in the CDS process.

equal social, political, and economic legacy of apartheid. Negotiations took place at four key sites. They include decision-making bodies of the city in the national system of governance, existing and purpose-built public-participation forums, the advice of external experts, and—the most hidden of forums—the structures of the ruling party. We turn to examine each of these (sometimes contradictory) sites of power in turn and the extent to which they proved to be influential in shaping city strategy. We begin by looking at the role of national government.

City Strategy in the National System of Governance

It would be easy to see the Joburg CDS as something of a watershed in planning practice, ushering in a new generation of engaged and reflective action that draws together in a more integrative fashion a range of interested and affected parties at the local city scale. Yet the reality is more nuanced. As the city implements its new developmental mandate, it draws increasingly on traditional tools and processes of city management, important parts of which are set nationally.[12] This suggests that the CDS marks a continuity in modernist state-centered planning (with uniform regulations and even budgets), rather than a break from it. This is especially true in service delivery (transport being a key example), but also in areas of environmental regulation such as fire protection or water standards, where there are nationally defined standards and regulations. However, modern centralism is not necessarily antithetical to development, as the case of the South African constitutional influence on urban policy shows.

Municipal councils may not contravene constitutional obligations. Regardless of what a local authority wishes, an unusually progressive South African constitution safeguards the interests of the poor and the excluded on issues of basic needs, gender and race discrimination, and democratic and accountable government.[13] The Constitution has enshrined the view of a particular generation of voters and bequeathed a rights-based approach to city development, within which vested interests must operate. As a result, there is no longer any legal space for the more extreme conservative views within formal local government.[14] The constitutional obligations effectively provide the philosophical point of departure for city-scale welfare support in the Joburg CDS (which includes, among other things, free water and electricity, as well as property-rate rebates). Other than the recognition of the right to basic services and the endorsement of the principle of nondiscriminatory distribution of benefits, the

Joburg CDS does not fundamentally challenge the modern conception of welfare support and leaves intact the expectation of universal support for basic service consumption.[15] Such assumptions presuppose a strong and direct role for the state in line with the more progressive tradition of grand modernism (Friedman 2001).[16] But the dark side of modernist planning is evident too, with the Joburg CDS slipping into the apartheid-style assumption that poor people for which the city could not provide could, somehow, be excluded from urban citizenship of Joburg.[17]

Still more evidence of the power of national government in setting the terms of Joburg's city strategy can be seen in the powers, functions, and resources of the city council. Municipal systems in apartheid South Africa, including the overall institutional design of departments, the broad pattern of committee structures, and the regulatory and zoning framework, owed much to the British model of modern town planning. Theoretically, this model changed in 1994 with the establishment of integrated developmental local government. Following the fiscal crisis of 1997, however, the Transformation Lekgotla (which controlled all council activities including spending and staffing) was appointed. The Lekgotla included some city officials and politicians, but was dominated by local and national government appointments as well as external advisers (largely supplied by the World Bank). Very significant technical decisions about the future of the city were agreed to by the Lekgotla as part of the iGoli 2002 process (including the principle of corporatization, key financial performance indicators, and political restructuring to create a single metropolitan system). As the city council endorsed the process and the outcomes of iGoli 2002, it is difficult to argue that national government overturned council agreements and exerted undue or unwanted power over the local municipality. However, behind the scenes it is quite clear that the Joburg leadership was strong-armed into accepting the salvage package offered by National Treasury once the city got into financial trouble. In particular, the fact that the Joburg council, having articulated an extensive spending plan favoring the poor after 1994, was, by 1999, cutting spending and endorsing the neoliberal national economic policy of GEAR (Growth, Employment and Redistribution), raises the question of the autonomy of the local state in South Africa.

The Joburg CDS is a useful barometer of the intergovernmental influence exerted on the city. Theoretically, local government in South Africa is an autonomous sphere of government. As we have already noted though, this autonomy is relative and can be challenged. Local autonomy only operates while a council is solvent. As the Johannesburg case demonstrated, even potential bankruptcy allows provincial and national intervention in the running of the municipality. There are further areas that point to the myth of the devolved power of the local state. The extensive responsibilities of the provinces in the big budget line areas of transport, health, welfare, and education mean that the capacity of the Joburg local authority to address poverty depends in large measure on effective intergovernmental engagement and capacity to spend within the city jurisdiction. Local government in South Africa has relatively limited powers and functions for investment (basic services being key), severely circumscribing the scope of the CDS. Housing, welfare, justice, policing, education, and most aspects of health and transport fall outside its responsibilities, although provisions were made recently for the creation of a metropolitan police force and for municipalities to be accredited as suppliers of housing. New areas of local government responsibility, however, include social and economic development and environment. The importance of crime and the HIV/AIDS pandemic as barriers to economic growth and poverty reduction in the urban context has seen the city extend its jurisdiction in these areas, despite the fact that they must be funded from locally generated revenue.

The Joburg CDS reveals that there is an ongoing tension between the central and local state, rather than the establishment of an independent devolved local state that is more attuned and accountable to global dynamics. The idea that it would be possible to exert power at the city scale simply by controlling local government is absurd—even for South Africa's most politically and economically significant city. Despite attempts at devolution, South Africa remains a highly centralized state. Even the powerful Joburg council is dependent on national government support. Against the picture of a strong nation-state, we now turn to explore the impact of the public forums set up to enhance civic engagement with the CDS and, more importantly, to entrench the principle of participatory governance envisaged under the developmental local government vision.

Public Participation in the Joburg CDS

Prior to 1994 most medium-term planning was conducted through the city planner's office in the city council and revolved around the structure plan. This tradition was ruptured with the post-apartheid introduction of the notion of Integrated Development Plans (IDPs). Although IDPs are linked to the medium-term budget cycle of three years, they remain effectively short-term operational plans. Yet the way that the planning is conducted draws on both participatory discourses and ideas of new urban management. As such, it was a simple shift to the idea of medium-term strategic plan or CDS. In the case of Joburg the need for a CDS emerged organically. The internal organizational structure that would handle the CDS and the associated public participation grew out of crisis management. A Corporate Planning Unit was created to manage the fallout of the highly politicized iGoli 2002 process.

iGoli 2002 was initially internally focused and had no public participation because labor was the key stakeholder and the primary dispute was between the city and the unions of its own employees. Others in civil society, including the Anti-Privatization Forum, objected to this narrow definition of interests. They argued that the city was excluding communities by reducing the dispute to a labor issue when the form of service delivery had wider implications for the poor.[18] Following the tense negotiations between the municipal unions and the city, it was decided to create a more open consultative forum to be known as the 2010 Steering Committee (phase 2 of the CDS; see the preceding table).

A proposal for the 2010 Steering Committee was already under consideration when, in August 2001, a city summit was held to get an agreement from all stakeholders in the city for the 2002 package. The national Congress of South African Trade Unions (COSATU) and the city could not reach agreement, and COSATU agreed to participate in the 2010 Steering Committee only if the terms of reference of that committee were extended. The city was instructed by the political leadership of the ANC to "open it up" and get a very wide mandate on the new city direction. Among the stakeholders sought out under the leadership of Joburg Chief Executive Officer Khetso Gordhan (who was brought in to manage the Johannesburg crisis) was business.[19]

The Transformation Lekgotla, the committee appointed to rescue the city from its financial crisis, nominated the political representatives to the 2010 Steering Committee. They included a spectrum of party views. In defining the stakeholders, the committee was influenced by the idea of social partners that had been used successfully elsewhere in South Africa.[20] Labor, business, government, and residents were defined as the four main social partners for the city strategy.

The constitution of the 2010 Steering Committee defined its purpose as:

- Serve as a representative working committee of the consultative stakeholders forum.
- Guide the implementation of the declaration of the iGoli Summit.
- Harness the collective experiences of stakeholders, and ensure that this experience informs and influences council's strategy and approach in a consistent manner.
- Facilitate the formulation of a long-term transformation plan that will determine future development and investment opportunities in Greater Johannesburg.[21]

In addition, the Terms of Reference specified that "The Steering Committee shall ensure buy-in from the residents and communities of Greater Johannesburg to the current process of transformation and be the ambassadors of such city programs."[22] Twelve meetings were held between 4 February 2000 and 3 November 2000. Membership of the Partnership Steering Committee consisted of the following representatives, nominated by the Transformation Lekgotla: six from the council; four from business; four from labor; four from civic and residents' associations; one from provincial government; and one from national government.

Leaving aside government, whose dominant role in the city we have already noted, let us look at the role of the other parties in the 2010 process. The story of the participation of the Joburg residents in 2010 is a fairly familiar account of elite capture, though it should be noted that although the city went to great lengths to avoid the marginalization of the poor, this was only partly successful. For the sake of brevity, I focus only on the roles of labor and business.[23]

Labor

Much has been written about the hotly contested relationship between the city and organized labor, especially over the iGoli 2002 proposals. The tension generated by iGoli 2002 over privatization spilled over into the rest of the CDS negotiations. For the purpose of the 2010 consultation labor was not defined as the local unions—the South African Municipal Workers' Union (SAMWU) and the Independent Municipal and Allied Trade Union (IMATU)—but as the national federation COSATU (although in practice the political power of SAMWU and IMATU in Johannesburg meant that all three were asked to participate in the 2010 Steering Committee). Since the unions had a defined constituency, they were the most representative group. After the first meeting, however, COSATU pulled out—not because of the substantive discussion under the 2010 process, but because the ongoing negotiations on privatization generated by 2002 restructuring were going badly. They therefore withdrew from all consultations.

Business

Fewer overt problems were encountered with getting business to sit at the 2010 negotiating table. Rashid Seedat, the director of the Corporate Planning Unit, recalls: "Business was easy because it was more organized than anyone else, although the informal sector was a problem to define. In practice white business interests dominated through the Johannesburg Metropolitan Chamber of Commerce and Industry (JMCCI)."

Formal, white-controlled business was reasonably involved in the affairs of the former Johannesburg and its suburbs (such as Randburg and Sandton) in the period before the 1980s.[24] However, for fifteen or more years from roughly 1980 onward, this part of the business sector tended to feel removed from the thinking of local government.[25] To that extent it joined other parts of the business sector during the period—restricted black business interests, especially in Soweto, that were suffering from long-standing race restrictions, such as the Group Areas Act, limited to Indian business, and from tightly controlled by-laws that constrained the burgeoning informal business environment. During the negotiation phase best-captured in the affairs of the Central Witwatersrand Metropolitan Chamber from 1991 to 1994 (Mabin 1999), it could scarcely be said that any of these business voices were heard in the emerging metropolitan context. Furthermore, an at-best strained relationship existed between business and city government after the elections of 1995.[26]

In quite obvious ways the CDS sought to end the estrangement of business from city politics and to extend the involvement of business in the city. The fiscal crisis and arrival of Ketso Gordhan as city manager seems to have had a signal influence on improving the business-local government relationship in the city, at least as far as the white-controlled part of the sector was concerned.[27] However, black, Indian, and informal business seems not to have developed an effective interaction in quite the same way.[28] The reasons for the difference can be found in a number of factors—weak organization, division, lack of capacity within organizations to interact effectively with the city, and, in some cases, lack of understanding of possible benefits of closer relations or of will to develop an interaction.[29]

In this environment, the course of business participation in the CDS processes is not surprising. The names of participants on the 2010 Steering Committee were proposed by the city, responding in part to voices of experience such as Cas Coovadia, the onetime anti-apartheid inner-city political activist and here representative of black business, and the JMCCI. However, and despite original vigorous participation by some individuals, it fell ultimately to the JMCCI to make the most significant inputs in the process—due to the combination of will, capacity, and real organizational practice in that quarter. Almost certainly only the JMCCI reported back effectively to its executive (if not its membership) on a regular basis, and it had an effective role in partially influencing the course of discussion in the 2010 Steering Committee.[30] By contrast, black business as represented by the National African Federated Chamber of Commerce and Industry (NAFCOC) and the Foundation for African Business and Consumer Services (FABCOS) either failed to take up the invitation or could not really contribute to the process, for reasons opposite to those affecting the JMCCI. International business representatives attended on some occasions, but played only a small role. Informal business was not directly represented at all, and indeed representatives such as the FABCOS delegates were inclined to argue for regulation and control over that sector, rather than its full incorporation into discussion.[31] Whereas a large organization like the JMCCI (3,000 members) may have the practice and capacity of reporting back, a culture of mandating representatives does not exist, since, once appointed, business leadership is expected to get on with the job.[32] Thus, rather different questions need to be asked about the nature and depth of participation in this case than in those of unions or civic organizations.

Business representatives do not argue that they determined the course of the CDS process, yet the greater openness to business that developed during the 1998–2000 period on the part of the city meant that there seems to have been a much enhanced inclination to hear business views and to incorporate business priorities into strategic thinking. The results are evident at least in some measure in the direction taken in the 2030 process, such as skills development and security. However, two caveats should be mentioned. First, business tends to consider a notoriously short time horizon, being far more interested in very short-term public issues, such as broken traffic lights, than in more academic questions of long-term vision. This makes business participation in processes like 2010 somewhat problematic and probably explains why business representatives tend to argue in favor of sector-specific contacts between themselves and city government, rather than broad fora.[33] Second, although the results of the CDS processes thus far in Johannesburg are superficially business-friendly, they are perhaps more driven by what public-sector officials in Johannesburg think business wants and needs than by what business (itself a poorly defined constituency) has actually been able to articulate itself.

From the 2010 Participatory Forum to Consultation in 2030

The shifting attitude of the council on the best ways to engage civil society in the CDS is of particular interest. With iGoli 2002 the city responded to the public who had been informed of the content of the CDS via the media, union and party structures, or civil society networks. This gave way in 2010 to a situation where the council tried to lead or facilitate the contributions of civil society through an organized forum of representatives who would make their views known to the council and then feed the agreements back to their constituencies. In practice this strategy broke down because of the boycott of key stakeholders. It was also subject to elite capture. In 2030 the city launched a coordinated strategy whereby the different constituencies were directly targeted to inform them of the proposed CDS strategy and solicit responses. There has been a substantial shift in thinking about participation within the city because of the 2030 process. Parks Tau, an ANC councillor puts it this way:

> The Mayoral Committee is committed to finding workable ways of enabling real participation. It seems part of the answer lies in soliciting participation on issues most relevant to local communities. For example, calling a meeting on strategic issues in the IT sector in Orange Farm [a peripheral squatter camp] seems unlikely to solicit meaningful participation. This becomes about "ticking boxes," and saying we consulted widely on IT, and had a meeting in Orange Farm attended by (x) number of people—rather than focusing on the quality of participation.

He argued instead for finding ways of avoiding the "ticking boxes" approach, building confidence in participatory processes, and ensuring that people are really heard. The shift in emphasis is seen in the move away from the broad stakeholder inputs that were sought on 2010 to the responses that were solicited to prepare 2030. For the council, this process remained participative. Kenny Fihla's comment again:

> We faced the question of when to allow participation. I didn't feel we should consult while formulating a first draft. Its better to have something to put on the table which stakeholders can respond to. We want to consult around real options—that makes the consultation more meaningful. We'll prepare different drafts of the same document—and that way will be able to get inputs from a range of stakeholders without intimidating anyone or patronising anyone.

Overall the participatory process appears to have frustrated as much as it has empowered those involved. One of the key participants in the 2010 Steering Committee, Lorraine Lotta, refused to be interviewed, indicating that she had already wasted too much time on the fruitless process. Her views, especially her environmental concerns, were heard and directly incorporated into the drafting of 2030.[34] Ironically, the representatives of poorer communities who had less impact offered less condemnatory evaluations of the 2010 Steering Committee. They too expressed frustration at the process.[35] The technical support team, the Corporate Planning Unit, and participants agree that, overall, the CDS participation in the form of 2010 was not a great success in creating a power base for the public.[36]

The core problem for the city seeking wide civil society involvement in the CDS lies in the very wide, metropolitan scale of the project. It is difficult to include all stakeholders in one forum because it involves too many people. Even in the limited 2010 Steering Committee, not all members found it easy to speak. It was difficult to identify who the real representatives were, especially in as large a city as Johannesburg. Interests of business, residents, and labor were not homogeneous and, at times, were even internally conflictual. It was especially difficult to identify representatives of unorganized communities, for instance, in the case of Johannesburg, gender interests, as well as the interests of colored and Indian residents and informal business. Crucially, it proved difficult to ensure that representatives formed liaisons with constituencies, and the South African National Civic Organization (SANCO) experience in this regard is germane.

The 2010 participatory process highlights the well-established difficulties of preventing elite capture—even within a sector such as labor or business. In Johannesburg, SAMWU headquarters disagreed with the Johannesburg branch on iGoli. Formal business dominated the agenda at the expense of the informal sector. It was also difficult to accommodate civil society structures that do not organize at the city scale, as in the case of nongovernmental organizations such as Planact or the Urban Sector Network.[37] It was even harder to get organized communities that did not perceive it as their concern to participate in a CDS—as in the case of churches in Johannesburg. Similarly, organizations whose base involves issues that lie beyond municipal competencies, such HIV/AIDS, were difficult to accommodate in the process. Finally, it was difficult not to blur the line between participation, consultation, and feedback.

Overall then, the purpose-designed public participation forum set up as part of the Joburg CDS did not provide an especially effective direct platform for any one of the constituencies. In an evaluation of the Joburg CDS, it was found that, despite its developmental objectives and design, it was difficult for the poor to make an impact in the purpose-designed participatory structure. However, the poor were able to influence the CDS with some success not through the participatory forum, but through more conventional mechanisms. First, democratic elections gave the representatives of the poor the majority of seats in the council through wards. Backbench councillors, especially in the 2030 process, made significant changes to the CDS proposals. Second, collective action and organization in civil society—as in the case of the unions whose boycott of the CDS was very successful—gave voice to the poor. Third, targeted focus groups also helped the poor. The fourth method involved statistically representative social research among poor communities. The fifth mechanism was the appointment of technical support structures whose instruction it was to ensure representation of all residents, especially the traditionally disenfranchised. Finally, the poor were empowered through the party political structures, a process we return to later. That said, although many of the avenues used by the poor to lobby on the CDS were long-established formal structures or conventional direct-action oppositional political tactics, the participatory forums of the CDS undoubtedly increased public knowledge of local government issues and served as a lightning rod for debate. But, the voices of Joburg residents had to compete not only among themselves and with business, but also with the outside experts advising on the CDS.

External Experts

Through the Constitution, national government was provided with a tight framework within which the overall direction of the Joburg CDS was forged. In the 1990s the problems facing South African cities were immense, and the technical details of urban management were poorly understood—leaving plenty of scope for donors, consultants, and other external players to influence the direction and detail of post-apartheid governance. This was especially true after the 1997 fiscal crisis, when the goal of getting the city to a position where it could achieve "growth with sustainability" was defined. At least initially (in iGoli 2002) the primary task of the CDS was to define what was needed to be done, technically, institutionally, and politically, to achieve this goal.[38]

Internationally much has been written about the influence of external neoliberal agencies such as the International Monetary Fund and World Bank, which, through their technical support, are able to dictate the policy direction of city governments, especially in the developing world (Munslow and Fitzgerald 1995; Bond 2000a; 2000b). In the absence of socially democratic alternatives that provide workable solutions to the challenges of large cities in middle-income countries, the off-the-shelf solutions to problems of pricing, billing, service delivery standards, and contract management have certainly fallen disproportionately to international consultants and donors, in Joburg as elsewhere. But just how much power did external experts have in the Joburg CDS?

The stereotypical view of the all-powerful role of lending institutions, donors, and consultants in city politics is not borne out by all the evidence in the Joburg CDS. It is true that the World Bank exerted a tremendously powerful influence in iGoli 2002 though personal relationships[39] and the technical advice it offered the Transformation Lekgotla (Savage et al. 2003). Yet not all donors, and indeed not the World Bank, had the ear of Joburg in the same way. Donors were known to complain that Joburg was reluctant to take any advice at all (Parnell 2004). A case in point is the background work done on poverty. Even before the CDS process began, the World Bank initiated substantial and expensive research in Johannesburg on service delivery and manufacturing. While the manufacturing work was fed into the 2010 process, it was not used as extensively as it might have been "because of data compatibility problems."[40] Furthermore, a large study on social exclusion was funded by British Department for International Development and was submitted to the Corporate Planning

Unit in July 2001 as part of the poverty mapping exercise for 2010.[41] Neither the Boston-based Monitor Group, which was the lead consultant on 2010 (Monitor Group 2001), nor Sandy Lowitt, the author of 2030, were even aware of the study.[42]

The most expensive research commissioned for the CDS was done by the Monitor Group, which ran the million-dollar research process around 2010. The impact of the various studies must be described as limited at best. While several of our respondents questioned the tendering process associated with the commissioning of the iGoli 2010 research and also the cost-to-quality ratio of the material produced by the subconsultants and main consultants, none doubted that the collection of primary data to inform a CDS might be worthwhile. The scope of iGoli 2010 was significantly wider than either iGoli 2002 or the 2030 process. All major aspects of council business were reported on. It is the very breadth of iGoli 2010 that appears to have led to its inauspicious reception.[43] Crudely, the process of reporting on 2010, which was rushed through in time for the December 2000 elections, did not provide a pithy enough summary or clear enough vision for rapid consumption by councillors.

There is a more general question about power implicit in the Monitor experience. Because of the election, the consultants were asked by the 2010 Steering Committee to fast-track an overall strategic direction for the city. This was a task they felt uncomfortable with, as it was beyond the terms of reference. Moreover, defining a city strategy short-circuited a process "that was not designed to deliver for an election."[44] What they did instead was to offer a "balanced" set of recommendations that built around the notion of "survive the bad, promote the good." The passive reception of iGoli 2010 was fueled by political turmoil within the ruling party. This climate of leadership uncertainty led to the setting aside (though not overturning) of the 2010 vision in favor of the formulation of a new process known as 2030. Significantly, signaling a greater ownership of the CDS direction, the 2030 documents were produced by a Special Contract appointment in the Mayor's Office, and not by an external consultant.

Formally, 2030 can be found in three documents—a foundation document, a vision statement, and a strategy report. Leading officials and politicians were open to the idea that the views expressed in 2030 might change in the light of public consultations.[45] In practice the most significant amendments to the draft document prepared on behalf of the Economic Development Directorate were included following the Mayoral

Selected Content Items in Joburg 2030 Changed by the Mayoral Committee

Item to Be Addressed	What Change Was Incorporated
HIV/AIDS	A paragraph was added showing how the Mayoral Thrusts complement the ten focus areas of 2030, and hence HIV/AIDS is a priority for the city.
Environmental sustainability	Paragraphs were included for the planning section and the utilities section, which argue that economic growth must be mananged so as to ensure sustainability in terms of the environment. The open space argument was expanded, as was the issue of alternative energy sources, water usage, and waste. A pollution argument was added to the public transport issue. On the utilities side it was added that the utilities need to coordinate sustainable provision with the relevant council functions as part of their strategic agenda.
Densification	The argument was added that densification must be appropriate and that the costs of upgrading infrastructure to support these new densities must be taken into account. The argument that different utilities have different operating parameters in terms of spatial location and usage was also added.
Township development	Three key catalytic projects were expanded and redefined specifically to focus on getting economic activity into the townships. The projects state that the council will act as the flagship on these, but there are additions to how other business will be crowded in.
SMME development	Two additional projects in this area were added: the skills partnership project with tertiary education facilities and a range of mentoring/incubator projects in the ICT field.
Issue of balance: social development	A section was added to cover what was mentioned in the workshop regarding no immediate budget reallocations necessitated by the 2030 strategy as well as issues relating to required changes in efficiency and focus rather than financial reallocations. A new section is being added to the paradigm to suggest a more balanced approach while not deviating from the logic of the paradigm.

Note: ICT = Information and Communications Technology; SMME = Small, medium, and micro enterprises.

Committee Lekgotla in December 2001. The Mayoral Committee amendments raised the profile of the otherwise subdued emphasis on poverty reduction, bringing the 2030 document more in line with the 2010 vision. More generally, the experience of 2030 suggests that, at the end of the day, it is crucial to understand the internal dynamics of party politics, especially when, as in the case of Johannesburg, the same party is in power at national, provincial, and local levels.

Party Politics

As the economic heartland of South Africa and the geographical center of internal political mobilization against apartheid, Johannesburg holds symbolic power. The future of the city is crucial to the international and national perception of the ANC's stewardship and the prospects of an African renaissance. The city's place as the hub of one of the world's poorest regions makes the future of Johannesburg a matter of great political importance—not least in the discussions around the continental policy agenda of the New Economic Partnership for African Development (NEPAD). The symbolic status of the city raises the political stakes of the Johannesburg CDS. It is therefore strange that, despite the extensive recent work on the city, nobody has specifically addressed the role of the ANC in city government. This section makes no pretensions to providing an analysis of this kind but does seek to highlight why party politics in general and ruling party politics in particular are critical sites of power in the city.[46]

It has been alleged that, despite the ANC's majority, the opposition Democratic Alliance continues to play a disproportionately important role through the effective use of council committee structures (Beall, Crankshaw, and Parnell 2002). To some extent the CDS experience reinforces this picture. In the absence of a formal information program, dissemination of the details of 2002 and 2010 were communicated largely through formal party political structures. This was certainly the case for the ruling ANC, where branch meetings saw lively debate on the issues. Opposition parties also relied heavily on reports from councillors. For example, Don Forbes of the Democratic Party reported back to his caucus and constituents every six months. Other members of the caucus also relied on his detailed briefings and presentations of what was happening in 2010 and reported similarly to constituents at iGoli briefing meetings, at which between 40 and 200 people attended. Within the New National Party (NNP) there were also strong lines accountability. However, the events leading up to the formation of the Democratic Alliance (between the NNP

Political Supporters and Shifting Focus within the Joburg CDS

	Pre CDS	iGoli 2002	City Development Strategy		
			iGoli 2010	2030	
Key concerns	Community participation	Financial viability	Data collection for integrated planning beyond crisis management	Municipal strategy and economic development
Content drivers	New post-apartheid officials and politicians plus poor communities	Provincial and national government, especially the Department of Finance, with World Bank advisors	Monitor (consultants), Khetso Gordhan (CEO), and Rashid Seedat (CPU)	Council appointment: Sandy Lowitt and Economic Development chair Kenny Fihla
Political patrons/ supporters	Newly elected grass-roots ANC coucillors	National ANC, business	Local ANC councillors	Reelected local and national ANC plus business
Most obvious political opposition	Affluent ratepayers	Unions, NGO leaders, and academics	Alliance partners, SANCO	Left-wing civil society
Areas of action	Extend infrastructure	Municipal restructuring, budget reform, privatization	Data collection, establish civil society forums	Skills development and crime reduction
Ideological emphasis	Redistribution	Cost recovery	Growth, efficiency, and poverty relief	Economic growth

Note: SANCO = South African National Civic Organization.

and the DA) had a major impact on local politics. At the time, legislation stipulated that councillors elected on a proportional representation list could not cross the floor without loosing their seats. This meant these NNP councillors would effectively loose their jobs if they broke ranks with changing NNP policy. The merger put a lot of strain on debates because of the divergent positions within the party structures at local level.[47]

At the party-political level, the ANC dominates the formal and informal politics of Joburg, although in the council the opposition Democratic Alliance exerts considerable leverage through its links with formal business and its historical involvement in white politics. As the home of old and new, black and white business interests, Johannesburg politics is highly sensitive to elite as well as to popular politics. The ANC, because of its size and its political history, embodies all of these contradictory interests. The ANC is thus simultaneously a government in power, a political party, and a social movement that embraces complex interests in formal and informal alliances. Unsurprisingly, there are internal tensions within the party, not least over how Joburg should be run. For example, it is clear that the debate over privatization unleashed by iGoli 2002 fundamentally challenged the parameters of the ANC's alliance with COSATU and the South African Communist Party. It is also likely that the current assessment of GEAR will influence and be influenced by the tone of the 2030 proposals in Johannesburg.

Splits within the ANC in both the province and the city can be crudely reduced to the debate over whether the Reconstruction and Development Programme (RDP) or the more neoliberal GEAR policies offer a better developmental path. The Johannesburg CDS has been a critical forum for the expression of these divisions, particularly through the relative importance ascribed to poverty over growth. What is abundantly clear is that there is as yet no hegemonic view within the ANC over how a city should be run (as shown in the table outlining the CDS's shifting focus). Even more important, it is obvious that the one site of power that straddles local city politics, grass-roots organizations in civil society, and even the selection, briefing, and appointment of external advisers is the ruling party itself.

Conclusion

Questions about urban power are not new, but their relevance is more potent when set against a context of a globally significant city that is governed by a transitional (national and local) state that has unclear human and financial capacity. Johannesburg is also in a region that is either pessimistically characterized as being dominated by war, famine, and political crisis, or alternatively as on the cusp of economic, social, and political reconstruction and renaissance. In this transitional, fluid, and institutionally unstable context, it is clearly important to understand who is the driver of change in the city and where that power is located institutionally.

The conventional assumptions and tools of urban theory, whether located in neoclassical, Marxist, or postcolonial thought, are necessary but not sufficient to the task of locating the institutional base of the powerful interests that shape city management under conditions of massive transition. The major reason existing approaches are insufficient is that, while it is widely recognized that urban power is contested (the cast of competing actors or players is generally fairly well understood), at the global periphery and under conditions of urban change the sites or arenas for negotiating power are either hidden and difficult to locate, have not yet been negotiated, or are not always known even to the actors themselves. Alternatively there are too many different institutional entry points into city politics, and it is not yet clear which are the primary conduits of influence. The premise of this essay is therefore that, under conditions of transition where the form and practice of municipal governance is evolving, we cannot effectively recognize or locate the actors in city government without knowing where to look for them and establishing which of the competing forums of governance are the most influential. This is not a simple case of, Find the stage and you will identify the actors and their interests. While clearly those who have power will ensure that the forums they select are given weight in dictating the direction of city governance, in transitional contexts like that of Joburg some actors may assume or lose power because they inadvertently select processes that become more or less important. Thus, while ultimately I am concerned about establishing who has the power to run the city, the intellectual device deployed for establishing the patterns of power and influence cannot fall only on the actors themselves but must also explore the various institutional forums that have emerged as platforms from which to influence city governance.

Gaining power in Joburg was not only a consequence of the interplay of the complex intergovernmental environment, and of global-local forces, but also the distillation of the varied and sometimes contradictory avenues for participation created under the guise of developmental local government. Ironically, while the transition to democracy has ushered in many new opportunities for the voices of the Joburg poor to be included in urban politics, the plethora of forums that marginal groups are now forced to engage in may have divided and dissipated their impact—at the very moment when the realities of Joburg's global positioning demands that they organize effectively to influence their urban futures. Set against the view of the competing sites of a centralizing state versus a bottom-up, civil-society-led urban politics are the realities of the less well understood arenas of international experts and internal party politics. If there is a lesson from Joburg about urban power in a global city in the south, it is that we need to know much more about the specific details of city governance itself before we can answer the question, Who runs the city?

Notes

The author wishes to thank Sophie Oldfield and Alan Mabin who participated in the original research on which this essay draws.

1. Just on Joburg, see Schmidt 1999; Bremner 2000; Mabin 1999; Tomlinson 2003; Swilling and Boya 1997.

2. Overall though informal politics is not yet a major force in large South African cities like Joburg.

3. This despite conscious efforts to reconceptualize and reinvigorate debate on the developmental role of the state. See Simon 1992; Tendler 1997; Heller 2001; Evans 1996.

4. See Mayekiso 1996; Sapire 1992; Seekings 2000.

5. Those close enough to provide a substantiated account of the internal party politics are sometimes reluctant to speak critically. Those outside are dependent on a press that rarely undertakes investigative journalism and is generally poorly informed about local government and city management.

6. But see the Cape Town literature: MacDonald 1997; Watson 1998.

7. There have been a number of donor-funded evaluations: Savage et al. 2003; Parnell 2004. The South African Cities Network also undertook a peer review of iGoli 2002.

8. See Beall, Crankshaw, and Parnell 2002, who argue that democracy is a precondition for uniting the divided city of Johannesburg.

9. On the nature of the local government transition, see Mabin in this volume.

10. For details, see Beall, Crankshaw, and Parnell 2002.

11. *Lekgotla* is a Setswana word meaning a gathering of elders—the term is widely used in South Africa to refer to special workshops, often away from town, that are scheduled to deal with important issues. In this case the full Mayoral Committee plus other key stakeholders met in the Drakensburg for five days to debate 2030.

12. For example, through nationally defined building codes and construction standards.

13. Under the Constitution, the purpose of local government is to provide democratic and accountable government for local communities; to ensure the provision of services to communities in a sustainable manner; to promote social and economic development; to promote a safe and healthy environment; to encourage the involvement of communities and community organizations in the matters of local government.

14. Surprisingly little of the South African civil-society literature tackles the issue of how the far-right wing organizes within a radical democratic environment at the city scale.

15. Unlike the National Treasury's Special Poverty Relief Allocation (SPRA), which breaks with the Western welfare tradition and embraces a community participation strategy that downgrades the role of the state to facilitator of development and does not envisage a universal roll-out of benefits. Instead the SPRA tries to develop a hybrid model of bottom-up development drawn from a livelihoods perspective and a traditional state-driven poverty relief strategy.

16. See also Beauregard and Tomlinson in this volume.

17. 2030, for example, assumes that poor people will either choose not to come to the high-cost economy of Joburg or will exclude themselves in the face of only the most basic of state support in designated informal reception areas (City of Johannesburg 2001).

18. Trevor Ngwane, Anti-Privatization Forum. Interview by S. Oldfield, 16 January 2002, for Parnell 2004.

19. Khetso Gordhan, former CEO of GJMC. Interview by the author, 21 January 2002, for Parnell 2004.

20. Specifically in National Economic Development and Labor Council (NEDLAC) where the public and private sectors joined with unions in a tripartite forum to settle disputes.

21. "Annexure A. 1999. Terms of Reference for the Transformation Partnership Steering Committee," in *Minutes of the iGoli 2010 Partnership Steering Committee*, 2nd Ordinary Meeting, 1 October 1999, 27–29.

22. Ibid., 28.

23. A full account can be found in Parnell 2004.

24. Gerald Leissner, Central Johannesburg Partnership. Interview by A. Mabin, 2 February 2002, for Parnell 2004.

25. Gerald Leissner, Central Johannesburg Partnership, and Marius De Jager, JMCCI. Interviews by A. Mabin, 2 February 2002 and 17 February 2002, for Parnell 2004.

26. Marius De Jager, JMCCI. Interview by A. Mabin, 17 February 2002, for Parnell 2004.

27. Steven Cohen, Centre for Development Enterprise. Interview by the author, 15 January 2002, for Parnell 2004.

28. Maduna Khoba and Cas Coovadia, Banking Council of South Africa. Interview by A. Mabin, 7 February 2002, for Parnell 2004.

29. See especially interview with Cas Coovadia.

30. See interviews with De Jager, Coovadia, and Khoba.
31. See interview with Maduna Khoba.
32. See interview with Cas Coovadia.
33. See interviews with Marius De Jager and Cas Coovadia.
34. Sandy Lowitt, 2030 author, City of Johannesburg. Interview by the author, 14 January 2002, for Parnell 2004.
35. Albert Musiye, SANCO/ANC-Freedom Park Informal Settlement. Interview by S. Oldfield, 17 January 2002, for Parnell 2004.
36. Rashid Seedat, Corporate Planning Unit, and Lone Paulson, 2010 Steering Committee facilitator. Interviews by the author, 18 January and 12 February 2002, for Parnell 2004.
37. Susan Carey, Urban Sector Network, and Sipho Simelani, Cope. Interviews by the author, 19 January 2002, for Parnell 2004.
38. For a review of iGoli 2002, see Savage et al. 2003.
39. Especially that between Junaid Ahmed, the World Bank's resident representative, and Khetso Gordhan, the CEO of Joburg.
40. Harold Harvey, Lead Consultant 2010. Interview by the author, 14 January 2002, for Parnell 2004.
41. City of Johannesburg 2001.
42. Harold Harvey, Lead Consultant 2010, and Sandy Lowitt, 2030 author.
43. This point was made in a number of interviews, for example: Joanne Murphy, Director of Strategy and Support, City of Johannesburg, interview by the author, 17 January 2002; Roland Hunter, Director of Finance, City of Johannesburg, interview by the author, 18 February 2002; Rashid Seedat, Director CPU, City of Johannesburg, all for Parnell 2004.
44. Harold Harvey.
45. See interviews with Parks Tau, Mayoral Committee, interview by the author, 21 January 2002; Kenny Fihla, Mayoral Committee, interview by the author, 14 February 2002; Roland Hunter, Director of Finance, City of Johannesburg; and Sandy Lowitt, 2030 author, all for Parnell 2004.
46. Donor reluctance to engage with or be seen to be supporting political parties is one reason for the neglect.
47. Sarel van der Merwe, former New National Party Councilor. Interview by A. Mabin, 17 February 2002, for Parnell 2004.

References

Beall, J., O. Crankshaw, and S. Parnell (eds.). 2002. *Uniting a Divided City: Governance and Social Exclusion in Johannesburg*. London: Earthscan.
Bernstein A., and J. McCarthy. 2002. *Johannesburg: Africa's World City? A Challenge to Action*. Johannesburg: Centre for Development and Enterprise.
Bond, P. 2000a. *Cities of Gold, Townships of Coal: Essays on South Africa's New Urban Crisis*. Trenton: Africa World Press.
———. 2000b. *Elite Transitions*. Johannesburg: Wits University Press.

Bremner, L. 2000. Reinventing the Johannesburg Inner City. *Cities* 17: 185–93.
Chipkin, I. 2003. "Functional" and "Dysfunctional" Communities: The Making of National Citizens in South Africa. *Journal of Southern African Studies* 29: 63–82.
City of Johannesburg. 2001. *Strategic Document for Attaining the City Vision of 2030*. Johannesburg.
City of Johannesburg Council. 2001. *Johannesburg: An African City in Change*. Johannesburg: City Manager's Office.
Evans, P. 1996. Introduction: Development Strategies across the Public-Private Divide. *World Development* 24: 1033–37.
Friedman, S. 2001. A Quest for Control: High Modernism and Its Discontents in Johannesburg, South Africa. Unpublished paper, Centre for Policy Studies, Johannesburg.
Gotz, G., and A. Simone. 2002. On Belonging and Becoming in African Cities. In R. Tomlinson, R. Beauregard, L. Bremner, and X. Mangcu (eds.), *Emerging Johannesburg: Perspectives on the Post-Apartheid City*, 123–54. New York: Routledge.
Greater Johannesburg Metropolitan Council (GJMC). 1999. *iGoli 2002: Making the City Work—It Cannot Be Business as Usual*. Metropolitan Corporate Services, Johannesburg.
———. 2001. *iGoli 2010*. Metropolitan Corporate Services, Johannesburg.
Heller, P. 2001. Moving the State: The Politics of Democratic Decentralization in Kerala, South Africa, and Porto Alegre. *Politics & Society* 29: 131–63.
Mabin, A. 1999. From Hard Top to Soft Serve: Demarcation of Metropolitan Government in Johannesburg. In R. Cameron (ed.), *Democratisation of South African Local Government*, 60–199. Pretoria: Van Schaik.
MacDonald, D. A. 1997. Neither Above nor from Below: Municipal Bureaucrats and Environmental Policy in Cape Town, South Africa. *Canadian Journal of African Studies* 31, no. 2: 315–40.
Mayekiso, M. 1996. *Township Politics: Civic Struggles for a New South Africa*. New York: Monthly Review Press.
Monitor Group. 2001. *Towards a Strategy for Building Johannesburg into a World Class City*. Proposed Strategic Framework for Development Through Delivery, Empowerment and Growth, Discussion Document Commissioned by the City of Johannesburg, February.
Munslow, B., and P. Fitzgerald. 1995. The Reconstruction and Development Programme. In P. Fitzgerald, A. McLennan, and B. Munslow (eds.), *Managing Sustainable Development in South Africa*, 17–26. Cape Town: Oxford University Press.
Parnell, S. 2004. Building Developmental Local Government to Fight Poverty: Institutional Change in the City of Johannesburg. *International Development Planning Review* 26: 377–99.
Parnell, S., and E. Pieterse. 2001. Developmental Local Government. In E. Pie-

terse et al. (eds.), *Democratising Local Government: The South African Experiment.* Cape Town: UCT Press.

Pieterse, E. 2003. From Divided to Integrated City? Critical Overview of the Emerging Metropolitan Governance System in Cape Town. *Urban Forum* 13: 1–24.

Pieterse, E., S. Parnell, M. Swilling, and D. Wooldridge (eds.). 2001. *Democratising Local Government: The South African Experiment.* Cape Town: UCT Press.

Sapire, H. 1992. Politics and Protest in Shack Settlements of the Pretoria-Witwatersrand-Vereeniging Region, South Africa, 1980–1990. *Journal of Southern African Studies* 18: 670–97.

Savage, D., G. Gotz, C. Kihato, and S. Parnell. 2003. *Strategic Review of iGoli 2002.* Project managed by the Program Director: Strategic Support in the City Manager's Office. Johannesburg.

Seekings, J. 2000. *The UDF: A History of the United Democratic Front in South Africa, 1983–1991.* Cape Town: David Phillip.

Simon, D. 1992. *Cities, Capital and Development: African Cities in the World Economy.* London: Bellhaven Press.

Simone, A. 2002. Going South: African Immigrants in Johannesburg. In S. Nuttall and Ch. Michael (eds.), *Senses of Culture: South African Culture Studies,* 402–34. Cape Town: Oxford University Press.

Schmidt, D. 1999. Organisational Change in Greater Johannesburg Metropolitan Area. In P. Cranko and D. Schmidt (eds.), *Organisational Change Theme Team, Local Government Learning Network,* 17–32. Cape Town: Oxford University Press.

Shubane, K., and M. Shaw. 1993. Tomorrow's Foundations? Forums as the Second Level of Negotiated Transition in South Africa. *Centre for Policy Studies* 33. Johannesburg.

Swilling, M., and L. Boya. 1997. Local Government in Transition. In P. Fitzgerald, B. Munslow, and A. McLennan (eds.), *Managing Sustainable Development,* 165–91. Cape Town: Oxford University Press.

Tendler, J. 1997. *Good Government in the Tropics.* Baltimore: Johns Hopkins University Press.

Tomlinson, R. 2003. Ten Years in the Making: A History of Metropolitan Government in Johannesburg. *Urban Forum* 10: 1–40.

Watson, V. 1998. Planning under Political Transition—Lessons from Cape Town's Metropolitan Planning Forum. *International Planning Studies* 3: 335–50.

———. 2002. *Change and Continuity in Spatial Planning: Metropolitan Planning in Cape Town under Political Transition.* London: Routledge.

Formal and Informal Structures of Power in Mumbai

Jim Masselos

The Mumbai Metropolitan Region

Mumbai at the end of the twentieth century was among the world's largest cities. The Mumbai Metropolitan Region in which it is located covers an area of some 4,355 square kilometers. The settled, or urban, area more than doubled from 234.09 square kilometers in 1968 to 575.48 square kilometers in 1987 (Bombay Metropolitan Region Development Authority 1995; Masselos 2003). Growth varied considerably throughout the metropolitan region: there was hardly any change in the oldest settled sections, but extensive development occurred in outlying and semiagrarian land. The overall increase in population in the region as a whole has continued to surge: from 12.6 million in 1991 to an estimated 15.1 million in 2001 (Tata Services Ltd. 2001). A 2004 UN survey ranked it as the world's fifth largest city in 2003 at 17.4 million and saw it moving to fourth largest in 2005 with 18.3 million and to second largest, after Tokyo, with 22.6 million in 2015.[1]

Mumbai at the beginning of the twenty-first century is a great city. Other descriptors may apply equally: among them megalopolis, postmodern, mega-city, heteropolis. Its geographic spread and expanding population all provide reasons for such naming, to say nothing of the social, economic, cultural, political, and productive diversities that exist within it.

Currently the city is known as Mumbai, although the name only became official in the mid-1990s when it was renamed from Bombay, a word going back to the earliest days when the British East India Company acquired the original seven low-lying adjoining islands on the west coast of India. On the southernmost tip the company established a settlement that acquired the name Bombay, probably through Anglicization of the name of the local dominant deity, the goddess Mumbadevi. Thereafter, in two of the city's regional languages, Marathi and Gujarati, it was referred to as Mumbai, in Hindi/Urdu as Bombai, and in English as Bombay. Bombay was the official name in the time of the British raj, a usage retained after Independence in 1947 through 1995 when the state government, an alliance of right-wing Hindu nationalist parties, the Shiv Sena and the Bharathiya Janata Party (BJP), officially renamed the city. It was a renaming that recognized the majority usage in the city, and was not a matter of great contention, though many city inhabitants continued to use both names interchangeably, often according to the language they were speaking at the time.

The nomenclature points to diversity in the city according to language and hence regional and cultural affiliation. The diversity is not, however, solely between the polar Marathi and Gujarati speakers, but encompasses other linguistic groups from the numerous languages and concurrent regions within the Indian Republic. Diversity is there too in terms of religious community, particularly of Hindu and Muslim, but also of Buddhists, Sikhs, Christians, Parsis, and Jains. There are also differences in caste and in other ascribed social divisions as well as in class and in geographic dispersions and locality concentrations within the city. Some of these differences are unique to India's complex social structure, others parallel what exists in other cities and in urbanization processes elsewhere.

Mumbai's headlong growth and its social complexities raise the issue of whether the city is to be understood as an agglomeration of fragmented and separate elements bound within the confines of urban settlement. What follows addresses the question by examining the city's urban structures of power as they existed and changed in a context of massive urban change. The city had from its origins been a location over which diverse formal and informal structures of power held sway. Did the dramatic changes in urbanization that occurred in the last decades of the twentieth century impact upon the patterning of power? Was the city less and less the object of state controls and more the field over which self-organizing networks established their sway, replacing earlier locality-based—and spatially delimited—patterns of controls? The argument of what follows is that patterns of power did change—and that a degree of consolidation and linkage occurred between them, all conducive to urban unification and reinforcement of strong and potent urban identity.

Formal and Institutional Arenas of Authority

A mixed variety of institutions wield formal power in and over the city. It is not at all an autonomous entity. Formally, its governance falls under the tiered hierarchy of the structures of the democratic nation-state and the limitations that accrue at each level of national governance. The central government wields power over the city in terms of its financial powers and its overall economic planning structures through various Five Year Plans. It also exerts control of those parts which involve national defense—in particular the naval dockyards and other military establishments that remain under its exclusive control, distinct of regional and local authorities. Through its charge over immigration, customs, and external trade, the center controls entry points into the city from abroad, namely the airport and the docks. Likewise, it controls the rail system, the suburban railways, as well as the two intra- and interstate lines out of the city into Maharashtra and the rest of the nation. Responsibility for major roads out of the city is shared with the state government.

The Maharashtra state government has clearer and more specific control over Mumbai space through responsibilities that accrue to it under the Constitution. State departments administer matters of major concern to the city—police, revenue, and other items of social and economic importance. Its overriding powers over the city are asserted in the Mumbai Metropolitan Region Development Authority (MMRDA), which it constitutes. The MMRDA has an overall planning role for the region, determining the form the city should assume into the future. Through public-interest and other litigation, the courts ensure the application of laws and notifications and the performance of their duties by the bureaucracy. Other administrative responsibilities vest in municipal corporations, particularly in matters of sanitation, sewerage, school education, and bus transport. Even in such matters, no single body covers the entire metropolitan region. In the early 1990s it was estimated that there were sixteen major authorities that further subdivided into some thirty-three subauthorities, each with specific regional jurisdiction.[2] The largest of these is the Brihanmumbai Municipal Corporation, the former Bombay Municipal Corporation, whose extent covers all of Bombay Island, the older suburbs adjoining it on Salsette Island, and much of the newly developed areas that have grown up over the last two decades of the twentieth century. Under separate municipalities are places like Kalyan, Thane, and Vasai, which were once outside and entirely separate from Bombay. New Mumbai, the planned city on the other side of the harbor, was from the outset constituted with its own administration. There are also autonomous official bodies like the Port Trust, which have independent jurisdiction over specific areas within the metropolitan region.

There is thus a variety of formal structures with administrative functions over or within parts of the city. None of them, no single institution among them, controlled or controls the city. Varied and variable responsibilities are prescribed by legislation to specific agencies and reflect developments that have accrued through custom and specific need over time. Some agencies have intersecting responsibilities, while others may have greater freedom to operate sui generis. Whichever, such official instrumentalities have a diffuse impact upon a complex urban field. The effect of their activities may be collusion and uniformity or it may be opposition and disjunction.

Patterns of Urban Politics

The structural complexities of formal governance are intensified by city politics and by political parties vying for control over urban life. The tiers of formal authority structures, national, regional, and local, are the main arenas for political contestation. Different parties may be in control in each arena.

Until May 2004 the central government was controlled by a coalition, the National Democratic Alliance, which was dominated by the Hindu nationalist BJP. Thereafter, following national elections, central power came to another alliance, the United Progressive Alliance, dominated by the Congress Party. The state—Maharashtra—government is another alliance, namely, of opponents to BJP. Thus, the chief minister is from the Congress Party, the oldest party in India and the party that led the struggle for independence. The deputy chief minister comes from another party, the Nationalist Congress Party (NCP), which split from the Congress Party over the foreign origins of its leader, Sonia Gandhi. A different mix operates at the municipal level. The largest of the municipal councils, the Brihanmumbai Municipal Corporation, is run by an alliance of the regionalist Shiv Sena as the largest party with the BJP a subordinate ally. There were thus different political mixes at different levels of government at the beginning of the twenty-first century, just as there had been previously.

Following the foundation of the Shiv Sena by the charismatic Bal Thackeray in the later 1960s and the decline of the hitherto electorally dominant Congress Party from the mid-1970s, it was rare from the 1980s for the three main government arenas to be controlled at the one time by the same party or even by the same coalition. Furthermore, parties might cooperate in one arena, as did the NCP and Congress in the state government at the end of the century, but they might also be in electoral conflict in other arenas, as in the 2002 Mumbai municipal elections when the two parties fought one another. Thus, any structural symbiosis between formal agencies of urban, state, and national government was largely subverted by the political differentiation between those who controlled different arenas. The city was one of the fields in which political parties deployed their forces and philosophies.

Other formal structures outside those derived from legal authority also influence decision making and city policy. In particular voluntary associations and interest and status groups of various kinds have an impact upon city life. Heritage bodies and nongovernmental organizations concerned with public health or working conditions, for instance, wield influence over aspects of city life. So too do a range of individuals who assume public roles, often and usually through such bodies, in order to voice concern with urban policy and try to influence it by persuasion or adversarial action. The influence of a handful of architects and other concerned individuals through the Indian National Trust for Art and Cultural Heritage and other heritage bodies has led, for example, to pressure to preserve localities deemed to have heritage or historical significance. Particularly prominent have been attempts to preserve and restore the Kalaghoda, Elphinstone Circle, and the University maidan precincts in the Fort area, thus affecting their appearance and usage and influencing ways in which the city functions (Horniman Circle Association 1999; Urban Design Research Institute Bombay First 2000; Marg Publications et al. 2000). What this has meant is that the tendency in the oldest parts of the city to remain unchanged due both to government planning processes and the effects of ossified rent laws and occupancies has been maintained, albeit with a significant nod in the direction of restoration and renovation.

Informal Power

Outside formal arenas, beyond the purview of legitimation by state-derived authority and its mechanisms of governance, there existed other locations in the city in which power was exercised. From the nineteenth to the twentieth century, prime locations for the expression of such power were street corners, and generally in the locality of the street and the local neighborhood.[3] Given a tendency for similar social groups to congregate together in particular neighborhoods, there was a degree of congruence between geographic space and social space. Members of similar or akin castes, or similar occupation, or religion, tended to live in common neighborhoods. The process of settlement aggregation was promoted partly by specific features of city life. Places of worship—temples, churches, and mosques—defined a neighborhood and attracted devotees. Similarly, the workplace—cotton mills, factories, workshops, markets, and so on—provided a focus for settlement based on occupational commonalities. Sometimes housing reinforced such patterns: cotton mills provided accommodation in large blocks (*chawls*) for their workers, and higher-caste cooperatives or wealthy magnates funded housing colonies for members of their group (e.g., Saraswat Brahmans or Parsis).

Adding to social complexity was some correlation between spatial settlement with a particular social group, ascribed social category, or occupation. Although never absolute, in terms of a religious index some areas could be seen as predominantly Hindu or Muslim or even Parsi, Jain, Jew, or Christian. After independence, Buddhist localities also appeared beginning in the 1950s, after the mass conversion movement sponsored by Dr. Ambedkar among Dalits (untouchables). In turn the broad religious division could break into specific castes or, as in the case of Muslims, castelike groups. Many such chose to live together in some city quarters, rather than others. Using other criteria, areas could have predominantly occupational characteristics: some were predominantly retail, wholesale, or trading in character, while others were industrial, populated by millworkers; and there were also jewelry markets, financial centers, and artisan locales. Using linguistic criteria, the ground plan of the city could be seen as a series of linguistic and cultural regions—Marathi, Gujarati, Hindi, Urdu, Konkani, and English among them. The layers intersected like templates, one above the other, and constituted mental urban maps variously used by people according to circumstance and situation.[4] Thus a predominantly Hindu area like Bhuleshwar/Kalbadevi was also predominantly Bania by caste, Vallabhacharya by sect, merchant by occupation, and Gujarati by linguistic region. A Muslim area around Mahomedali Road could be Konkani Muslim by castelike group, Konkani by language, and merchant or laboring by occupation. Such localities, known as *mohallas* or *wadis,* had distinctive identities and were so named and understood. Consequences followed thereby.

The spatial concentration of akin groups, through ascribed social identity—caste or castelike group, or occupation, language, region, or religion—engendered cohesion. It also promoted caste or community organization and the expression of concomitant forms of traditional authority. Thus the collectivity accepted social authority as represented in caste councils or castelike gatherings (*panchayats* and *jamats*) and through them or separately in headmen or group leaders. The role of priests, *purohits, maulvis,* and monks could be an additional element in the structures of social authority present in street localities where akin groups settled. A variety of terms applied to localities. Apart from a neighborhood's specific name, such as Pydhonie, or a particular street name, other words carried a terminological notion of locality.

A locality might be identified as a *galli* (literally a lane or alley),[5] a *wada* ("a division of town, a quarter, a ward"),[6] or a *wadi* (originally an enclosed field, or a cluster of huts in a village, or "a division of the suburban portion of a city");[7] sometimes *chawl* ("a long and narrow building; . . . also a row, line, or series [of shops or uniform houses]")[8] might be used. These Marathi words usually connoted Hindu-dominant localities; for Muslim localities *moholla* was applied. Free of religious connotations was the bazaar, which was not only a marketplace but a distinctive locality. Of these *wadi, moholla,* and *bazaar* were most common in conveying an idea of a street-corner community, a neighborhood entity.

Neighborhood solidarity manifested itself in various ways. Among them was the sharing of public religious symbols during festivals, symbols that required locality organization for success: the ten-day public installations of God Ganesh for Hindus or of model tombs for Husain and Hasan for Muslims during Mohurrum had this effect, as did the nine nights of street dancing during Navratri among Gujarati Hindus. After Independence, secular national festivals could provide occasion for locality integrity, as in the annual flag-raising ceremonies within and specific to localities on the morning of Independence Day, 15 August. There was also the role played by traditional social or religious leaders in giving a *mo-*

halla or *wadi* cohesive identity, a role some used to achieve personal prominence.

Other locality leaders, or *dadas*, built their positions differently by ignoring traditional authority structures and attracted followings from local gymnasiums, student clubs, teashops, and other gathering places. The followings became street gangs, usually intensely loyal to their *dada* (elder brother), and enabled him to control physical force in locality life and to use or threaten to use it, when necessary. The *dada*'s power came from the capability of might and enabled him to move into the subterranean worlds of gambling and protection, and to manipulate "fund raising" for festivals, such as Mohurrum and Ganesh Chaturthi, to his own advantage. Success in such areas gave him further funds, further control of resources—and further power.

While gang leaders and traditional authority figures were potentially in conflict, conflict between them was not the norm within the *moholla* or *wadi*. More often than not, a via media was established, an accommodation in which both functioned simultaneously. Conflict outside the locality was another matter: it was commonplace for neighboring localities to be rivals—and for their *dadas* also to be opposed. Though outright violent confrontation between them was not frequent, there were times when hostilities did break out—often during religious processions as in the Mohurrum processions of the early twentieth century.

Localities were also an element in more prominent nineteenth-century disturbances, in extended riots between Hindus and Muslims (1893), or Parsis and Muslims (1874; Wilson 1940). In them the locality modules came together to create larger hostile blocs, which joined in the confrontations and violence characteristic of such events. Into the twentieth century, locality hostilities continued as a major factor in the various eruptions of crowd violence. They were there too in the 1950s in the riots between opposed linguistic groups over whether Bombay should be the capital of Gujarat or Maharashtra, new states constituted on linguistic grounds out of the former Bombay province. Conflict in the city assumed spatial form in major battles between adjacent but linguistically different Gujarati and Marathi neighborhoods.

At the end of the twentieth century, much of the locality differentiation survived in Mumbai, in its overall pattern, if not in all its specific detail. Despite the city's expansion into new space, the tendency for akin groups to congregate together continued as a feature of urban life. In the newer parts there was a concentration in terms of status and wealth. In what were once the outer reaches of Greater Mumbai on Salsette Island and in Navi [New] Mumbai, clusters of large high-rise apartment blocks with their characteristic postmodern designs mushroomed in the final two decades as sleeper suburbs for a growing affluent middle class. The less affluent gathered in other, less grandiose, housing colonies. While such settlement patterns suggest status or class polarization rather than social ascription, the trend was reduced after the 1992–93 riots when Muslims who had moved into middle-class areas found themselves specific targets for attack. Many in consequence returned to Muslim-dominated localities, particularly in south Mumbai, thereby intensifying the prevailing concentration of Muslims. Much of the older part of the city retained the flavor of its past. The merchant trading or commercial financial characteristics of many areas survived, while conversely the character of former millworker areas dissipated as mills closed and major redevelopment began to turn them into middle-class enclaves. Housing colonies dedicated to specific social groups, however, continued to operate largely on exclusive criteria. The earlier religious, regional, and linguistic characteristics of many quarters survived, even as new linguistic concentrations became evident, as for example that of Hindi speakers from northern India in sections of Ghatkopar, Kurla, Malad, and Borivili.[9] Even in slums, spatial differentiation existed between social groups: in Dharavi there was a clear demarcation between Hindu and Muslim quarters. While there was by no means anything approaching a total correlation between locality and social group, the shape of the city's multiethnicity was discernible in its settlement pattern. The relentless growth of Mumbai had not resulted in an amorphous agglomeration of people but in a complex patterning of ethnicities and identities.

Traditional social authority retained a presence in the localities. Although the tighter social controls that had operated in community or caste structures in the nineteenth century were less apparent at the end of the twentieth century, they sometimes featured in the new circumstances of urban life. In specific castelike groups, as, for example, among the Daudi Bohras, conflict between reformers and the religious or social head of the community surfaced in the 1990s, a reminder not only of festering disputes present over the preceding century but a signal of the continued role of traditional leadership. That locality structures were still important was also demonstrated in other ways. A potent sign of the significance of traditional leadership within the *moholla* and the *wadi* was evidenced in 2001 by those people on whom Mumbai's new joint commissioner of police chose to exert pressure in order to prevent the city from suffering violent repercussions from the Afghan crisis: he went to *moholla* Muslim leaders and local-level Hindu leaders in order to ensure maintenance of public order in the city.[10]

Intersecting Structures

While local power structures and powerful individuals still featured in the *mohollas* and *wadis,* that world was linked into wider patterns of urban power structures and India-wide issues. The *moholla* was not a world entire unto itself. By the final decade of the century, it was less frequently only local in character and more often part of wider phenomena so that the street corner had a place both in city politics and in extended citywide criminal organizations. The locality was not a microcosm, but was part of the macrocosm.

Throughout the 1990s the press would erupt with accounts of yet another criminal gang murder, either of a member of a rival gang or of a victim.[11] During the mid-1990s four citywide gangs vied for control. Led by Mafia-like bosses in absentia from abroad or, in one case, from within a Pune jail, organized crime had extended its 1950s base of gambling and illicit liquor into gold smuggling and later into drugs. In the process the structure of citywide crime controlled by a single individual through secondary bosses, each with his own territorial jurisdiction and particular specialization, had split into at least four main gangs fighting for control. By then, organized crime had its fingers in almost every aspect of Mumbai's economic activities: the film industry, land development, extortion and protection rackets, horse racing, and numbers gambling games—and politics. While the gangs drew on, and related to, specific localities, they also established links with politicians that went beyond what had hitherto been the case. A writer to the *Times of India* saw that "a complete transformation has occurred in the relationship between coercion and violence, on the one hand, and politics and business, on the other. For instance, in the sixties or seventies, politicians patronized criminals because they needed muscle power in electioneering or booth-capturing. Business would engage them to break strikes and smash unions" (Bidwai 1995, 10). Today, businessmen in certain sectors deploy this Mafia as a direct economic input, for example, to steal electricity, or to corner markets physically and control the competition. Criminals are also used to mediate in disputes over unaccounted-for monetary transactions. The working of the construction industry is inconceivable without black money and the use of coercion to evict legal tenants or squatters in inner-city areas, which are then taken over, developed, and sold at astronomical rates. Political collusion is integral to this.[12]

The communalization of politics in the 1990s equally had implications for the nexus of urban informal leadership and political party structures. Local leaders were not quarantined from the political environment or from assertions of separatist identity. The spread of Hindu nationalism and fundamentalism was largely also the story of the rise of the all-India political party, the BJP, its message of Hindutva, "Hinduness," and its association with Hindu organizations like the VHP (Vishwa Hindu Parishad, or World Hindu Organization) and more belligerent and activist groups like the Bajrang Dal (Army of Monkeys). The effect of their activities was a coalescing of social attitudes and political behavior along religious criteria. Through the VHP, funds and support were garnered from overseas Indians, some satisfactorily domiciled in and nationals of other countries, and others away on limited sojourns. How far expatriates when they returned influenced the power structures of the city is unclear, although they did bring with them funding for new and more elaborate housing, like that to which they had become accustomed in their former Western homes. Some of the building boom in the new suburbs drew upon the middle-class life expectations of nonresident Indians who sought to maintain a second base in their former homes. Other building activity was likewise required to satisfy the new businesses attracted to the city after the national economy was liberalized from the early 1990s. These created business enclaves attempting to remain free of the complexities of power at work in the city, though perhaps not especially successfully. They too were subject to the established patterns and seem to have learned quickly the ground rules of their new operational areas and to have established ways to accommodate and work with the forces active in the city.

Adding to the mix in Mumbai was the city's own party, the Shiv Sena (Shiva's Army or Shivaji's Army). The Shiv Sena championed the interests of Marathis whom it asserted had been denied opportunities taken by other linguistic groups. From the late 1980s the Shiv Sena focused on Muslims, pinpointed as alien and hostile. In doing so, the Shiv Sena benefited from the dominant spread of fundamentalist attitudes.

In Mumbai, an effect of BJP and Shiv Sena activism was an increase of religious devotion and its expression through public worship and ceremony. The numbers of Muslims participating in Friday prayers expanded dramatically in the early 1990s—reaching the point where mosques could not hold all those wanting to pray, so that the faithful spilled onto surrounding streets and appropriated them temporarily for prayer, thereby stopping traffic and causing inconvenience and annoyance. Hindu attendance at temples also seems to have increased, and during the time of heightened communal tension in January 1993 mass participation in religious worship in the form of *maha aartis* at and around temples attracted large numbers of people. The practice of religion became a rallying cry in the city and was a means through which street-level attitudes were expressed and organized.

There were other, more grave ways to express hostility. Anti-Muslim sentiment reached a flashpoint in December 1992 when right-wing Hindu elements from various parties and religious organizations destroyed the Babri Masjid at Ayodhya. The result was not merely heightened communal tension; major riots occurred around the nation, including particularly serious outbreaks in Mumbai in December and again in January 1993. The January riots were the largest and most extensive the city had seen. Violence and destruction broke out in virtually every part of the city with people of all classes subject to attack. People in slums were attacked and killed, and their dwellings burned. Muslims in high-rise apartments were targeted by groups of men who selectively picked out their victims where they lived. Shops were destroyed, cars burned, and people killed. Estimates of the total number of deaths vary, but it is likely to have been between 500 and 1,000 people. Some 250,000 people fled from the city as refugees. What took place was particularly complex and no single explanation covers the variety of horrors evident in the January riots. In terms of this discussion, the riots illustrate two aspects of locality politics and power (Masselos 1994; 1996).

There was a clear targeting and direction in the nature of the attacks on people and property. In a row of shops in a market, for instance, only the Muslim shops would be looted, shops on either side being left untouched. When gangs went to apartment blocks they knew who they wanted and on which floor and in which apartment their selected Muslims lived. Much of the violence was focused and showed detailed knowledge of the area. It bore the marks of a pogrom, a concerted attack on Muslims. The leader of the Shiv Sena, Bal Thackeray, talked in TV interviews at the time of young men from branches of the party being involved and stated they were exacting justice for what the Muslims had done. Newspaper accounts support an interpretation of men from the local branches of the Shiv Sena having been involved. The Shiv Sena was very much a wielder of influence within the locality, but in such mass disturbances its cadres had a more potent weapon—physical force.

The widespread burning of huts in the slum areas illustrates a different aspect of locality power. Huts were valuable commodities. The people who lived in them did not have title or right to where they were, though their squatting wrested for them quasi title. The longer they stayed, the greater their right to remain, and the more difficult to remove them. On the other hand hutment dwellers were subject to shanty patterns of power that involved obligations to pay rent for the space they occupied. Their rents went to a landlord who equally had no title to the land or to the rent—excepting that he had physical force at his disposal to ensure payment. Thus land or space was a commodity in hutment areas and was controlled through elaborate systems of extortion. The extortion in, and overall control of, such precincts were enforced by gangs usually controlled—or, at the least, employed—by shanty landlords. In their turn landlord and gang often linked into the more extensive citywide gangs.

The torching of the shanties during the 1993 riots thus did not occur in a *terra nullius,* a place untrammeled by rights and ownership, but in a place where a tiered structure of rights was exercised in different forms over the space of the hutment, from occupation to rent, from gang to slum landlord, and onward. What occurred in the slums in that January therefore was largely intended, and of consequence. Some of the burnings may have been related to the fundamentalist attitudes prevalent in other incidents of those days, yet the flames were consuming resources, capital investment, and productive enterprises. Alternate benefit had to come from the flames. They may therefore represent attempts by the slum landlord to drive out the former occupants, resume the land, and rent it to new tenants at higher rates and on payment of key money—in other words, for the slum landlord to achieve a capital gain from the territory he controlled. An alternate explanation suggested at the time is that the torchings were initiated by the actual owners of the land, those with legal title, who employed *goondas,* gangsters or strong-arm men, to set fire to the slums. The objective was for the landlord to resume control of his property and build new *pukka* (permanent) middle-class buildings on the site.

In more quiet times, some localities continued to be subject to gangs who operated their various rackets within and outside it. As for the political parties, they too sought to maintain a presence in the *moholla* or *wadi* and monitor and guide its politics. Apart from whatever specific benefits derived from the locality, it had a place in electoral politics—less at the national level, more at the state level, and most at the municipal level where a locality's vote could be particularly influential in determining outcomes. Thus, moves in late 2001 to clear slums immediately adjacent to the city's international airport were stayed because of the effect they would have upon voting in the coming municipal elections in early 2002.[13]

While most parties had some sort of space in various localities from which they pursued their work, perhaps the Shiv Sena's grass-roots activity was the best organized. The Shiv Sena had a highly visible profile in the neighborhoods. It had branches (*shakas*) throughout much of the Marathi-speaking areas of the city, in middle- and lower-middle-class areas as well as in working-class and shanty neighborhoods. With facades usually decked out as a fort, the *shaka* had locality presence. It was a gathering place for young Marathi men and thence a base to initiate group action. While the Shiv Sena may have asserted regional identity belligerently, it also showed concern for its own in grass-roots level activities with a distinct social welfare objective—through running ambulance services and blood donation camps, and finding work for the unemployed. It looked after its own. It was as if its members were protected by a larger, and caring, entity. A Shiv Sena member from the Rajya Sabha, the upper house of the central Indian parliament, articulated the sentiment in a 2001 municipal electioneering speech in Mumbai: "[J]oining the Shiv Sena is like being a part of the mainstream. Once you are with the Shiv Sena, you will have no fears and insecurities."[14]

The *shakas* were potent in Marathi localities because of their promise of security in a threatening and insecure environment. As a collectivity, the *shakas* could be powerful instruments in citywide politics and contestations of various kinds. Other parties along the political spectrum variously tried to achieve similar exposure but were less successful; even the BJP in Mumbai could only admire the Shiv Sena achievement and hold it out as the role model for municipal corporators. Part of a speech of the BJP vice-president at a 2002 municipal victory rally in Mumbai is worth quoting for its insights into what should be expected: "A BJP corporator must be looked upon by the general public as a court of appeal. For any grievance, people must turn to you. If you work in a constructive and honest manner, people will stand by you in every situation."[15]

The speech highlights the blending of formal and informal political roles—the corporator should be a locality leader, handling locality grievances as much as a politician operating in the formal sphere of municipal government. The two roles blended into one another at this level, just as locality leadership of authority and force had also linked into citywide structures of power. The pattern was Foucauldian in its netlike nodes, each of which interconnected between levels and between different kinds of power.

As for the *shakas* and locality branches, their success would seem to be proved by the victory of the Shiv Sena in the 2002 Brihanmumbai Municipal Corporation elections. The Shiv Sena–BJP combine won 132 seats out of 226, with the BJP, the dominant party in the nation's parliament, very much the minor ally in this election with its tally of 35 seats. The Congress won only 61 seats, and the NCP, its municipal rival but state government ally, won 12. Had the two not fought hostile campaigns they might well have won more seats. The results were clearly a victory for the Shiv Sena and its tactics and would seem to show the viability of its underlying structures and the nature of its appeal. In terms of votes cast, however, the figures reveal a different pattern. Of 3,368,420 voters, the Shiv Sena–BJP alliance attracted 1,252,039, while the Congress and the NCP together attracted 1,318,495 voters.[16] Had they allied, the final result in terms of corporation seats could have been different—certainly the marked disparity between the parties in the corporation chambers would not have eventuated. An explanation for the result lies in the impact of the fragmentation of anti-Hindu nationalist sentiment. It also suggests that issues as much as locality organization were important in electoral situations and also perhaps that the achievement of the Shiv Sena locality branches was not as significant as my analysis would suggest. The *shakas* after all were located mainly in Marathi-speaking areas, and Marathi speakers were outnumbered in the city, even though they may have been vociferous in politicking.

The Power of People

Finally, but not least among urban locations for power, was the power that came from the people themselves, when people expressed their needs or acted spontaneously. Then they could act on their own, without direction from any set of structures, formal or informal. Agitations over a matter that concerned everybody in the city, the running of the suburban trains, provides an example of the ad hoc, but potent, expression of people's power.

First let us consider an example of the opposite, a politically focused agitation. At the end of February 1992, a Shiv Sena corporator began a rail *roko* movement designed to stop the running of trains and thus bring pressure to bear upon the central and state governments, both run by the Congress Party at the time. The movement, which involved demonstrators sitting down on the rail lines in front of the trains was effective in that it directed attention to the Shiv Sena and opposition to Congress, but it did nothing to remedy the situation for train commuters. It was essentially a political protest using an issue of concern to build up political support. While party organization was behind this *roko*, it was not present in other incidents involving the railways. In July 1993 commuters stopped all trains on the Central Railway line because one particular train was delayed, and riots broke out at Ambernath. On the same day on the Western Railway line, because trains were canceled due to a cable fault, crowds attacked trains up and down the line. In September 1994 at Churchgate station, passengers turned "berserk" after six trains were canceled. Some destroyed their season tickets, others stoned stationary trains, and others attacked platform furniture as well as the stationmaster's office.[17]

These reactions are not untypical and are reminders that in the structures of power in the city there was a power wielded by the people themselves, rather than devolved or given up to others. People could act when they were directly affected in matters of immediate concern. No intermediary of locality organization or locality personality was needed to energize them when the situation became sufficiently intolerable—nor any political party either. Theirs was a spontaneous assertion of how the city should be run; expressed in the way it was over suburban trains, it was a voice that could not be ignored. Such incidents also suggest an increased tendency for mass mobilization regardless of city power structures and even directed against them. It was a mobilization that was based not upon locality agendas and groups, nor upon party and organizational aggregations, but upon people gathered together by one specific interest or some immediate and apparently ad hoc cause. They need not even know one another or be linked through organization. In this sense, such agitations were reactions against the firming of structures and the increased linkages between the various levels of power emerging within the city.

Such events highlight the complex ways in which various forms of power interacted in the city. There were different levels with different leaders and different issues. Increasingly, however, as the twentieth century came to an end, it would seem that local leadership, whether formal or informal, traditional or nontraditional, was less an isolate within the locality but was much more linked into a wider network of power and influence. The ways in which political parties and other organizations brought the locality into a wider urban context meant that the locality as isolate was less and less frequent a phenomenon. In the globalized postmodern—and continuously expanding—city, there may well have been social fragmentation and intense social confrontation, but there was also social and political integration, as well an increased potential for horizontal mobilization by the people themselves on issue-oriented matters.

Notes

1. UN 2004 survey data as reported in the *Australian*, 26 March 2004, 9, and the *Weekend Australian*, 22–23 May 2004, 2.

2. A full list appears in Bombay Metropolitan Region Development Authority 1995, 63.

3. For a fuller exploration of these structures, see Masselos 1977; 1982.

4. For a fuller exploration of mental templates, see Masseolos 1991.

5. *Molesworth's Marathi-English Dictionary*, corrected reprint (Poona: Shubhada-Saraswat, 1975), 228.

6. Ibid., 745.

7. Ibid.

8. Ibid., 280.

9. See Ambarish Mishra, "Sena No Longer Eyes Only Marathi Manus, Set to Woo Banarsi babu," *Times of India* (Mumbai), 1 January 2002, 3.

10. See interview with V. N. Deshmukh, 2001. Today, neither side wants trouble. *Mid Day* (Mumbai), 6 December 2001, 11.

11. See, for example, the lead stories in *Outlook*, 29 November 1995, and *Sunday*, 26 November–2 December 1995.

12. Bidwai 1995, 10.

13. Archana Sharma, "Politicians Did Not Want to Alienate Airport Slum Dwellers before Civic Polls," *Times of India* (Mumbai), 7 December 2001, 7.

14. Speech of Sanjay Nirupam cited in Misra, "Sena No Longer Eyes."

15. Speech of Gopinath Munde, National BJP vice-president at a BJP victory rally in Mumbai, in "Follow Sena's Example, Munde Tells BJP Cadres," *Times News Network*, 14 March 2002, in *The Times of India Online*, "Mumbai," www.timesofindia.com (accessed 10 April 2002).

16. The figures are from the report by Uma Upadhyaya, "BMC Polls Highs and Lows," *Mid Day*, http://midday_chalomumbai.com/02-23-2001/images/show Article.php?id=9687 (accessed 13 March 2002).

17. See *Times of India* and *Indian Express* (Bombay), 29 February 1992, 1 and 3 March 1992; *Times of India*, 27 July 1993 and 29 September 1994.

References

Bidwai, B. 1995. Crime-Political Nexus. The Crucial Business Link. *Times of India*, 29 November.

Bombay Metropolitan Region Development Authority. 1995. *Draft Regional Plan for Bombay Metropolitan Region, 1996–2011*. October, Bandra (East).

Horniman Circle Association. 1999. *Restoring a Banking District*. Bombay: UDRI.

Marg Publications et al. 2000. *Buildings of the Kala Ghoda Art District*. Bombay: UDRI.

Masselos, J. 1977. Power in the Bombay "Moholla," 1904–15: An Initial Exploration into the World of the Indian-Urban Muslim." *South Asia* 6: 75–95.

———. 1982. Change and Custom in the Format of the Bombay Mohurrum during the 19th and 20th Centuries. *South Asia* 5, no. 2: 47–67.

———. 1991. Appropriating Urban Space: Social Constructs of Bombay in the Time of the Raj. In S. Freitag (ed.), Aspects of "the Public" in Colonial South Asia. Special issue. *South Asia* 14, no. 1: 33–63.

———. 1994. Postmodern Bombay: Fractured Discourses. In S. Watson and K. Gibson (eds.), *Postmodern Cities and Spaces*, 199–215. Oxford: Blackwell.

———. 1996. The Bombay Riots of January 1993: The Politics of Urban Conflagration. In J. McGuire, P. Reeves, and H. Brasted (eds.), *Politics of Violence: From Ayodhya to Behramapada*, 111–26. New Delhi: Sage.

———. 2003. Defining Moments/Defining Events: Commonalities of Urban Life. In S. Patel and J. Masselos (eds.), *Bombay and Mumbai: The City in Transition*, 31–52. Delhi: Oxford University Press.

Tata Services Ltd. 2001. *Statistical Outline of India, 2001–2002*. Mumbai.

Urban Design Research Institute Bombay First. 2000. *Ballard Estate: A Corporate District*. Bombay: UDRI.

Wilson, Cp. H.H. 1940. Account of the Word's Mughal Origins. In A. C. Ganguli and N. D. Basu (eds.), *A Glossary of Judicial and Revenue Terms*, 499–500. Calcutta: Eastern Law House.

Legitimating Power Structures in São Paulo

Sueli Schiffer and Csaba Deák

The remodeling of the decision-making processes in urban planning of the São Paulo Metropolitan Region since the early 1990s is discussed in this essay as being a result of the spread of neoliberal ideas and practices in most social and economic sectors in Brazil. Formerly prevalent comprehensive urban planning was replaced first in the late 1970s by less comprehensive planning, therefore called "sectoral," to be replaced in its turn in the early 1990s by a new approach to spatial organization under the name of "strategic" planning. This was supported by a discourse that sought to disqualify the state as an (efficient) provider of basic infrastructure and social services. At the same time, it sponsored new, institutionalized partnerships between the urban administrations and the private-sector or civil-society organizations to implement projects even in sectors that came by constitutional law under public responsibility.

It is undeniable that the previous urban and social policies had induced a very segregated and unequal urban structure in São Paulo, with prevalence of infrastructure and social equipment in the higher-income areas, and this begged urgent changes in the spatial policies. We argue, however, that the shifts in the nineties did nothing of that sort and, on the contrary, were introduced precisely to sustain the same historic process, namely, hindered accumulation (Deák 1988), that has been restraining the development of the Brazilian economy since the colonial period. In this way they became new means of reproducing the old status quo, in which the privileges of the dominant class—an elite, as distinct from bourgeoisie—take precedence over collective interest.

The institutional and legal framework set up during the 1990s, had the declared purpose of achieving the goals of social development, based on the ideological principles henceforth prevailing. In the realm of urban management, the new laws were targeted to legitimize new forms of partnership between public administration and private organizations in the implementation of social and urban projects. Additionally, the local level was raised to the status of the most legitimate instance to deal with urban planning and (local) social inequalities, and the participation of civil society in the decision-making processes of the government bodies of public administration was legally guaranteed.

This essay describes the experience of the past decade and seeks to assess whether it led to more equal participation of the less favored groups, or to any consistent improvement in the social-economic conditions or in terms of infrastructure provision of the majority of the population of São Paulo.

The Power Structures in Brazil Resulted from the Process of Hindered Accumulation

The Brazilian economy has been undergoing changes since the early 1990s in the name of adjusting to the requirements of international trade and financial transactions, customarily called globalization of the economy. Now globalization at best represents an increase in the number and value of cross-border economic transactions (for instance, in trade and finance), but it is not—as is often implied—a new stage of capitalist development.[1] Dupas (2000, 1) already noted that in a context of a greater cross-border mobility of large amounts of capital "the room for the operation of public policies is drastically reduced," since both the domestic monetary and fiscal policies and government spending are squeezed by the requirements of inflation control to ensure "the trade competitiveness of the domestic products."

Such economic arguments have been used to justify the shrinking participation of the state in the provision of social wage and basic infrastructure (power generation, telecommunications, roads, etc.), and implicitly legitimize the enlargement of the market sphere to act as a strong partner in alleviating the worsening of an already very unequal social structure. The latter has been part of Brazil's history since colonial times, when the Portuguese metropolis took up slave labor to achieve tight political and economic control over the colony by preventing the emergence of local social forces that could get loose from its command. This socioeconomic status quo was maintained when Brazil broke away from Portugal

(1822). This was eloquently illustrated by the fact that Independence was proclaimed by the heir to the Portuguese throne, in a move aimed at the preservation of the previous relations of production and at perpetuating a ruling class modeled on the former colonial basis. This would imply giving continued preference to the external market at the expense of sovereign national development.

Such is the background of the Brazilian elite society, which, in contrast to a bourgeois society that has as its moving principle the free development of productive forces, is rooted precisely in the containment of the development of homegrown production, as an ultimate means of control over the national accumulation process. Deák (1988) argues that the Brazilian social formation can be characterized as an elite society due to the prevailing overprivileges of a small ruling class—the elite—which are allowed to take precedence over collective interests, and are sustained by the recurrent reimpositions of a process of hindered accumulation (see Deák and Schiffer in this volume).[2] The omission of providing adequate social services, the maintenance of low salaries for the great majority of the population, scarce investments in technology, and low priority given to education at all levels are some of the major consequences resulting from hindered accumulation.

The power structures behind city management and infrastructure provision are also determined by the features of the elite society, contributing to the prolongation of deep and chronic social and urban inequalities. The strengthening of cross-border economic relations in the last decades of the twentieth century represented no inflection in this historical process; indeed, they became one of its many movements. Subsequent concentrations of capital and wealth were nothing but the expected outcomes of an ever-exclusionary economic path once again imposed in Brazil during the 1990s, ideologically anchored this time in the spread of the neoliberal project of the core economies.

Neoliberal Policies of the 1990s and Effects on the Urban Institutional Framework

The period from the 1960s to the early 1980s was a time of comprehensive, or development, plans, when planning rhetoric clearly stated its purpose as supporting economic and social development. This planning went hand in hand with detailed instruments of spatial control, such as zoning and building regulations.

In this way, public, or collective, interest was clearly established at the level of spatial organization and city management. Exactly how close state intervention came to the proclaimed principles in actual practice is another matter—and, indeed, there always were glaring differences at the level of infrastructure provision, for example, between the privileged southwestern sector of São Paulo and the half-abandoned periphery. However, these could as yet be seen as mere imperfections, probably stemming from underdevelopment or dependency of a system that in essence was still oriented toward the goals of collective interest and social equity.

After the Brazilian miracle (1968–74), a period of high economic growth rates, the time of comprehensive planning, whether national or urban, was over, and planning became sectoral, or single-purpose, focused on specific issues such as transportation, sewerage, or land use. This period was followed by the worst recession in Brazilian history (1981–83) and planning became merely "anatomy of poverty," restricted largely to the elaboration of diagnoses, but with little or no concrete action due to a general feeling of lack of resources.

The wave of neoliberalism reached Brazil and held full sway through the nineties, a time when the inefficiency and bankruptcy of the state were declared. The basis of the economic process that followed, equivocally attributed to globalization, is best summarized by Paulo Nogueira Batista Jr.:

> To countries like Brazil, that still carry significant trends of a colonial past, the debate [about the outcomes of globalization] is always problematic. The ideology of "globalization," particularly in its more extreme versions, constitutes a considerable and fallaciously modern reinforcement of the deep-rooted subservience of several sectors of the ruling class of the country, always ready to act as agents of the dominant international interests and to collaborate in a passive and subordinated integration to the international economy. In this context, the "globalisation" is used as an *alibi* for traditional behavior of the local elite. (Batista 1997, 44)

The elite society adopted the neoliberal discourse in order to justify the fact that sectors previously controlled by the state would now be opened to the market. As already noted, a considerable part of public works was privatized, such as electricity, telephone (both fixed and mobile), optical cable, and motorways. Urban planning even abandoned sectoral planning and the metropolitan scope and left the place to fragmented municipal and submunicipal plans focused on strategic planning and based on public-private partnerships.

New agents—or pressure groups—emerged to replace or act as a partner of the public sector in a wide range of social projects and the supply of urban infrastructure. These agents were organized in a variety of loosely defined associations, consortia, councils (generally with the participation of government bodies), cooperatives, and nongovernmental organizations (NGOs) of all sorts. Legal instruments were introduced, some of them changing constitutional edicts, to allow the strengthening of the partnership between public and private sectors, justified by yet another ideological argument pointed out by Batista (1997, 46), namely the "inevitable downsizing of the state." This statement, which eventually turned into a generally accepted credo of the "scarcity of public funds," was then used to justify the retraction of the state from its duty to design and implement social policies.

The rise of new entities—frequently referred to as actors—participating in the decision-making processes of the public policies occurred mainly at the level of local government and gave rise to equally new forms of associations or partnerships. The new focus on local policies reflects a shift in the Brazilian institutional framework that started with the Constitution of 1988. The latter provided a redistribution of funds and attributions in favor of the municipalities. The municipalities—hitherto a part of the federated states—were also made "constitutional entities," on a footing equal to that of the federal states and the federation itself. Thus the changes were not just in the share of the tax revenues among the union, the federated states and the municipalities, but imported in fact in a complete about-face from a model that prevailed since the 1960s and that allowed for the nationwide administration and implementation of social policies. The new approach led to the increased fragmentation of the state apparatus, justified in the name of enlarging civil participation and the role of private partnerships in urban decision-making process.

The achievement of greater influence of private groups in public projects was institutionally backed by other federal laws as well, starting in 1990 with the Programa Nacional de Desestatização (National Program of Denationalization),[3] followed in 1995 by the Lei Geral das Concessões[4] (General Law of Concessions of Public Services) and in 1998 by Law 9.636, which legislates on social organizations (Azevedo 1999).

Basic infrastructure, such as the water supply, sewage system, and public transportation are the main public services that fall, by force of the 1988 Constitutional Law, within the duties of local administration. Local administration, however, can implement them through concessions to private companies. This law thus allows for the transfer of provision to private companies to be carried out "by their own investment and risk" (Azevedo 1999, 68). As providers, such companies may charge users directly for the services they use.

Although the regulation and quality control of services provided by concessionaires remain the obligation of government administration, "which must act in accordance with the collective interest" (Azevedo 1999, 71), the recent evolution of tariffs leaves obeyance to this rule very much in doubt. As the chart illustrates, a steep increase—almost trebling—of the share of the price of public services compared to the household income (which remained stationary) has occurred in the major Brazilian metropolitan regions. During this same period, concession contracts for electric power distribution were signed and some public services, such as fixed and mobile telephone services, were privatized after they were no longer defined by the constitutional order as "essential public utility services." Many public companies were privatized, and many of these were absorbed by foreign corporations.

The enormous spread of fixed lines and mobile telephones after priva-

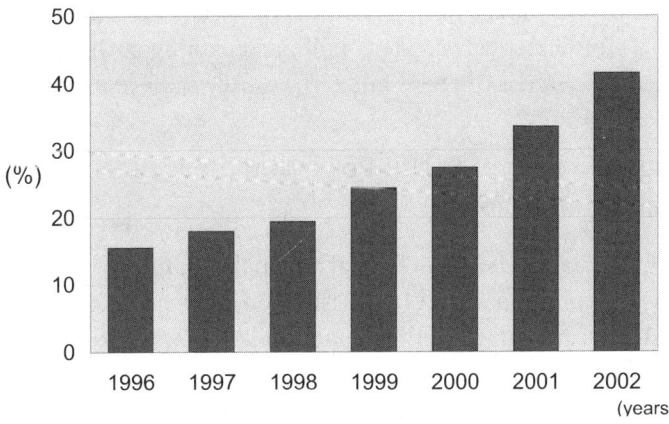

Brazil: metropolitan regions. Share of spending on public services in household income (1996–2002). Source: G. Dupas, data from Instituto Brasileiro de Geografia e Estatística (IBGE): Pesquisa de Orçamentos Familiares (POF) and Pesquisa Mensal de Emprego (PME), 2003.

tization is a telling example of the hindered accumulation process in Brazil, commanded by the elite and largely supported by foreign capital. If some development of the productive forces is required to maintain a minimum level of domestic accumulation, one of the means to achieve it is to extend infrastructure supply to the low-income population, usually a couple of decades after this utility had become accessible to all in the developed countries. Thus, a few years after privatization, fixed telephone lines reached the low-income peripheral areas at a very low price, but at much higher rates. The enormous increase in rates not only contributed to the rise of family expenditure on public services but also to increasing default rates in the payment of bills.[5]

At the same time, a drastic improvement in digital networks linking the largest Brazilian cities, especially São Paulo, to other international metropolises through satellites and optic fiber connections was implemented (Schiffer 2002). This guarantees the country—and specifically the elite—integration into the global world economy as well as favorable conditions for the headquarters of foreign multinational companies, which in the 1990s rapidly increased their share in the ownership of domestic firms to settle down in São Paulo.

In short, the Brazilian legal framework reflects the characteristics of the elite society that stands behind it. On the one hand, this framework is constantly being improved—always in the name of the collective interest—with new social controls, participatory processes, and stricter public regulation of the provision of public services. On the other hand, the same laws simultaneously create conditions enabling powerful pressure groups to pursue their interests and successfully achieve their goals.

The Fragmentation of Urban Policy and the Rise of Social Organizations

The 2001 Estatuto da Cidade (a federal law on the Statute of the City)[6] gave municipal governments general jurisdiction over urban land property rights, land use, and the enforcement of building regulations. In its general guidelines the law establishes that "the cooperation between public administration, the private sector, and other sectors of society in the urbanization process must aim at the provision of services in the public social interest" (article 2°-III).

Although the law leaves most details unregulated—leaving this task to the municipal *planos diretores* (master plans)—two sections of the Statute of the City deal specifically with possible exceptions to building restrictions. The first (section IX) enables municipal administrations to sell burden rights, which in practice means allowing higher building densities in an urban area than as prescribed in a zoning law, in exchange for a supplementary payment or other compensation by the beneficiary. This implies that the municipality can overrule the federal general urban laws with respect to questions such as zoning regulations. The second (section X) allows for *operações urbanas consorciadas* (urban operations in consortium), which is a form of urban intervention based on consortia between public bodies and private enterprises. This can work as a loophole allowing an interest group to legitimize actions in the name of the public interest and even tap public funds, even if this means action in fact contrary to concerns such as the overall urban structure or environmental degradation.

Another form of nongovernmental association fit to enter into a partnership with public bodies was opened up by the Federal Law 9637/98,[7] which created and regulated the entity "social organizations." The stated aim of the law was to "create a juridical instrument to allow the transference to nonprofit private corporate bodies certain activities that have been performed by the public sector . . . without the submission to the Concession Law" (Azevedo 1999, 72). Social organizations are restricted to a number of social activities, usually belonging in what is known as the third sector—namely, education, scientific research, technological development, protection and conservation of the environment, culture, and health. Under the rules established in each individual contract, public management can transfer to a legally constituted social organization public revenues, as well as public assets, in the name of ensuring the satisfactory performance of the program contracted.

Under the current law, NGOs are characterized as nonprofit private organizations. Although their legal organization can follow one of two possible institutional formats, social organizations or foundations, according to the Brazilian Association of NGOs (ABONG), only around 5% take the latter form. The main actors and focus of NGOs have changed since the mid-1960s, when pioneer NGOs were linked to Christian churches and aimed at helping low-income groups attain access to education, promote neighborhood social movements, and realize trade-union demands. Currently there is a great diversity in their objectives and participants, though the primary activity is consulting (more than 40% of the ABONG associates), followed by popular education and citizenship education (around

14% each). About 75% of their funding comes from abroad, through non-governmental international cooperation agencies (Landim 1996).

Although there are many NGOs and social organizations earnestly working in poor communities on educational programs, environmental issues, urban conservation, and other relevant issues, the lack of an effective public control over their activities made possible the emergence of organizations that use the law merely to cover profitable private activities, oriented toward individual rather than to collective interests. This, however, is not a specifically Brazilian problem, as pointed out in a recent newspaper article quoting the French researcher Guy Sorman: "Some NGOs use fake scientific foundations to terrorize naive persons, presenting overestimated environmental dangers just to obtain grants and donations, mainly from multinational corporations."[8]

The number of social organizations in Brazil grew during the nineties.[9] Social organizations have an impressive share in a range of social activities, from day nursery for poor children to technical courses or first-aid health care assistance, among others. Most of these services are indeed poorly rendered by public administration, but the NGOs just scratch the surface of the issues they address, such is the scale of scarcity involved. Here we again encounter one of the constant features of Brazilian society: the level of reproduction of the labor force is kept to a minimum and very little public action is devoted to mitigating scarcity and the poor quality of public-service provision to low-income groups.

Around 40% of the partnerships between civil organizations and public bodies were established at the municipal level (Landim 1996). This reflects the general assumption that municipalities are most able to deal with social assistance programs due to their proximity and knowledge of local problems as well as facility in engaging in, and overseeing, partnership programs. Marques (1999) reckons that the basis of this assumption is an implicit misconception, which associates decentralization of social programs with democratization, for the sole reason that those programs usually imply some popular participation in decision-making processes. Effective social control of the provision of public services is, however, far from being achieved, and there is no adequate program of social participation that would take into account the extreme inequality in formal education and political influence of the diverse income groups, or the disparities in size and revenue of the municipalities.

Marques also pointed out the risks associated with the fragmentation of social programs due to their "municipalization." He stressed that "to allow the consolidation of several Brazils through the atomization of social programs can be an additional factor in destroying the nation. This is because, in spite of all the problems associated with centralization, there is no doubt that the process of construction of the Brazilian social protection was, simultaneously, a process that allowed the unification, under the right means, of the labor force of the whole country" (Marques 1999, 109).

In short, the fragmentation of public policies during the 1990s, from the provision of social services to urban infrastructure and development, is nothing other than a new means of reproducing the process of hindered development. This time, it is based on the dispersion and fragmentation of social forces within the great urban agglomeration, which undermines their capacity to organize and mount an effective challenge to the continued reproduction of the status quo. The guardian of the status quo is the elite, most of which is based in São Paulo, the economic heart of the country.

Changes within the São Paulo Power Structures

The São Paulo Metropolitan Region was formally instituted in 1973 (along with eight others throughout Brazil) and was composed of thirty-eight municipalities (now thirty-nine), but it was never endowed with political and economic power, and it always fitted rather awkwardly into the three-level federal administrative structure of the country. Even so, comprehensive metropolitan plans were sponsored from time to time by the Metropolitan Planning Enterprise, forming part of the São Paulo state administrative structure. Through the 1970s and most of the 1980s, specific urban plans were also developed for the main municipalities of the region in isolation. Basic infrastructure items, such as water, sewerage, electricity, and telecommunications, along with such social services as education and health, were provided by public institutions and enterprises operating in most cases at state level and at varying levels of coverage and quality of service. This rather precarious planning process lasted until the late 1980s, when the plans in practice were disqualified for good by the new constitutional entity status of the municipalities referred to earlier.

In the absence of a metropolitan governing body or legislation, and although there are a few projects based on a consortium of municipalities, focusing on the São Paulo Metropolitan Region in terms of decision-making processes and partnership projects would require, in fact, assessing thirty-nine separate municipalities. Thus the assessment of the currently existing formal and informal power structures that follows is centered on the municipality of São Paulo, which concentrates some 60% of the population and a yet greater share of the economic power of the metropolitan region.

Since the early 1990s the main changes in the formal structure of São Paulo have been related to the adaptation of local legislation to higher-ranked legal norms, particularly to the rights and duties enshrined by the Constitution of 1988 and recently also to the guidelines of the Estatuto da Cidade (Statute of the City) of 2001. Among the most relevant changes regarding the introduction of new approaches and actors into urban decision-making processes are the São Paulo *Strategic Master Plan*, the administrative decentralization into thirty-one subprefectures, and the legal instrument of "urban operations."

Besides the formally enacted juridical instruments, the urban decision-making process also has been influenced by emerging informal power structures, namely, by civil-society groups—a result of the effective political (economic) structure. The defense of the hegemony of the elite is thereby guaranteed through a variety of pressure groups. This causes correspondent reactions of some other civil groups trying to mitigate the perverse social effects of the economic model imposed.

The changes in the power structures in São Paulo also experienced the usual discontinuities resulting from the alternation of political parties in charge of the municipal government. The late 1980s saw the election of the first mayor from the Workers Party, or PT (Luiza Erundina, 1988–92). In the next two elections, two mayors belonging to the conservative Partido Popular Brasileiro, or PPB (Paulo Maluf, 1993–96, and Celso Pitta, 1997–2000), were voted into office. The PT reassumed municipal government in 2001 with Marta Suplicy, but in 2004 the conservatives came back into power.[10] The main difference between left- and right-wing governments is that the PT traditionally has a strong social orientation in its urban policy making, particularly with respect to the legalization and urbanization of *favelas* and the promotion of diversified social housing projects and financing lines. In contrast, the PPB has favored market-oriented public projects, such as urban highways and slum clearance, especially in higher-income areas. Although the general focus and rhetoric of these two parties point in very different directions, the difference in the end result of their terms in office is frequently overestimated. In practice, the policies of both had to fit into the neoliberal framework prevalent in the last decade of the twentieth century, which doomed to failure any attempt at effectively increasing the social welfare of the majority of the municipal population.

The São Paulo Master Plan

The urban plan for São Paulo city, *Plano Diretor Estratégico* (*Strategic Master Plan*), was approved by the city council in 2001. It introduced two important new legal procedures into the municipal decision-making process, namely participatory budgeting and increased autonomy of decentralized subprefectures. The municipal budget forecast was formatted to allow participation of the community or their civil representatives in the decisions over public investment priorities. Administrative decentralization was implemented after a municipal law of 2002 split the city management into thirty-one subprefectures, each ruled by a regional mayor and with a greater degree of autonomy than the previous regional administrations, enabling it to define its own master plan with local project proposals and investment priorities. One of the tasks of the subprefectures is precisely to set up their local plans (with some experimentation in participatory planning and budgeting), while they also take charge of the running of schools, first-aid stations, and public-space maintenance.

The objectives of the *Master Plan* underwent significant changes in the nineties, as already mentioned. In the earlier conception, the plans should "propose short-, medium-, and long-term measures and actions, approved by law, according to a prospective diagnosis for the future socioeconomic and spatial organization of land use, and of infrastructure networks development" (Villaça 1999, 238).

This concept is similarly expressed in the 1988 Constitution, although it has been frequently observed that it was never really put into practice in Brazilian urban planning, which has produced more discourse than project proposals, due to the behavior of the elite, "in this case represented by the real-estate pressure groups, which ignore the *Master Plan* because they can represent an opportunity for discussing the 'urban problems,' whereas they prefer to ignore it . . . supporting nothing but general principles, guidelines, or policies, and definitely nothing that could be self-applied" (Villaça 1999, 240–41).

These are precisely the principles and objectives that, now more explicitly, form the basis of the so-called strategic plans in general, and the current strategic master plan of São Paulo is no exception. The latter, in accordance with the national trend, abandoned even sectoral planning and the metropolitan scope, and replaced it with fragmented municipal (and, in this case, even submunicipal) plans in the spirit of strategic planning, isolated initiatives taking the form of urban operations, and public-private partnerships, which address mainly particular issues within the urban agglomeration raised by narrowly based pressure groups expressing private interests (such as downtown reclaiming, Operation Água Espraiada, Faria Lima—big new avenues in place of old streets, rivulets or *favelas*—neighborhood preservation and enclosure, for a few examples).

The authority of a subprefecture is confined to activities that fall within its geographical limits. This legal determination can generate considerable divergence of policies and actions within the municipality, contrary not only to municipal but also to metropolitan integration, which has been for so long experimented with. The fragmentation of the decision-making process is strongly felt when each subprefecture proposes and coordinates its own master plan (under the general guidelines of the municipal *Master Plan*) and the related participatory procedures. Indeed, recent (at the time of writing still ongoing) experience of drawing up such plans has yielded extremely uneven results in terms of diagnosis, level of detail, investment propositions, social participation, and prospects for each area.

Yet another aspect of administrative decentralization is the structural weakening of the collective as opposed to private interests. The major arena for disputes over urban issues is the city council. The creation of the subadministrations came to introduce a new level in those disputes. Considering the reduced autonomy of subadministrations and the comparatively greater capacity of organized pressure groups to participate and influence the design of plans, the resulting shift of balance is, once again, very much to the advantage of the more powerful and organized interest groups.

"Urban Operations"

Urban operation projects, included in the Statute of the City of 2001, already had been developed in São Paulo for more than a decade, in accordance with previous municipal rules. The four projects so far implemented, named after the areas involved, are Faria Lima, Água Branca, Águas Espraiadas, and Centro (the historical center).

According to Section X of the Statute of the City, any municipality can enact a specific law circumscribing an area to be subject of an urban operation in accordance with its master plan. This legal instrument, formally termed "urban operations in consortium" is defined as "the joint actions and measures under the coordination of the municipality, with the participation of the landowners, inhabitants, users, and private investors, with the aim at achieving within a [delimited] area structural urban transformations, social improvements and the environmental valorization" (article 32 &1).

In view of those goals the municipality can in each urban operation "exceptionally" overrule its own urban legislation. For instance, it can allow higher construction density, exceptions to established land use restrictions, or regularize formerly illegal buildings or allotments. The funding of an urban operation is a combination of public finance complemented with private funds obtained by selling certificates of burden rights to build above established density limits, named Cepacs (Certificates of Additional Building Potential). As a rather weak compensation for the collective interests being overlooked, if not squarely violated by the operations, the amount collected from Cepacs is remarked for reinvestment in local infrastructure to help upgrade the area subject to the urban operation.

The current São Paulo *Strategic Master Plan* proposes nine new urban operations, in the declared purpose of creating public space and dealing with the main local problems, such as demand for public transport, infrastructure, or social housing.

Extensive academic research and numerous surveys have been conducted to assess the earlier urban operations, particularly Faria Lima and Águas Espraiadas.[11] All of them conclude, unsurprisingly, that those areas went through a manifold price increase and real-estate valorization after public improvements in local infrastructure and private investment in higher-standard buildings, resulting, on the whole, in local gentrification.

Actions of Civil Society Groups

The informal power structures in São Paulo, composed of organized civil society groups, as pointed out earlier, are rooted in the behavior of the elite, which systematically prevents the adequate design of social and urban policies aimed at the collective interests and works to open a space for its own maneuvering. In other words, members of organized civil society who do not feel themselves represented by government bodies in specific matters are allowed to act on their own initiative. The result is the emergence of particular pressure groups, such as noninstitutionalized philanthropy, social movements, or even individual efforts toward a less unequal society, but also of middle- and higher-income groups. The latter form their informal organizations simply to promote their own interests, such as neighborhood associations that want to preserve or to improve their neighborhoods, or yet to protect themselves against violence, which has been increasing *pari passu* with the spread of neoliberal policies since the 1990s.

The amplitude of the scope and the diversity of partnerships in São Paulo is boundless, but a few emblematic examples may illustrate them. In the first group, there are widespread activities of the Catholic Church, which, in cooperation with local people in very poor or violent neighborhoods, led to the creation of community centers in the periphery of São Paulo. They then demand from the municipality bodies all sort of local improvements, such as child care and schooling, technical courses, and youth or elderly assistance. A second example refers to the biggest São Paulo *favela*, Heliópolis, where more than 80,000 people live. It has received aid from volunteers working with organized local groups to improve the area in a variety of ways, such as implementation of sport grounds, street lighting, and even development of a child chorus. The municipality contributes with the pavement of some streets and provision of a police station.

In the second group, a few recent examples of informal actions, aimed at influencing the urban decision-making process in order to improve the local environment in higher-income districts, include:

- To promote facade renewal of historical buildings located downtown, help is provided by university students and small shopowners, who stand under the supervision of the municipality and a group linked to the Programa Ação Local (Local Action Program). This initiative of the Associação Viva o Centro (an NGO) was created in 1997, aimed at organizing the downtown community as "caretakers" of the historical center, mobilizing the neighborhood, and denouncing any irregularities, such as illegal commerce or land use.
- Parks and traffic improvements and land use control in a middle-income area in the southwestern region of the city were performed by a neighborhood association, named Sajape (Sociedade Amigos dos Jardins Petrópolis e dos Estados). The main objectives were to implement green-area projects and appeal to the formal institutions for an improvement of the living conditions of a neighborhood of about 6,500 people.
- Inhabitants living in one of the most wealthy areas of São Paulo suc-

cessfully protested against the official approval of a luxurious high-rise building above the legally allowed maximum height.
- Upper-middle-class groups have increased their private security all over the city, with the use of security equipment, such as cameras, local telephone network, and even private police of a size comparable to the municipal and São Paulo state police forces, when taken together.

Regarding environmental protection or conservation of historical assets, some social organizations or NGOs have acted as powerful pressure groups to induce the public sector to deal with these issues. The funding of restoration of historical buildings and monuments comes mainly from private companies, but always in association with the public administration. Some of the recent examples in São Paulo are the rehabilitation of the Estação da Luz railway station, the conversion of another railway station into a concert hall, the Sala São Paulo, and several former bank headquarters converted to cultural exhibition centers, all of them situated in the downtown area.

Among the examples of projects for urban renewal, powerful social organizations, such as Associação Viva o Centro and Centro Vivo, are active in trying to revitalize the historical center of São Paulo within an urban operation proposal (Operação Urbana Centro).[12] The former concentrates on multinational banks and large Brazilian corporations, while the latter promotes popular movements to restore dwellings. Two other associations, namely, Associação Paulista Viva and Movimento Colméia, have the purpose of improving the two main secondary centers of São Paulo, at the Paulista Avenue and Nova Faria Lima Avenue. The latter had already been the object of the urban operation Faria Lima. Recently a group of executives formed the Movimento Colméia and proposed to the municipality a new form of partnership. This consists in a financial contribution to a proposed improvement of the area by planting trees in the central area of the Faria Lima Avenue and by constructing a road link to the Berrini Avenue, a major location for the headquarters of large Brazilian and foreign companies. This partnership is quite unique since part of the works will be within the former area of the Faria Lima urban operation, which means that Cepacs can be sold by the municipality to raise funds toward the required public investment, while part of the investment and of the land required by the renovation project will be donated by members of the Movimento Colméia.

Besides private capital and social organizations, multilateral development banks are a third group of relevant partners in the decision-making process related to the spatial organization of São Paulo—but also of many other Latin American cities as well. In fact, the major funding agency for urban conservation projects in Brazil is the Inter-American Development Bank (IADB). The operational framework of this bank, in theory, covers all aspects related to social and economic development. Since 1995 the IADB has been applying an institutional resolution that allows up to 5% of its capital to be earmarked for direct financing to the private sector, without demanding the previously required governmental guarantees (IADB 2001). At the same time, the IADB not only extended the customary credit line for public works in infrastructure, but also introduced loan contracts for historical center conservation projects that can be taken on simultaneously by the public and private sector. Recently the São Paulo municipality signed a 300 million USD funding agreement with IADB to revitalize the historical center, which also involves private enterprises and social organizations.

Conclusions

Since the 1990s, formal partnerships between the public sector and private capital, social organizations, and NGOs have been encouraged in Brazilian law and planning practice, in accordance with general neoliberal economic and social policies. Such partnerships are justified as being part of a more participatory, or more efficient, approach to the achievement of collective interest. Lack of public funds is also invoked to promote new forms of city management, as in the case of São Paulo, that experimented with a variety of new public-private partnerships[13] in the name of chronically tight budgets and scarce resources to design, implement, and manage urban development.

In fact, the introduction of these new partners in decision-making processes does not represent a real shift in the Brazilian socioeconomic process. It is, rather, a new attempt to legitimize an existing process of the elite society, whereby the mediation of the interests of the dominant class through the figure of public interest, as administered by a neutral bureaucracy, has always been seriously impaired by the structural—and deliberate—weakness of the state apparatus and the constant direct interference in its workings by specific pressure groups and individual members of the elite. In this light, the new planning procedures appear merely as new forms for old processes.

The same can be said also of urban planning and administration regarding their recent transformations. The current shift in the share of resources and responsibilities among the three governmental spheres shows a shying away from development plans in favor of strategic planning within municipal limits, or fragmented even further to within submunicipal boundaries, as in the case of São Paulo where in the early 2000s the municipality was subdivided into thirty-odd subprefectures. Similarly, most of the federal legislation concerning urban policies is sent to the local administrations to be filled in with specific detail. The justification for this procedure is the idea that local administrations are more adequate to deal with and to legislate about their own affairs. This is only a partial truth, however, for although it is true that the municipal, or even submunicipal, administration should be able to handle local development constraints more easily than, say, the federal level, it is also true that decentralization goes frequently into an ideological discourse merely as an excuse for the withdrawal of the various levels of government addressing social and urban problems.

The question remains whether the greater participation of nongovernmental actors (civil society groups, social organizations, neighborhood associations, NGOs, etc.) in the power structures dealing with urban management or the provision of social services has resulted in any improvement for a substantial part of the population. There is no evidence whatsoever to allow an affirmative answer to this question, although it is also true that most new forms of social organization and public-private agreements so far have had so short a life and have been so specific in scope that any attempts at assessing their overall outcome is seriously impaired. This is true especially in light of the extremely deep-rooted inequalities of Brazilian society, which require large-scale—and long-term—improvements.

The question that ultimately remains, therefore, is whether a broader participatory process with the inclusion of new actors into decision making is a mechanism that will help to overcome the disproportionate power of elite interest groups and reorient the domestic accumulation to contribute to an unrestrained process. Or, alternatively, can the hindrances of Brazilian development be removed by the very same elite that had imposed it for such a long period? For this last question to be answered in the affirmative, the elite would need at last to realize that hindered accumulation is not sustainable any longer, for this would imply lowering further the already very low subsistence level of the labor force, the consequences of which can be readily observed in everyday urban life and in unemployment numbers, violence rates, and the proportion of the population living in slums and *favelas*. And, certainly, such social outcomes will not be fended off with private security forces, armored cars, or towering walls.

Notes

1. See Deák 1994 for a critical review of the acceptance of globalization of the economy as a new stage of the capitalist accumulation, also referred to briefly in Deák and Schiffer in this volume.

2. For a further assessment of the process of hindered accumulation and the behavior of the Brazilian elite society, see Deák 1988 and Fernandes 1973. Schiffer 1992 focused on the impact of this process on the Brazilian spatial organization.

3. Federal Law 8.031/90, reformulated by the Law 9.491/97, aimed at allowing private capital to own the former state companies, the major Brazilian capital goods industries, such as metallurgy and iron industries.

4. Federal Law 8.987/95, supplemented by Laws 9.074/95 and 9.648/98.

5. Estado de São Paulo, 24 July 2003.

6. The Federal Law 10.257/01 Estatuto da Cidade is assessed by Souza 2005.

7. The Federal Law 9.637/98 authorizes the federated states and municipalities to create their own regulation as far as they do not explicitly contradict its general terms.

8. Folha de São Paulo 2002, 2.

9. Although there are no official statistics, the number of all nonprofit organizations in Brazil in 2000 is estimated to be more than 250,000 throughout the country, based on several federal registers, according to an ABONG e-mail answer to this question.

10. For an early assessment of the prospects opened up by Marta Suplicy's election, see Deák 2001.

11. For the first case, see Campos-Pereira 2002 and Bella 1998, and for the second, see Fix 2001.

12. Note that this project—or operation—is concerned with local intervention only, as though the dynamism or revitalization of the center would not depend crucially on improving its accessibility to the overall urban structure, as discussed briefly in Deák and Schiffer in this volume.

13. The final form and details of the federal law that will regulate public-private partnerships (PPPs), including regulation for large-scale projects such as power plants, railways, roads, and seaports, is still being debated in Congress, so they cannot be assessed yet.

References

Azevedo, E. de A. 1999. Parcerias no serviço Público Municipal. In Fundação Prefeito Faria Lima-Cepam, *O Município no século XXI: cenários e perspectivas*, 65–76. São Paulo.
Batista, P. N., Jr. 1997. Mitos da "globalização." Coleção Documentos. Série Assuntos Internacionais 52. São Paulo: Instituto de Estudos Avançados da Universidade de São Paulo.
Bella, L. M. 1998. Operações urbanas em São Paulo. Estudo de caso Faria Lima-Berrini. Master's thesis, Faculdade de Arquitetura e Urbanismo da Universidade Mackenzie, São Paulo.
Campos-Pereira, R. C. R. 2002. A operação urbana Faria Lima: estudo de um mecanismo de parceria entre Estado e capital na cidade de São Paulo nos anos 90. Master's thesis, Faculdade de Arquitetura e Urbanismo da Universidade de São Paulo.
Deák, C. 1988. The Crisis of Hindered Accumulation in Brazil. BISS 10. Bartlett International Summer School on the Production of the Built Environment, Cidade do México, *Proceedings BISS 10*, 253–59. London, 1989.
———. 1994. Globalisation or Global Crisis? Paper presented at the XIII World Congress of Sociology, Bielefeld, International Sociological Association. www.usp.br/fau/docentes/depprojeto/c_deak/CD/3publ/94glob-cr (accessed 10 October 2003).
———. 2001. The Partido dos Trabalhadores in São Paulo. *Soundings* 18: 41–52.
Dupas, G. Economia global exclusão social: pobreza, emprego. Estado e o futuro do capitalismo. 2nd ed. São Paulo: Paz e Terra.
———. 2003. Data Presented on a Speech for the Ipiranga Corporation. São Paulo. Mimeo.
Estado de São Paulo (ESP). 2003. *Governo quer reajuste de até 17,24% na telefonia*. 24 July.
Fernandes, F. 1973. *Capitalismo dependente e classes sociais na América Latina*. Rio de Janeiro: Zahar.
Fix, M. 2001. *Parceiros da exclusão: duas histórias da construção de uma "nova cidade" em São Paulo: Faria Lima e Água Espraiada*. São Paulo: Boitempo.
Folha de São Paulo. 2002. *O perigo da proliferação indiscriminada*. 21 July.
Inter-American Development Bank (IADB). 2001. About IADB. www.iadb.org/exr/english/ABOUTIDB/about_idb.htm (accessed 8 February 2004).
Landim, L. 1996. *Notas para um perfil das ONGs*. São Paulo: ABONG. www.abong.org.br/novosite/biblioteca (accessed 18 June 2006).
Marques, R. M. 1999. O lugar do município em tempos de globalização e questionamento dos sistemas de proteção centralizados. In Fundação Prefeito Faria Lima-Cepam, *O Município no século XXI: cenários e perspectivas*, 105–10. São Paulo.
Schiffer, S. 1992. A territorialidade revisitada. Brasil pós II PND. Associate Pro-

fessor Thesis, Faculdade de Arquitetura e Urbanismo da Universidade de São Paulo.

———. 2002. São Paulo: Articulating a Cross-Border Region. In S. Sassen (ed.), *Global Networks, Linked Cities*, 209–36. London: Routledge.

Souza, C. 2005. Tensions between Global Demands and Local Needs: Urban Governance in São Paulo. In K. Segbers, S. Raiser, and K. Volkmann (eds.), *Public Problems—Private Solutions? Globalizing Cities in the South*, 363–78. Aldershot: Ashgate.

Villaça, F. 1999. Dilemas do Plano Diretor. In Fundação Prefeito Faria Lima-Cepam, *O Município no século XXI: cenários e perspectivas*, 237–47. São Paulo.

World Bank. 2003. *Brazil at a Glance*. http://www.worldbank.org (accessed 10 April 2004).

From "State-Owned" to "City Inc."
The Case of Shanghai
Fulong Wu

The global city region is the best place to observe how Castells's (1996) "spaces of flows" are being "reterritorialised" into local politics (Brenner 1999). For Scott (2001) global city regions represent a new economic and political order. Economically, the global city regions see new concentrations of post-Fordist industries. This is because these city regions "are invariably important centers of resourcefulness and invention for all sectors of production, but especially for post-Fordist industries where the basic conditions leading to these outcomes are so abundantly concentrated" (Scott 2001, 820–21). Politically, the neoliberal governmentality is becoming dominant and traditional citizenship is "vigorously and increasingly in question" (Scott 2001, 821). Globalization has introduced new actors into local politics. It has also transformed existing actors in the city. In the case of European cities, business interests are being restructured at this scale along with the extension and the deepening of market logics (LeGales 2002). Organized interests are becoming more territorialized: for example, chambers of commerce and industry, as powerful local actors, have successfully invoked the principle of economic competition as the organizing principle for political actors. The dominance of powerful business leaders is a major feature of entrepreneurial urban politics (Peck and Tickell 1995).

Saskia Sassen views this changing governance as a process of "making claims on the city" (UNCHS 2001): global capital has made claims on nation-states, and in consequence the changing power relationship often "contributes to strengthen the advantages of certain types of economic actors and to weaken those of others" (UNCHS 2001, 75; Sassen 1996). While the American version of an entrepreneurial city shows a strong role of chambers of commerce and industry and business elites, the European model suggests greater involvement of the local government and its strategic coalition with business in reorientated local politics. The making of new claims on the city does not always mean the dominance of multinationals and the weakening of local politics. Instead, the transformation of power structures could be more driven by proactive local governance as an institutional response to the challenge brought about by economic globalization. It must be reminded that the state is not necessarily a static entity. Rather, it can actively transform itself into a new structure, often through localization and territorialization, and thus survive or even consolidate its presence.

China, as a previous state socialist country, represents a totally different context. Globalization, decentralization, and marketization are major processes that capture profound social and economic changes since the market reform initiated in 1979 (Logan 2002). The remaking of global city regions has been seen in several megalopolises such as the Hong Kong–Shenzhen–Guangzhou and the rest of the Pearl River Delta, Shanghai-Nanjing-Hangzhou and the lower Yangtze River Delta, and Beijing-Tianjin-Tangshan and the cities along the Bohai Bay. The emergence of global city regions indicates the spatial reorganization of the Chinese economy and changing governance in the transition toward a more market-oriented economy and greater integration with the global economy. In the postreform period, the Chinese city is witnessing the formation of territorially based entrepreneurialism, which is associated with the reglobalization strategy, that is, using globalization as an opportunity to transform the role of the state and, in turn, to legitimize its presence in the economic sphere (Wu 2003b). In this process, the spatiality of the globalizing city becomes the important medium and vehicle to achieve the aspiration of the state. Overall, on the surface, Shanghai departs significantly from the classical neoliberal project, which emphasizes the triumph of the market and minimization of state intervention. However, in essence, the case of Shanghai only suggests some variation of this worldwide spread of neoliberal governance under globalization (Tickell and Peck 2003), because we have to situate the state in the new structure of power so as to understand the novelty of state functionality.

This essay will begin an investigation of changing power structures—both formal and informal arrangements—in Shanghai since the early 1990s. The changing power relationships are understood through the changing strategy of accumulation, which in turn is a local response to globalization and the global city in the making. Rather than returning to the much-heated debate on globalization and the waning nation-state, I attempt to understand how the national state is rescaled and territorialized into the global city region and how the local state is reconfigured to suit the changes in governance. It is argued that although globalization imposes a similar threat and imperative to all cities, the local response is historically and geographically contextualized. The four case cities (Johannesburg, São Paulo, Mumbai, and Shanghai) in this project all belong to the periphery and hence can be seen as the frontier of globalization. They are globalizing cities in developing countries. Their responses vary according to the interaction between historical legacies and new visions of change.

The Shanghai case suggests that situated in this periphery of globalization, the state's capacity to take the lead in the building of both physical and institutional environments is critical in the formation of the global city region. While globalization is the critical factor in triggering off a series of changes in power structures, the context of "postsocialism" and hence of strong state intervention is also a codeterminant in the trajectory of urban changes in the Chinese case. Changes in the global periphery are now being incorporated in a bigger picture of unfolding neoliberalization in the contemporary world, but the exact process that occurs at locales at the periphery varies (see other contributions in this volume). In the case of Shanghai, we see active decentralization of administrative and fiscal duties and continuing utilization of state policy instruments to enforce economic restructuring in Shanghai (Wu 2002; 2003b).

Rescaling the State and Changing Formal Power Structures

The City as New Spatiality of Governance

The power structure under the former socialist regime was characterized by its vertical hierarchy, which formed the basis of the command economy. This structure was dominated by a system of state work units, tied up vertically with government departments (Lieberthal 1995). This structure enabled the state to realize the state-led industrialization necessitated by the Cold War confrontation. Such a strategy determined the pivotal role of the central government and dominant economic planning as the mechanism of resource allocation. Under this centralized power structure, the key actors were the central government and its agencies and various "state production units" (known also as "state work units"). The effective concentration of resources in the system of state production units provided a basis for implementing economic planning.

Moreover, the Chinese Communist Party (CCP) was integrated within the government and the work units. The organization of the city, representing the ideal of industrialized society, was separated from that of rural areas. This was effectively implemented through compulsory household registration (Solinger 1999), similar to the internal passport of the former Soviet Union (Andrusz 1996). The city was a totalized society where the division between the state and society was not clear-cut, and with the former penetrating into the latter. The party-state, household registration, and state work units were the three pillars of socialist urban governance (Wu 2002). Such a power structure implied a weak territorially based coordination mechanism. Hence, the concept of the city itself was different from that under capitalist regimes: the latter organizes collective consumption under the Keynesian welfare state (Castells 1983). In essence, the socialist city stood for no more than a collection of production sites.

The power structure has changed since the adoption of economic reform and open-door policies in China. The market-oriented reform is characterized by reengineering power relationships, first, between the central and local states and, second, between the public and private sectors. First, the change in fiscal arrangement has led to greater autonomy of local governments. Economic decentralization is said to be the recipe for fast growth of the Chinese economy (Chung 1999), and the rearrangement of central-local relations has been widely documented (Kwok et al. 1990; Naughton 1995; Wong, Heady, and Woo 1995).

Under the centralized socialist regime, Shanghai made a substantial contribution to national industrialization and fiscal balance. In the 1970s Shanghai's industrial output value accounted for one-seventh of the national total, and its fiscal revenue was about one-fourth to one-sixth of the national total. Because of this high-weighted status in national economies, economic reform in Shanghai was cautiously delayed until 1990 when the central government announced the development of the Pudong New Area, a massive underdeveloped area across the Huangpu River.

Second, the relationship between the public and private sectors changed. With the reform of state-owned enterprises, production units are allowed to retain their surplus profit and have been separated from government departments. Although there was no large-scale privatization in China, the reform of property ownership into shareholding led to the decline of state ownership. Foreign invested firms and domestic private enterprises today occupy an increasingly larger share in the economy. The private sector is particularly active in the service sector such as restaurants and catering and small businesses and production.

Fiscal Decentralization

Decentralization of the fiscal system went through three stages in Shanghai (J. Chen 1999). During the first, from 1978 to 1984, expenditure was linked to revenue and the total proportion of revenue submission to the central government was revised on a yearly basis. During the second, from 1985 to 1993, the central government relaxed control over local expenditure and the baseline of expenditure was raised from 2 to 3.5 billion yuan. Meanwhile, revenue submission was fixed to 10.5 billion yuan in 1988, and Shanghai was allowed to use its surplus revenue. During the third stage, from 1994 onward, the tax-sharing system was operated and the Shanghai municipal government had an independent tax base and autonomous expenditure. The fiscal reform created progressive institutional innovations through which local government agencies have been mobilized. Similar to other places in China, local governments are now becoming ambitious actors who are subject to harder budget constraints. Consequently, their behavior is transformed into that of "industrial firms" (Walder 1995). The operation mechanism is very different from the one characterized by the "soft budget" under state socialism (Kornai 1992). What is different is Shanghai's strategic importance as China's "dragonhead" and gateway to connect to the global economy. It has thus regained its favorable position in fiscal deals with the central government.

Behind the increase in local revenue and expenditure is the strong determination of the central government to create an international Chinese economic, finance, and trade center in the Yangtze River Delta. This is known as the "dragonhead" strategy. The expansion of local autonomy can be seen as the willingness of the central government to reformulate its economic strategy rather than as the result of hard negotiations by local government to gain more freedom in economic decision making. For example, an often neglected fact is that some working teams composed of senior officials were sent by the central government to Shanghai to help it prepare a better deal (Yang and Han 1999). The increasing presence of Shanghai officials in the central government in the 1990s (e.g., Jiang Zemin, Zhu Rongji, Wu Bangguo) further strengthened the voice of Shanghai in its request for more progressive arrangements.

Corresponding to fiscal decentralization, Shanghai has launched a series of institutional reforms to further mobilize lower-level agents. The urban districts, formerly with limited functions, gained a whole array of administrative powers, including planning, public works maintenance, the approval of local foreign trade deals, and commercial administration. Since the mid-1990s Shanghai has begun to adopt a new structure of local government, namely "two levels of government and three tiers of management." The two levels of government refer to the municipal and district governments, and three tiers of management refer to municipal, district, and subdistrict (or street office) management. The street office is not a level of government, but rather the agency of district government. The rise of the private sector, the inflow of rural migrants, and increasingly mobile individuals require the establishment of governance beyond the formal work-unit system. In order to manage those who are not formally affiliated to a state work unit, the street office has been given a new role of comprehensive management. This level of government has thus become an active participant in governance and has begun to manage its own economic base by attracting and registering enterprises. The result of economic decentralization is that multiple actors have been created at the levels of local government.

In addition, the decentralization of power from the central government to the municipal, district, and finally street office has forged the formation of horizontal linkages through which the urban level is "substantialized." Accordingly, the relationship between the state and society is experiencing profound changes. To be economically competitive, the government has realized the need to reduce the burden of comprehensive welfare provision to state-owned enterprises. The reform of social service in essence is the stripping of services attached to workplaces and making them operable in the market and the whole city, instead of just in individual work units. This economic incentive is coupled by the necessity brought about by social problems such as rising unemployment rates and "floating" rural migrants, for which the traditional omnipotent state does not have a control mechanism. In order to cope with these practical needs, Shanghai is among the first few cities that are experimenting with "community construction" (*shequ jianshe*).

Community Construction

Community construction, as defined in the government policy, is a discursive strategy to consolidate the state's penetration into the grass-roots level and to maintain a governable urban society in order to support the strategy of global city remaking. In practice, this policy emphasizes a shift of many functionalities previously taken by the state work units—pension distribution, unemployment support and poverty relief, property management, and organized consumption—to local street-level organizations. While the policy sometimes does promote self-organization of mass and local democracy, in the practice of service privatization, retrenchment of the welfare function, and consumption-oriented urban development, the shift in fact favors those who have purchasing power and thus form the consumer groups, such as the homeowners' association. This policy is in part a response to the impact of globalization, which has exacerbated the mobility of resources and population and economic restructuring and, in turn, created challenges for the state to manage a changing society. It is increasingly impossible to accomplish these functions through the top-down approach. As a result, many responsibilities are transferred to the communities. Three processes are strengthening local-level governance.

First, as mentioned earlier, the role of the street office has been strengthened and in many ways even professionalized. In the old planning era, the agents of communities (i.e., street office) and of neighborhoods (i.e., residents' committee) were peripheral to urban governance—retired people or housewives looked after individual workers or the self-employed without any workplace affiliation. Now, young and qualified social workers are appointed to take charge of the office.

Second, community service centers have been set up to provide property management, community cleaning and sanitation, leisure and recreation, and social welfare services. Up to the end of 1999, Shanghai had 10 district-level community centers, with a staff of 112. At the subdistrict level there were 122 community centers with 3,946 professional workers (SAEB 2000, 490). These service centers are operated with various companies under the principle of "big society and small government." New experiments are now being tried to increase base-level democracy by establishing residents' self-governing bodies. Elected residents' representatives are introduced into a residents' committee (a neighborhood organization, legally defined as "autonomous organizations of mass"). For example, sponsored by the Social Development Bureau of Pudong New Area, the Luoshan community service center has been developed as a nongovernmental organization (NGO) to provide various services to residents.

Third, in the commodity housing estates, when the percentage of private owners exceeds 30%, Shanghai Residential Property Management Regulation requires the establishment of a homeowners' association. The homeowners' association has begun to play an active role in appointing property management companies and thus takes over some responsibilities traditionally shouldered by the government. In some places, however, the homeowners' association comes into conflict with the residents' committee, as the latter is associated with the street office and district government. Especially after the professionalization of the residents' committee, its nature as a mass organization is being transformed. More often than not, the residents' committees become the "legs of local government."

In summary, globalization together with a more market-oriented development approach has forced the state to adopt a more decentralized power structure. This process is not very different from those seen in other parts of the world, although different routes and forms are taken. If there is something unique in the postreform context, the process is actively driven by the state itself. In this sense, it is more a process of reterritorialization of the state itself rather than just reterritorialization of mobile capital.

Making Coalitions with Capital: Informal Power Structure

While the formal structure does not give a prominent status to external investors, in the competition for investment overseas investors have begun to show increasing leverage by forging relationships with local political elites. It is observed that the making of "relationships" (*guanxi*) blends the traditional practices of gift exchange with the new context of entrepreneurialism. For example, Hsing (1998) attributes the success of Taiwanese investors in mainland China to their cultural and linguistic affinity with the local elites. This allows "footloose" capital to be embedded into local politics through informal and often fragile coalitions.

The informality of the relationship between local elites and business actors should not, however, be romanticized, and cultural practices play a role of lubrication rather than determination. In questioning China's *guanxi* capitalism, Castells (2000, 311) argues that the reason why overseas Chinese business networks play such an important role is "not that they and their southern China partners both like steamed cod. It is because China's multiple link to the global economy is local, that is, it is performed through the connection between overseas Chinese business and local and provincial governments in China." This is accompanied with a simultaneous transition in China's local governance toward decentralization, as discussed earlier. Changing central-local politics have now been extensively documented with reference to decentralization of property rights and changing budgetary and fiscal systems (Walder 1995; Oi and Walder 1999). But these changes had been so far mainly attributed to China's economic reform and internal changes in the central and local relationships. Shanghai's case suggests that interplay between globalization and localized networks.

The interplay can be observed from two angles. First, the interplay reflects the change in professional services under globalization—in this case, the prominent role of so-called global intelligence corps (GIC, i.e., elite architectural firms)—in the production of mega-projects (Olds 2001) or the "citadels" of global cities (Marcuse 1997). These GIC firms are solicited by the Shanghai municipal government in its international planning consultation and thus play a key role in Shanghai's global publicity. For example, four GIC firms (Massimiliano Fuksas, Tokyo Ito, Dominique Perrault, and Richard Rogers) individually prepared the conceptual plan for the Lujiazui central financial district.

Second, the interplay is made possible by key politicians who overcome institutional hurdles and build progrowth coalitions on a project-by-project basis. Fu (2002) described in detail the development process of the site in the Lujiazui central financial district, which is used for the Shanghai World Financial Center. This involves very intimate interactions between Japanese property tycoon Minoru Mori and vice mayors and mayor of Shanghai. Recognizing the heavyweight development of the projected world's tallest building, the Shanghai government gave a special concession at a reduced 15% income tax rate, which is normally only for the manufacturing sector. The municipal government swiftly relocated households and work units to the site. When the national tariff-waiver policy began to change in 1995, former premier Zhu Rongji (who was the mayor of Shanghai before being promoted to the central government) gave a personal exemption, allowing Forest Overseas Company Ltd. to continue enjoying the tariff waiver policy (Fu 2002, 118). The changes in the landscape of Lujiazui testify how this "project-based, implicitly progrowth coalition" actively plays its role in urban governance.

The development projects reveal the informal power structure built upon coalitions between the state and capital. The transformed local politics are now more oriented toward undertaking the "central task of economic construction," without "questioning whether such a road leads to capitalism or socialism," as urged by Deng Xiaoping, the architect of China's economic reform.

The Changing Relationship between the Public and Private Sector

Marketization has changed the relationship between the public and private sector. The omnipotent state and state-owned enterprises have retreated from comprehensive welfare provision to households. The market mechanism has been introduced into housing consumption and urban services provision. After the abolition of in-kind work-unit housing, commodity and low-profit economic housing become major housing sources. In services provision such as water, gas, and electricity, service and utility companies have gradually replaced government-funded public works and diminished their monopoly position through increasing user charge. For example, as early as the 1980s, Shanghai adopted an installation fee for gas provision. The initial installation fee amounted to 1,500 yuan plus a compulsory 500 yuan construction bond, which was equivalent to 50% of annual household income by that time (Lu 2002, 20). This innovative practice has greatly eased the capital bottleneck and increased investment in infrastructure. Since the 1990s the user-charge practice has been widely used in bus fares, gas supplies, waste water discharge, and municipal sanitation services. Utility companies have been set up to take over responsibilities of service provision. The Shanghai Urban Construction Investment and Development Company, established in 1992, used a variety of financing mechanisms, such as construction bonds, the stock market, and service concession, to raise capital, and its funds accounted for about 90% of Shanghai's total urban infrastructure revenue in 1996 (Yusuf and Wu 2002, 1230).

Recently, the *entrepreneurial city* (literally translated from Chinese as, the "city of business management") has become a popular term. The concept emphasizes the use of market instruments to manage urban assets—both physical and symbolic—so as to fund urban development. The government can cooperate with the private sector by transferring its physical assets (e.g., land) or institutional assets (e.g., the right of naming and franchising). Private funds are encouraged to purchase and operate public works and services. For example, the Shanghai Urban Construction Investment and Development Company recently sold the operation rights of the Nanjing-Shanghai highway, recovered its original investment, and further invested in new projects.

There is an observable shift from the public to private sector in terms of GDP composition and investment in fixed assets. The state-owned economy has declined from 86.2% in 1978 to 54.4% in 2001, while the nonpublic sector increased from just 1% to 28.6% in the same period. In terms of investment in fixed assets, the percentage of state-owned investment in total decreased from 58.4% in 1995 to 38.1% in 2001, while foreign investment and investment from Hong Kong, Macao, and Taiwan accounted for, respectively, 13.8% and 4.3% in total in 2001. Another major source of investment is from the stock market. In 2001 shareholding contributed 29.1% of total investment in fixed assets. The consequence of the change has been the increasing role of the private sector in urban development.

Multiple Actors in Action

Foreign and Overseas Investors

Since the adoption of an open-door policy, China has received rapidly growing foreign direct investment (FDI). By the mid-1990s China became the largest recipient of FDI. Newly gained World Trade Organization membership injected a strong stimulus for the continuing inflow of foreign investment. Foreign investors, owing to their high mobility, gained bargaining power in their interaction with the local government, as the latter is driven into the intercity competition for external capital. The accompanying tables show the growth, source, and distribution of foreign investment in Shanghai. The inflow of foreign investment was slower in the 1980s when the opening up of Shanghai lagged behind southern China, but began to speed up since 1990 when Pudong was designated as the largest new development area in China. It can be seen that dramatic growth occurred after 1992 when Shanghai promulgated the new policy to open up the real-estate sector to foreign investors. Consequently a building boom appeared in the mid-1990s. In 2002 Shanghai approved 3,012 contracts of FDI, a 22.5% increase from the previous year. Contracted FDI reached 10.576 billion USD and realized FDI amounted to 5.03 billion USD. Up to 2002, the accumulative realized foreign capital utilized in Shanghai was 40.415 billion USD.

In terms of the place of origin, Hong Kong ranks the highest, ac-

Growth of Foreign Capital and Direct Investment
in Shanghai, 1980–2001

	Realized Foreign Capital (billion USD)	Among which FDI (billion USD)
1980	0.015	—
1985	0.115	0.062
1990	0.78	0.177
1995	5.298	3.250
2000	5.391	3.160
2001	7.410	4.391

Source: Shanghai Statistical Bureau 2002.

counting for 26.4% of investment in 2001 and 30.7% in accumulative FDI. The next two largest sources are the United States and Japan, which account for respectively 12.75% and 12.83% of accumulated FDI. Germany and Singapore accounted for 4.0% and 4.33% of realized FDI. Compared to cities in southern China, Shanghai has seen a greater diversity in terms of place of origin, and more multinationals from the United States and western Europe.

While the manufacturing sector continues to be strong, accounting for 60% of the total realized foreign investment, the tertiary sector, especially real estate, finance, and research and development, began to attract foreign investment. Among the list of manufacturing multinationals are Hitachi, Phillips, IBM, DuPont, Alcatel, General Motors, and Volkswagen. The real-estate sector attracted 16.4% of realized investment. Its proportion in total investment decreased from 27.5% at the peak before the Asian Financial crisis in 1997. The list of clients of the Lujiazui central finance district, arguably the most globalized part of Shanghai, includes both domestic and overseas giant players, including branches of the central bank of China (Peoples' Bank of China) and four major domestic banks and a couple of foreign financial institutions.

Foreign and overseas investors have become some of the most active actors, because they bring about much needed capital and technologies. Foreign investors also help to open up Shanghai to the world market and thus stimulate export. Although China has maintained a high rate of capital formation, the underdeveloped domestic private sector has seriously constrained the contribution of nonstate capital in economic develop-

The Source of Foreign Direct Investment
in Shanghai, 2001

Country/District	Accumulative, 1980–2001 (billion USD)	Percentage
Hong Kong	10.872	30.72
Taiwan	1.685	4.76
Japan	4.541	12.83
Korea	0.417	1.18
Singapore	1.531	4.33
Thailand	0.119	0.34
Germany	1.414	4.00
United Kingdom	0.806	2.28
France	0.316	0.89
Italy	0.053	0.15
United States	4.510	12.75
Canada	0.233	0.66
Australia	0.276	0.78
Total	35.385	100.00

Source: Shanghai Statistical Bureau 2002.

ment. After fiscal decentralization and the decrease in state budgetary investment, foreign investment thus has become a new source of investment, thereby triggering a series of institutional changes through the interaction with local government. Although foreign investors are not dominant as they are in the countries where neoliberalization policy has been vigorously forced by international financial organizations, the interaction between investors and local government officials is discursive. Shanghai, as well as other Chinese local governments, frequently organizes overseas business and trade fairs to establish informal relationships, as discussed earlier. Most business-friendly practices first were experimented with in the development zones and then extended into other areas, becoming the norm. In the Pudong New Area, foreign investment receives one-stop comprehensive services, with the time of approval shorter than ten working days. The Shanghai municipal government has set up a Foreign Investment Commission (FIC), a powerful branch above government departments, similar to other commissions such as the Development and Planning Commission. The FIC provides speedy and

The Distribution of Foreign Direct Investment by Economic Sectors, 2001 (billion USD)

Sectors	Investment in 2001	Percentage in the Year	Accumulative Investment, 1981–2001	Percentage in Total
Primary	0.017	0.38	0.073	0.21
Secondary	2.650	60.34	18.403	52.00
Manufacturing	2.628	59.83	18.189	51.40
Tertiary	1.724	39.25	16.909	47.79
Transport and communication	0.218	4.96	0.820	2.32
Wholesale and retail	0.168	3.83	1.169	3.30
Real estate	0.720	16.39	10.809	30.55
Social services	0.213	4.85	1.929	5.45
Total	4.392	100.00	35.385	100.00

Source: Shanghai Statistical Bureau 2002.

unified services to foreign investment. Before the FIC was set up, foreign investors, like all domestic projects, needed to deal with various government departments. The FIC replaced these departments and has become the front window of government services. This in essence means that foreign investors enjoy a simplified procedure of project approval, which is not available to domestic projects.

As an emerging global city region, Shanghai is different from the export process zone and has seen the presence of larger corporations rather than lower-ranking, labor-intensive material processing projects. These corporations are particularly interested in China's potential market rather than cheap labor. At the end of 2002, 174 multinationals from among the Global 500 developed 328 large investment projects in Pudong. Among the big names are Shanghai General Motor (GM) Company Ltd., Shanghai Huahong NEC Company Ltd., and the Krupp Stainless Steel project, which all exceed investment of 10 billion yuan. Kodak (China) Company Ltd. invested nearly 10 billion yuan.

Pudong is also a site for experiments in many new practices. For example, foreign banks and financial institutions are clustered in the Lujiazui Financial and Trade Zone, including twenty-six foreign banks that are allowed to operate domestic renminbi currency business. The state council has given approval for the establishment of three Sino-foreign joint ventures specializing in foreign trade, including CNTIEC-SK, Lansheng-Daiwoo, and Dongling. The structure of foreign capital shows Shanghai is attractive in the placement of regional headquarters. In Pudong foreign banks from different countries established their branches.[1] The clustering of foreign bank branches in Shanghai provides a critical mass of producer services for foreign-funded manufacturing industries, attracting them to select Shanghai as their location.

Foreign investors are important to Shanghai not only because they contribute to capital formation, but also because they constitute the critical linkage through which Shanghai connects to the rest of world. Multinationals located their production sites in the Yangtze River Delta and Shanghai and, to be near to production sites, placed their regional headquarters in Shanghai. This has integrated Shanghai into the global economy and is attracting more investment through the clustering effect. Their importance should be understood with Shanghai's attempt to realize its ambition of becoming a global city.

Local Governments

Economic decentralization has mobilized multiple lower-level government actors. The devolution of governmental functions from the central to provincial government levels (of which Shanghai has an equivalent status) is a major feature of the postreform political landscape (Chung 1999). After a series of property rights reconfigurations, which allow de facto land users to draw legitimate benefits, land development has been taken through localized negotiations between land users and potential developers. This effectively means that while the national state still retains ownership in name, actual disposal rights have been decentralized to local government, and the right of drawing economic benefits is shared between the land occupier, developer, and government. This very pragmatic approach reduces the resistance for urban redevelopment, because the organization that uses the land can be compensated for the transfer of land use rights. However, such practice does not favor individual households that were not affiliated to a workplace or could not be represented by an organization in order to gain disposal rights over the land. These households are mostly private homeowners, who owned the houses before the reform.

Economic decentralization requires urban governance in general and land management in particular to be scaled down to lower levels. Local governments of different levels are engaged in promoting economic growth and providing social services. Enterprise reform stripped some work units of social service functions and transferred them to local governments. For example, for those who gave up formal employment in the state institutions, their "personnel dossiers" were henceforth transferred to a city "human resource exchange center," and local governments took greater responsibility in managing urban residents. Since the adoption of "two levels of government and three tiers of management," the lower levels of government at the district and street office levels have been given greater autonomy to operate their economic activities. The practice of returning 1% to 2% tax from the district government to the street office has greatly stimulated the latter to expand the so-called community-based economy and to transform the street office from a subordinated branch of district government to a substantial level of administration. These lower levels of government are becoming active economic agents. In 2001 there were 101 street offices powered by administrative decentralization.

Since local government became "autonomous" and a substantial actor, it has begun to engage in forceful place promotion, using various tactics commonly used in a business environment to market the city or district, as if the latter were a brand of commercial product. Place promotion is widely seen in the post-Fordist entrepreneurial city in the West (Hall and Hubbard 1998). Different tactics, however, must be used because of varying local strengths and weaknesses. City market strategy often focuses on image creation and marketing ranging, but this could be organized into a more structured response to enhancing city competitiveness, including institutional changes and strategy preparation. The tactics used by local governments range from image enhancement (e.g., glossing skyscrapers as advanced investment environment), entrepreneurial discourse (speedy, friendly, and transparent government and preferential treatments), designation of development zones (providing special business environment), land leasing instruments (concessions on the land fee and planning restrictions), leadership from the mayoral office and strong development coordination (corporative government and low-resistant communities), and public investment in infrastructure (strategic improvement of key infrastructure with the guarantees from the government) (Wu 2003a). Some innovative Web-based methods to target potential investors are utilized, along with the new effort of promoting on-line government service. The Shanghai city government actively exploits the chance of organizing large international spectacles and fairs such as Fortune Global Forum, APEC (Asia Pacific Economic Cooperation) meetings, and World Expo 2010 to attract media attention. On the Web site of the Shanghai municipal government (www.shanghai.gov.cn), the city is portrayed as a cosmopolitan metropolis. Meanwhile the popular culture is producing the nostalgia for the "Paris of the Orient" of the 1920s and 1930s.

Local Business Corporations

In the socialist regime, because the private sector was constrained, there were virtually no independent business interests outside the state sector. The state departments operated many kinds of service provision. For example, the municipal and district housing management bureaus were responsible for allocating housing to those who were not qualified for receiving workplace-based housing. Along with the progress of market reforms in the 1990s, state bureaucrats spontaneously went into business and many bureaus set up sideline businesses. This behavior is best seen as entrepreneurial because it is engaged in direct, profit-seeking, risk-taking economic activities (Duckett 2001, 33). The objective in market-oriented reform is to "separate the enterprise from the government," and accordingly part of managerial departments have been converted into companies, for example, from housing management bureaus to property management companies. In Shanghai, the Minghang District Bureau of Park Management has been divided into an administrative bureau, a park management institute, and the Shanghai Shenzhou Greening Ltd. Previous industrial bureaus of different sectors have been changed into respective industrial corporations.

New super land corporations, similar to those in the United Kingdom, have been created to take charge of land development. This was first tried in the development of special zones such as Economic and Technological Development Zones (ETDZs). For example, the Shanghai municipal government established Shanghai Hongqiao Joint Development Ltd., with the capital of the Bank of China Shanghai Branch and the Bank of China Corporation Hong Kong Branch, to manage the assets of the Hongqiao ETDZ. Similarly, in the development of Pudong, the Shanghai municipal government, as the owner of the state land, injected land assets into three large corporations: the Jingqiao Export Processing Development Zone Corporation, the Waigaoqiao Free Trade Zone Development Corporation, and the Lujiazui Finance and Trade Zone Development Corporation. After processing the land assets, these corporations began to finance land development by using the land asset as collateral to obtain bank loans.

These new development corporations are responsible for infrastructure provision. They manage their assets in a way different from the government. It is more convenient for them to use market approaches to mobilize capital and to maximize the economic benefit. This hard budgetary constraint imposed by the market increases the incentive for enhancing asset values. The establishment of the development corporations not only opens the channel to absorb capital from overseas and from the domestic stock markets but also shifts the role of government. Along with the establishment of the stock market in China, about 1.2 billion USD have been raised through listing development projects in the market since the 1990s (L. Chen 2002). The contractual relationship offered by the development corporations to the clients gives some stability and certainty to investors and thus boosts their confidence. Today Pudong has about fifteen major development companies, including the Lujiazui (Group) Company Ltd., the Jinqiao (Group) Company Ltd., and the Zhangjiang Hi-Tech Park Development Company. Each plays a key role in development management.

Both global and local actors participate in urban development. The two tallest buildings in the Lujiazui central financial district in Pudong, Shanghai's new central business district, illustrate the diverse source of capital in the remaking of China's dragonhead. The 88-floor Jin Mao Tower is currently the tallest building, reaching the height of 421 meters. From floors 3 through 50 are offices. The Grand Hyatt Shanghai occupies the top 38 floors with 555 rooms. The project, completed in 1998, was supported by fourteen ministries, departments, and corporations, including China's Ministry of Foreign Economy and Trade Cooperation. The Shanghai World Financial Centre is designed to be the tallest building in the world, reaching 492 meters and 101 floors. The project was resumed in 2003 and is invested in by Forest Overseas Company Ltd. and thirty-three Japanese corporations under the legal representative of the Shanghai World Financial Centre Investment Ltd. The two buildings are both designed by internationally renowned architectural firms and serviced by various global companies specializing in areas such as fire protection and interior decoration.

Local Communities

The legacy of state socialism means that the grass-roots communities are weak. Under socialism, the dominance of the state work-unit system virtually diminished the need for interest articulation outside of the formal state machine. The interests of households were traditionally articulated through workplaces. In the new formal and informal power structure, grassroots interests are again marginalized due to two reasons. First, market-oriented development and hence the overwhelming logic of economic competition have placed an emphasis on flexibility and market-friendly management. With the changes in the land use system from an administratively allocated system to a land-leasing system, the right of controlling urban space has been transferred from work units to municipal governments, and then to external developers. Although planning and a quasi type of zoning (i.e., development control plan) have still been carried out, their materialization is now subject to intense progrowth politics and distortion in order to make a more preferential deal for external investors. In the competition for the control of space, the practice of selling space means that mobile capital has a competitive edge, as investment can generate immediate changes and hence an impressive record in office for political elites.

Second, economic restructuring, especially the dismantling of state-owned enterprises, means the weakening of the work-unit system, which has begun to retreat from comprehensive welfare provision. There has been very little resistance to the swift reduction made in traditional manufacturing industries such as textile, light manufacturing, and shipbuilding industry. Of 5.73 million employees, 257,200 were registered as unemployed in 2001, giving an unemployment rate of 4.3% (Shanghai Statistical Bureau 2002). However, it is estimated that the number of unregistered laid-off workers is much higher. In 1999 registered laid-off workers in the street offices amounted to 410,000 (SAEB 2000, 490). Laid-off workers are detached from the channels through which their interests have been traditionally represented and articulated. Their detachment leads to isolation from the rest of society rather than freedom of choice. The recent attempt to build communities through strengthening base-level organization such as the street offices reflects the trend of reestablishing the linkage between those detached segments of the population and the system of government management. This has also led to the emergence of various community or nongovernment organizations. Recently, NGOs have been emerging in urban communities. Homeowners' associations are one type of such organization, but they are often initially organized by the property developer. Public participation in this sort of organization is still inadequate, which often only represents a fraction of residents who are better-off and becoming property owners.

Community resistance is weak in the face of urban restructuring. This is because grass-roots level organizations have been weak under state socialism. In former times, the state, or more precisely, the state work units, represented their interests. Now globalization has transformed the state: it rescaled the level of representation and reoriented the focus of the functionality of representation. With the retreat of the state, community interests have become unorganized. Confronted with powerful coalitions of private and public sectors, individual households are less capable of making their voices heard. Moreover, the logic of economic competition advocated by the neoliberals regards this as the inevitable cost of urban growth.

Rapid real-estate development and the construction of public infrastructure such as underground and elevated roads have generated a large amount of displaced residents. The accompanying table shows the number of households relocated from 1985 to 2001 and housing space demolished. It can be seen that more than 70,000 households have been relocated per annum, so as to make space for new commercial uses, modern offices, and productive infrastructure, which are all critical elements for a global city. Although these households are generally compensated because of strong tenancy rights under state socialism (Marcuse 1996), they are often relocated to the suburban areas where the housing price is cheaper. So far there had been no such phenomenon as "not-in-my-backyard," which is very active in the most advanced Western economies. But the formation of homeowners' associations began to activate the consciousness of self-interest. In some areas, the associations are actively bargaining with developers and local governments for better service provision, higher security, and less pollution.

Different actors have different perceptions about Shanghai's future. Overseas investors see Shanghai as a major window through which they can access the vast Chinese market. The cosmopolitan past of the city adds to the affinity. Local communities are so far bought into the vision of global city. But the tension will inevitably increase along with the sacrifice asked in order to make the space for global capital. Local business corporations see the development of a global city as an excellent chance to capitalize the land value, develop a base for export, access the global market, and even form China's own multinationals. What is remarkable here is the reterritorialization of the state, as the local governments, under the support of the central government, successfully depict a glorious urban future. The pragmatism together with a flexible institutional structure so

The Number of Households Relocated and Property Floor Space Demolished, 1995–2001

	Total Number of Households	Space Demolished (million sq. m.)
1995	75,777	3.227
1996	89,132	3.429
1997	79,857	4.797
1998	78,205	4.522
1999	75,185	3.425
2000	70,606	3.657
2001	73,728	5.156

Source: Shanghai Statistical Bureau 2002.

far has successfully mobilized various actors to participate in an essential state project (Wu 2003b).

Conclusion

The development of Shanghai suggests a strong dimension of local politics in the formation of global city regions. Because of the weak community, the state is able to set the agenda without much resistance from below. Residential relocation has been carried out swiftly (Wu 2004a), making space for global capital. Industrial restructuring has generated redundant workers in traditional manufacturing industries such as textiles, iron and steel production, and traditional light industries. The property right of land under state socialism enables a monopoly position of the municipality, which has been used as an instrument to solicit development projects.

In terms of formal power structure, Chinese cities have seen a clear trend of decentralization. The decision-making process and organization of actual developments have been shifted from the central government to local municipalities, from municipalities to subordinated district governments, and further down to development corporations. Rapid growth is attributed as much to strong governance capacity as to decentralized initiatives. The local state always maintains a steering role in growth management and is active in reshaping the institutional framework so as to maintain economic competitiveness.

Rather than simply viewing the impact of globalization as if the city were passively transformed by imposed forces, this essay attempts to understand how the local politics—changing power relationship and emerging actors—have been facilitating the remaking of global city regions. Unlike the western European model, where association and social movements are strong in local politics (LeGales 2002), and the North American "growth machine"-type of politics (Logan and Molotch 1987), where the Chamber of Commerce and Industries orchestrates the coalition of progrowth actors, the Chinese city has seen strong input of the state, similar to the "development state" in other East Asian countries. Originally developed in Japan as a latecomer among industrialized nations in the world (Wade 1990), the concept of the development state emphasizes the role of the state in making industrial and financial policies in order to restructure the economy. Recent studies on Tokyo and Seoul (Hill and Kim 2000) set off the debate about the alternative trajectory of becoming the global city region. It is suggested that the distinct local structures must become active themselves rather than just accommodating the global forces.

In this periphery or semiperiphery of globalization, the role of the state is critical in initiating strategic and institutional transformations so as to meet the challenge of globalization. The state's intervention in the economy is not seen as a negative force but rather a positive factor. This case study shows that a series of institutional changes has led to reconfiguration of formal power relationships and further changes in informal power relations between the state, markets, and society. In this process, multiple actors including foreign and overseas investors, local governments, local business actors, and communities have been created and engaged in complicated gamelike negotiations (Wu 1999). The state, now in the form of decentralized and downward-scaled actors, still maintains a critical role in the process.

However, the case of Shanghai does not simply follow the development state model. Seemingly, the dominance of the state in urban development contradicts the global trend toward neoliberalism (Tickell and Peck 2003). But when the role of the state is examined in the transformed power structure, formally and informally, it is clear that the city is a variant to the neoliberal city (Wu 2003a). This does not necessarily mean a convergence to the universal global, neoliberal city. Rather, Shanghai perhaps represents a more advanced stage of neoliberalization, where the state plays an active role by using its governing function to support the market. The reterritorialized state can better support the market and pave the way to new methods of capital accumulation.

Although the state retains or has even consolidated its role in governance, the transformation of the power structure shows that this is no longer the model of state-led growth. More specifically, the state no longer owns the means of production and does not seek to treat the city as a state-owned asset. Instead, the city is now becoming an entrepreneurial, gigantic "City Inc." Or, in other words, the city itself is becoming the site of new governance. So far the transformation of the power relationship is asymmetric, in the sense that the local community is weak and that capital is better accommodated to the project of global city building. Institutional and market forces reinforce marginalization and have led to a "poverty of transition" (Wu 2004b). However, the power structure is not fixed. The relationships forged in the entrepreneurial state project will be continuously contested along with the changing external and internal political economic environments.

Note

1. The geographical distribution of major banks and financial institutions shows that there are 18 branches from Asian countries and areas (Japan: 9; Korea: 3; Hong Kong: 2; Indonesia: 1; Malaysia: 1; Taiwan: 1; Thailand: 1), 21 branches from Europe (France: 5; Germany: 5; Holland: 4; Italy: 2; United Kingdom: 2; Belgium: 1; Spain: 1; Switzerland: 1), 4 branches from the United States, and 1 from Australia.

References

Andrusz, G. 1996. Structural Change and Boundary Instability. In G. M. Andrusz, M. Harloe, and I. Szelenyi (eds.), *Cities after Socialism: Urban and Regional Change and Conflict in Post-Socialist Societies*, 30–69. Oxford: Blackwell.

Brenner, N. 1999. Globalization as Reterritorialisation: The Re-scaling of Urban Governance in the European Union. *Urban Studies* 36: 431–51.

Castells, M. 1983. *The City and the Grassroots*. London: Edward Arnold.

———. 1996. *The Rise of the Network Society*. Vol. 1. Oxford: Blackwell.

———. 2000. *The End of Millennium*. Vol. 3. Oxford: Blackwell.

Chen, J. J. 1999. *Local Revenue Growth*. Shanghai: Shanghai Social Science Academy Press.

Chen, L. Y. 2002. *Shanghai's Modern Urban Construction and the Reform of Investment and Capital Formation*. Shanghai Mayor's Speech delivered at the 35th annual meeting of the Asian Development Bank. Shanghai.

Chung, J. H. 1999. *Cities in China: Recipes for Economic Development in the Reform Era.* London: Routledge.

Duckett, J. 2001. Bureaucrats in Business, Chinese-Style: The Lessons of Market Reform and State Entrepreneurialism in the People's Republic of China. *World Development* 29: 23–37.

Fu, Z. 2002. The State, Capital, and Urban Restructuring in Post-Reform Shanghai. In J. R. Logan (ed.), *The New Chinese City: Globalization and Market Reform,* 106–20. Oxford: Blackwell.

Hall, T., and P. Hubbard. 1998. *The Entrepreneurial City: Geographies of Politics, Regime and Representation.* Chichester: John Wiley.

Hill, G. C., and J. W. Kim. 2000. Global Cities and Development States: New York, Tokyo and Seoul. *Urban Studies* 37: 2167–95.

Hsing, Y.-T. 1998. *Making Capitalism in China: The Taiwan Connection.* Oxford: Oxford University Press.

Kornai, J. 1992. *The Socialist System: The Political Economy of Communism.* Princeton, N.J.: Princeton University Press.

Kwok, R. Y., W. Parish, A. G. O. Yeh, and X. Xu. 1990. *Chinese Urban Reforms: What Model Now?* Armonk, N.Y.: Sharpe.

LeGales, P. 2002. *European Cities: Social Conflicts and Governance.* Oxford: Oxford University Press.

Lieberthal, K. 1995. *Governing China: From Revolution through Reform.* New York: W. W. Norton.

Logan, J. R. 2002. *The New Chinese City: Globalization and Market Reform.* Oxford: Blackwell.

Logan, J. R., and H. L. Molotch. 1987. *Urban Fortunes: The Political Economy of Place.* Berkeley: University of California Press.

Lu, H. L. 2002. Governance of Urban Public Life and Urban Residents. In Z. Yi and H. L. Lu (eds.), *Urban Governance and Quality of Citizen,* 1–37. Shanghai: Shanghai Social Science Academy.

Marcuse, P. 1996. Privatization and Its Discontents: Property Rights in Land and Housing in the Transition in Eastern Europe. In G. Andrusz, M. Harloe, and I. Szelenyi (eds.), *Cities after Socialism: Urban and Regional Change and Conflict in Post-Socialist Societies,* 119–91. Oxford: Blackwell.

———. 1997. The Enclave, the Citadel, and the Ghetto: What Has Changed in the Post-Fordist U.S. City. *Urban Affairs Review* 33: 228–64.

Naughton, B. 1995. *Growing Out of the Plan: Chinese Economic Reform, 1978–1993.* Cambridge: Cambridge University Press.

Oi, J. C., and A. G. Walder. 1999. *Property Rights and Economic Reform in China.* Stanford, Calif.: Stanford University Press.

Olds, K. 2001. *Globalization and Urban Change: Capital, Culture, and Pacific Rim Mega-Projects.* Oxford: Oxford University Press.

Peck, J., and A. Tickell. 1995. Business Goes Local: Dissecting the "Business Agenda" in Manchester. *International Journal of Urban and Regional Research* 19: 55–78.

Sassen, S. 1996. *Losing Control? Sovereignty in an Age of Globalization.* New York: Columbia University Press.
Scott, A. J. 2001. Globalization and the Rise of City-Regions. *European Planning Studies* 9: 813–26.
Shanghai Almanac Editorial Board (SAEB). 2000. *Shanghai Almanac 2000.* Shanghai: Shanghai Almanac Press.
Shanghai Statistical Bureau. 2002. *Shanghai Statistical Yearbook 2002.* Beijing: China Statistical Press.
Solinger, D. J. 1999. *Contesting Citizenship in Urban China: Peasant Migrants, the State, and the Logic of the Market.* Berkeley: University of California Press.
Tickell, A., and J. Peck. 2003. Making Global Rules: Globalization or Neoliberalisation?" In J. Peck and H. Yeung (eds.), *Remaking the Global Economy,* 163–81. London: Sage.
United Nations Centre for Human Settlements (Habitat) (UNCHS). 2001. *Cities in a Globalizing World: Global Report on Human Settlements, 2001.* London: Earthscan.
Wade, R. 1990. *Governing the Market: Economic Theory and the Role of Government in East Asian Industrialization.* Princeton, N.J.: Princeton University Press.
Walder, A. 1995. Local Governments as Industrial Firms: An Organizational Analysis of China's Transitional Economy. *American Journal of Sociology* 101: 263–301.
Wong, C. P. W., C. Heady, and W. T. Woo. 1995. *Fiscal Management and Economic Reform in the People's Republic of China.* Hong Kong: Oxford University Press.
Wu, F. 1999. The Game of Landed-Property Production and Capital Circulation in China's Transitional Economy. *Environment and Planning A* 31: 1757–71.
———. 2002. China's Changing Urban Governance in the Transition towards a More Market-Oriented Economy. *Urban Studies* 39: 1071–93.
———. 2003a. Transitional Cities. *Environment and Planning A* 35, no. 8: 1331–38.
———. 2003b. The Entrepreneurial City as the State Project: Shanghai's Reglobalisation in Question. *Urban Studies* 40, no. 9: 1673–98.
———. 2004a. Intra-urban Residential Relocation in Shanghai: Modes and Stratification. *Environment and Planning A* 36: 7–25.
———. 2004b. Urban Poverty and Marginalization under Market Transition: The Case of Chinese Cities. *International Journal of Urban and Regional Research* 38, no. 2: 401–23.
Yang, Y. Q., and H. J. Han. 1999. *The Open-Door Strategy.* Shanghai: Shanghai Social Science Academy.
Yusuf, S., and W. Wu. 2002. Pathways to a World City: Shanghai Rising in an Era of Globalisation. *Urban Studies* 39: 1213–40.

4 | Contested Future
Discourses and Images in City Regions

Making a global city is not simply about installing and modernizing infrastructure. It also has a lot to do with image creation that in turn spurs interest and investment in the region and also engenders local support for the project. Hence, when talking about the "making" of global city regions, one may assume an underlying marketing strategy, designed to promote a city's goal of becoming a global city. And, indeed, due to the general shift of urban policies toward entrepreneurship and competitiveness, there has been a steady growth of city marketing strategies around the world. Such campaigns usually aim at reinventing the image of a city. Cities like to present themselves as modern, economically successful, and culturally diverse. In order to strengthen a city region's position in the worldwide competition for capital, know-how, and tourists, city administrations strive to highlight the specific local qualities that portray their cities as unique places with a high quality of life.

Images are linked to discourses. Both shape the way in which people, including key actors, perceive and interpret reality. Images can serve as a powerful engine to mobilize investments of different kinds. In this function, the creation of a positive image is mostly geared toward the outside world. Discourses in turn are employed to set frames of reference through the definition of relevant issues and problems, and subsequent delimitations and visions. Discursive rhetoric is actively used by politicians to build legitimacy for their policies and instill citizens with the "right" attitude (see Beauregard and Tomlinson in this chapter). However, alternative discourses may compete with the usually dominating official discourses for the power of definition. After all, the majority of the population does not necessarily benefit from a new city image. Instead, the general population may be more concerned with the high costs of living associated with modernization and restructuring. It may worry about gentrification and social fragmentation and also stress the need for environmental protection or highlight the insufficient provision of basic services. These concerns, however, are rarely discussed within the framework of the official marketing strategies.

The following contributions on the discourses in the four cities develop a deeper understanding of the interrelationship between discourses and image creation. In Shanghai the dominating and prevailing image is that of a rapidly growing future global city. This has triggered immense foreign investment in the city region. In São Paulo, on the contrary, the vision of becoming a global city does not even appear in the new Master Plan of the city administration. Instead, strategies for inclusion of the marginalized are being developed. And while the administration in Johannesburg crafted the 2030 strategy in order to become the future "world-class city in Africa," in Mumbai the situation is more accurately described as a completely fragmented discourse between "internationalism and locality."

The city administration of Johannesburg aims at making Johannesburg the world-class city in Africa. In the light of this vision, the instructive study of Robert Beauregard and Richard Tomlinson explores the discursive qualities of the new governance regime. Trying to create the image of an attractive and successful global city, city officials avoid addressing conflicting issues. Consensus is assumed and local government is depoliticized. Symptomatically, the people of Johannesburg are viewed as customers and government becomes a technical management exercise. According to the authors, this approach reduces the spectrum of governance and deliberately excludes alternative narratives and discourses. In addition, it clearly departs from the earlier discourses, which emphasized the redistribution of wealth and the provision of basic services to the poor.

In Mumbai/Bombay the discourse is rather fragmented, determined by such factors as language, religion, locality, and economic and cultural background. The city administration seems unable to integrate the different discourses into one coherent self-image. Consequently, a resolution to the question of how the city is to be reinvented remains elusive. Instead, as Ranjit Hoskote depicts, different groups have diametrically diverging visions of the city. Those who insist on calling the city Bombay promote a progressive image of universality, pursuing the reopening of the city to the outside world. The contending, locally oriented discourse, however, backed by Hindu-nationalist parties like Shiv Sena, is identified by politics of ethnic segregation and exclusion, aimed at shielding the city from any potential risk from the outside world. Tellingly, the name of the city has officially been changed to Mumbai, pronouncing its function as capital of the linguistically homogeneous province of Maharashtra. Thus, no single driving self-image of the city exists today.

São Paulo in turn does not necessarily have to create the image of a global city anymore, because it has been the most important city in South America for decades. Nevertheless, as Pedro Jacobi points out in his contribution, there are two strongly competing discourses. On the one hand, there is the global discourse—supported in particular by the real-estate sector and the traditional elite. It emphasizes the international aspirations of the city and demands more investments into an infrastructure that accommodates the needs of the global elite. On the other hand, there is the local discourse, led by civic organizations, trade unions, and other actors. It stresses the need to fight poverty and strengthen participatory practices. The city administration under the Workers Party, in turn, tries to mediate between the two competing discourses. It thereby sets different priorities than its counterparts in Johannesburg and Shanghai. While aware of the city's regional hub function, the administration seems to be more conscious of the sharp inequalities within the city. Hence, the new Master Plan, adopted in 2002, does not promote the vision of a global city, but instead focuses on socioeconomic, human, and urban development as well as environmental issues.

Finally, Shanghai is probably the best example for a successful strategy of aggressively promoting the vision of becoming a global city. Zhongxin Sun shows in her study the dramatic transformation of Shanghai during the 1990s from being the model socialist city under the tight supervision of the central government to the emergence of the global city vision in 2002. This transition was underscored when Shanghai won the bid for the World Expo 2010. The global city discourse has strongly influenced the image of the city, internally as well as externally. The city administration, backed by the central Chinese government, today actively pursues the new vision, which is symbolized through the planned construction of the world's tallest building, its longest bridge, and its deepest seaport. The unconditional promotion of this image has historical reasons, for until the late 1930s Shanghai used to be a major international metropolis—the gateway to China. While the city administration seeks to reclaim that position, the contending voices and alternative "indigenization" discourses do not seem to be strong enough to seriously challenge the newly created image.

Thus, while there is a strong lobby supporting the discourse on "making" a global city in all four city regions, this image is actively promoted only by the city administrations in Shanghai and Johannesburg. In turn, the alternative and locally oriented discourses are strongest in São Paulo and Mumbai. On the whole, it seems that the successful promotion of the global city vision is most likely if alternative discourses are disregarded, contained, or even controlled. A powerful city government with the backing of a central government and a strongly articulated official vision apparently is best suited to glamorously reinvent the image of the city, as has been the case in Shanghai. Participatory mechanisms, however, at first glance seem less conducive to the making of global city regions. In the long run, though, a shared vision of leaders and citizens may prove inevitable for sustained success as a global city region.

Simon Raiser and Krister Volkmann

The Discourse of Governance in Post-Apartheid Johannesburg
Robert A. Beauregard and Richard Tomlinson

Anticipating the end of apartheid in the early 1990s, South Africans came together to debate the formation of new local governments that would treat all racial groups and political jurisdictions in an equitable and just fashion (McCarthy 1992; Robinson 1998; Swilling, Humphries, and Shubane 1991). The subsequent shift from an apartheid to a post-apartheid regime generated a series of administrative transitions aimed at merging previously existing white local authorities with black townships. "One city, one tax base" was the overarching goal.

The backdrop to these changes was the injustice of apartheid and the inequalities that had been etched on the landscape. Apartheid's memories and the expectations created by the political dispensation of 1994 pervaded public deliberations. Changes in governmental practices, moreover, unfolded in parallel with the political entrenchment of the African National Congress (ANC) and the marginalization of the grass-roots civic organizations that had been so central to the resistance movement. The demise of the apartheid regime also opened South Africa to global influences, particularly neoliberalism's promarket and antigovernment biases, and engendered aspirations that the country and its major cities would become actors on the world stage. Within this context, elected officials, municipal labor unions, grass-roots groups, and various publics experimented with new forms of governance. Out of this debate emerged an image of Johannesburg as both a world-class city and a city yet deeply rooted in Africa, an image embraced mainly by the ANC, local government, and corporate interests.

The purpose of this essay is to explore the discursive qualities of this new governance regime. Forging governmental practices, whether road paving or bill collection, is more than a matter of organizational charts, revenue sources, voting procedures, and service delivery schemes. Governance also entails crafting the legitimacy of new structures and practices and instilling citizens with compatible qualities (Joyce 2003). Much of this work is discursive. Through public representations, government and city leaders solidify their authority, justify their performance, and create new citizens (Lester, Nel, and Binns 2000; Salskov-Iverson 1997; Stenson and Watt 1999).

Our specific concern is how Johannesburg's leaders have represented their efforts and thus how they have negotiated the contradictory pressures operating on local government. In order to lessen these tensions, government officials have mounted a discursive strategy to constrict governance. The intent of their pronouncements is to characterize the government as a deliverer of public services and a contributor to economic growth. The focus is on government's formal properties. By contrast, governance is generally conceived as inclusionary, less concerned with the efforts of bureaucracy and officials than with the enhancement of local democracy through the incorporation of diverse communities. Governance is constituted by social mechanisms that operate across the state, civil society, and the economy and that provide for social stability, the welfare of the people, and justice (Mayer 1995). Government and governance, of course, are not mutually exclusive. Emphasizing the former, however, has the effect of consolidating political power rather than diffusing it.

Our analysis focuses on two aspects of local government: its current performance and its vision for the future. In order to maintain a consistent point of view, we confine our attention to specific types of texts. To assess the representation of government performance, we use recent mayoral addresses and annual budget reports (see appendix A). To assess how local officials view Johannesburg's future and its potential for world-city status, we draw on Joburg 2030, the city's vision statement (see appendix B). Ideally, these texts would span from before the 1994 political dispensation to the present. Between 1994 and 2000, however, the Johannesburg local government was in a constant state of reorganization. Executive speeches and "state of the city" reports were either not produced or the texts lost, while the publication of long-term planning documents was suspended.

Discourse and Governance

One cannot grasp the possibilities and difficulties of governance without an understanding of the discursive interplay between government and its constituents. Discursive interventions—speeches, reports, plans, public hearings, press releases—are as much "government" as are legislation and public services. Public representations enable political leaders to create legitimacy across multiple groups, stabilize governing coalitions, and assure the compliance of citizens (Edelman 1988). Consequently, how government and governance practices are represented to the public by bureaucrats and elected officials is of major importance. What governments do and how they present themselves discursively, either in anticipation or as ex post justification, are inseparable. Convincing people to change their behavior, respect laws, or engage democratically involves shaping their expectations about the consequences of acting (or not acting) in specific circumstances (Kaplan 1986; South African Cities Network 2004; Throgmorton 1996).

Meaning, though, is never fixed (Hastings 1999). Governmental discourse is constantly being revised as people act in response and as the efforts of governments fall short of or exceed expectations. Consequently, what government officials say cannot be treated as transparent renditions of either past conditions or proposed actions (Roe 1994; Yanow 1996; 2000). At root, they are attempts to persuade listeners and readers of a specific view of the world. The analytical issue is how substantive themes and arguments are rhetorically constituted and presented.

Our analysis is designed to reveal three basic dimensions of urban governance in Johannesburg: the search for and maintenance of legitimacy (an issue tightly tied to governmental performance), the creation of the kinds of citizens most appropriate for the type of governance being proposed, and the positioning of the government in relation to the economy and civil society.

The Johannesburg government faces these tasks in the context of a post-apartheid reality where race continues to influence urban development and the commitment to "one city" remains elusive (Beavon 1997; Bremner 2000; Tomlinson et al 2003). Internal power struggles among the ANC-led government, the South African Municipal Workers Union (SAMWU), and oppositional political parties have created a contentious political environment, while the national government's embrace of a neoliberal economic policy has had repercussions for local fiscal affairs and development agendas. And, though many black communities still have thriving civic associations, much of their leadership, so prominent during the anti-apartheid years, has been absorbed into the ANC (Beall, Crankshaw, and Parnell 2002; Heller 2003). Finally, persistent housing shortages, racial and class segregation, high levels of crime, and now HIV/AIDS tarnish Johannesburg's image and make it difficult to attract foreign tourists and investors and stem the decentralization of households, retail activity, and industrial investment from the inner city.

Background on Local Government

Following local government elections in 2000, the newly titled city of Johannesburg (hereafter city) adopted a metropolitan form of government. Prior to that time, a variety of governmental structures were used to effect the transition from an apartheid to a post-apartheid regime (Beall, Crankshaw, and Parnell 2002, 63–106; Christopher 2001; Tomlinson 1999a, 2005; Tomlinson et al. 2003).

The city government is charged with two primary tasks: service provision and social and economic development. It is also required by law to provide democratic and accountable government, promote a safe and healthy environment, and encourage community involvement in its activities. To this end, the city is engaged in an array of local government functions—water and sanitation, electricity, waste removal, and other municipal services; participates in the delivery of low-income housing; and is responsible for such social services as libraries and recreation.

The government is led by an executive mayor, a mayoral committee that functions as an executive committee, and a city council. A city manager oversees daily operations. These operations are organized into public agencies (e.g., city parks), utilities (e.g., Johannesburg Water), departments (e.g., police, health), and corporatized entities such as Metrobus. Staff functions include economic development and planning.

Critical to any understanding of local government is that the city exists in a precarious fiscal environment. In 1997 the government was on the verge of bankruptcy. The combination of a weak economy and low levels of rate and utility payments constricted revenue streams while persistent poverty and unemployment generated heightened demands for services. The commitment to "one tax base" revealed a structural shortfall in revenue sources. Persistently stark socioeconomic inequalities and enduring spatial segregation by race and increasingly by class further undermined fiscal stability. In the inner city, formerly white neighborhoods are now mostly occupied by black households, office activity has shifted downward to low-value uses, and high-end retailing in the central business district has collapsed (Tomlinson 1999b).

Particularly salient for local government has been the national government's shift away from direct responsibility for the social well-being of the country's citizens, a commitment generally imputed to the ANC's Reconstruction and Development Programme. This program was replaced in 1996 by the central government's Growth Employment and Redistribution (GEAR) policy. In accordance with this policy, and stemming directly from the Local Government White Paper of 1998 that called for "developmental local government," local governments are encouraged to contract out services, engage in partnerships with business, minimize tariffs and regulations, and focus on business investment and job growth. They are also intended to be more democratic and accountable. This policy compels the city to trust that the benefits of economic development will trickle-down to mitigate enduring poverty, high unemployment among black Africans, substandard housing, and spatial segregation. As a result, the city has to maintain legitimacy with its residents and meet their basic needs while under fiscal constraints and central government pressure to dampen expansive government and ignite economic growth.

Government Performance

Each year, the executive mayor (hereafter, mayor) of Johannesburg releases an annual budget report for public review and accompanies this release with a speech before an audience of local dignitaries. The mayor's remarks are reported in newspapers and on television and radio and made available on the city's Web site. Here is the government speaking to the people, summing up for them its past accomplishments and future objectives. Hence, these texts are a useful, even if partial, view of local governance. They represent the understandings that elected and appointed officials wish to have adopted by the general public. They do not give voice to counterarguments; their function is to garner support and legitimacy.

While Johannesburg officials frequently employ the term *governance*, they use it in such a way as to narrow collective decision making. As we will see, governance is reduced to the actions and decisions of the local government as it pursues economic growth for the city, rather than broadened to encompass various types of non-business-related partnerships and civil-society organizations jointly engaged in collective endeavors and in reproducing the conditions for democracy (LeGales 1998). In Johannesburg, governance is constricted. This is evidenced by the assumption of consensus, the depoliticization of government, the treatment of citizens as customers, and the marginalization of grass-roots organizations.

As expected, the annual mayoral speeches and budget reports assume a citywide consensus as to what government should do and how it should do it. Johannesburg appears here as politically unified. Disagreements are suppressed and, when mentioned, are portrayed as deviations from shared interests or as only temporarily unresolved. Municipal labor union resistance to privatization and downsizing in the late 1990s receives only the briefest of mentions, and dissent across party lines is dismissed as an aberration and an impediment to progress. In 2001, for example, the mayor commented that relations with the trade unions and municipal workers had been "strained" in the previous year. He then noted that the government planned to "appeal to the unions to work in partnership with management to implement a joint vision of transformation for the city."

Citizen dissent is treated similarly; recognizing it indicates not a fissure in governance but the sensitivity of the leadership to resident concerns. These are not texts of policy conflict. Rather, their intent is to publicize the city government as well led and committed to the unitary interests of the city, interests that benefit all of its residents. For example, making Johannesburg a world-class city, the mayor noted in 2001 in his 2002/3 budget speech, "necessitates that we have one common goal and vision for the entire city. . . . Let us march into the future as one."

What becomes overwhelmingly clear in reading the speeches and reports is that the mayor, his council, and staff have erased the distinction between their positions and the government as an institution. They portray themselves less as stewards of an entity that the electorate has created than as actors whose leadership is unquestioned and essential. Given a "clear mandate to govern" (Office of the Executive Mayor 2003, 1), they are the government.

Such rhetoric attests, in part, to the fact that these officials were popularly elected. It also attests to the dominance of the ANC in the local government and the corresponding weakness of the other political parties (Parnell in this volume). There is little serious dissent within the city council. The "official opposition" is the Democratic Alliance (DA), but it shares many of the goals of the ANC in respect to outsourcing service delivery, concurs with the majority of ANC policies, and generally supports the ANC's vision for the city's future (Democratic Alliance 2003). Consequently, the DA's opposition mostly consists of complaints regarding mismanagement, budgetary decisions, failure to assure payment for services, and the lack of consultation by the ANC. The DA basically functions as a "watchdog."

Inside the government, then, a consensus exists. Consensus enables officials to treat the government as a mechanism for the realization of shared goals rather than as a contested terrain. This is one component of a more important rhetorical move—the depoliticization of local government; that is, the portrayal of governing as solely an administrative task.

To this end, the texts portray elected officials as good managers and government as a technical enterprise guided by competence and expertise. Dispassionate and objective, the tone is managerial and draws on the Western tradition of business-like government whose task is to deliver services in the most efficient manner. Problems are carefully analyzed and policy designed to address them. For example, the mayor frequently draws a link between budget and policy decisions and prior planning studies: "The budget we present this afternoon is not simply a numbers game," the mayor stated in his 2003/4 speech, "[i]t is guided by the Joburg 2030 strategy and underpinned by the Integrated Development Plan" (p. 11). In this way, current decisions are justified and made legitimate. The government proceeds rationally and in the best interests of the city.

In fact, elected officials "recognize the discipline and commitment that is required of [them]" (Office of the Executive Mayor 2001, 2). Over and over, the texts note the ways in which the mayor and his councillors have maintained their focus on making government better. Officials have not succumbed to (unnamed) tangential debates or political disagreements. In 2002, for example, the mayor called on all people to act jointly regardless of political affiliation; "each political party is free to express its views and voice its criticism . . . as long as we remain vigilant about the principle of serving above self." His appeal was to a broad public interest and the importance of consensus (Office of the Executive Mayor 2002).

Reinforcing this managerial and consensual perspective is the tone of the texts; they are mainly intent on reporting. From year to year, each speech and budget report follows a fixed format. They describe what has been done and what will be done, note challenges and accomplishments, schematically review expenditures and revenues, and discuss future plans. The texts are essentially closed. They tell the public what already has been decided; they are not meant to be debated. Of course, it is in the nature of such speeches and reports to gloss over disagreements and to tout the accomplishments of those who lead. On the other hand, in such a sharply segregated city with a history of robust political debate, the muted attention to the political and contested qualities of governance is noteworthy.

Only infrequently do these speeches and reports break from the flat affect and distant tone of managerialism. For example, one recent budget report (2003/4) offered a more personalized view of government by actually including citizen comments submitted to the local newspaper and the city's Web site. A. G. Katz is quoted as regards poor infrastructure: "I concur with Rosemarie Krantz that probably 40% of our water is lost due to the bad state of pipes" (Office of the Executive Mayor 2003/4, 5). Mabuza Shabalala's comments are used to document the lack of enforcement of bylaws to buildings: "Most flats in Joburg are in a state of collapse" (p. 5). The inclusion of these personal remarks softens the managerial tone and bridges the gap between efficient government performance and basic needs.

That tone is further mediated by a commitment to addressing widespread and lingering poverty. About one-third of the households in Johannesburg are so poor that they cannot afford to pay for water and electricity, live in decent housing, or (if owning a home) pay for rates. To address these conditions, the ANC has a free basic-services policy that provides for free water and electricity up to a certain level of consumption, free waste removal, and rate rebates for properties whose assessed value is less than 20,001 rand. These items are central to local government's indigent policy. The free services and the widespread failure to pay for services above the level for which services are free are funded through cross subsidies in the water and electricity sectors, cross subsidies from rate payments for free waste removal, and, for the rates rebate, through cross subsidies from the general account. When the mayor declares that "poverty is a central goal" of the city, however, it is not only these initiatives to which he refers. The reduction and even elimination of poverty is also a motive for the city's commitment to economic growth, a point to which we will return.

One of the most important discursive thrusts of any governmental text is the creation of citizens compatible with the mode of governance being expounded. Just as the end of apartheid engendered new governmental structures, it resulted in new citizen claims as well (Sassen 1999). Consequently, citizenship itself has had to be reimagined.

The citizen envisioned by these reports appears in two ways: first as a resident, with qualities that enable the government to function well, and, second, as a customer. For example, in presenting the city's "social package"—that is, its utility and rate subsidies to the poor—the mayor noted that residents are obligated to be disciplined in their use of utilities and in their utility and rate payments. In 2002 he also pointed to the need for residents to act responsibly: "Too often we see people dropping litter, or stealing out in the middle of the night to dump rubbish" (Office of the Executive Mayor 2002, 16).

Patience, specifically on the part of residents, is of major importance and a repetitive theme of the texts. The government's capacity to effect the underlying causes of poverty and unemployment is limited and funds for addressing basic needs are scarce. In commenting on a new call center for citizen complaints, the mayor noted that "[w]e cannot expect an infant born yesterday to rise and run. This will be against all the laws of nature" (Office of the Executive Mayor 2002, 7). The comment applies to all government performance. The city's residents are expected to participate in community meetings and voice their concerns, but not to lose patience or turn to protest. Moreover, they should report crimes, conserve and pay for electricity and water, use the freely provided trash bins only for storing trash (and not for housing chickens), and avoid the unsafe sex that exacerbates the HIV/AIDS epidemic.

Relatedly, the mayor talks incessantly about a "better future." "Changing the trajectory of the economy and changing the skills of the labour force cannot yield results in anything but the long-term," the mayor said in 2003. Speeches and budget reports are forward looking. The city's enduring problems will eventually be solved, but only if—these texts imply—a patient and understanding electorate allows it to happen.

At the same time, the texts construct the "ideal" Johannesburg resident as a customer. As the mayor stated in his 2001/2 budget speech, "[w]e are investing heavily in customer relations, and good governance" (p. 10). Worries about fiscal balance, efficiency, rates, staff training, and intergovernmental grants all focus on the primary function of government: the provision of public services. To provide services efficiently and effectively, the government and the private companies it oversees must embrace an "ethos of customer care." Good customers are also needed; that is, customers who register their satisfaction or dissatisfaction, thus providing useful feedback, but also "do the right thing and pay for the services they consume" (Office of the Executive Mayor 2002/3).

A customer, of course, is not the same as a citizen (Bender 1996; Friedmann 2002, 67–86; Isin 2000). A citizen is known by his or her political rights and, in many countries, by his or her social rights to housing, social services, and employment (Marshall 1964). A citizen has a moral relationship to the government, a customer a monetary relationship. A customer engages in a specific type of exchange in which value is traded for (equal) value. There, the relationship ends. Neither side to the transaction is otherwise obligated. A service is provided, a rate or utility bill is paid.

Johannesburg's residents do enjoy rights—access to water, education, health care services, a clean environment, adequate housing, dignity—as citizens. Such rights are embodied in the country's Constitution. Local government discourse, however, marginalizes them. Obligations are displaced by market-type exchanges as the defining element of citizenship.

This crafting of residents as customers seems incompatible with the city's insistence on good governance. Governance usually involves multiple actors with shared responsibilities for the city's well-being (Chipkin 2003). By contrast, the exchange of services for rate payments is less about sharing responsibilities than about being responsible to one's role either as a service provider or as a customer. Exchange is a weak form of sharing. Thus, to commit to good governance and to cast residents as customers is, at best, a constricted portrayal of what governance entails.

Residents-as-customers makes sense, though, when one realizes that the government is being portrayed as an appendage to the commerce of the city. Over and over, the implication is that economic growth in Johannesburg will improve the quality of life for residents. Economic growth will create more business and employment opportunities and expand the wealth of the city. To this extent, quality of life is what constitutes evidence of good governance: "[A]ddressing basic needs and providing local economic development . . . [are] . . . two sides of the same coin" (Office of the Executive Mayor 2001, 2). Governance is defined in terms of its consequences—residents with a high standard of living who are "proud" of their city and, as important, proud of their government.

Given this model of good governance, it is surprising that so little attention is paid to economic growth in these speeches and reports. No data are presented on the expansion of jobs, increases in leased office space, or the formation of new businesses. Moreover, local economic development initiatives—city improvement districts, capital investments, private-public partnerships—are seldom mentioned.

In more recent speeches, though, the mayor has challenged the city council to think of itself not as a manager of services but as "an agent of economic growth." This is seen as the only way for the city to achieve good governance. The Democratic Alliance concurs. The ANC and the DA champion economic growth as the solution to Johannesburg's social problems and the government's fiscal instability. Growth, it is assumed, is the preferred and only path to a vibrant and prosperous city. Additionally, both political parties want residents to take personal responsibility for their lives, a theme that evokes the ANC's call for responsible customers.

When the ANC ascended to power, it absorbed many civic leaders and embarked on solidifying its position as the country's dominant political party (Heller 2003). Once in partnership, civics are now viewed mainly as useful forums for citizen feedback. While new civic associations have emerged to provide a counterweight to government (and thus the ANC), they are not included within government in the same way that they were prior to the new metropolitan government. Public forums still exist, but public politics is meant to focus on achieving efficient government and economic growth, not to challenging governmental policy. From the City's perspective, the issue is customer satisfaction and a citizenry receptive to the direction that the city provides.

Political opposition to this view of local governance does exist, but, as already noted, does not come from political parties; DA policy is not antithetic to ANC positions. Rather, opposition comes from local civic associations (Beall, Crankshaw, and Parnell 2002), the SAMWU, and various protest movements organized around utility rates and privatization. The SAMWU has been particularly vocal in its resistance to efforts to allocate government functions to the private sector, a policy that began with the city's first vision statement, iGoli 2002 (Pape 2001; SAMWU 2003). The issue is GEAR policy, the same policy that provides the rationale for economic growth. Economic growth is meant to stabilize the economy, so that South Africa can enter global markets. Economic stabilization, moreover, requires fiscal stabilization, with fiscal stabilization pursued through job attrition, wage reductions, and the outsourcing of work.

SAMWU's discursive opposition is crafted around workers' rights, the need for greater democracy (specifically, meaningful consultation with community groups), and the greater benefits of government service provision when contrasted with private provision. For these reasons, the SAMWU is active in the antiprivatization movement, a movement that includes the Anti-Privatisation Forum, the Municipal Services Project, the Peoples Budget Campaign, the South African Council of Churches, and Congress of South African Trade Unions, among others (Anti-Privatisation Forum 2003). Rejection of privatization rests on two rhetorical points: the extent to which privatization expands capitalist control and the contradictions attendant to providing "social" goals through "private" entities. In addition, the city's desire to be a world-class city is used as an indicator of its indifference to peoples' needs. For the Anti-Privatisation Forum, governance is the issue.

The city, however, seems intent on constricting the terrain of governance in Johannesburg. The texts have biases: conflict is erased (or hidden), government is represented in managerial terms, citizens are conceived as customers, and grass-roots organizing is discouraged. Governance is centered in the local government, rather than being the framework in which the city operates.

Vision and Governance

The annual budgets and mayoral speeches are short-term statements. They are meant to depict needs and ongoing commitments and to indicate how both will be addressed in the immediate future, usually within the next year. Yet, the discourse on urban government (and governance) also draws on a long tradition of city planning, extending back to the early twentieth century, that argues for simultaneous attention to a more distant future (Friedmann 2002; Sandercock 1998). Ideally, a long-term policy perspective will guide short-term decision making. South Africa is no exception (Mabin and Smit 1997). Over the past twenty years, planning's future perspective has been joined by visioning, that is, the development (usually with citizen involvement) of expansive and innovative future scenarios (Rogerson 1996).

Beginning in 1995, development plans were required of all South African municipalities, and in 2000 the Municipal Services Act mandated Integrated Development Plans. Such plans became the basis for a number of key documents that led eventually to a vision, a dynamic urban image, for the city—Joburg 2030 (Hossack 2002a; 2002b).

The path to Joburg 2030 involved two prior steps: iGoli 2002 and Joburg 2010. iGoli 2002 was launched in 1999 as a short-term response to the need for government reorganization, the restoration of the city's fiscal health, and the development of the management capacity that would enable Johannesburg to be a unified and prosperous city. The intent was to engage in a major reorganization of the government's service delivery and financial functions. Solving these problems would establish the foundation for an African world-class city.

Recognizing the need for a corresponding long-term perspective, the city instituted Joburg 2010. This document was designed as a strategic framework for future policy decisions. In 2001, however, government officials deemed it inadequate, having too short a time horizon. They replaced it with Joburg 2030.

The long-term goal is to develop "Johannesburg as a world class city in which all our citizens will be able to enjoy increased prosperity and quality of life by the year 2030" (City of Johannesburg 2002, 3). The city's commitment to this vision is supported by the corporate business community and such pro-city organizations as the South African Cities Network; it is opposed by the various groups involved with the antiprivatization movement, groups leery of the connection between world city status and globalization. To make this vision a reality, the report goes on, the city must be situated "on the road to a high level of sustainable economic growth." This means encouraging the "right kinds of long-term economic activity" (ibid.). Only in this way can the city's quality of life be improved.

The optimism of Joburg 2030 is based on a belief that "[w]e live in one of the most dynamic and exciting cities in the world." It is, the report claims, "[a] city of possibilities and promise, excitement and hope for the future" (ibid.).

As envisioned, the road to a "better city" requires that the city council "be a well-governed, robust and dynamic agent of economic development" (ibid., 9) rather than solely a provider or insurer of services. In addition, the city must harness the economies of urbanization and localization that emanate from the agglomeration of economic activities in this largest of South African cities. The accompanying strategy involves creating an environment conducive to investment (specifically, reducing crime and engaging in skills development), enhancing the efficiency of investment so as to bolster corporate profitability by improving telecommunications, and accelerating growth within the city using better city-based data, small business development, industrial sector targeting, and "catalytic projects."

After setting forth this framework, the report documents an economic model for the city and leads the reader through a multitude of proposed tasks, each with corresponding performance criteria and targets. The approach is methodical and the tone is analytical, with the emphasis on managing the city government. Local government, Joburg 2030 claims, must develop an economic policy that merges macroeconomic policy with microeconomic planning concerned with actual households and businesses. Of central importance is the assumption that, in cities, "the distinction between economic variables and non-economic variables is considerably blurred" (City of Johannesburg 2002, 7). To put it more bluntly, the social conditions under which people live cannot be separated from the state of the economy.

The road to a world-class city entails negotiating innumerable government responsibilities, each one making its contribution to the overall goal of sustainable economic growth. Comprehensive and dispassionate, the city's vision is based on a foundation of deep concern for the fate of the city and the quality of life of its residents. And, since the report rests on previous development plans and the citizen participation upon which they drew, the vision has legitimacy.

What does it mean, though, for a city to develop a vision statement? How does such a vision contribute to good governance?

Obvious to any reader of Joburg 2030 is that its authors avoid offering a fantasy Johannesburg, "a utopian shopping list of all that is nice in the world" (City of Johannesburg 2002, 6). Rather, their vision is a "realisable" (ibid., 12) trajectory of development that adheres closely to the present. Drastic changes in institutional practices, novel social arrangements, innovative urban forms, or new economic activities are absent. To this extent, the vision is less visionary than cautious and practical. What the city's officials and planners propose is the erasure of current problems and the strengthening of weak institutional capacities. They want a world in which the city has reached its "full economic potential." An appropriate subtitle for Joburg 2030 would be "a better today, tomorrow."

What is being assumed is that the city will undergo no fundamental changes. Joburg 2030's vision is anchored in the city's current "weaknesses, strengths, opportunities and threats" (City of Johannesburg 2002, 11). Growth, not development, to use a common distinction, is the objective. No new inventions (such as the World Wide Web or cell phones) are predicted to be commercialized in the city, no new products will be developed to provide exports, corporate organization will be static, and political alignments will remain as is. The Johannesburg of the future will be "improved" but not alien to current residents who live to see it realized.

From this perspective, Joburg 2030 can be distinguished from the provincial growth plan known as Blue IQ (Gauteng Provincial Government 2002). The differences are attributable, in part, to resources; Johannesburg's capital investment allocations are sufficient only for basic projects, whereas Gauteng province has the financial capacity to mount regional initiatives. But the tone of Blue IQ is also different. It proposes to create Gauteng's own Silicon Valley (the Innovation Hub), develop a regional rapid transit system, and undertake major tourism projects. None of this is visionary, but, when compared to Joburg 2030, it seems less tied to the present, less conservative in outlook.

In addition, the authors of Joburg 2030 have assumed that the world outside Johannesburg will be unchanged in thirty years' time. They fail to recognize that the San Francisco's and London's that serve as the models to which Johannesburg aspires are themselves developing vision statements and acting to improve their position and global competitiveness. The text is insular. There is too little awareness of the dynamics of social change within and outside the government, within and outside Johannesburg and the country.

Thinking of Joburg 2030 in this way might lead the cynic to conclude that the vision is another instance of trivial planning—that is, planning done simply for symbolic purposes and wholly without consequences for policy making. This is not the case; the mayor's annual speeches and budget reports are replete with references to the city's vision and how it shapes current decision making. Moreover, Joburg 2030 is attentive, maybe too attentive, to resource constraints and actions that will enable the city to achieve sustainable economic growth and world-class status. Each goal is addressed with specific tasks, and each task is set within a performance appraisal framework contained in the Integrated Development Plans. Joburg 2030 is a practical guide for city government.

At the same time, the vision is less attentive to the problems and weaknesses—and the apartheid legacy—that it hopes to resolve. The assumption seems to be that poverty and unemployment among Africans, rate collection shortfalls, and crime, among other issues, are temporary. They are not viewed as endemic to prevailing and enduring institutional relationships. If there is a utopian quality to this vision, it lies precisely in this assumption that the government and the city's residents can be perfected.

What makes this attitude toward the future incongruous are the momentous changes that have occurred in South African society since the 1970s when apartheid was at its peak. National political arrangements have been transformed, the racial composition of the government has changed dramatically, and Africans, Indians, and coloreds are now full citizens of the country. Once oppressed, racial groups have wholly novel expectations of government, and many harbor vastly different visions of the future for their children. These are people and places in flux. Joburg 2030 ignores this history.

Such an approach to the future has one, very salient consequence: it does not require that the current governance structure change in any significant way. Despite worldwide debates about the meaning of citizenship, the expansion of the democratic sphere, the creation of public spaces in which differences can be confronted and collective action deliberated, and the incorporation of civil society into governmental institutions (Holston 1999), the Joburg 2030 vision contains no major rupture in local government or current governmental practices. Government will become more efficient, citizens will be less dependent on it, and economic growth will be sustained, but otherwise it will be the same government as in 2002. Prevailing power relations and political party alignments will be undisturbed.

From a governance standpoint, having a vision conveys a sense of strong leadership. Leaders do not drift; they do not make ad hoc decisions or act impulsively in response to daily challenges. Visionary leaders act in the present guided by an image of the future. They are not motivated by partisan interests, but instead draw their inspiration from the unitary interests of the city and the people who comprise it.

In effect, the audience for Joburg 2030 is asked to believe that adherence to a vision is the only way to achieve a "better future." More to the point, in the context of Joburg 2030 and the mayoral speeches and budget reports discussed earlier, vision is what distinguishes governance from government. Government involves the provision of services and the collection of rates and fees. It is inward looking and technical. Government with vision is governance. Governance looks outward to society and escapes from the pressure of short-term action. Governance is institutionally and historically expansive. The development and publication of vision statements by cities is thus a signal that its leaders, and the government that they represent, are engaged in a larger project for the greater good of society.

Yet, the city of Johannesburg's vision does not broaden public decision making; it constricts it. In order to coordinate political gains, convey a sense of political stability, and shift peoples' attention from current problems, it looks to a future that can be achieved without destabilizing prevailing social and institutional relations. If economic growth ensues and spreads evenly throughout society, the city's future will be better. The current balance of political power and leadership, however, will not be disturbed.

Concluding Comments

In the city's Integrated Development Plan for 2003/4, the tasks of good governance are described (p. 36). They include involvement in the South African Local Government Association, the sharing of "best practices" with other cities, compliance with employment equity and skills development legislation, the stabilization of labor relations, anticorruption initiatives, financial risk management, and consultation with the public. Contrast this with Friedmann's (2002, 114) more widely shared understanding of governance: "Governance refers to the various ways by which binding decisions for cities and city-regions are made and carried out. . . . [It is] considerably more inclusive than traditional government . . . and reflects the fact that increasingly a wider range of participants exists in these processes than has . . . been the case."

The city of Johannesburg reduces governance to good government. Its focus is the formal mechanisms by which public decisions are made. Through annual mayoral speeches and budget reports, governance is recognized but constricted. The texts assume consensus, treat government as a technical function, are managerial in tone, and generally depoliticize not just public services but the meaning of basic needs and the sharing of power. Citizens are turned into customers, and centralization substitutes for democracy (Friedman 2003). These underlying themes are reinforced by the city's sense of Johannesburg's future, a future whose attainment requires no fundamental change but only improvement along previously established paths. Economic growth reigns as the goal and rationale for local government. (Parenthetically, concerned about the economic focus of Joburg 2030, in 2004 the city began formulating a Human Development Agenda for Johannesburg.)

All of this puts in doubt the advisability of a commitment to Johannesburg as a world-class, African city. This desire is clearly a response to the unavoidable discourse of globalization and its core belief that city regions thrive on the basis of global competitiveness (Beauregard and Pierre 2000). It is also, as mentioned in one mayoral speech, a response to studies that have claimed Johannesburg as the only world city in Africa and to the memory of South Africa's international isolation—its pariah status—in the 1970s and 1980s. Johannesburg's leaders do not envision the city as a global city on par with New York or Tokyo, but they do imagine that it can be a significant economic force in southern Africa if not the larger region. Most important the notion of a world-class city conjures up a city participating in global prosperity through its access to trade, global production, and international finance. The city's hosting of the World Summit on Sustainable Development in 2002 and the ICC Cricket World Cup in 2003 reinforced the belief that Johannesburg can attain world-class status.

The notion of Johannesburg as an "African" city is more problematic. In its apartheid form, Johannesburg was essentially a European city and "Europeans"—the English and Afrikaners—still dominate corporate boardrooms and control most of the country's wealth. Economic growth, moreover, is concentrated precisely in the northern suburbs where Europeans reside. Johannesburg, though, is and has been an African city; it is in Africa, the majority of its residents are black Africans, there is an enduring ethnic and tribal culture, and the inner city is almost entirely occupied by black households and businesses and by African immigrants from neighboring countries. The puzzle is how to reconcile these two heritages and then how to translate them into strategies of development and governance.

In numerous ways, Johannesburg exhibits the qualities of a city government that has joined the global trend to neoliberalism (Bernstein 2003; Tickell and Peck 2003). It views government as an appendage of the economy, quality of life as a matter of individual opportunity and choice in labor and investment markets, citizens as customers, and the future as shaped by globalization. In addition, Johannesburg's political leadership, mainly the ANC but also the DA, are interested in consolidating power. Downsizing government, touting individual responsibility, and fostering economic growth are the means to this end.

This Johannesburg variant on neoliberalism differs not just in motive from the neoliberalism extant in the United States and Great Britain. The ANC came to power in South Africa after decades of political unrest. A new regulatory regime, one that would offer stability as well as opportunities for individual social and economic advancement, was unavoidable. Achieving this while consolidating power and position seems to have dictated a discourse that constricts, rather than expands, governance. In this context, a discursive strategy that sets the local government as an agent of economic growth and economic growth as the path to good governance makes sense.

Appendix A: Mayoral Speeches and Budget Reports

Greater Johannesburg Metropolitan Council. 2001. Budget 2000/2001: Enroute to a Unicity. Office of the Executive Mayor, Address by Executive Mayor at Council Meeting, 30 January 2001. Photocopy.

Office of the Executive Mayor. 2001/2. Mayoral Budget Speech: Building an African World Class City. www.johannesburgnews.co.za/budget_2001/menu.html (accessed 15 May 2004).

———. 2002/3. Mayoral Budget Speech. www.joburg.org.za/may2002/budget_speech.stm (accessed 15 May 2004).

———. 2002. State of the City Address by the Executive Mayor at Council. 31 January.

———. 2003. Official Opening of Council Executive Mayoral Address. 30 January.

———. 2003/4. Mayoral Budget Speech. www.joburg.org.za/2003/budget_speech.stm (accessed 15 May 2004).

Appendix B: Plans and Vision Statements

City of Johannesburg. 2001/2. *City Development Plan, 2001/2002*. www.joburg.org.za (accessed 5 May 2004).

———. 2002. *Johannesburg 2030*. Johannesburg: Corporate Planning Unit.

———. 2003/4. *Integrated Development Plan, 2003/04*.

Gauteng Provincial Government. 2002. *Blue IQ: Annual Report*.

Greater Johannesburg Metropolitan Council. 2000. *iGoli 2002: Making Greater Johannesburg Work*.

Johannesburg 2030: Q & A. www.joburg.za/joburg_2030 (accessed 5 May 2004).

Note

We would like to acknowledge the assistance of Judith Briggs, Democratic Alliance Councillor, city of Johannesburg, for her help in obtaining various speeches and reports and in providing a description of the Democratic Alliance's policy positions.

References

Anti-Privatisation Forum. 2003. www.apf.org.za (accessed 3 May 2004).

Beall, J., O. Crankshaw, and S. Parnell. 2002. *Uniting a Divided City: Governance and Social Exclusion in Johannesburg*. London: Earthscan Publications.

Beauregard, R. A., and J. Pierre. 2000. Disputing the Global. *Policy & Politics* 28, no. 4: 467–78.

Beavon, K. S. O. 1997. Johannesburg: A City and Metropolitan Area in Transformation. In C. Rakodi (ed.), *The Urban Challenge in Africa*, 150–91. Tokyo: United Nations University Press.

Bender, Th. 1996. Clients or Citizens? *Critical Review* 10, no. 1: 123–34.
Bernstein, A. 2003. New Urban Paradigm Revitalizes Cities. *Business Day*, 11 June.
Bremner, L. 2000. Reinventing the Johannesburg Inner City. *Cities* 17, no. 3: 185–93.
Chipkin, I. 2003. "Functional" and "Dysfunctional" Communities: The Making of National Citizens in South Africa. *Journal of Southern African Studies* 29, no. 1: 63–82.
Christopher, A. J. 2001. *The Atlas of Changing South Africa*. London: Routledge.
Democratic Alliance. 2003. www.dajhb.co.za (accessed 5 May 2004).
Edelman, M. 1988. *Constructing the Political Spectacle*. Chicago: University of Chicago Press.
Friedman, St. 2003. Only Inclusive Democracy Can Make Promise a Reality. *Business Day*, 21 October.
Friedmann, J. 2002. *The Prospect of Cities*. Minneapolis: University of Minnesota Press.
Hastings, A. 1999. Discourse and Urban Change. *Urban Studies* 36, no. 1: 7–12.
Heller, P. 2003. Reclaiming Democratic Spaces: Civics and Politics in Post-Transition Johannesburg. In R. Tomlinson, R. Beauregard, L. Bremner, and X. Mangcu (eds.), *Emerging Johannesburg: Perspectives on the Postapartheid City*, 155–84. New York: Routledge.
Holston, J. (ed.). 1999. *Cities and Citizenship*. Durham, N.C.: Duke University Press.
Hossack, C. 2002a. Joburg 2030—The High Road to Growth. www.joburg.org.za/feb_2002/30year_plan2.stm (accessed 3 May 2004).
———. 2002b. Next Generation Jo'burg—Africa's San Francisco? www.joburg.org.za/feb_2002/2030.stm (accessed 5 May 2004).
Isin, E. (ed.). 2000. *Democracy, Citizenship and the Global City*. London: Routledge.
Joyce, P. 2003. *The Rule of Freedom: Liberalism and the Modern City*. London: Verso.
Kaplan, Th. J. 1986. The Narrative Structure of Policy Analysis. *Journal of Policy Analysis and Management* 5, no. 4: 761–78.
LeGales, P. 1998. Regulation and Governance in European Cities. *International Journal of Urban and Regional Research* 22, no. 3: 482–506.
Lester, A., E. Nel, and T. Binns. 2000. South Africa's Current Transition in Temporal and Spatial Context. *Antipode* 32, no. 2: 135–51.
Mabin, A., and D. Smit. 1997. Reconstructing South Africa's Cities? The Making of Urban Planning, 1900–2000. *Planning Perspectives* 12: 193–223.
Marshall, T. H. 1964. *Class, Citizenship, and Social Development*. Garden City, N.Y.: Doubleday.
Mayer, M. 1995. Urban Governance in the Post-Fordist City. In P. Healey et al. (eds.). *Managing Cities*, 231–41. Chichester: John Wiley & Sons.
McCarthy, J. 1992. Local and Regional Government: From Rigidity to Crisis to Flux. In D. M. Smith (ed.). *The Apartheid City and Beyond*, 25–36. London: Routledge.

Pape, J. 2001. A Public Sector Alternative "SAMWU's Efforts." *South Africa Labor Bulletin* 25, no. 4: 45–50.

Robinson, J. 1998. Spaces of Democracy: Remapping the Apartheid City. *Environment & Planning D* 16, no. 5: 533–48.

Roe, E. 1994. *Narrative Policy Analysis*. Durham, N.C.: Duke University Press.

Rogerson, Ch. M. 1996. Image Enhancement and Local Economic Development in Johannesburg. *Urban Forum* 7, no. 2: 139–58.

Salskov-Iversen, D. 1997. A Discursive Perspective on British Local Government's Response to Change. *Discourse & Society* 8, no. 3: 391–415.

SAMWU. 2003. www.samwu.org.za (accessed 3 May 2004).

Sandercock, L. 1998. *Towards Cosmopolis*. Chichester: John Wiley & Sons.

Sassen, S. 1999. Whose City Is It? Globalization and the Function of New Claims. In R. A. Beauregard and S. Body-Gendrot (eds.), *The Urban Moment*, 99–118. Thousand Oaks, Calif.: Sage.

South African Cities Network. 2004. *Pilot Peer Review Visit to the City of Johannesburg, 27–31 May 2002*. www.sacities.net (accessed 3 May 2004).

Stenson, K., and P. Watt. 1999. Governmentality and "the Death of the Social"?: A Discourse Analysis of Local Government Texts in South-East England. *Urban Studies* 36, no. 1: 189–201.

Swilling, M., R. Humphries, and K. Shubane (eds.). 1991. *Apartheid City in Transition*. Cape Town: Oxford University Press.

Throgmorton, J. A. 1996. *Planning as Persuasive Storytelling*. Chicago: University of Chicago Press.

Tickell, A., and J. Peck. 2003. Making Global Rules: Globalisation or Neoliberalisation? In J. Peck and H. Yeung (eds.), *Remaking the Global Economy*. London: Sage.

Tomlinson, R. 1999a. Ten Years in the Making: A History of Metropolitan Government in Johannesburg. *Urban Forum* 10, no. 1: 1–40.

———. 1999b. From Exclusion to Inclusion: Rethinking Johannesburg's Central City. *Environment & Planning A* 31: 1655–78.

———. 2005. Reinterpreting the Meaning of Decentralization in Johannesburg. In K. Segbers, S. Raiser, and K. Volkmann (eds.), *Public Problems—Private Solutions? Globalizing Cities in the South*, 327–66. Aldershot: Ashgate Publishing.

Tomlinson, R., R. Beauregard, L. Bremner, and X. Mangcu. 2003. The Postapartheid Struggle for an Integrated Johannesburg. In Tomlinson, R. Beauregard, L. Bremner, and X. Mangcu (eds.), *Emerging Johannesburg: Perspectives on the Postapartheid City*, 3–20. New York: Routledge.

Yanow, D. 1996. *How Does a Policy Mean? Interpreting Policy and Organizational Actions*. Washington, D.C.: Georgetown: University Press.

———. 2000. *Conducting Interpretive Policy Analysis*. Thousand Oaks, Calif.: Sage.

Versions of a Postcolonial Metropolis
Competing Discourses on Bombay's Image
Ranjit Hoskote

> Bombay was not an indigenous Indian city. It was built by the British expressly for maintaining trade links with India and was never perhaps expected to become a large town. Thus, it was neither oriented nor situated around a sacred place, nor was it structured in relation to the cardinal points and directions as a traditional Indian town might have been built. In fact, being primarily set up as a port, it developed looking out to the ocean with the quay as its focus.
> —*Sharada Dwivedi and Rahul Mehrotra*

Acts of Naming

The tension between a global and a local identity was inscribed into the nature of Bombay/Mumbai at its foundation. As an international port and center of trade and manufacture developed by the British colonial administration in India, it looked outward to the widespread international framework in which it played a role. At the same time, as an island situated off India's west coast, whose native inhabitants were connected by ties of ethnicity, occupation, worship, and exchange to the hinterlands of Maharashtra, Goa, Gujarat, and Karnataka, the city also maintained an association with the realities of the subcontinental environment. Bombay/Mumbai's heritage is that of a colonial town that served as an interface between India and the world. This, combined with the geographical circumstance of it being an island-city, holds the key to the cultural intricacies and political turbulences that inform the city's present. Indeed, in describing Bombay (which was officially renamed Mumbai in the mid-1990s) as a city confidently poised to play its role as a global megalopolis, commentators often overlook the fact that, as a postcolonial metropolis, it occupies an unstable and ambiguous position between the global and the local. This is the result of an unavoidable paradox: when the state of Maharashtra was carved from the former Bombay Presidency and the princely state of Hyderabad, as an entity premised on the linguistic primacy of Marathi, a Maharashtrian cultural identity, and the interests of a largely rural economy, Bombay became its capital. The highly Westernized, multicultural and multilingual urban center could not have been more alienated from the state over which it would preside.

For the purposes of this essay, I shall refer to the city by the dual name, Bombay/Mumbai,[1] to emphasize this complex urban predicament, and to signify the two major competing claims that have been asserted over this prosperous, vibrant, and populous[2] metropolitan region in recent decades. *Bombay* symbolizes an openness to an inclusive cosmopolitanism and diversity of experience, alluding to the city's colonial history and often, though by no means necessarily, incarnating an elite sensibility. This name incarnates the designation, *Bom Bahia*, or "Good Bay," that the Portuguese gave to the outpost when it was ceded to them by the Gujarat Sultanate in 1534. Passing to Britain as part of Catherine of Braganza's dowry when she married Charles II in 1661, the outpost was leased to the East India Company and so inaugurated the trajectory that would culminate in metropolitan status (Tindall 1992). *Mumbai*, on the other hand, tends to downplay or even robustly reject this colonial history as an alien contamination, insisting on a more nativist vision that roots the city in a Marathi and tacitly Hindu ethos. The name memorializes the mother goddess, Mumba-Aai or Mumbadevi, whose worship was prevalent in precolonial times and continues in the city today. It thus serves as an ideological rallying point for groups who assert the ideal of cultural purity, and who oppose any dilution of the city's supposed core identity by other linguistic, religious, or ethnic constituencies (Kosambi 1995).

While both names were simultaneously in popular use,[3] the city was officially renamed Mumbai in 1996 by the government of Maharashtra, a coalition formed by two right-wing parties: the national-level Hindu-majoritarian Bharatiya Janata Party (BJP) and its regional-level ally, the Shiv Sena, which colors its majoritarianism with a distinct autochthonist shade. Thus, *Mumbai* became formally reinforced as the symbol of a parochialist ideology, while *Bombay* came to signalize the cosmopolitan resistance to such an ideology. The schism between Bombay and Mumbai underscored an ideological polarization between a democratic politics of inclusion and a demagogic politics of exclusion that took place in the metropolis from 1995 to 1999, during the tenure of the BJP-Sena government; this period also marked the high noon of the epoch of organization, when profound economic changes transformed Bombay/Mumbai. The interweaving of the right-wing coalition's simultaneous neotraditionalist desires and its globalist aspirations with the effects of organization was to bear seismic sociocultural consequences, which I will delineate in the course of this essay.

The competition between the claims of Bombay and Mumbai surfaces in everyday metropolitan experience: in conversational exchanges, humor, artistic gestures, graffiti slogans, and such public-sphere performances as demonstrations and protest marches. The cosmopolitan ideal enshrined in *Bombay* is rhetorically presented, by its opponents, as the preserve of an elite: the charge tends to be persuasive because, while large numbers of citizens do indeed subscribe to the cosmopolitan ideal in practice, its theoretical elaboration is left to members of the articulate classes, who sometimes render it in self-defeatingly narrow terms as a programmatic rejection of the local. The parochialist agenda manifest in *Mumbai* is maintained by the Shiv Sena (Hansen 2001, 8–10), which propagates a virulent brand of identity politics, promotes a "sons-of-the-soil" policy, has unhesitatingly used violence in the service of populism, and yet combines its militant Hindu communalism with an emphatically urban vision of the local. Its founder and supreme leader, Bal Thackeray, has openly professed his admiration for Nazism.

Between these two extreme positions, Bombay/Mumbai exists in a range of versions: there are as many images, visions, and discourses of the city as there are interest groups, for Bombay/Mumbai is a powerful cultural imaginary, variously conceived and constructed. Each version conveys the narrator's emotional and material investments in the city: whether it is a member of the transethnic English-speaking elite that views Bombay as a Westernized island incidentally moored off the forbidding and backward mainland of Maharashtra. Or the Marathi-speaking millworker or bourgeois intellectual of central Bombay, to whom Mumbai is an inalienable extension of Maharashtra. Or the inner-city Gujarati or Parsi merchant, whose ancestral trade linkages connect him to the pre-Maharashtra past of the Bombay Presidency and to a present that crosses the state boundary to connect Bombay with Surat, Ahmedabad, Baroda, Rajkot, and other commercial and industrial centers in Gujarat. Or the "south Indian," a broad and inaccurate classification that includes communities from Karnataka, Kerala, Tamil Nadu, and Andhra Pradesh, across a spectrum of social and cultural locations, among them hoteliers, journalists, publishers, booksellers, artists, film makers, traders, accountants, and craftspersons. Each group has its specific nostalgia for a charmed period in the city's history, its own urban foundation mythology, and a special belief in its authority to define the city's nature. Connections among these constituent groups and acknowledged overlaps among their specific self-images are, however, infrequent, except where such groups are bound together in a common economic or cultural practice.

Therefore, what strikes even a casual observer of the current debate over the identity and future of the Bombay/Mumbai Metropolitan Region—at the core of which is the question of whether it ought to be more securely anchored in the local; whether it must reorientate itself toward acquiring the infrastructure, amenities, and style of a global city; or whether some reconciliation between these opposed imperatives may be achieved—is that there is no single dominant image of the city, no broadly shared civic vision, no common discourse regarding policy objectives, no agreement on the greatest common good of the metropolis. What prevails, in place of such consensual unities, is a kaleidoscopic circle of images in a state of perpetual contestation, varying from citizen to citizen and community to community, and determined by such factors as language, religion, ethnicity, locality of habitation, and economic and cultural capital.

The context within which this debate has unfolded, since the early 1990s, is that of a perceived need for metropolitan regeneration. Toward this end, a variety of political parties and nongovernmental organizations, civil-society groups, bureaucratic committees, and corporate initiatives have attempted to address the crucial issue of Bombay/Mumbai's further evolution. Alongside the cultural questions considered here, these circles also underscore administrative and infrastructural concerns. Can the metropolis survive its unplanned expansion? Will the island-city continue to turn its back on the needs of the migrants who arrive daily in their thousands, while extending itself to the mainland across Thane Creek? Or will it strive toward the desired status of global city, its elite imagining a clean, sophisticated, highly automated environment from which all traces of inefficiency, pollution, and human unpredictability have been erased? What modes of governance would best serve these mandates: a more responsive and participatory civic administration on the one hand, or a more ruthless technocratic oligarchy on the other?

Communicative Disengagement

In a city so divided along differentials of politicized identity, tacit influence, and active power, there can be no single platform on which the city's future can be discussed by all the interest groups concerned. Important civic questions do circulate in Bombay/Mumbai, but this is a fragmentary and episodic discourse conducted across a gamut of venues, including the academic symposium, the administrative committee, the NGO activist meeting, the political rally, the ethnic enclave, and the civic-affairs supplements of the newspapers. Often, too, the languages in which this discourse is conducted pass each other by. In a literal sense, because the public spheres representing the city's major languages—English, Marathi, Gujarati, Hindi, and Urdu—do not form a coherent ecumene. Also, in a figurative sense, since there appears to be little in common among the idioms and preoccupations of such participants in the debate as the urban planner, the professional geographer, the municipal councillor, and the public-interest activist. Even within the same constituency or faction, sometimes there are strong differences of emphasis, so that activists may be divided between the preservation of historic urban built form and the resettlement of slum residents, or planners may be torn between a community participation and a top-down model of metropolitan regeneration.

I would argue that this condition—the lack of a common platform and language among urban actors, and the consequent inability of their fragmentary civic discourse to translate itself into durable proposals or projects—is not, in itself, the main problem afflicting a metropolis that hovers indecisively between the alternatives of stagnation and revitalization. I believe it, rather, to be symptomatic of a more fundamental malaise: the crisis of Bombay/Mumbai lies in its incoherence as a corporate polity, resulting from an increasing communicative disengagement that has come to characterize the relationships among the groups that constitute the city's collective life since the 1960s. I would suggest that this mutual alienation among the city's constituent groups became intensified during the 1990s, in correspondence to the divergence in their material interests and cultural orientations, political ambitions, and economic aspirations, in a moment shaped, as remarked earlier, by the contradictory pulls of neotraditionalism, global aspiration, and the stresses of organization. In this moment, a metropolis that had been celebrated for its richly multiple yet coherent identity—to the extent of becoming an iconic standard of progressive values and hospitality to cultural experiment (da Cunha 2003; Prakash 2003)—exploded in a series of unmanageable antagonisms. Bombay/Mumbai's customary cogencies, already placed under pressure by the persistent communal and class violence of the 1970s and

Contested Future 263

1980s, were disrupted by a new array of factors, the most prominent among these being:

1. The conflict between the city's old and new economies (often termed the "sunset" and "sunrise" sectors, respectively) and their personnel, with the advent of organization, and the difference in degree to which communities have been benefited or placed at a disadvantage by the processes of organization
2. The city's inability to integrate its disparate interest groups, especially its relatively recent immigrant populations, into a single hospitable conceptual space regulated by consensual authority structures
3. The marginalization and attempted disenfranchisement of groups such as the Dalits, the Muslims, and migrant labor
4. The phenomenon of competitive populism, a political manipulation by various parties of these material and emotional dissatisfactions, from which an identitarian politics of resentment is generated

Let us examine these four factors in some detail.

Conflict between Old and New

In Bombay/Mumbai, the convenient shorthand term *local/global* has not described a smooth interface so much as it has marked a ragged border between several sets of opposed classes, interests, and milieux. It may be translated through various binaries, such as: industrial subaltern / information elite; informal economic sector / organized economic sector; recycling economy / throwaway economy. One of the major causes of the communicative disengagement that has kept Bombay/Mumbai's various communities and factions apart during the past fourteen years is the difference in degree to which communities have been benefited or placed at a disadvantage by the economic liberalization inaugurated by the Congress government led by Prime Minister P. V. Narasimha Rao in 1991, and pursued by successive national governments to accomplish the opening-up of the Indian economy to global market actors. The discourse staged around organization in Bombay/Mumbai engages with this economic asymmetry as its central topos: it dramatizes the conflict between the so-called sunset sector (the defunct or flagging textile mill, manufacturing, and shipping industries) and the sunrise sector (banking, finance, and information technology), playing up the mutual antagonism of the constituencies associated with each.

Bombay/Mumbai's flourishing textile mill industry, with which the metropolis was once synonymous, was founded in the 1850s. Its collapse may be dated to the total strike called by the influential trade-union leader Dr. Datta Samant in 1982–83, which no subsequent negotiation could resolve. The principal effect of this crisis was that thousands of millworkers were rendered unemployed, and their families forced into petty enterprise or crime; the large reserve army of resentful youth that grew out of this predicament was recruited, less than a decade later, either into the Shiv Sena, or into one or another of the city's criminal Mafias. Over the 1990s, as real-estate prices in Bombay climbed steeply to rank among the highest in the world, the mills in the heartland of the metropolis fell into ruin. The mill lands became, nonetheless, the focus of conflict among millowners, the longtime residential population of millworkers, real-estate developers, and criminals who extorted protection money and offered hired killers to settle disputes outside the purview of the law (D'Monte 2002).

Successive state governments, both Congress and BJP-Sena, called upon to arbitrate, failed to adopt policy measures to resolve this crisis; housing experts and visionary architects who had proposed solutions were ignored; and millowners eager to sell these blocked assets began to adopt extralegal approaches to effect land resale. At the time of writing, no clear policy has been adopted to resolve the issue, but the mill lands are being leased out piecemeal, informally, to developers establishing high-rent apartment blocks and office premises—the operational bases of the sunrise sector inserted, through a process of gentrification, into the old working-class districts still occupied by the remnants of the sunset sector. These are the visible manifestations of the transformation through which the city's textile mill economy, driven by local capital, has yielded before a different, yet incipient economy: one dominated by the avant-garde of global capital, specialist entrepreneurs, and professionals who work for transnational banking and financial services, media, entertainment and advertising agencies, software corporations, and knowledge enterprises.

The uneven transition from the mill-driven economy to the services-oriented economy, signaling a dramatic social shift as it does, has accentuated the conflict between the affluent and the disempowered classes. This conflict is fueled by the anxiety and frustration caused by the most visible outcome of organization: the opening-up of a new market for consumer goods and the spread of conspicuous commodity fetishism. The demonstration of purchasing power among the affluent triggers, in turn, the aspirations and frustrations of the classes whose modest incomes exclude them from the consumerist market. At an everyday level, the new stresses in urban culture are enacted through an antagonism between alternative identities, idioms of belonging, and modes of self-assertion: a collision between old local mythologies and new global ones, each distorted, fractured, and reshaped on impact with the other. The global is incarnated in the invitations of cyberspace, the flashy neon advertising logos of Nike, Benetton, Reebok, and Microsoft, and the Coke-and-pizza youth subculture. The local is identified with the politics of ethnic segregationism promoted by parties such as the Shiv Sena; it is articulated through the reengineering of the sacred as a revanchist means of mass mobilization, especially through "mythological" television serials[4] and public religious observances that reinvent folk traditions of festivity (Hansen 1999). Indeed, this simultaneity of mythological frames—their collision and mutation—points to the manner in which Bombay/Mumbai generates alternative and competing versions of modernity, even countermodernities, which feed into the circuit of versions from which images of the metropolis are constructed in the popular imagination.

Inability to Integrate

This reflection leads us to take note of Bombay/Mumbai's increasing inability to integrate its disparate interest groups, especially its relatively recent immigrant populations, into a single hospitable conceptual space regulated by consensual authority structures. Since no common basis or shared program has emerged to replace the ethnic, regional, or religious world-views of the city's constituent groups *as a psychological reality* (the rule of law and the force of civic sanction, themselves in danger of breakdown under pressure of circumstances, do not propose themselves as a substitute), these world-views invariably play a divisive role. I would remark here on the city's inability to develop new forms of ritualized authority that are widely acceptable as mechanisms by which antagonisms may be resolved; so that, in the absence of legislative innovation, dissensions among groups are dealt with in informal settings that range from the benign neighborhood committee (the *mohalla* or *patti*, a traditional locality recast as a civil-society initiative) to the kangaroo court of the criminal arbiter-enforcer (the *dada* beloved as an antihero in popular Hindi cinema, and the exemplar for the Shiv Sena's brand of rough streetside justice). Thus, the cadences of *communitas* that we hear in contemporary

Bombay/Mumbai are not, in every case, evidence of renewed civic energy. Sometimes, they are pragmatic and rhetorical improvisations based on cultural categories representing classical power relationships, such as those of insider/outsider, local/alien and legatee/upstart.[5]

Through the 1990s, Bombay/Mumbai has received a dual traffic of people from two opposed processes: those of rural immiserization and organization. On the one hand, there is a steady influx into the city of ecological and economic refugees dispossessed from rural India: these immigrants are recruited into the informal manufacturing and service economy, or into organized crime, and play a vital role in the city's vast informal sector as an unorganized working class. They provide the metropolis with its domestic help, casual labor, construction workers, storekeepers, commercial-sex workers, and the anonymous bangle manufacturers, leatherworkers, shoemakers, and tailors whose wage slavery disappears behind the glitter of upmarket brand names.[6] Despite their contribution to Bombay's economy, they are denied basic rights and the aegis of citizens' entitlements: as uncertain inhabitants of Bombay's interstitial spaces, their squatter settlements are built on encroached land, their electricity and water connections are illegal; their lives are at the mercy of the local bully, the land-shark, and the municipal demolition squad. On the other hand, transnational corporations disperse their operations within India, taking advantage of the low-cost intellectual and physical labor available, thus generating a "sweatshop economy, incarnated both in the physical grind of the informal sector, and in the tight, time-zone-adjusted, night-into-day routines of medical transcript recorders and telephonic client-services outsourced from the Western to the Eastern Hemisphere.

While Bombay/Mumbai's nineteenth-century modernity, both as process and as myth, was inclusive and generalized, engaging all sectors of society in its elaborations, its twentieth- and twenty-first-century postmodernity has been, both as process and myth, exclusive and restricted: as we have noted, it engages only certain highly specialized sectors of society in its elaborations while ignoring others, bringing about an entrenchment of privilege and an asymmetry of opportunity and entitlement. While Bombay/Mumbai's modernity was a process of maximizing profits from labor, it was also, even if by default, a mode by which individuals could liberate themselves from the burden of a feudal past. Both elite and subaltern classes were involved in the project of modernity, and their interests were intimately interlinked. This is why, in the early, Victorian phase of Bombay's expansion, a significant number of millowners were dedicated to "good works": to the creation of an infrastructure for health, education, transport, and cultural uplift, to housing and the provision of amenities and employment to the poor. By contrast, Bombay/Mumbai's postmodern elites place personal comforts first; being of mixed ethnic composition, nonlocal, and often on the move across the globe, they concentrate on optimal conceptions of their own well-being, largely shutting out any thought of the city's subaltern classes. For the upwardly mobile elite groups, the public sphere is to be abandoned in favor of a retreat into "civil privatism," in Habermas's phrase. For the subaltern groups, the public sphere is rejected in favor of a resort to defensive ethnicity and violent self-assertion, to recover the dignity and purpose denied them by a changing society, as well as an aggressive or criminal appropriation of opportunities and entitlements withheld by the sate.

This split between the Old and the New would have been a textbook case of a passage from reality and modernity to virtuality and postmodernity, had it not been for the fact that Bombay's cityscape, shaped by a counterpoint between frozen rents and leaping real-estate prices, creates a unique system of stresses: a chain of hybrid spaces in which freehold owners, tenants, illegal tenants, squatters, encroachers, and pavement dwellers may all be found in the same neighborhood. The subaltern and the elite are not, therefore, always geographically separated: affluent enclaves and dilapidated ghettos are not set wide apart, but are set interstitially alongside one another. A typical Bombay/Mumbai stratigraphy shows bungalows and high-rises on the crest of a hill; apartment blocks on the level below; *chawls* or mass-housing tenements and old-fashioned middle-class community housing at a further remove; the *basti*s and *jhopadpattis,* the shanties and slums, on the wrong side of the tracks. This is as true for the Janus-like dualism of Cumballa Hill / Forjett Street, with an elite residential area backing on to a commercial and working-class one, as it is for the more apparent Lower Parel / Upper Worli divide, where the former name indicates a mill land that is gradually being gentrified into the locale signified by the latter name. Such proximity generates a circuit of aspiration, frustration, contempt, and resentment—which sharply dramatizes the disparity of skills and rewards, opportunity and entitlement, the differentials in housing, education, employment, and social welfare in the city (Hoskote 1996; 1999).

In such an interstitial situation, transgressions of delicate boundaries and confrontations over control of sites and resources are an ever-present danger: conflicts erupt periodically, in forms ranging from the epic scale of ethnic rioting and the commandeering of public space for violent demonstrations, to the miniature level of commuter riots at railway stations and incidents of stone throwing on train commuters by slum dwellers across the tracks. Such conflicts could have been contained by the state. However, during the mid-1990s, the state in Bombay/Mumbai increasingly delegated its authority as an arbiter to extraconstitutional sources of force, either political enforcers or criminals, not accountable to the electorate. During the BJP-Sena regime (1995–99), the state turned into a clearinghouse and placeholder for influential class interests, rather than an instrument for achieving public welfare. This alarming phenomenon of a routinely practiced parastatal method of conflict settlement—when disagreements over real-estate deals, prolonged litigation under the Rent Act and the Land Ceiling Act, and unclear deeds of lease and ownership created a situation in which landlords and tenants resorted to strong-arm measures—underscored the erosion of legitimate conflict-resolution mechanisms in Bombay/Mumbai.

Marginalization

Through the 1990s the majoritarian-autochthonist ascendancy succeeded in gradually marginalizing and effectively disenfranchising the city's oppressed Dalit caste groups, the Muslim religious minority, and the migrant-labor communities, who form a substantial proportion of Bombay/Mumbai's population. While the Dalits, who once had a powerful radical leadership but now lack such active direction, have fluctuated in their political loyalties (they have, most recently, been courted by their traditional enemy, the Shiv Sena; see Omvedt 1995, 72–80, and Hoskote 2004a), the Muslims have tended to retreat further into a ghettoized solidarity. This process of ghettoization was exacerbated by the December 1992–January 1993 riots following the destruction of the Babri Masjid in Ayodhya, northern India, by Hindu right-wing militants. A still-unaddressed guilt attaches to this phase of the city's history, when its Muslim population was sought to be contained if not erased by a tacit coalition of forces, including elements among the Congress state government, the Hindu-dominated state bureaucracy and police, Shiv Sena militants, and hired criminals. The pogroms launched by these forces were multipronged, aimed at Muslim homes, Muslim-owned shops and factories, and the Urdu press. The twin objective was to displace Muslims from ethnically mixed residential and commercial areas and to silence the Muslim intelligentsia. Through the 1990s, observers reported unwritten sanctions practiced in Hindu-dominated cooperative housing societies, by which Muslims were discouraged from seeking occupancy. Through an insidious demographic shift since December 1992, large numbers of Muslims have gravitated toward *mohallas* in the inner-city and Muslim-majority suburban neighborhoods, thus partitioning the city spatially and eliminating a measure of that interstitiality by which religious communities shared their everyday lives (Hansen 1999; 2001, 160–93).

For the Dalits—whose vanguard radical formation, the Dalit Panthers, challenged the Shiv Sena at street level in the early 1970s, only to join their erstwhile adversaries in the late 1990s (Hoskote 2004b)—the events of July 1997 carry a significance parallel to that borne for Muslims by December 1992. In July 1997 riots broke out in the city after a paramilitary unit fired on a crowd of Dalits protesting the desecration of a statue of their celebrated leader, the social revolutionary B. R. Ambedkar, in the northern suburb of Ghatkopar; the findings of the inquiry were never satisfactorily implemented (not least because no Dalit leader, neither among the former Dalit Panthers nor the more mainstream Ambedkarite Republican Party of India, possessed the necessary authority to demand this), and the event has become symbolic of the marginalization of Dalits in Bombay/Mumbai's civil space. Useful as vote banks during elections, the Dalits find themselves neglected in the sphere of educational opportunities, housing, and medical welfare.

Beyond even these groups are those immigrant labor groups referred to earlier, largely drawn from rural Bangladesh, Bihar, Mithila, Uttar Pradesh, Andhra Pradesh, northern Karnataka, and Telengana, who contribute productively to Bombay/Mumbai's informal sector, but live outside its institutional networks and are not granted any civic rights. They are shadows on the census, if they count at all: vulnerable in the matter of competition for labor opportunities and markets in the informal sector, they have been targeted by the Shiv Sena, both in rhetoric and in actuality. They, too, were attacked, uprooted, and in large measure expelled, under the fictive rubric of "Hindu-Muslim riots" during the 1992–93 pogroms. As a result of these traumatic events of the early 1990s, Bombay/Mumbai's traditional image as a stable economic center and a tolerant, multicultural city was considerably damaged. The damage was worsened by the fact that scarcely any improvements were made in the civic infrastructure and the restrictive taxation and levy patterns by successive state and city governments during the 1990s. The flows in international investment and business opportunities, which might have helped the city to reinvent itself, moved instead to other, emergent metropolitan centers in India,[7] and Bombay/Mumbai became further mired in its irresolutions. The slow breakdown of Bombay's engines has been grimly cataloged: the city remains plagued by a lack of policy initiatives in a range of areas, including water and electricity supply, transport, housing, telecommunication, and education; and in the securing of environmentally effective legislation on the coastline, heritage areas, energy consumption, and slum rehabilitation. The city region's development has also been hampered by the uneven rhythm of collegiality and dissension between a municipal government that has been consistently dominated since 1985 by the Shiv Sena, and a state government that has been alternately controlled by the Congress, the Congress–Nationalist Congress Party (NCP) coalition, and the BJP-Sena combine, during the same period. Its future as a global city region remains a tantalizingly potentiality, while the means of actualizing it have yet to be addressed (see Guzder 2003).

Competitive Populism

The material and emotional dissatisfactions that we have noted, as generated in a context of swift economic change, have been politically manipulated by various actors in Bombay/Mumbai during the 1990s and to the present. This has resulted in the emergence of the model of an aggressive, even annihilationist identitarian politics of resentment, whether practiced from an autochthonist-majoritarian platform by the Shiv Sena, a majoritarian-revanchist standpoint by the Vishwa Hindu Parishad and the Bajrang Dal,[8] or a subalternist-radical basis by the Republican Party of India. Rightist, centrist, and leftist forces have all deployed this identitarian politics of resentment in a quest for microlevel as well as macrolevel gains, so that it is sometimes difficult to disentangle a supposedly liberal agenda from a conservative one, since they rival one another in the practice of competitive populism (da Cunha 2003).

The centrist Congress–Nationalist Congress Party (NCP) alliance in Maharashtra has often outdone the Shiv Sena in its virulent advocacy of Maratha warrior-caste sentiment (Hoskote 2004c), while the Shiv Sena has outwitted the Congress in flamboyantly espousing the Dalit cause (Hoskote 2004a). These political manipulations have fractured what I have earlier described as the city's cogencies, overturning the customary understanding between Hindu and Muslim neighbors and altering the caste configurations on which the city's main political entities, the

Congress–Nationalist Congress Party coalition and the BJP-Sena combine, have traditionally depended. Over a period of time, as rightist and centrist politicians have exchanged positions, either from conviction or expediency, their caste bases have also shifted, so that the anti-Muslim, anti-Dalit Sena spokesperson of the 1980s is the NCP savior of the Muslims and Dalits in the 1990s (Hansen 2001, 83–84).

In studying the patterns of stimulus and response by which politicians and their constituencies, governments and their opponents, administrators and their publics have addressed one another in Bombay/Mumbai during the 1990s, we find that the emphases of governance shift constantly, according to the changing rhythm of competitive populism. This phenomenon has deepened Bombay/Mumbai's crisis of governance, exploiting the city's pervasive communicative disengagement and subverting civil space by resorting to emotive appeals to caste-group feeling and ethnohistorical sentiment. The interrelated problems of communicative disengagement and disrupted cogencies, competitive populism and fragmentary discourse lay within the problematic matrix of electoral democracy as it operates in a society whose members exhibit primal self-identities based on an allegiance to their caste-group, ethnicity, and/or religious denomination (albeit that these self-identities and allegiances are constantly updated, recast and realigned). Any electoral mobilization, in such a society, is inevitably predicated on such divisive premises, to the detriment of a more consensual, broad-based interest transcending interest groups. In the context of contemporary Bombay/Mumbai, the operations of this pervasive identitarianism have had serious repercussions on the very conception of civil space, the space occupied by citizens in the pursuit of their private aims within the greatest common good. When a conscriptive citizenship, rather than one based on the recognition of dignity of the individual, is imposed upon the individual, what is at stake is the essence of participatory democracy, the sense of being at home.

Desired City, Undesirable Citizens

The foregoing reflection leads us directly to the central questions of inclusion and exclusion: Who really belongs to Bombay/Mumbai? Who can legitimately claim it as his or her city? The government of the city region has increasingly been obliged to speak in many tongues, adapting its polyphony to the expediencies of demography and the variability of its audiences. This is sharply evident when it addresses its electoral power base in the city's working-class, slum, and shantytown areas: it adopts a strict "sons of the soil" logic for the consumption of the Maharashtrian proletariat and unorganized floating labor, while fabricating schemes of reassurance that seem to include the long-settled migrant specialists in the restaurant business, the building trades, and small-scale industry, who came to the city, originally, from coastal Karnataka, Andhra Pradesh, Gujarat, and Tamil Nadu. In a tendency that began during the early 1990s, the rhetoric of the city government and the state government has had to balance between the charade of localism and an effort to attract global capital to invest in Bombay/Mumbai. In these circumstances, the definition of the "ideal citizen" varies widely, changing with the passage from a rhetorical to a pragmatic context. In a cultural discussion, the Marathi-speaking person of Maharashtrian ethnicity may be privileged as a guarantor of authenticity, while the non-Maharashtrian who has blended into the environment may be praised as a symbol of assimilation; in a politically charged discussion, the Bihari or Bangladeshi migrant laborer is typically denounced as a burden on the city and a potential criminal, while members of the transnational elites active in banking, finance, and information technology are regarded as harbingers of prosperity, the species of high-level migrants that the city ought to attract.

These contradictions were made manifest, for instance, during the violent agitation that the Shiv Sena led against "outsiders" in November–December 2003. North Indians, mainly from Bihar and Uttar Pradesh, who had come to Bombay/Mumbai to take an examination for posts in the lowest grade of manual labor in the railways, were brutally assaulted and forced to leave the metropolis. When challenged, Shiv Sena activists and apologists insisted that, by outsiders, they meant unskilled laborers from Uttar Pradesh and Bihar; they were eager to clarify that the Shiv Sena had nothing against the high-level migrants who came into the city to staff the managerial-technocratic apparatus of the knowledge and finance sectors. In truth, it may well be a repressed dislike of the empowered immigrant presence at the elite level—which is both desired and resented—that is expressed through rage directed at the helpless immigrant presence at the subaltern level, the marginal population that staffs the informal sector. Indeed, given the endemic asymmetries of the island-city's economy, it is the immizerated north Indian and Bangladeshi laborers who service the metropolis; the global citizens whose advent is so ardently desired, even by localist sentiment, do not arrive in great numbers, simply because Bombay/Mumbai's civic governance cannot ensure refined amenities—the absence of pollution, well-regulated traffic, the quality of life, and the opportunities for leisure—that such cities as Singapore, Hong Kong, or Shanghai can, as metropolitan centers that have self-consciously programmed themselves as global city regions. In such a situation, the reimagining of the "new citizen" who is most appropriate for the governance regime must necessarily shuttle between actuality and desire.

The dream of the global city is the one shared platform in a city of divergences, a common motivation that brings together social and political actors who are otherwise bitterly opposed. It unites, in peculiar if momentary alliances, the old social elite, which articulates itself through the discourses of heritage conservation and the restoration of public spaces; the new political elite, which speaks from a neotraditionalist viewpoint, asserting the claims of local, regional culture; the new global economic elite, whose material interests have altered the sociology of transport, entertainment, media, and expressive culture in the city; and public-interest activists, who more typically oppose the other three groups. While the various idioms of political imagination embodied by each group remain in competition, they tend to overlook their differences as well as the city's tensions, to engage discursively with each other in projecting Bombay/Mumbai as that supreme object of desire, a global city. The localist Shiv Sena and the globalist corporate houses, the connoisseurial urban heritage movement and the NGOs working to ensure community participation in cleanliness campaigns, the developmentalist bureaucracy and the urbanist discussion circles—all these groups voice the need for Bombay/Mumbai to transform itself. What prevents this transformation is the fact that, while their desires converge, their interests—as well as those of the communities and constituencies not represented in their deliberations—do not coincide.

Closer scrutiny does indeed reveal an intriguing parallelism among some of the least similar of these groups. The *localist* desire to keep Mumbai, in the Shiv Sena phrase, "safe from outsiders," is not unrelated to the *connoisseurial* desire to preserve the "look" of a Bombay frozen within the colonial imagination: though far from identical in their political aims, both these lines of desire culminate in implicit or explicit demands for the near-impossible physical closure of the city to migrants, and the more sinister and plausible deportation of undesirable segments of the population. So that, despite appearances, the mutually disdainful Shiv Sena and the heritage movement have more in common than they would consciously admit; unfortunately, such parallelisms cannot serve as a basis for constructive civic action and urban regeneration, and can scarcely conduce toward the evolution of a global city (Hoskote 2002).

Successive administrations that governed Maharashtra and Bombay/Mumbai through the 1980s and 1990s optimistically held up Singapore as an ideal to be emulated, without pointing out the discipline—not least the self-discipline practiced by the political class—necessary to accomplish this aim. Nor was reference made, by the various proponents of the Singapore dream, to the distinctive sociopolitical order of that Southeast Asian nation-state, its intricately balanced ethnic relationships, its authoritarian management of state, economy, and society. Certainly there was not the slightest effort to discuss the practical, near-obsessive attention to detail exhibited by the People's Action Party government of Singapore in its distribution of people, resources, spaces, and technologies from the smallest to the grandest level (George 2000, 13–24). What prevailed instead was the urban beautification rhetoric of "Clean Bombay, Green Bombay," espoused by the Shiv Sena city government in the 1980s (Hansen 2001, 205–11), and the hectic construction of more than sixty soaring flyovers in the mid-1990s by the BJP-Sena state government, at an expenditure of 15 trillion rupees (approximately 300 million euros) for a project that would benefit only 12% of the population, which owned private transport, while ignoring the urgent need for mass rapid public transport to convey the other 88% of Bombay/Mumbai's citizens. In the same vein, private developers convinced the Congress-NCP state government of the viability of a scheme to insert skyscrapers into the congested central Bombay/Mumbai area of Tardeo, imagining into existence a nearly science-fictional landscape of towers, private bridges, and elevators built into Tardeo's overpopulated, overbuilt hills, while ignoring the overflowing gutters, pavement dwellers, and overstretched railway system below (Guzder 2003). For Bombay/Mumbai's various elite groups, the First World model provides only a look, an appearance, a monumental cityscape; practical details impede the momentum of the dream.

Conclusion: Cartographies of Dislocation

The shifting emphases of governance in Bombay/Mumbai, and their underlying tensions, reflect the larger conflicts inscribed into the transitional situation in which India, and even South Asia, found itself at a historical juncture when the turbulences of postcolonial self-definition became overlaid and rendered more complex by the processes of organization (Appadurai 1996). I have tried to show how these processes have sometimes exacerbated existing social conflicts, while also engendering new genres of oppression and competition in metropolitan India.

A city is as much a product of the political imagination as it is a product of economic and cultural processes. While economic and cultural processes bear a large-scale momentum and an impersonal materiality, the political imagination is characterized by a certain intentionality, a human agency directed toward self-governance. The political imagination works through an ongoing process of negotiation and transaction, understanding and misunderstanding among various sectors of society, including caste groups, classes, neighborhoods, and occupational leagues. Ideally, it embodies their commitment to a contract, by which they agree upon the central myth of their city, its driving self-image. Usually, the political imagination is developed by a city's elite groups and enforced by the state. By allocating every sector of society a share in the city's myth, the political imagination acts as a guarantor of group identity and group alliances; it also acts as a mode of managing potential conflict among groups over competing interests.

When the political imagination of a city fails, when the contract embodied by it breaks down, what results is a chaotic scenario of fragmentation, in which the various sectors of society abrade one another through antagonism, while the city collapses as a collective entity—both in material terms and in terms of its identity. In Bombay since the early 1990s, as we have seen, the antagonisms have multiplied faster than they could be managed, while the alliances have not endured. This civic collapse represents a failure of the political imagination on the part both of the city's constituent groups, especially of its elites, and of the state, as embodied both in the city and the state government.

The failure of these forces to navigate Bombay/Mumbai out of its crises is all the more appalling by comparison with their counterparts during the 1890s: an establishment that represented a benign Victorian model of governance and capitalism with a tradition of philanthropy, justice, and institution building to offset its colonial exploitation and its profits in opium, war provisioning, silk, and cotton. While Bombay/Mumbai's 1890s elite was dedicated to long-term visionary investment for the public good, the emergent elite of the 1990s has remained preoccupied with short-term gain; as such, strategic responses to the question of how the city is to be reinvented remain elusive, and the city region's denizens attest to a debilitating sense of powerlessness and incoherence as they search in vain for resources of hope by which they may reimagine the urban condition. In this sense, Bombay/Mumbai is a microcosm of the Indian nation, in that it represents a proliferation of group interests, some of which achieve articulation through legitimate channels, while others find deviant, underground, dissident, or criminal modes of expression, without confronting the vital questions: How are these differing interests to be reconciled within a political dialogue aimed at securing equity? And if a single collective image cannot be achieved, is it not possible to establish, at the least, a relatively stable anthology of images, in place of the constantly altering kaleidoscope of images that currently obtains? The anthology is not inappropriate as a model: for it is open-ended without being unstable; it prizes multivalence within a consistency, rather than permitting ambivalence and uncertainty, so ensuring the continuity of that social dialogue, that intersubjective communication that can be the only enduring basis for a humane metropolis. Only when this basis has been secured can Bombay/Mumbai begin, meaningfully, to integrate the needs and aspirations of its citizens into the dream of a global city.

Notes

1. For a concise history of the origin and development of Bombay as a British colonial metropolis, see Tindall 1992. For an exhaustive history of Bombay from the earliest times to the present, accompanied by maps and photographs, see Dwivedi and Mehrotra 2001.

2. The official estimate of Bombay/Mumbai's population stands at nearly 18 million, although it is probable that the actual figure is somewhat higher.

3. The Hindi variation, "Bambai," also enjoys wide currency: like "Bombay," it connotes a cosmopolitan vision.

4. For a study of the role played by mythological television serials in sustaining the Hindu-majoritarian upsurge of the 1990s in India, see Rajagopal 2001.

5. For an account of a parallel phenomenon of emergent cultural patterns in a changing urban terrain based on an artisanal economy, see Kumar 1994.

6. For an account of the complex, largely unacknowledged role of the shanty-town in Bombay/Mumbai's informal-sector economy, see Sharma 2000.

7. Among these locations in India, which were more inviting to global capital, were Hyderabad in Andhra Pradesh and Bangalore in Karnataka, cities and states whose governments have been strongly committed, across political lines, to a technocratic organization since the early 1990s.

8. The Vishwa Hindu Parishad and the Bajrang Dal are militant front organizations of the Rashtriya Swayamsevak Sangh, the foundational organization of Hindu majoritarianism, of which the BJP is also an affiliate.

References

Appadurai, A. 1996. *Modernity at Large: Cultural Dimensions of Globalization*. Minneapolis: University of Minnesota Press.

da Cunha, G. 2003. Decline of a Great City. *Seminar*, no. 528: 14–18. City of Dreams, a Symposium on the Many Facets of Bombay. New Delhi.

D'Monte, D. 2002. *Ripping the Fabric: The Decline of Mumbai and Its Mills.* New Delhi: Oxford University Press.

Dwivedi, S., and R. Mehrotra. 2001. *Bombay: The Cities Within.* New ed. Bombay: Eminence Designs.

George, Ch. 2000. *Singapore: The Air-Conditioned Nation, Essays on the Politics of Comfort and Control, 1990–2000.* Singapore: Landmark Books.

Guzder, C. 2003. The Free for All City. *Seminar*, no. 528: 28–30. City of Dreams, a Symposium on the Many Facets of Bombay. New Delhi.

Hansen, Th. B. 1999. *The Saffron Wave: Hindu Nationalism and Democracy in Modern India.* Princeton, N.J.: Princeton University Press.

———. 2001. *Urban Violence in India: Identity Politics, "Mumbai," and the Postcolonial City.* New Delhi: Permanent Black.

Hoskote, R. 1996. Hyphens and Ellipses: Popular Appropriations of Ceremonial Spaces. In R. Mehrotra and G. Nest (eds.), *Public Places-Bombay*, 37–43. Bombay: Max Mueller Bhavan Bombay/Urban Design Research Institute.

———. 1999. Cartographies of Dislocation: Civic Tensions and the Redistribution of Civil Space. Paper presented at the international conference Global Flows, Local Fissures, World Academy of Local Democracy, Istanbul, May.

———. 2002. Consommation patrimoniale, processus culturel/Heritage as Commodity, Culture as Process. In J. Nouvel (ed.), *L'urgence permanente/The Permanent Emergency*, 116–19. Marseille: Galerie Enrico Navarra/Galerie Patrick Seguin/levaporetto.org.

———. 2004a. Their Journey from Ambedkar to Thackeray. *Hindu*, 29 March, 13.

———. 2004b. The Dalits' dilemma. *Hindu*, 4 April, 16.

———. 2004c. Politics and the Cult of the Chhatrapati. *Hindu*, 1 April, 13.

Kosambi, M. 1995. British Bombay and Marathi Mumbai: Some Nineteenth Century Perceptions. In S. Patel and A. Thorner (eds.), *Bombay: Mosaic of Modern Culture*, 3–34. New Delhi: Oxford University Press.

Kumar, N. 1994. Urban Culture in Modern India: World of the Lower Classes. In I. Banga (ed.), *The City in Indian History: Urban Demography, Society, and Politics*, 191–205. New Delhi: Manohar/Urban History Association of India.

Omvedt, G. 1995. *Dalit Visions: The Anti-Caste Movement and the Construction of an Indian Identity.* Hyderabad: Orient Longman.

Prakash, G. 2003. Blitz's Bombay. *Seminar,* no. 528: 22–27. City of Dreams, a Symposium on the Many Facets of Bombay. New Delhi.

Rajagopal, A. 2001. *Politics after Television: Hindu Nationalism and the Reshaping of the Indian Public.* Cambridge: Cambridge University Press.

Sharma, K. 2000. *Rediscovering Dharavi: Stories from Asia's Largest Slum.* New Delhi: Penguin.

Tindall, G. 1992. *City of Gold: The Biography of Bombay.* Reprint, New Delhi: Penguin.

Two Cities in One
Diverse Images of São Paulo
Pedro Jacobi

As a metropolis at the periphery of the capitalist system, São Paulo must come to terms with the effects of globalization: a crisis of economic centralization, fiscal predicaments of various kinds, and a change in the profile of the metropolis from an industrial to a service center. São Paulo at the same time is one of the three largest cities in the world. It is a focal point of entrepreneurial decision making and the headquarters of financial systems and specialized services such as advertising, fashion, design, health care, and higher education. Undoubtedly, it is the most important link between the national and international economy of Brazil. The city today incorporates all of the most advanced tertiary activities of the larger region. Yet the transition from an industrial to a service center that occurred in the 1980s and 1990s also contributed significantly to social polarization, increasing the share of low-skill jobs. This development has had a decisive impact on the land market, the dualization of space, and the structure of consumption.

São Paulo is shaped both by historical and structural determinants, and in recent times also by the international economic process. The current discourse on São Paulo, represented by authors like Ferreira (2003), accordingly likes to depict São Paulo as a global city. A global city is a connecting point between a national economy and globalized flows of capital. It is a financial center, the headquarters of large transnational corporations, and the core of a complex network of highly specialized modern services backing global transactions.

For the critics of this ideology, upon careful empirical study São Paulo does not fit the image of a global city. Poverty and inequality persist and contrast strongly to the wealth at the center of the city. According to these critics, there is a need to strengthen participatory practices in São Paulo.

Discourses on São Paulo range from the aforementioned discourse that valorizes São Paulo as part of the network of global articulations, and others, like the one just described, that hold that São Paulo is marked by a dualistic urban structure and consequently put forward the normative expectation that this dualistic structure should be overcome (Marques and Torres 2005). They call for structural reforms promoting progress, social equity, and environmental preservation. The following contribution presents both types of discourses.

São Paulo's Transformations: A Global City and Its Contradictions

The wealthiest city in Brazil is undergoing significant economic change. Economic transformations, together with intermittent recessions and changes in the technical productive structure have modified São Paulo's centrality. In 2000 the city concentrated 60% of the metropolitan region's population, in contrast to 72% in 1970. Once an industrial metropolis, it is quickly becoming a center of tertiary activity. In 2000 the share of tertiary activity in São Paulo's economy reached more than 75% (EMPLASA 2002). The economic conversion of the city has produced contradictions in the urban space and essentially given rise to two coexisting cities in the same space. One is a mega-city participating in globalized economic relations. The mega-city is home to the same type of highly qualified professionals that can be found in global cities around the world. The other city is home to low-skilled laborers who find themselves at the periphery of the overall city economy. In recent years, the already existing polarization of the labor market increased, and due to the freezing of per capita income, inflation, recession, and unemployment, more than 60% of the inhabitants of São Paulo today live in substandard housing. Accordingly, images of the city contrast "global citizens" living in gated communities and strictly monitored, protected spaces with "excluded citizens," who are segregated and live in the periphery.

São Paulo has proved incapable of effectively implementing urban transformation to overcome its duality. Instead, the pattern of fragmented ghettos has been reinforced. The city's administration has been much less interested in global discourses than in real-estate prices and the interests of the entrepreneurial sector as such. For their part, entrepreneurs aim to increase the number of bank headquarters and transnational corporations in São Paulo in order to create so-called new urbanized areas with the most modern technologies (intelligent buildings) that encourage the most immediate links with the global system. They are responsible for effective marketing that encourages public investment in infrastructure that will guarantee São Paulo's global ties.

Notwithstanding the impact of structural transformation, São Paulo has not lost command of major national corporations, despite the relocation of some of their headquarters. São Paulo is a preferred destination for transnational corporations and the financial system, where they can develop a hub in the network of globalized transactions (Marques et al. 2003).

Traditional explanations based on the idea of class differences no longer are adequate in explaining the pattern of segregation and social asymmetry in São Paulo. Segregation is instead based in the framework of a complex metropolis, where the concentration of private property in a few hands contributes to social polarization (uneven income levels, differences in formal education, and professional qualifications).

One of the most striking effects of the present socioeconomic reality is the increasing level of urban violence, especially homicides, tied in to the lack of access to economic and social rights. The problem is so serious that homicide is one of the main causes of death of male adolescents between sixteen and twenty-four years. The rates have been growing (Cardia, Adorno, and Poleto 2003), and the differences between regions are very significant. Where poverty is dramatic, the rates are higher, suggesting a link between social deficits and the rate of homicides. Violence affects the population unequally, reinforcing economic, social, and cultural inequality. An indicator called Index of Juvenile Vulnerability (SEADE 2002) reveals the asymmetries between the population of central areas and the intermediate and peripheral areas in terms of the rate of juvenile homicides per 100,000 inhabitants. The variability is between 0 in the wealthiest neighborhoods to 531 in the poorest districts of the city. Most of the peripheral districts average around 200 and 300 homicides. Urban violence has a very negative and complex impact on the populations' daily life, contributing to a loss of confidence in the police and judiciary system and the uncontrolled growth of private police. It also contributes to the expansion of an ideology of fear, the abandonment of public spaces, and the decline of neighborhoods. An indicator of this problem is the number of daily episodes of violence in the city in 2003. The rate reached 309 crimes against persons, 1,206 deliberate homicides, and 118 car burglaries and thefts. The rate per 100,000 inhabitants is 4,020 deliberate homicides in the whole year, 1,344 thefts and 1,139 burglaries and 87,492 car burglaries and thefts (State Government of São Paulo-Secretariat of Public Security). These data indicate the extent those problems linked to violence and crime have reached in the city, and this has influenced the way in which the media deals with the issue and how people make choices to protect themselves from insecurity.

Images and Visions

One of the most recurrent discourses on São Paulo is associated with its ethnic diversity. São Paulo is said to be a city of 1,000 nationalities, one that has integrated a highly diverse body of immigrants. São Paulo has also always been seen as a locus of entrepreneurship. With the significant changes the city has undergone, private investors of the globalized economies search to invest in a city that offers an adequate environment for businesses. The picture of the 1970s—of a city with low rates of unemployment, violence, and pollution and with an adequate urban infrastructure—has changed.

São Paulo presently is confronting the challenge by striving to reduce social exclusion, improve distributive policies, and attract investments of the globalized economy.

Today the city offers a complex combination of modern economic activity and a qualified consumer market. Economic activity is located in dynamic clusters where the logistics of transportation and communication correspond to consumer and producer needs. São Paulo has strengthened its image as a strategic site for investment of national and international reach. The city today is widely viewed as the main market of Brazil and Mercosul. According to research done by influential publications within the business community, almost a quarter of top executives consulted in 2002 indicated São Paulo as the best city for business in Latin America (Municipality of São Paulo 2002, 80). This strong international image is attributed mainly to three factors: consumption potential, infrastructure, and qualified manpower. São Paulo's centrality and interaction with the global economy reinforce its importance as the most active stock exchange of Latin America (Bovespa, i.e., the futures stock market, which is the sixth in the world in the volume of negotiated contracts). The city is the site of 70% of national and regional headquarters in the country, 100%

of the international banks and finance corporations, 85% of the largest banks, and 90% of the most important publishing houses (Municipality of São Paulo 2002). The metropolitan region of São Paulo receives almost 20% of the external investments of multinational corporations in Brazil. It also accounts for 375 multinational enterprises or joint ventures with foreign capital in the industrial sector. São Paulo has been named as the eleventh global center for the control of operations of multinational corporations. Sixty-six companies are located in the city. Of all the business fairs and exhibitions in Brazil, 70% take place in São Paulo (Municipality of São Paulo 2002). Furthermore, São Paulo is seen as the country's largest center of production of information and culture, as an archipelago of global modernity (Wilheim 2001). Due to this overall economic strength, the city has also become a location of tourism linked to business activity and today attracts more than 4.2 million annual visitors (Indicators-Data from Web site of Municipality of São Paulo).

Notwithstanding its comparative advantages, the image of the main economic and technological center of the country stands in sharp contrast with its social and environmental problems. The challenges for urban policy are clearly visible in light of growing social inequalities, the fragmentation of the urban fabric, and the precarious situation of labor. The question arises for planners how to implement large-scale transnational projects in a territory that has not even implemented a basic platform of urbanization. The city government's discourse has been emphasizing, notwithstanding the administration at stake, its openness to global influences, and its administrations have been implementing since 2001 social actions that will increase the quality of life in the city and hence attract further investment. The big challenge is to reinforce the role of the city in defining behavior, cultural patterns, and trends within the country and Latin America.

Two former city administrations (1993–2000) devoted their attention to the expansion of public works projects—urban highways, tunnels and overpasses, and emblematic housing and transportation projects—with very little social impact. The administration of the PT, or Workers Party (2001–4), however, made an important move to combat poverty and social exclusion in the peripheries through social policy and investments in the improvement of infrastructure for public transportation—special roadways for buses around the city and improvements in wealthy neighborhoods to direct the flow of traffic. It has developed policies that are open to negotiation with the national and international elites, but it has also reinforced the privileges of an ethnic elite that is conscious of its social role, and is also very aware of the demands of the new international reality and the logic of the multiple demands of a complex and diverse society.

The discourse of the local government has been centered since 2001 on the renewal of certain areas of the city and the need to "incorporate a vision that connects private investment to a reversal of growth based solely on income and opportunities concentration" (Web site of Municipality of São Paulo). The present administration (2005–8) has also emphasized the need to rejuvenate neighborhood centers and other parts of the city as a way to strengthen São Paulo's image as a global city. The discourse is centered on the concept of development, economic and social, and São Paulo is characterized as a "laboratory of experiences." On the one hand it is oriented toward high-tech industry, and on the other it is concerned with social inclusion through measures such as the improvement of educational infrastructure in the peripheral areas, digital inclusion initiatives, investments in land regulation, programs to generate minimum income and work alternatives for the unemployed, and the restructuring of the degraded transportation system that has been corruptly managed for many years.

However, problems become really complex when there is extreme disparity and inequality within the dispersed and badly integrated nuclei (Marques et al. 2003). São Paulo centralizes decisions in a reduced number of centers that are tied into the global urban network. The city's dynamic thus increasingly has become a dynamic of two cities, global and local, existing side by side. The first is structured by its own logic and the market (mainly real estate) but is sustained by infrastructure maintained by the state. This is also the area where most shopping centers and the economy of consumption are located. The globalized sectors are willing to strengthen partnerships to revitalize areas and to create healthy environments for investments based on the combination of economic attractiveness and the improvement of social asymmetries. Here the present administration has focused on investments rejuvenating neighborhoods and improving the population's access to services. The continuous loss of purchasing power of the wage earners and the increase of unemployment has had an effect on the geographic space, increasing the number of people living in inadequate housing.

São Paulo defines urban spaces inserted in the global network as spaces of capital. The image of modernity is linked directly to regions that have absorbed most public investments, lately in the southwestern part of the city. Here a type of vicious circle of income and wealth concentration arises. The consolidation of this growth vector is the outcome of public investment patterns—investments in tunnels, construction of avenues, and improvement of urban infrastructure, all of which favor large corporations and high income families with extensive use of individual transportation. Between 1994 and 1997, 27.5% of all investment in the municipality was devoted to the southwestern region of the city, indicating a very conscious decision to favor the wealthy sectors (Fix 2001). Some investments were also made in the poorer areas of the city, but the sums spent were considerably smaller. The concentration of investments from 1993 to 2000 in the urban rapid road system is proportional to the reduction in municipal investment in services and public works that could produce a positive effect in terms of the distribution of income, wealth, and quality of life in the city. The municipal government became the main partner of the private sector in the urban renewal of some areas, acting as a real-estate promoter, socializing risks and costs, and privatizing benefits (Fix 2001). The trend has been the polarization of urban growth, and the enlargement of social disparities has not ceased. The differences between districts are significant in terms of access to infrastructure and urban services and quality of life.

During the PT administration (2001–4), the PT promoted a committed discourse to reverse the presence of unacceptable inequalities and to strengthen the capacity of public administration in managing the public policy of the city. It worked at developing mechanisms to increase revenues within a redistributive perspective, emphasizing, for example, the burden right to over-build. Within this perspective, the proposals of land use adopted a holistic understanding of the urban scenario. The concept of urban planning was based on an integrated definition of priorities, involving the promotion of new centralities; new zoning directives; new political-administrative structures to help decentralize the city (via decentralized municipal governments or subprefectures); increased equality and neighborhood identity; and a view of land as a heritage of the municipality and of development of urban operations as instruments of urban renewal of degraded and less developed areas of the city. These initiatives call for partnerships with other public and private agents centered on the mobilization of social capital and well-defined goals. The implementation of a new urban policy was intended to offer decentralized alternatives to sectors of the population affected by the new logic of capital. The administration also favored initiatives to democratize the access to social benefits through participatory budgeting and more progressive urban land taxes. This, however, called forth strong reactions from the middle classes.

The administration proposed an active and entrepreneurial attitude, politically informed and open to the world, but conscious of its importance to reduce inequalities. The public discourse intended to demonstrate political leadership that is legitimate, democratic, well informed, and up-to-date, and open to the new tendencies of the international scene. It would have liked to be seen as respecting the rights and interests of the population, especially the portion of the population that historically has been marginalized and excluded from the mechanism of decision making and the programs of urban promotion. Social and urban responsibilities were prioritized. Planning capacity with popular participation was promoted, and rights to citizenship were stimulated.

The Debate on the *Master Plan* from 2000 to 2001 — Discourse Negotiated

Within this complex and unequal socioeconomic and spatial context, the definition of master plans could, in the future, reverse social exclusion and produce what Rolnik calls "an anti-exclusionary urbanism" (Rolnik 2001). The experience of the *Master Plan* in São Paulo during PT's administration gives insight into the competing visions and strategies with respect to the future of the city. The *Master Plan* does not actually promote the idea of a global city, but it recognizes the fact that São Paulo has the typical characteristics of a global city and that these intensify the contradictions inherent in a dualistic and peripheral economic structure with chronic social deprivations. Within this perspective, the *Master Plan* strongly emphasizes the implementation of a basic platform of urbanization, as the city suffers from the effects of the globalization of economic activities, negative social dynamics, and poor labor relations. Some parts of the city are more in the "global city" sphere than others, and this intensifies the contradictory nature of the process. The former city administration focused on a set of initiatives intended to develop the national and international relations of São Paulo with other cities, between private organizations and the city, as well as with national and regional government. Additionally, it sought to build networks with multilateral institutions to promote partnerships, accords, and cultural exchange. It also stated that it sought to shape policy that is more inclusive, but also internationally oriented.

There was increasingly a clear understanding that the previous model was exhausted due to the convergence of several crises: a decrease in economic activity, an increase of social asymmetries with respect to the urban social fabric, public space, and local politics and administration. The tertiary metropolis implies an increasing socioeconomic insecurity for a large portion of the population, resulting in social duality.

Besides the mobilization associated with the demands of the excluded, there are important initiatives of the middle classes to protect their neighborhoods and of the business community to renew the central areas of the city.

The discussions prior to the approval of the São Paulo *Master Plan* in 2002 evidence the visions held by the various economic and social actors in the city. The approval of the plan was a very complex process, and although some criticisms are justified, it followed a highly participatory strategy, where all involved sectors expressed their opinions. Despite the openness of the process, the real-estate and building sector was able to express its demands with more forcefulness and organizational capacity than other groups.

The *Master Plan* is based on six principles including the redistribution of urban land rent costs, public-private partnerships, solidarity with the poorest sectors, recuperation and environmental preservation, the implementation of housing policies from a social perspective, the mobility and accessibility by public transportation, and the strengthening of the public sector in its planning and regulatory function. Based on these basic principles, directives and actions for socioeconomic development, human development and quality of life, environment, and urban development have been created.

The *Master Plan* tries to deal with several problems, mainly a more efficient use of land and control of the growth of regions with precarious urbanization. The growth of the periphery, not only in the municipality of São Paulo but also in the larger cities of the metropolitan region, has affected areas that should be environmentally protected, since they are situated near water basins. The poorest of the poor dwell in these areas, due to a lack of alternatives and the high cost of housing in the central areas. Other problems addressed by the *Master Plan* relate to transportation and traffic, the high cost of daily commutes, and the unequal distribution of existing infrastructure, some of which is left idle.

To deal with these problems, the *Master Plan* defines objectives and divides the city into zones of intervention. It also defines the instruments and strategic actions needed to concentrate housing in the consolidated areas and to contain growth in the already precarious and environmentally protected areas.

The former city government understood the *Master Plan* as a possibility for greater control of the development of the city and the real-estate market, where the administration will be able to determine the rhythm of growth in the city and metropolitan area. The municipality will have more instruments to influence the real-estate market. Some instruments will be important in creating improvements in the city (constructive potential, created land, and the "burden right to overbuild").

The *Master Plan* implements the Statute of the City approved in 2001 by the National Congress, mainly on issues such as property and its links to social dynamics. The concept of the social function of property is contained in legal instruments concerning the comprehensive regulation of informal settlements and private and public urban areas. This function will be defined in detail by municipal urban legislation. The basic idea is that it is the task of municipal governments to control the process of urban development through the formulation of land use policies in which the individual interests of landowners necessarily take into account the social, cultural, and environmental interests of other groups and of the city as a whole. The *Master Plan* furthermore creates Special Zones of Social Interest that facilitate the improvement of squatter settlements and the construction of social housing for the low-income population. The instrument of these zones allows the municipal government to occupy empty properties in areas with existing infrastructure and to intervene in the real-estate market.

The *Master Plan* introduces conditions for more planned urban expansion through specific urbanization measures. It represents an important step toward the definition of strategic objectives for the city. According to Bonduki (2003), a council member who played a central role in the process, the *Master Plan* "stimulates housing in consolidated areas, establishes limits to urban expansion, defines zones of environmental preservation, and proposes structural development, urbanization, and regularization of the periphery." The city government intends to reduce the growth of areas around water basins and expects to create conditions for a denser city center and to revitalize the more deteriorated neighborhoods close to the inner city. The *Master Plan* also extends land valorization to investments of social interest and promotes the regularization of illegal settlements and slums that represent almost half of the housing in the city.

An important aspect of the *Master Plan* is its approval by the municipal council after a process of debates with stakeholders. It thus represents a democratic outcome following inputs by different representative institutions of society—the larger community, NGOs, social movements, real estate, industry, the business community, and academics. According to analysts, notwithstanding the outcome, the municipal government had a weak performance as to social dialogue during the preparation of the *Master Plan*. As the discussions were conducted by segments, only the Secretariat of Planning had the whole picture of the process. In the end, the only stakeholders that really influenced the final format were the real-estate sector. The social movements had too little access to information in order to be able to really get involved. However, many of their demands were already considered through the inclusion of issues previously called for by the Statute of the City. In the discussions in the municipal council, the largest polemic centered on the rules of use and occupation of land, especially in the most expensive areas of the city. Some issues were also taken out of the discussion, such as zoning, in order to avoid complex issues from aborting the process.

At this point in time there is little dialogue linking the São Paulo *Master Plan* and the planning of the metropolitan region. After the 1970s, dialogue was promoted only by one metropolitan proposal in 1994, which had almost no effect (EMPLASA 1994). Although the solution of the structural problems in almost any municipality depends on a solution at the metropolitan scale, the existing problems are not being confronted in an integrated process. With the exception of some municipalities, the *Master Plan* is being elaborated despite three bottlenecks: the overall housing deficit, transportation, and basic sanitation. The lack of a larger metropolitan approach implies that the solutions that should be proposed are not being put forward. This is especially the case for transportation, a regionwide impasse. The current discourse on the metropolitan region stresses the need for cooperation in order to solve the main problems that affect the region as a whole. There have been a handful of innovations, such as the ABC Consortium (a gathering of municipalities—among them Santo André, São Bernardo do Campo, and São Caetano do Sul—that have been implementing cooperative policies on some issues, such as basic sanitation and regional development in the southeastern industrial belt of the metropolitan region). This takes place thanks to the initiative of civil society and the existence of institutions for cooperation that opened space for dialogue and cooperative management. The lack of federal incentives for mayors to cooperate and the heterogeneity of the municipalities in the region reinforce the autarkic municipalist logic. Another hindering factor is the lack of clearly defined financing, which is tied to the fact that there is little agreement on the political status of the metropolitan region in the first place.

During the debate on the *Master Plan,* the segment representing organized civil society participated in the defense of the public interest. The main issues at stake were linked to the need to guarantee the social function of the city and property. Specifically, the National Forum of Urban Reform sought to combat real-estate speculation, to guarantee access to urban services to all citizens, to democratize the municipal management process, and to open channels of participation. The main argument was the need to change the vision of the city, emphasizing the will to reduce inequalities, strengthen centrality, and create mechanisms that promote redistributive policies. Criticisms of current policy making were directed to the noninclusion of Special Zones of Social Interest in valued areas. The movement became an effective participant in the debate, thanks to the support of NGOs, which contributed their conceptual and technical skills.

The segment representing real estate defended specific interests. Its main criticism regarding the Statute of the City and the accompanying instruments concerned the "burden right to overbuild"—an instrument that increases the cost of real-estate production. Their criticism was mainly directed at those aspects that put constraints on the potential for further real-estate development. The lobby criticized the inflexibility of the proposal and obtained positive outcomes when the *Master Plan* was voted. They considered it to be the "possible plan, but not the one the real-estate market wished, as it will have impacts on the creation of value in the city."

Another important economic sector in the city, the Business Trade Board, did not participate actively in the debate, but its main goal was to ensure the renewal of the central area, reducing the degradation and the chaotic use by vendors, as well as fighting the increasing level of violence and delinquency.

The academic and corporative (Architects' Association) segment played a very active role, defending the importance of the Statute of the City and the active participation of society in the debate.

In the São Paulo process, notwithstanding the criticisms that always arise, different segments supplied vital input to the process. Also, the administration took a more proactive role than in former situations. The real-estate segment, always polarizing, was much more open to negotiation than formerly, and it was encouraged to be so by recent changes in the Statute of the City. In São Paulo, the regional plans currently under elaboration will be implemented by each of the thirty-one decentralized municipal governments, which were created in 2002 in order to induce more decentralized decision making in the city.

Conclusions

The City of São Paulo is global, but it is also marked by increasing urban and social segregation. The process of peripheralization is the main structuring feature of space in the metropolis. The main pattern is a center-periphery pattern intensified by a spatial separation of different social groups.

The Workers' Party administration's (2001–4) discourse and practice aimed to lessen inequalities and to strengthen the capacity of public administration to plan and implement public-policy measures. The administration showed an active and enterprising attitude toward urban management: politically informed and open to the world, but also conscious of its role in the reduction of inequalities; and aware of the need to demonstrate political leadership that is democratic, up-to-date, and open to new tendencies in the international arena. It thus aimed to represent and respect the rights and interests of various sectors of the population.

The *Master Plan* for São Paulo, an important and negotiated outcome for the city, introduces several essential, innovative, and redistributive measures centered on four aspects—recovery, containment, structuring, and urbanization. It also signals the end of three decades without central city planning. The *Master Plan* provides a vision and orientation for the next ten years in city administration, but also for economic actors, civil society organizations, and citizens in general. Its strategic actions aim to improve land occupation, preserve the environment, and improve the access of more excluded segments of society to services and urban resources.

The changes proposed by the *Master Plan* are an important source for the social and urban transformation of the city. This pact to ensure the future of São Paulo is an articulation of a discourse led by the PT administration that sought to manage the city in a more democratic and equal way. The *Master Plan* is accompanied by a set of structural reforms for the city—administrative, political, and fiscal. The great challenge is the institutionalization of these reforms, most of which already were approved by the municipal council between 2001 and 2003.

Because social and urban inequalities increased over the past decades, exaggerated by the loss of population in the central districts and population growth in the periphery, the former administration's discourse understandably focused on the need to reverse this trend. The main arguments were that the aforementioned was an unjust and illogical process and also contrary to the economic interests of local government.

The main question in São Paulo is how both winners and losers can be included in the logic of the global network. For those who have a positive perspective, it seems that they will indeed benefit from the prevailing economic dynamics with the increasing flexibility and opening of markets combined with technological development in production and communications. Their discourse does not consider that this logic impacts the production and organization of urban space, affecting individuals with a less positive outlook. The effects can lead to both exclusion and segregation.

Those critical of such a reductionist world view emphasize the concept of public policy and investment. Globalization is seen by these critics as a much more complex and multifaceted process than many proglobalization supporters would suggest. It is argued that in developing countries the myth of a global city may work as an instrument to impose the logic of the urban market on realities, thereby exacerbating social inequality, the precariousness of jobs, and social segregation. These critics argue that the example of Asian cities does not apply to the São Paulo case, given the differences in terms of global flows and given that most of the main real-estate agents are national. They see the label of global city as a manipulative term. The discourse on global cities is useful primarily to the real-estate sector, not only because of the glamour and profit potential tied into the concept of global cities, but also because it legitimizes the channeling of public investments to promote real-estate valorization in the already well-serviced business districts, thereby multiplying profit rates in this sector. This is an ideologically constructed discourse that intends to promote the specific interests of a few sectors in the "islands of the first world."

The former São Paulo administration has assumed an aggressive attitude toward the world, emphasizing its profile as both a global city and a city that intends to reduce the extent of social inequality (SEMPLA 2002). The main challenge for São Paulo is bridging the gap between the need to maintain strong global linkages and simultaneously to confront inequities and social problems.

The fact that opposing discourses exist is very problematic, and the current city administration needs to consider the reality that São Paulo will always have to deal with its historically grown contradictions. Municipal government will have to change the prevailing logic, thus working toward the nonreproduction of urban segregation and a concentration of investments in the most populated areas. It needs to work toward renewing living environments and reducing social and urban deaggregation.

References

Bonduki, N. 2003. City Councilor of São Paulo. Interview by the author, 12 May. Tape recording.

Cardia, N., S. Adorno, and F. Poleto. 2003. Homicídio e Violação de direitos humanos em São Paulo. *Estudos Avançados* 47: 43–73. São Paulo: IEA/USP.

Empresa de Planejamento Metropolitano SA (EMPLASA). 1994. Plano Metropolitano da Grande São Paulo-1994/2010. São Paulo: EMPLASA.

———. 2002. Sumário de Dados da Região Metropolitana. www.emplasa.sp.gov.br.

Ferreira, J. 2003. *São Paulo, o mito da cidade-global: ideologia e mercado na produção da cidade.* Annals of VI International Seminar of Urban Development promoted by Mercociudades, Buenos Aires, 3–4 July.

Fix, M. 2001. *Parceiros da exclusão: duas histórias da construção de uma "nova cidade" em São Paulo: Faria Lima e Água Espraiada.* São Paulo: Boitempo.

Jacobi, P. 1992. *Movimentos Sociais e Políticas Públicas.* São Paulo: Cortez Editora.

———. 2000. *Políticas Sociais e Ampliação da Cidadania.* Rio de Janeiro: FGV Editora.

———. 2001. The Metropolitan Region of São Paulo—Problems, Potentials and Conflicts. *DISP* 147, no. 4: 20–24. Zurich: ORL Institut.

Marques, E., and H. Torres (eds.). 2000. *São Paulo: segregação, pobreza urbana e desigualdade social.* São Paulo: Editora Senac.

——— (eds.). 2005. *São Paulo: segregação, pobreza e desigualdades sociais.* São Paulo: Editora Senac.

Marques, E., et al. 2003. Pobreza e espaço: padrões de segregação em São Paulo. *Estudos Avançados* 47: 97–128. São Paulo: USP-Instituto de Estudos Avançado.

Municipality of São Paulo. 2002. Document Postulating São Paulo for 2012

Olympic Games. Theme 1, item 1.8: *Economic Resources and Dynamics of the City*. Mimeo.

———. www.capital.sp.gov.br (accessed 7 November 2003).

Rolnik, R. 1997. *A cidade e a lei: legislação, política urbana e territórios na cidade de São Paulo*. São Paulo: Studio Nobel.

———. 2001. Estatuto da Cidade—Instrumento para as cidades que sonham crescer com justiça e beleza. In R. Rolnik and N. Saule, *Estatuto da Cidade— novas perspectives para a reforma urbana*, 69. Cadernos Polis 4. São Paulo: Polis.

Sassen, S. 1998. *As cidades na economia mundial*. São Paulo: Studio Nobel.

SEMPLA (Municipal Secretariat of Planning). 2002. *A economia da grande cidade: os desafios da política urbana em São Paulo*. São Paulo. Mimeo.

———. www. prefeitura.sp.gov.br/sempla.

Sistema Estadual de Análise de Dados (SEADE). 2002. Indice de Vulnerabilidade Juvenil. www.seade.gov.br.

State Government of São Paulo-Secretariat of Public Security. www.ssp.sp.gov.br.

Wilheim, J. 2001. *Tênue esperança no vasto caos: questões do proto-renascimento do século XXI*. São Paulo: Paz e Terra.

Shaping Perceptions of Shanghai
Discourses, Images, and Visions

Zhongxin Sun

The biggest city in China, Shanghai covers 710 years' worth of history.[1] There is no doubt that the rapid development of the Chinese economy has had profound effects on urban development since the government adopted its reform policy in 1978. Since 1990, with the deepening and furthering of reform and the opening-up policy being applied throughout the country, Shanghai has witnessed its own rapid economic, social, and spatial transition in the context of globalization. It has reestablished its prominent role at home and abroad.

This essay contextualizes the emergence of Shanghai's discourses, images, and visions in relation to globalization and Chinese social transition since 1990. Its findings are based on recent interview research and literature studies conducted in 2003.[2]

Shanghai's Discourse

Shanghai's city culture is characterized as Hai-pai, which loosely translated means "sea style." Literally speaking, it means that the sea receives hundreds of rivers. Hai-pai also indicates that the city has close connections with the Western world, an innate connection with market economy as well as innovative ideas, and thus has the most modern image among all Chinese cities. All discourse on Shanghai and the origin of Hai-pai culture can be traced back to the unique historical and geographical characteristics of this city.

Historical Context

Shanghai is known by its Chinese nickname Hu. A *hu* used to be a fishing tool created by fishermen who live along the Songjiang River (today's

Suzhou Creek) and the coast of the East China Sea during the Jin Dynasty (fourth–fifth centuries). By combining the name of the fishing tool and the then term for an estuary of a big river, they coined a Chinese character Hu to name the place as it sits at the mouth of the Yangtze River, the longest river in China.

The mid-nineteenth century to the mid-twentieth century was an important time for Shanghai as its industries took on their leading roles in Asia. After the Opium War in the mid-nineteenth century, Shanghai served as a major trading port and gateway to inland China. With the invasion of the big powers from across the world, Shanghai was then turned into a semifeudal-colonial city. Prior to 1949, Shanghai had become the financial, trading, and economic center of the Far East. People from foreign countries and other Chinese areas started to come to live or work there, turning Shanghai into a city of immigrants. Capitalist-style development was interrupted for a time by the Communist Revolution in 1949, but modern Shanghai remains influenced by the expansion of the world capitalist system, which is reflected in many aspects of social life in today's Shanghai.

Geographical Context

No city can be understood outside of its geographical context, Shanghai included. Contemporary city culture is the outcome of the interaction of forces at work on regional, national, and global scales. In Shanghai's case, the geographical context was cited often in terms of Hai-pai culture. Most literature emphasizes Shanghai's location—the estuary of the Yangtze River as it flows into the East Sea. The names of the city in the Chinese language suggest Shanghai's open-mindedness and its ability to welcome the diverse cultures and peoples from other areas both in China and the outside world.

The national-geographical context is an important approach in understanding Shanghai's urban changes. These changes in the postreform era can be traced to changes in the whole political economy in China since the Chinese government adopted its reform policy in 1978. Before the reform era, the whole country functioned under a central, authoritarian socialist system in which the vertically controlled party system penetrated every corner of society and in which local governments exercised little power over domestic affairs. It was also a system fundamentally isolated from both global and capitalist systems. Under such a political economy, it would have been impossible for Shanghai to make any significant change without a tremendous shift in the central government's policy. Nevertheless, Shanghai established itself as a big socialist model city before the reform era. Since the reform era of the 1990s, the city has reconstructed its leading role among all Chinese cities.

Global influence is significant for understanding Shanghai's discourse as well. China's door was opened at a time when the pace of globalization had sped up at all levels around the globe. When Shanghai pushed its reform and opening-up policies in the 1990s, and especially since the Pudong New Area of Shanghai launched its new development plan with national support, the whole city has reflected an increasing acceptance of free markets and private enterprises as the principal mechanisms for promoting economic activities. Globalization relates to three spheres of society: the economic, the social, and the cultural (Lie and Lund 1999). Globalization affects the trade in goods and services, foreign investments, capital flows, and migration patterns, among other things. The influence of the outer world therefore touches upon all levels of the city's society.

With its historical and geographical conveniences available for the whole world under the reform and opening-up policy, Shanghai has witnessed marked progress in its social and economic development since the 1990s. Now, the city is striving to turn itself into one of the economic, financial, trade, and international shipping centers of the world.

From the Early 1990s to 2003

Since the early 1990s, Shanghai has been experiencing dramatic change, revealing itself to China and the rest of the world as a prosperous and ambitious city. Taking the social transformation of Shanghai as the background, the discourses of Shanghai are elaborated in the following four aspects.

Joining the Reform Era: "Elder Brother" versus "Dragonhead"

The rapid development of the Chinese economy has had profound effects on China's urban development since the Chinese government adopted its reform policy in 1978. At the Third Plenum of the Eleventh National Congress of the Chinese Communist Party in December 1978, Deng Xiaoping's followers unveiled plans for a new course for the country. From then on, China was to abandon such leftist slogans as "Taking class struggle as the key link," and "Politics to take command." Instead the general orientation would be shifted toward economic development. The overall goal of the reform was to achieve the Four Modernizations—in industry, agriculture, science and technology, and national defense. Two general principles guided the reform program: "To the outside, adopt openness; to the inside, enliven the economy." With these, China then entered the era of reform and opening-up.

The reforms started in agriculture. Operating under the Maoist line of producing grain as the key task for attaining local self-sufficiency, land had not been farmed to its best advantage. Individual incentive was hampered by an egalitarian work point system of income distribution that failed to relate reward to effort. The household responsibility system, whereby each household was made responsible for its production within the whole and then given a commensurate share of the rewards, produced the most remarkable transformation of the rural economy since the rural reform.

The urban reforms, ushered in by the long-awaited "Decisions on the reform of the economic system" in December 1984 marked the second stage of China's reform program. In 1979 the Deng government reformed national economic policy and ideology. Essentially, it chose to open the country to global capitalism, albeit in a limited and gradual manner. Pursuing employment creation, technology and management expertise transfer, and capital investment, China's government began its reform policy with the Special Economic Zones (SEZs) program. The aim was to attract industrial transnational corporations looking to expand operations by offering extremely competitive primary factors of production, such as labor, raw materials, and land. The Chinese government initially targeted industrial enterprises from Hong Kong, Macao, and Taiwan. Not only were enterprises from these areas geographically close, but Beijing was also hoping to take advantage of overseas Chinese links, as kinship and village ties remained extremely pervasive (Lever-Tracy, Ip, and Tracy 1996).

From an economic perspective, by 1990 the SEZ program was considered a success, with the effect of expanding employment opportunities, increasing income and living standards, and, most important, increasing foreign-currency earnings. Encouraged by this, the central government began to expand the zoning program. However, reform did not benefit Shanghai at first. Urban reform occurred gradually, as along the coast four special economic zones and fourteen open cities were created to attract overseas investment, trade, and management practices. South China's development attracted the most attention at that time with places like Shenzhen, for example, rapidly growing from a small fishing town into a modern city.

Shanghai was viewed as a model state socialist city under the planned economy system and tightly supervised by the central government. Due to its contribution and "sacrifice" to the whole country before 1990, Shanghai was known as "elder brother" (*lao-da-ge*). Culturally and linguistically, this referred to the city's important conservative role while the whole country underwent reform and opening-up. It was also an expression that strongly urged the city to take the lead in the new reform era.

Shanghai lagged behind at the beginning of reform era. This was evident not only by the change in economic growth itself, but also in the social discourse related to the local Shanghainese's own reputation for social life. For example, in 1991 leading newspapers published a mass discussion titled "The New Image of Shanghainese in the 1990s." The Shanghai statistics bureau conducted a survey that revealed that people from other provinces did not have a good impression of Shanghainese. At that time, even neighboring areas like Jiangsu province experienced faster economic growth. Shanghai was the last "old castle" in the reform era, but Shanghainese still retained their sense of privilege and looked down upon people from other provinces. Hence their image in other provinces was quite negative: conservative, discriminating against outsiders, clever and witty but not smart, and nearsighted.

China's reform unfolded gradually, and Shanghai's urban development did not speed up drastically until 1990. At this point the central government decided to develop the Pudong New Area in Shanghai (east of the Huangpu River), with the expectation that Shanghai would become an international economic, financial, and trading center, and the leader in Yangtze River commerce. This decision greatly advanced Shanghai's economic development, demonstrating the central government's determination to revitalize Shanghai's past of the 1920s and 1930s as the world-class city. The whole Pudong area transformed itself from farmland into a modern city of steel and glass. New skyscrapers went up, foreign investment poured in, corporate headquarters settled, and expensive housing complexes sprung up everywhere. The whole city gained a higher status in China, as well as impressing the world. Today Shanghai has become the "dragonhead" of the Yangtze River area, setting its goal to develop into a global city while retaining the city's traditional advantages.

As both the gateway for the outside world to the huge Chinese market and to the outside world for China, Shanghai positioned itself toward urban development in the reform era. As the Tenth Five Year Plan of Shanghai states: "Complying with the new trend of economic globalization and China's entry into the WTO, we will participate in the international economic and technical cooperation and competition within a wider range, concerning more fields and at a higher level; speed Shanghai's development when melting into the whole world and serving the country; and form a new circumstance at all aspects" (Chen 2003).

On the morning of 9 November 2002, when attending the discussion by Shanghai delegates for the Sixteenth Chinese Communist Party National Congress, Jiang Zemin pointed out that since the reforms and opening-up to the outside world, Shanghai had conscientiously implemented policies from the central government. The development of Shanghai was supported by the whole nation, and it should "actively explore new methods for a linkage development with Yangtze Delta regions . . . , enthusiastically probe new methods to participate in the Western Development and integrate the advantages of technique, personnel, and management in Shanghai and Eastern China with those with rich natural resources and huge markets in Western China so as to make contributions for economic and social development as well as for ethnic unity of the nation" (Chen 2003).

From the old, conservative elder brother during the first stage of the reform era (1978–90) to a young, ambitious, lively dragonhead of China's reform and opening-up since the 1990s, Shanghai seemed to experience its discourse conflicts superficially, even while reconfirming its important role within the whole country and in the globalized modern world.

The Principle of Opening-up: "To Act in Accordance with International Rules" versus "Indigenization"

With its unique Hai-pai culture and its position vis-à-vis the rest of China, Shanghai has many advantages in establishing its global position. This culture explains its readiness to adopt outside rules or practices to benefit its own development. From the standpoint of international capital, Shanghai is the gateway to what is potentially the world's biggest market. It is said that the product that catches Shanghai catches the whole of China. Multinational corporations tend to view Shanghai as the key entrance point into the Chinese market, a place to set up their affiliates in order to facilitate business on the mainland.

"To act in accordance with international rules" became a popular slogan in government documents and the mass media during the 1990s. This is a well-known discourse among ordinary Chinese people in Shanghai, too. However, there was resistance toward this discourse when it is accompanied by "indigenization/localization." The market reform and opening-up policies of the 1990s further exposed Shanghai people to the outside world, offering alternative views about how the city's social and economic life can be organized. With foreign investment and labor pouring into Shanghai, the city has to think about how to communicate and cooperate with different cultures, since the flow of international capital has not only changed the economic structure of ownership dramatically, but also, perhaps more important, has changed the social structure of this city, including attitudes and behaviors of the city's municipal government and its people.[3]

From the standpoint of the foreign investor, the common problems that investors face have been frequently noted: the language barrier, the incompatibility of Western and Japanese management styles with Chinese practices, the distinctive bureaucratic organization of the workplace, the difficulties of hiring—and firing—workers and eliminating inefficient work practices, low labor productivity, poor quality control, and differences in negotiating practices and the long time-frame needed for their completion. Most of all, investors cite the lack of an established legal framework (Lever-Tracy, Ip, and Tracy 1996, 67). As one of my interviewees remarked:

> I remember that when we launched our business a few years ago, since most of our employees were mainland Chinese, we had to spend much time to train the employees. Mostly, other than the skills, it was about their attitudes toward work. For example, the workers here used to be the "master" of the factory and state, and the work culture under planned economy is very different from the market economy. We had to work hard to improve the efficiency of the workplace and let our employees understand and adjust to our company's culture. In the last years, things improved a lot. Maybe because the employees have now had experience working with foreign companies. Generally, they speak English better, and some of them even have an MBA degree, too. Their working skills are much better now. We've hired more local people to be middle-level and high-level managers now. (foreign businessman, age 48, working in Shanghai)

From the standpoint of the government, with the opening-up policy, especially the entry into the World Trade Organization and the deepening of Shanghai's market reform, it is an important task to attract international capital to promote urban development. As the biggest city in China, Shanghai has to compete with other cities in China and even with those in other countries. To prevail over other competitors, a so-called better investment environment and the crucial principle "To act in accordance with international rules" were adopted. This principle extended its meaning to aspects other than just economic development. For example, during the past thirteen years of Pudong's opening-up and development, this discourse was frequently used in government documents and various meetings concerning Pudong's development plan at every level. International rules have been used to stand for the higher criteria to which city governance is held.

These concerns were recently addressed by the mayor of Shanghai in a government report in which he stated:

> [Shanghai should] stick to carrying forward internationalization, market-orientation, [information technology] and constitutionality in a whole [sic], and improve the soft environment of city development greatly. [Shanghai should also] speed up the creation of managerial systems and operational rules in conformity with international practices, make great efforts to establish the city managerial environment and living environment for people at home and abroad to work and live in, ... improve operational mechanisms in keeping with the development of socialist market economy ... carry out the guideline of governing the city according to laws, improve the governmental legal system, promote the principle of administration by law, [and] do a better job of strengthening the constitutionality standard of Shanghai. (Chen 2003)

Resistance accompanied the application of "the international rules and practices." According to my interviews, Shanghai's attitude toward the principles of international accord found a serious impediment in the indigenous culture and the historic trend to use that culture as a rationale for local behaviors that might seem unpleasant or unreasonable to outsiders. This "indigenization," as it is referred to in China, comes in two forms: the first in feedback from the use or overuse of these international rules and practices; the second from focusing on developing local strength from many aspects.[4] It seems some Shanghainese feel frustrated by the use or overuse of international standards. For example, at a meeting to discuss the city's culture that I attended with some editors and scholars in 2002, when comments were made about some people's bad habits in the city, such as smoking in public places like buses without asking for the permission of the other people around, spitting on the street, and talking loudly in restaurants while eating, one participant chimed in:

> I am tired of those comparisons of China and the developed foreign countries. Yes, foreigners might not feel happy if some Chinese do this in front of them. But why should we do things to please foreigners? Why should we follow their practice? We have our own traditional culture and local rules. (male professor, age 35)

The resistance against "acting in accordance with international rules or practice" often emerges in critiques of the city governance. As an interviewee commented:

> You cannot imagine how much Shanghai wants to be a "global city." Thus government does things based on some international rules or practice. They hardly realize that this was a current form of the old term "to worship and have blind faith in things foreign." . . . those pretty French parasol trees of Huai-hai Road were cut off, replaced with many modern high-rise buildings built with glass, in order to fit the standards of global city. (female college student, age 22, born in Shanghai)

Although it seems that there is conflict between the two discourses, unlike the big brother and dragonhead discourses (each indicating the same importance of Shanghai in a nationwide stage during different eras), "international rules or practice" and "indigenization" are actually integrated in many ways. Resistance toward the latter remains powerful, with the former still taking the prevailing role. Recent government documents illustrate this principle clearly, talking about "making Shanghai a city suitable for the domestic and foreign people working and living here . . . [and] making the Shanghai's mother river . . . the Oriental Seine" (Chen 2003).

Globalization in the social and cultural spheres has been marked by discontinuities and contradictions (Lie and Lund 1999). Even in a city where Western influences seem relatively strong, they have often been adapted to an indigenous style, and so also within the domain of city governance. On the one hand, Shanghai has strength in its tendencies to be open-minded, to welcome diverse cultures, to learn new things from the outside world, and as a city it happily embraced Western influence by taking the forefront during the reform era. On the other hand, it struggles hard to search for a development road with its own characteristics. In principle, both discourses are double-edged swords, but in practice it is believed that the city has become more rational in choosing what it really needs to realize its development goals.

Local Governance, Community Construction: "Small Government" versus "Big Society"

In the past few years, the Shanghai municipal government proposed and gradually initiated a new system of municipal administration known as "two levels of government, three levels of administration." The new administration system, operating on the principle of "small government, big society," has become an important governance principle over the years. In keeping with the requirements of a socialist market economy, the street office (*jie-dao*) and the residents' committee, the two lowest government administration organizations, practice and improve the overall governmental administration and grass-roots "community construction." Thus, the phrase "community construction" or "community development" has emerged in both government documents and in research papers from various social science fields in Shanghai during these years.[5]

Before the reform era, Chinese urban management took a totalitarian pattern, which meant an almighty government covered all fields of society and economy. It employed a vertical hierarchic management system in local urban governance: city district–street office–residents' committee (Wu 2002). The street office was the representative organization of city district government, and residents' committees became practical representative organizations of the street offices. Most people were organized according to their work units, not by their street office or residents' committee. Work units regulated social resource distribution and were burdened with a great deal of social functions, such as education, employment, and other social services. Shanghai, like other Chinese cities, used an upside-down, pyramid-like administrative system, wherein the upper government controlled almost all socioeconomic resources, made decisions, and pushed forward urban development with a "command-obedience" pattern (Wu 2002).

Market reform continued to weaken the base of this pattern. A more independent market led to the collapse of the work-unit society. Most importantly, the work units waived the responsibility of social security and housing welfare. At the same time, with the increasing number of migrants coming to Shanghai, unemployment became one of the biggest social concerns, creating a need for housing policy reform. Likewise, all those changes have demanded a different administration to solve the problems. Therefore, the traditional vertical government system could not satisfy the social demands.

Practically speaking, the current urban governance that is taking place inside the vertical district-office-committee administrative system was widely advocated in most cities after the 1990s. It adopted the characteristic "government builds up the society," which typically is the "two levels-three levels" system, with the municipal and district level being the two levels of government. This means that the municipal government transfers responsibility and power for public affairs from a high to a lower governance level, either street office or residents' committee, while at the same time it strengthens the power of local government to improve its capacity of distributing socioeconomic resources.[6]

In fact, this strategy of administration implies that Shanghai government has been trying to put both street offices and neighborhood organizations into a more important administrative position, with both organizational levels potentially defined as footholds in urban governance. Research shows the change the two levels have been experiencing. For example, Zhu (1997) described how powers of the street offices in community service, education, sanitation, social security, social safety, and so on are increasing through these policies. In Shanghai, the government also advocated the concept of "the fourth level operation," which was implemented to make the residents' committees carry out more government tasks.

According to the 1989 Residents Committee Organic Law, residents' committees are mass organizations, which are supposed to be autonomous institutions, designed to help residents to be self-serving, self-managing, and self-educating. In practice, and in the opinion of many Chinese residents, it is not their committee but rather a government-backed organization whose function is nothing but administration and policy implementation, as well as charging various kinds of fees (Sun 2003). It has, however, evolved into an instrument for government policy implementation and an extension or even local substitute for government organization.

Since the 1990s, Chinese urban society has been experiencing a structural transformation that requires more democratic methods to handle local affairs, rather than the top-down control and mobilization that have been employed by the Chinese state for more than fifty years. Obviously, the transformation of the power structure is still within the vertical administrative system, so the street offices and the residents' committees are strengthening their roles as local governments. Residents' committees are burdened with too many government tasks, and this greatly weakens their effectiveness and deviates from the autonomy target. However, the practice and ideology of community construction have made Shanghai a model throughout the whole of China in this field. After all, Shanghai has already started implementing processes that suggest that upper government should retract its administrative power from lower levels, specifically street offices and residents' committees, and both levels should empower other social organizations to deal with concrete business and public affairs as well.

With the increasing autonomy of residents' committees, faster development of nongovernmental organizations, a greater level of citizens' participation and self-administration, grass-roots democracy and its concurrent democratic monitoring, and the rise of property ownership associations after housing policy reform in Shanghai, the structure of the city's local governance at the community level has been gradually changing.

Discussion on City Spirit: "Material Civilization" versus "Spiritual Civilization"

On 3 December 2002, after three years of persistent effort, Shanghai won the bid to host the 2010 World Expo. Buses plastered with slogans proclaimed, "Grant us an honor, and Shanghai will reward the world with more splendor." According to various newspaper articles and government documents, it was hoped that Shanghai, by hosting the World Expo, could promote Shanghai and also realize fundamental modernization by accelerating the pace of building itself into a global city.

Meanwhile, discussion themes such as "2010 World Expo and Shanghai's further reform" or "2010 World Expo and Shanghai's City Spirit" appeared among the works of scholars and officials. Many articles have been published in newspapers and academic journals by researchers and professors from major universities and academic associations in Shanghai.

Most Chinese would agree that "attaching equal importance to both material and spiritual civilization is important" in shaping Shanghai's city spirit in modern times. As reported in one government publication, in order to complete the Five Year Plan for Shanghai it is necessary to:

> Further implement the ideology of running the country by the rule of virtue, intensify the ideological and ethical construction, advocate the traditional virtues of patriotism and contribution [to society] . . . ; speed up Socialist cultural development, carry forward the mental outlook of intensive and pioneering effort . . . ; strengthen direction by public opinion and education in the law, [and] try to form [a] good social atmosphere of . . . competition on the basis of justice and diligence and curiousness. (Chen 2003)

Essentially, the city's spirit discourse is about the quality of the people who live and work in Shanghai.

This discourse as it is currently appearing has its own contexts. First, Shanghai started to conceptualize the traditional importance of spiritual civilization in a new way. Although there was always the slogan about "attaching equal importance . . ." since the advent of the reform and opening-up era, in fact only material civilization was stressed. For example, the goals of the Four Modernizations in the 1980s (industry, agriculture, national defense, science and technology) applied to the content of material civilization. However, with the process of modernization under social transition from a planned economy to a market economy, people realized the importance of spiritual civilization as not just a slogan but as the soul of material civilization (Yu 2003).

Second, Shanghai started to realize the importance of "software construction" in city development. Since the reform era, the comprehensive strength of Shanghai has been visibly enhanced, with much development acceleration evident. The image of Shanghai is very modern with its good metro system, railway stations, Grand Theatre, Oriental Pearl TV Tower, the highest building groups in Luijazui Center, and the bridges across the Huangpu River. All of these could be termed the "hardware" of the city. Shanghai is proud of its hardware construction these years, and justifiably so.

It is all the human factors, including the legal systems, management and service levels, and people's quality of life, including relevant social skills, during modernization that can be called the software of a city. When talking about the dramatic changes happening in Shanghai, people tend to focus only on the hardware aspect. Growing construction says Shanghai is growing, just as the lamp project says Shanghai is brighter. Yet the discussion on the city's spirit keeps asking, "What do you feel about the city when you are pushed in and out when taking the metro in

Shanghai? What do you feel about the city when you hear loud noises in a concert? What impression will you have of Shanghai if a man or woman spits while riding his or her bicycle past you on the street?" There is a growing sense that human factors (software) should be elements of a city's spirit.

Third, the discourse of city spirit is directed against the image of Shanghai people. Despite the rapid development of the city, its people still retain their negative image in China. Many inhabitants are willing to refer to themselves as Shanghainese, but some are not (Li 2003). Shanghainese used to be thought of as rational market people, snobbish, clever but not wise, discriminating against outsiders (Chinese people from other provinces). Now they must pay more and more attention to their own image and try to "be a lovable Shanghainese," as a propaganda poster in the city advertised.

Fourth, the preparation for and hosting of the World Expo 2010 is considered an important opportunity for city development that will "boost all works to a new and higher level, and show Shanghai's amazing charm to the world" (Chen 2003). To many I interviewed, Shanghai's winning bid to host the World Expo shows the world's acknowledgment of Shanghai's achievements since the 1990s. Meanwhile, Shanghai also realized that it has weaknesses when compared with other global cities like New York, Tokyo, Paris, or London. For instance, if Shanghai wants to be a global city, the city needs more green space, better air quality, cleaner drinking water, and even an improvement in the ordinary citizen's English level. More important, the city should not just be a good place to work but also a nice place in which to live (Hu 2003). At the same time, some scholars argued that Shanghai should develop its traditional strengths and connect its spirit with the whole country's development. For example, Wang (2003) defined this city's spirit as "taking the whole country's situation as a priority, receiving hundreds of rivers like [a] big sea"(*Da-ju wei shang, hai na bai chuan*).

Under this context, the discourse of the city's spirit contains the following aspects:

- The combination of traditional strength and modern value, which is embodied in Hai-Pai culture. Shanghai has the broad-minded vision needed to adjust to all diverse cultures while emphasizing the modern values of science, law, and reason.
- The advantages of an immigrant city. Shanghai should take advantage

of the characteristics of an immigrant society, dare to explore new stages of the city development, and provide everyone with an equal opportunity to achieve success and a good life.
- The combination of the general and specific character of the global city. Shanghai should learn from other global cities, while developing its own characteristics.
- The citizens' legal, moral, and spiritual civilization education. This includes the value of running the country "by law," citizenship education, and credit education. As the latest Five Year Plan states, one of the main tasks is to "advocate social public virtue, professional ethics, household virtue, and promote the overall citizens' ethic level. Deepen the credit education, legislate education, national defense education and science popularization education, [and] continue to carry out the activities to establish civilized community, village or town" (Chen 2003).

This will have the effect of "strengthening the construction of the socialist spirit culture" (ibid.).

Conclusion: Vision of Shanghai and the Global City Positioning

Shanghai has been subject to dramatic change in very recent years. While a gap still remains, Shanghai already possesses many of the key features common to the world's major metropolises. Shanghai's city identity has been international for a long time. However, only since 2002 has the idea of Shanghai as a world-class city or global city emerged in various discussion fora and both informal and formal literature. The preceding discourses seem to be intertwined and function as the city's strategic framework toward this most recent objective.

The new strategic blueprint to build a world city, as unveiled by Jiang Zemin when participating in a discussion within the Shanghai delegation to the Sixteenth Chinese Communist Party National Congress, is based on structural adjustment, functional upgrade, and distribution optimization. After the plan was authorized by the central government for Shanghai, the "world city" discourse has been influencing its 16 million residents.

This influence can be easily seen in modern Shanghai. It is scarcely possible to walk down any major street without encountering at least one sign of global influence, from trendy fashions to the ubiquitous McDonald's golden arches. The tallest building in Shanghai was designed by a Chicago firm, and even the popular sports icons are liable to be current NBA players. The modes of dress, and even those of social or community gatherings, have begun to reflect a more cosmopolitan standard. You are just as likely to see a young woman in blue jeans drinking her latte at a Starbucks in Shanghai as you would be in Seattle.

There have been, in recent times, the addition of other, more globally recognized franchises and fashions on the streets of Shanghai. These include an increase in Western-style restaurants, and the daily parade on the local youth channel of various fashion models, walking endlessly to Chinese-dubbed commentary, as the current fashion shows of New York and Milan are displayed for Shanghai consumption.

That said, it should also be mentioned that much of this influence is, for better or worse, American, and that when many young people seek to emulate Western models, it is the American model that comes to mind.[7] There seems to be little recognition that the American modes of affluence may not be best, a dilemma that harks back to the argument of "material versus spiritual" civilization. There are also very real limitations as to the current state of Shanghai's efforts to transform itself, not the least of which is a sizable gap between the average Chinese of reasonable prosperity and the resident ex-patriate society.

Shanghai is not, at current, an integrated, global city in this regard. It lacks, for example, the cosmopolitan flair or even simple diversity that you might find in most Western cities. The Shanghai version is going to be mostly young, college-aged students and foreigners. Western restaurants, especially the pricier ones operated in the vein of trendy European or American hot spots, cater almost exclusively to the ex-pat community, with very few Chinese patrons in sight. The Chinese community and the international community revolve in different circles here, with little overlap. This is changing, to be certain, but the gap exists and presents a real obstacle to any attempt by Shanghai to become a truly global community.

The same holds true for the current crop of successful young entrepreneurs, always buying more and attempting to form a personal image relative to that of foreign counterparts, even to the point of buying a personal automobile, despite the woeful state of Shanghai's infrastructure. Moreover, while you might find a European business leader also engaged in community and political affairs, such cross-level interests are less likely here. The focus of business stays on business, with many business owners more concerned about their own bottom line than getting involved in any sociopolitical arena. There is no concern of material over spiritual; it's all material. This tendency means that there is often a striking lack of diversity when it comes time to discuss the city's direction.

It is important to note that any amount of global influence is tempered by acquiescence to the central government's plans. What China (and more specifically Beijing) says should be the model for Shanghai is what will be the model. Based on the current strategy, experts and even nonexperts in Shanghai believe that the forthcoming five to ten years will see key development acceleration for the city as an international economic, financial, trade, and shipping center, enhancing its competitiveness and influence in the world economy. To make this vision work, Shanghai is promoting these large-scale measures and plans to encourage the rise of new world-class industries and establish a firm economic foundation to achieve its goal of world city. To fit this position, which will depend much more on the integrated radial effects of other metropolitan circles, Shanghai plans to accelerate the construction of the new system with numerous neighboring small and mid-sized satellite cities: "The further outlook is that the collaborating Yangtze River 15-cities orbit, covering Shanghai as the core . . . , becomes the sixth largest metropolis orbit after New York, Toronto and Chicago, Tokyo, Paris and Amsterdam, and London and Manchester" (Chen 2003).

At the same time, Shanghai still faces many conflicts and problems during its development, and there are shortcomings and imperfections in city governance too. As the government work report states, the main problems are cultivating the functionality of the city with regards to establishing a single center for finance, trade, and shipping; ensuring that changes in the city's architecture and infrastructure are compatible with its culture; and taking full advantage of science and technology (Chen 2003). The recurring problems of unemployment, social welfare issues, and the reformation of formerly state-run enterprises must also be addressed with an eye on the government offices and officials responsible for such areas.

While most of my interview data show the Chinese's optimistic view of Shanghai's bright future in the world stage, a few of them expressed slightly different opinions on Shanghai's future. The data demonstrate a further combination of the discourses we discussed on Shanghai's role in China and abroad, local governance, the opening-up principle, and the city's spirit, and show their attitudes ranged from very optimistic to conservatively optimistic toward Shanghai's future.

It is no doubt that Shanghai is and will be one of the most rapidly developing and most lively cities in the world. (male professor, age 35)

With the support from all over the country, Shanghai can retain its leading role in Yangtze River area and even the whole China. However, Shanghai has its own arrogance and narrow-mindedness to overcome, otherwise it will block its development. Shanghai can squeeze into the rankings of global cities only when China gets strong in the world. In this sense, I hold a conservative opinion towards Shanghai's future. (female student, age 22)

As a Shanghainese, I am very proud of Shanghai's development these years. But we should also admit that to some extent, Shanghai is covered by the superficial prosperity. People tend to be hoodwinked by the economic growth; many social problems have been ignored. Some of the government's practices have become a mere formality. So there are some hidden perils, which will block the city's future development. (male white-collar worker, age 29)

Of course, the city is developing quickly. I think this trend will keep for several years. While it flourishes there are many deep problems that need to be resolved. One question that is often put out is that the city's business costs have risen greatly during the past several years, which would probably create a disadvantage in attracting investment. (male government official, age 32)

Shanghai is the best city of China. The city's spirit (open-mindedness, efficiency, reason) is most suitable for our institutional and political reform. The city will have a great future if we strengthen the reforms. (male, government official, age 32)

For the whole country, the first two decades of the twenty-first century are a period to build a better, all-around society. For Shanghai, the plan is to transform the city into a modernized socialist international metropolis and an international economic, financial, trade, and shipping center by 2020. The current discourse of world city or global city has Shanghai functioning no longer solely as the center of the national economy but as an international command and control center, home to a complex of financial firms and corporate headquarters (Sassen 1991; Knox and Taylor 1995). To face the world, Shanghai attaches importance to its comprehensive strengths in strong competitiveness and influence in the world economy. To face China, the city claims, "Shanghai is the whole country's Shanghai." Shanghai positions its development toward "serving the whole country and melting into the world."

From the early 1990s, in a context of globalization and the rapid Chinese social transition, different public and private actors have deployed the various sets of discourses of Shanghai, such as the Hai-pai culture, elder brother, dragonhead, to act in accordance with international rules, small government but big society, city spirit, material civilization and spiritual civilization, and, more recently, a world-class city. Each of these discourses, and the others discussed in this essay, has proposed forms and directions for the city's governance, financial and industrial practices, and the shaping of Shanghai's urban reality and identity in many ways.

It remains to be seen which of these discourses will prevail in the twenty-first century, or whether a new discourse will emerge to help transform Shanghai into the city it wants to be. Of the discourse presented here, the one that will have the greatest chance of survival is the vision of Shanghai as a global city. The reasons for this are historical, as Shanghai was once a major international metropolis, only losing its place on the world stage due to decades of self-imposed isolation. As it seeks to reclaim this position, it will by necessity embrace many of the modern world's current trends, which may also lead to the survival of the "international rules" coda, as well as an emphasis more on the material than the spiritual, a condition that is persistently prevalent in many locations today.

The outlook for Shanghai remains optimistic in this regard, as it is felt that by better integrating with the global community, the needs of Shanghai and of China can be better met. It should be pointed out, however, that the future of Shanghai is closely tied to that of China itself. Much, if not all, of the current impetus for change in Shanghai has come with support from the central government, and a withdrawal of that support, or some other drastic change in the stability of China as a whole, would be equally disastrous for Shanghai. Current trends would seem to argue against any impending social or political catastrophe, but this is China, and the past hundred years have been ones of remarkable change. Still, the outlook for Shanghai looks, to this observer, to be quite positive, with Shanghai adjusting to its recaptured role of international city with both energy and enthusiasm. It is hoped that future observations will bear out this optimism, and that Shanghai will continue to adapt to the needs, and the discourses, of both China and the global community.

Notes

1. Shanghai began as Hua-ting County, an administrative district established in AD 751. In AD 991 Shanghai Town was set up in the county. During the period from 1260 to 1274, the town evolved into an important trading port, and in 1292 the central government of the time approved the establishment of Shanghai County in this area, which has been widely deemed as the official beginning of the city of Shanghai.

2. The interview data cited in this paper were collected in Shanghai, between May and June 2003. I interviewed a wide range of people, via phone, email, and face-to-face, including people from different age groups, occupations, educational backgrounds, and genders. (The ages, economic, and educational backgrounds of informants varied from seventeen to sixty-three, from nearly illiterate to accomplished university professors, from unemployed to wealthy.) Twenty-three people were interviewed, and each interview lasted about one hour.

3. Take industry, for example. When the government introduced the reform policy in 1978, there were only two kinds of ownership in Shanghai: state-owned and collective-owned (run by the local government). From the point of view of ownership, Shanghai has become a mixed economy with foreign-funded enterprises as the most rapidly growing sector. Foreign direct investment has become an increasingly important factor in the restructuring of Shanghai's economy (Logan 2002, 115).

4. According to *Merriam Webster's New Collegiate Dictionary*, "indigenization" is the act of causing something to have indigenous characteristics. In China, however, the term has come to stand for the principal that "local is better," an attitude that has been a prominent factor of the Chinese cultural psyche since at least the arrival of the first European emissary.

5. The definition of "community" in Shanghai or other Chinese cities includes both governmental and geographical meanings, and specifically means the local street office or the residents' committee.

6. At the 1996 Meeting of Neighborhood Work in Shanghai, a new administrative strategy was put forward which is called "two levels of government, three levels of governance, and four levels of network." In this new strategy, municipal government reconfirms the system of two levels of government.

7. Based on an informal survey among high school seniors concerning where they saw themselves in ten years.

References

Chen, L. (Mayor of Shanghai Municipal People's Government). 2003. *Government's Work Report*. First Session of the Twelfth Shanghai People's Congress, 6 February.

Hu, W. 2003. Xiandai guoji da doushi yu renwen jinshen [Modern International Metropolis and Humanist Spirit]. *Tan Suo Yu Zheng Ming* [Exploration and Free Views], no. 5: 9.

Knox, P. L., and P. J. Taylor (eds.). 1995. *World Cities in a World-System*. Cambridge: Cambridge University Press.

Lever-Tracy, C., D. Ip, and N. Tracy. 1996. *The Chinese Diaspora and Mainland China: An Emerging Economic Strategy*. London: Macmillan Press.

Li, T. 2003. Zhidu zaojiu de "Shanghai Ren" [Shanghainese: Made by an Institution]. *Tan Suo Yu Zheng Ming* [Exploration and Free Views], no. 4: 11–12.

Lie, M., and R. Lund. 1999. Globalization, Place and Gender. *AI & Society*, no. 13: 107–23.

Logan, J. R. (ed.). 2002. *The New Chinese City: Globalization and Market Reform*. Oxford: Blackwell.

Sassen, S. 1991. *The Global City: New York, London, Tokyo*. Princeton, N.J.: Princeton University Press.

Sun, Z. 2003. Pu Dong guo ji shequ yanjiu baogao [Research Report on Pudong International Communities]; related conference paper: Community Change: A Study on Pudong International/Foreign Communities, at "Towards Area-Based Global Studies: Shanghai Studies," Sophia University, Tokyo, Japan, 14–15 March.

Wang, B. 2003. Chengshi jinshen yu chengshi shehui fazhan [City's Spirit and City Social Development]. *Tan Suo Yu Zheng Ming* [Exploration and Free Views], no. 5: 9.

Wu, F. 2002. China's Changing Urban Governance in the Transition towards a More Market-Oriented Economy. *Urban Studies* 39, no. 7: 1071–93.

Yu, W. 2003. Shanghai chengshi jinshen tantao zhi wo jian [My Opinion on the Probe into Shanghai City's Spirit]. *Tan Suo Yu Zheng Ming* [Exploration and Free Views], no. 4: 7–10.

Zhu, J. 1997. Cheng shi jie qu de quan li bian qian: Qiang guo jia yu qiang she hui mo shi [Changing of Power in Local Urban Area: Strong Government and Strong Society]. *Zhan Lue Yu Guan Li* [Strategy and Management], no. 4: 28–30.

5 | Comments by Senior Officials

The insider perspective of senior officials is of outstanding importance in the context of "making" a global city. This perspective sheds light on constraints faced by city administrations in times of scarce financial resources. Senior officials point to difficulties in formulating a coherent development strategy for their city. And they often feel obliged to defend the policy agenda of their administration. Therefore, their opinion may differ in some respects from the assessment by members of the academic community.

This holds true for the four selected city regions, too. The respective senior officials do not always agree with the views expressed in the previous chapters. This is not surprising, first, considering their function as city representatives; second, in view of their additional sources of insider information; and, third, taking into account the pressure on them to respond to the changing and often contradicting demands of higher levels of government, citizens, lobby groups, business leaders, and international institutions. The perspective from a city manager for this reason markedly differs from that of a university scholar. However, an exchange between these two groups has in many respects proved to be fruitful for both sides. Hence, by introducing the perspectives from practitioners, we seek to bridge the generally felt divide between research and practice. In the following chapter, one senior official from each city region very briefly analyzes the current status of his respective city region on its way to becoming a global city. Each official also comments on the contributions in this volume from his respective city.

The four comments underscore the particularities of each city, be it in the assessment of whether a respective city region aims to become a global city region, or be it in the discussion of the studies. While coming to different conclusions, they demonstrate in our view that the exchange between theory and practice should be intensified for the good of each city.

Simon Raiser and Krister Volkmann

Johannesburg
Roland Hunter

Johannesburg's vision is to become an African world-class city. This is a matter of setting high standards for the city, of asserting that Johannesburg can be as good a city as any other. However, the purpose of this is to provide good working and living environments to its residents; and to fulfill its responsibilities to South Africa as a whole. Since some 16% of South Africa's national product is generated in Johannesburg, that responsibility is considerable.

The city's vision does not, however, consciously target global city status as a specific objective—particularly if this is interpreted to mean some form of separation of Johannesburg from the rest of South Africa (see Mabin in this volume). Most officials and political officeholders are too preoccupied with the immediate challenges of delivery (i.e., rapidly improving the distribution and quality of services, including activities to promote economic development, to a population increasing at more than 4% per year) to prioritize such an objective.

It is these very challenges that drive both pronouncements made in official documents, and the actual practices that will tend to promote Johannesburg as a global city. This may not be a matter of "promoting development in the shop window and managing poverty in the back shop," as Mabin suggests, but rather, the imperatives of promoting development in the "back shop" are forcing an engagement with the "shop window." Capital spending has to increase in order to meet the infrastructure needs of the city. For this purpose, the capital markets have recently been approached to raise debt finance by issuing bonds. This has created a new constituency for the city, one that is measuring its progress with "shop window"–type indicators. However, the constituency has only been created because of the need to meet development challenges.

If the global city status is not being sought for its own sake, nevertheless, a consciousness of the position of Johannesburg within a network of world cities has developed inside the city administration, as well as an understanding of the potential significance for Johannesburg if any change in this status is emerging. Indeed, Johannesburg's responsibility to South Africa includes maintaining and developing the global city status. This will inform a forthcoming revision of Joburg 2030, the city's long-term (economic development) strategy. For it was clear when Joburg 2030 was put together that periodic revisions would be required, probably every five years, to take stock of progress, to review strategy, and to accommodate any changes of emphasis associated with a new mayoral term.

Care should be taken to make the correct inferences from official council policy documents (the Budget, the Integrated Development Plan, and also the Annual Report and financial statements). Such documents are drawn up by officials, and pass through an exhaustive process before entering the committee system, ultimately to be adopted by the full council. What is produced is an official council document. Thus the IDP and budget documents set out the adopted priorities and programs of council. The Annual Report similarly is a report on the successes and failures of council entities in the financial year concerned. While it cannot be claimed that these are "white-wash" documents (adverse audit opinions, for instance, were fully included in the 2003 Annual Report), they do represent the council's official view.

It is then possible to track the changes made in such documents as they go through their various stages to draw inferences regarding local politics. However, care should be taken not to deduce too much from this. For example, Parnell describes in detail content changes to the 2030 document after a Mayoral Committee meeting, which she ascribes to the "internal dynamics of party politics." But such changes are possible for more mundane reasons, including editing, clarification, and changes of emphasis by the author.

In general, Parnell is correct to seek the answers to the question "Who runs the city?" in the internal dynamics of ruling party politics. This is an important means by which intergovernmental influence is brought to bear. But the way such internal politics is played out will vary over time. For example, whereas during the iGoli 2002 period the city operated with a single multiparty executive across five councils (clearly a transitional measure), after the election the city benefited from the legitimacy associated with the establishment, finally, of a single council with authority over the whole city. The executive mayor now has a single-party executive, which clearly has implications for the daily practice of ruling party politics.

Beauregard and Tomlinson certainly draw conclusions more weighty than the evidence can support in their analysis of the texts of the official documents. Underestimating the challenges of simply getting "government" right, they decry an alleged lack of attention to "governance." They seem to feel that the tone of the documents is incorrect, and even that the documents should become "texts of policy conflict." This is to misconstrue both the purpose of the documents (whose content, by the way, is prescribed) and the nature of local politics. The various players in the wider local governance discourse have their own means of bringing their influence to bear, some of it very effective. It is not realistic to expect the formal council documents to become platforms for general political discourse.

Furthermore, it is also not legitimate to infer from formal council documents that "governance is constricted" because to do so is to ignore too much information. If the reading of official documents had been supplemented by a few interviews, it would have become clear that the council is deliberately seeking to improve governance rather than to constrict it. "Good governance" being a mayoral priority, a wide-ranging program has been implemented that seeks to enhance the working and accountability relationships with different constituencies as well as to advance internal accountabilities. For example, this program has given rise to public events in which the entire Mayoral Committee supported by senior officials, faces public meetings every month, sometimes involving thousands of people, in which residents/customers/citizens line up to question the performance and policies of council entities. Similarly, the executive mayor has met and continues to meet many social groups as part of the ongoing governance program. Such meetings have definite consequences internal to the administration. These efforts may not show up in the tone and content of the IDP and budget documents, but they exist nevertheless.

Parnell provides a broadly accurate account of the development of various strategies and strategy documents in Johannesburg over several years. Some caution is required: it is not as if the relationship among the three strategies making up what Parnell describes as a City Development

Strategy was preplanned. In fact iGoli 2002 was an administrative restructuring process that was well underway before work even began on the longer term strategy, 2010. There are also some quibbles: both Parnell and Mabin err in describing the iGoli 2002 program as being under World Bank direction. Notwithstanding personal relationships between key individuals, this was a homegrown initiative to which international donor agencies lent support.

It should be stressed that in developing city strategies, budget consultation processes, good governance programs, and other complex processes, the city makes a serious attempt and then seeks to improve on that effort each year. Thus it is possible to discern a rapid evolution and development of the content of the various official documents. Joburg 2030, too, will be revised and developed while keeping its economic essentials intact. Elements of the good governance program are developed and improved upon as experience yields suggestions for improvement.

The management of conflicting priorities and contradictory interests is the essence of government. The inhabitants of the city are citizens as well as customers; and they are workers and managers as well as residents. Poor residents seek certain kinds of performance from the city, and investors want to see other kinds. The council must, of course, strive to be effective and efficient as it attempts to rise to these challenges and manage these contradictions.

Mumbai/Bombay
Vidyadhar K. Phatak

Mumbai (or Bombay) has a latent desire to emulate Hong Kong and Singapore and become a global city. The latter cities are Asian port cities, like Mumbai, and both of them experienced severe housing shortages in the past, which they by now have overcome successfully. The desire to emulate Hong Kong and Singapore has been strong in many quarters of Mumbai, especially among politicians, bureaucrats, and industrialists. Yet the process of globalization—as is now understood—depends more upon macroeconomic policies than on city aspirations.

In the past, India had a centrally planned economy. Liberalization occurred only in 1991, compelled by a fiscal and balance-of-payment crisis and the granting of an International Monetary Fund (IMF) loan. Liberalization enabled private investors to set up new businesses in Mumbai without significant restriction (such as licenses and permits—in the past India had been described as "license and permit raj"). It opened up the possibility of foreign direct investment (in infrastructure and other projects) and also made it possible for foreign institutional investors to invest in Indian stock markets. Recently, Special Economic Zones (similar to Chinese SEZs) have been promoted in order to attract an increasing volume of foreign investment. Also, Indian companies have been listed on the New York Stock Exchange and NASDAQ.

A by-product of liberalization has been the weakening of labor protections and trade unions. After liberalization many industries, public enterprises, and nationalized banks introduced voluntary retirement schemes in order to reduce the size of their labor forces. Mumbai lost its traditional textile industry in the eighties and with it a significant proportion of employment in this sector. However, immediately after the macroeconomic liberalization and particularly after the establishment of new private-sector banks, Mumbai experienced rapid growth in the financial services sector. The Mumbai Metropolitan Region Development Authority (MMRDA) responded by designating its Bandra Kurla Complex as the International Finance and Business Center (IFBC), which was previously planned as a site for relocating offices from the congested Fort (South Mumbai) area. IFBC's locational advantages attracted many new financial institutions like ICICI, which was later to become the first universal bank and National Stock Exchange providing screen-based trading facilities in shares and debt instruments on a nationwide basis. The ICICI building virtually has become the new icon of Mumbai. Private initiatives to establish offshore banking facilities in Mumbai, however, have not yet succeeded indicating that such matters are clearly within the domain of the national government. Along with financial services, information technology has grown significantly. However, as they do not depend on agglomeration by physical proximity but on communication connectivity, growth in this sector has led to redevelopment of old manufacturing sites away from the traditional central business district and other suburban locations. Textile millowners have been trying to sell their real estate. In some cases the mill structures have been converted to shopping malls as a new symbol of globalizing Mumbai.

Against this background the answer to the question "Does Mumbai aim to become a global city?" will have to be no. Mumbai as represented by city or state government does not deliberately aim to become a global city. But the macroeconomic framework that has been put in place by the national government has prompted the city, perhaps at the behest of the business and services sector, to begin to become global.

Economic liberalization was concurrent with political decentralization in India. The seventy-third and seventy-fourth constitutional amendments of 1992 formally recognized local city government as the third tier of the federal structure. The amendments set forth the organizational structure of local government, the democratic process of electing citizens' representatives, taxation powers, and the duties of local government. Planning for social and economic development was included in the charter of local government, in addition to planning for traditional civic services. To coordinate the complexities of planning in metropolitan areas with multiple local governments, the constitution additionally provided for metropolitan planning committees. Despite this empowerment in city administration, today's Municipal Corporation of Greater Mumbai does not have a specific vision of Mumbai and certainly not one that sees Mumbai as a global city. There are two reasons why this is the case.

First, nearly 50% of Mumbai's population lives in squatter settlements devoid of basic civic services. Elected leaders at the city government, state, and national levels are called upon to attend to this problem (not necessarily in terms of policy initiatives, but by allocating funds at their disposal). Elected representatives therefore are shy of working toward making Mumbai a global city, since initiatives in this direction are likely to be seen as contrary to the interest of poor slum dwellers.

Second, the Municipal Corporation of Greater Mumbai does not have professional planners on its staff. Its engineers, for instance, are preoccupied with meeting increasing infrastructure demand. In addition, weak finances hinder city government from drawing up large-scale projects or incentives to promote certain types of development.

The state government of Maharashtra, of which Mumbai is the capital, however, has initiated two significant programs to help Mumbai. One is the construction of flyovers in Mumbai and the other is the provision of free housing to all slum dwellers who were resident in slums on 1 January 1995. The former program had a visible impact on the increasing number of car owners in Mumbai. The latter granted slum dwellers the dream of owning a house in Mumbai. Leaving aside the economic rationale or feasibility, these programs were politically correct. Though initiated by the Bharatiya Janata Party and Shiv Sena government, the slum scheme extended to all slum dwellers irrespective of their caste, religion, or language (that is perhaps the strength of the Indian democratic system).

In their plan of 1996 some planners, notably in MMRDA, recognized the need to rejuvenate Mumbai's economy and ensure Mumbai's competitiveness. Perceiving the prospect for growth in the liberalizing economy, the Bombay Chamber of Commerce and Industries, inspired by London First, established Bombay First as a lobbying group. Bombay First, of course, was careful to articulate its positions based on research and professional advice. In 2003 Bombay First engaged McKinsey & Company, Inc., and the two entities jointly published a report titled *Vision Mumbai—Transforming Mumbai into a World Class City*.[1] The report used the phrase "world class city" and recommended obvious measures such as the improvement of infrastructure (public and private transportation, water supply, sanitation, education, and healthcare) and an increase in low-income housing. It also proposed boosting economic growth to 8–

10% per annum and emphasized the need for more efficient governance. More significantly, the report also strongly recommended the enablement of "implementation through committed public-private resources led by the Chief Minister" and making "key government organizations accountable for results." Bombay First presented this report to administrators and political leaders and ensured that a task force was established to follow up on the report. The task force has the chief secretary of the state government of Maharashtra as its chairman and a senior bureaucrat as its secretary.

It would thus seem that whether Mumbai will truly become global depends upon the macroeconomic policies adopted by the central government. The recent reshuffling of union government has enabled left parties to play a more decisive role in the formulation of policies and slogans such as "economic reforms with a human face." This development may slow down the process of an Indian city becoming global. In reaction to this, the political leadership in Mumbai would have to strike a balance between supporting new economic activities that may attract foreign investment and protecting labor engaged in sectors such as the textile mills. If public resources are committed to the latter type of activities by way of subsidies, finding resources for the former would also become difficult. It remains to be seen how macroeconomic policies shape the way in which the state government makes its choices for Mumbai in the context of new policies.

Since Mumbai is going through the initial stages of becoming global, its local government has yet to respond to these forces. State government still decides most of the policies for Mumbai, be it the redevelopment of textile mills, the rehabilitation of slums, or the FSI (Floor Space Index) and land use zoning. Surprisingly, local leadership does not seem to assert its powers in this respect either, though guaranteed the right to do so by the Constitution. However, the Bombay First initiatives is an indication of the increasing role that will be played by the private sector in governance in the future. But notable in these efforts is the fact that the Bombay First has always approached state government for support, thereby bypassing city government.

I now turn to the findings of the three essays on Mumbai and their relevance for the city administration. The first essay by Sujata Patel is essentially a descriptive and interpretative presentation of Mumbai. The interpretation is from a leftist's perspective. For example, the decline in the textile industry began in 1982 almost a decade before the liberalization process began. The reasons for this also included the militant trade unions, the price and physical quota restrictions imposed by the government, and competition by the power loom industry, which due to its small and informal status could escape government control. However, these are not analyzed dispassionately. Similarly, the existence of slums and dilapidated *chawls* is highlighted, but some of the causes for this state of affairs—namely, rent control, urban land ceiling, and excessive restrictions on FSI—are not mentioned. Implicit in the argument is a bigger role for government, including the use of subsidies. How such an approach would be feasible for a local government that has barely managed to come out of serious revenue deficit and for a state government that faces an increasing debt burden is not explained. The essay also fails to anticipate the inevitability of globalization that would occur through the World Trade Organization. If that is likely to accentuate the deprivation, the author has not provided any practical course of action that could mitigate such deprivation. I therefore do not consider that the findings of this essay are of any practical help to the city administration.

The second essay by Jim Masselos rightly points out that various national state and local authorities have their own domain in Mumbai and that there is an absence of a single agency having authority over affairs of Mumbai. It also points toward the complexity added by different levels of government being ruled by different political parties. The increasing activism of nongovernmental organizations devoted to a single aspect of the city such as heritage, environment, open spaces, or slum housing is also noted. After describing the locality- and ethnicity-based social organizations of the early twentieth century, the author interprets the traumatic experiences of riots in the early 1990s. The conclusion of the essay is as follows: "In the globalized postmodern—and continuously expanding—city, there may well have been social fragmentation and intense social confrontation, but there was also social and political integration, as well an increased potential for horizontal mobilization by people themselves on issue-oriented matters." This does not purport to provide any practical advice to the city administration.

Ranjit Hoskote uses the change of name from Bombay to Mumbai as a metaphor to explain many manifestations of tensions that most metropolitan cities face in the process of economic transformation. However, renaming the city or more accurately restoring the original name has occurred in many other places as well: Peking became Beijing, and within India Calcutta became Kolkata (West Bengal), Madras became Chennai

(Tamilnadu), and Trivandrum became Thiruvananthapuram (Kerala). Interestingly two of these changes occurred in states ruled by communists, where no chauvinists, caste, or class motives could be attached to the act of renaming the city. In terms of evolving governance, the essay raises a polemic of two extremes—a more responsive and participatory civic administration or a more ruthless technocratic oligarchy. The practical option would obviously lie in between in the functioning Indian democracy. The interpretation of what is happening in Mumbai is woven around four questions—namely, conflict between old and new economies; integration of recent immigrants; marginalization of Dalits, Muslims, and migrants; and competitive populism that manipulates material and emotional dissatisfaction. However, resistance to migrant labor is not unique to Mumbai as seen by the recent U.S. reaction to outsourcing of business operations and perceived threats of job losses. Such outbursts are usually ephemeral. The main governance issue in Mumbai today is consensus building that could best be illustrated by the example of textile mills. The millowners wish to close the mills and sell the real estate. The workers and trade unions, however, want a decent retirement package and a share in the profit. Town planners, in turn, see this as opportunity to get land for public purposes. The heritage lobby wants the old mill structures to be preserved. Environmentalists want to convert the mill land into parks and gardens. Sadly, the essay does not provide any practical clues as to how such consensus could be brought about.

Note

1. *Vision Mumbai—Transforming Mumbai into a World Class City*, Bombay First-McKinsey Report, Mumbai, September 2003.

São Paulo
Jorge Wilheim

São Paulo can easily be discussed and identified in terms of its peculiarities, but can only then be compared to other metropolises like Shanghai, Johannesburg, and Mumbai. They are all different, facing similar characteristic perplexities, but finding distinct solutions to their own problems.

In the Brazilian case, as is correctly pointed out by Deák and Schiffer, the social context extends well beyond the fact that the ruling class is an elite (and not a European-type bourgeoisie) and that Brazil's economy may be considered a "hindered accumulation." To understand this, one should take into account the fact that Brazil, being an American country (like the United States or Argentina), was born from the encounter of nomad Indian nations with a small number of Portuguese and some other European settlers. The Portuguese crown did not colonize the new territory but tried to exploit it, counting on very few men, and almost no women, for this enterprise. The impossibility of enslaving nomads and the death by germs and arms of several million Indians (probably more than 6 million), brought along the enslavement and traffic of Africans, which meant the introduction of another very significant contribution to Brazil's intense ethnic fusion and acculturation process.

In this immense territory, low population density and the greedy search for supposed hidden treasures moved people to live either on farms or in towns. The European village life-style was never known in Brazil. People roamed through the territory, moving around but also up (and even sometimes down) the social ladder. This physical (geographical) and social permeability created an elite that copied the standards of European aristocracy only by the fact of owning land and being arrogant.

But, contrary to an aristocracy, anyone can eventually be a landowner, get rich, and enter the elite ruling class in Brazil. To this social flexibility one should add another anthropological feature, typical of roaming societies in large territories: the spirit, ethics, and behavior of a migrant culture.

These characteristics of Brazil are very typically expressed in the urban history and development of São Paulo, fully pointed out by Pedro Jacobi. They cannot be forgotten when analyzing the spirit of this place. As Shakespeare wrote, "What is a city, but its people . . ." And the building up of what is today considered "the Brazilian people" was the consequence, both unpredicted and upsetting, of the colonialist project of limiting the new country to serve as a mere mechanism of wealth production.

For the purpose of identifying and then comparing cities, it might also be useful to add that São Paulo was born as a highland base for the conquest of the hinterland, on a small triangular hill, defended by the valleys of two rivers (Tamanduateí and Anhangabaú). It remained a very small town for three centuries. From 1860 on, coffee plantations in its province hinterland boomed. The slave traffic brought slaves from the Brazilian northeast, and railroads were established by the British to take the product down to the port of Santos. As the original hill could not be reached by the railroads, a station was built "outside" the core city. The urban occupation and street network naturally started to move toward the station and the adjoining land (creating the "new city," including the districts of Campos Eliseos, Bom Retiro, and Brás).

The very late abolition of slavery (1888) and crisis of European agriculture around the Mediterranean at the end of the nineteenth century brought about a large wave of immigration of families who came till the land. São Paulo had 65,000 inhabitants in 1890 and 265,000 in 1900. One million Italians marched through the city on their way to the hinterland, and many eventually came back to take up other activities, mainly industrial, in town. Thus, Brazilian industry was born in São Paulo. The capital and banking system originated where coffee exports were present, but mainly also where the entrepreneurial capacity of the prevailing migrant culture was present too. The increase of population set up a local market for industrial products. At the beginning of the twentieth century, 92% of industrial workers were immigrants and of these 81% of Italian origin. The Portuguese spoken in São Paulo, differently from the accent spoken in Bahia or Rio, has a Mediterranean sound; and even some of its peculiar grammar comes from Italian.

Another feature must be taken in account, since it is quite different from the situation in Mumbai or Johannesburg. Although a new immigrant always looks for and receives the support of people of the same origin, in Brazil the immigrants did not constitute closed colonies or self-appointed ghettos. The second generation already married outside of ethnic borders, and their kids were "just" Brazilians. "Cultural anthropophagi," expressed in the *Anthropophagi Manifesto* of the 1922 Week of Modern Art in São Paulo, was not only a cultural image created by Oswald de Andrade and other intellectuals and artists. It was the intuition of a much broader significance.

And now, a comment on globalization, in anticipation of the local government's position toward global cities. Among other innovations of the current period of historical transition, new communications technology, merging computer and satellite technology, has created an almost instantaneous global connectivity. I propose that globalization means "the environment of global connectivity" in which we all live. In this virtual field, all processes of transformation are being accelerated. Cultural exchanges, consumers habits, new paradigms of industrial production, and financing decisions all are furthered by global connectivity.

Several authors have focused on the enhanced role of cities in an urbanizing world, pointing out the existence of some cities whose worldwide importance is determined by their concentration of decision making, high-consuming life-style, and presence of imposing and global political power entities (public or corporate). Different authors have listed between ten to thirty-four cities complying with this description and have called them global cities. They are almost all situated in the north (developed countries). But when we look at the whole picture of urbanization, one also identifies twenty-five mega-cities with more than 10 million inhabitants, and twenty-one of them are in the south (developing and less developed countries). Only a few mega-cities of the south are considered to be in the bracket of global cities. São Paulo is among them. Yet are these classifications significant? Are they new? Do global cities or mega-cities constitute network units? I doubt it, although other afterthoughts might be useful for building a theory.

Globalization did enhance a global urban network: a "virtual archipelago" of islands on which modern urban consumers share similar habits and behaviors, consume similar products and services, communicate in computer-English, live an accelerated life of speedy decisions, and have a sufficient family income to thrive in this life-style. These islands of modern consumerism are surrounded by oceans of excluded "swimmers" or "drowned" people, that is, the realm of excluded people. In New York or Berlin, the islands might be large and the ocean small; in Mumbai and Lagos, the islands are small and the ocean large. Tiny Zurich is a global city, while huge Lagos is not. São Paulo might be considered half the way between Mumbai and New York. Somehow a little nearer to this latter . . .

The 2001–4 local government did not "aim" to turn São Paulo into a global city. It did not focus its energy on creating exterior dependability. But it was certainly fully aware of the convenience of enhancing global links; in other words: we knew that we live and act in the environment of global connectivity, which is what we call globalization. It is unavoidable unless for any weird reason one chooses to unplug and live isolated from reality. Yet we consider this plugged-in life as a means, a necessary tool, and not our central aim. The real aim is human development for all. To reach this aim in Brazil (as well as in Latin America) one needs to make the economy grow but also to fill in the prevailing gap between rich and poor, to include the excluded. If this does not happen, production and wealth might be enhanced, but income concentration and exclusions too. For this purpose we have to use several tools, including global connectivities: export, international financing and investments, enhanced tourism, cultural exchanges, worldwide research, language-knowledge expansion, and tolerance and understanding of diversities.

Globalization for us is not synonymous with neoliberal policies. It is just the environment of global connectivity. One should make the most of this era of communication to foster human development. We acknowledge the fact that the present neomonopolistic phase of capitalism is characterized by making intense use of this connectivity to enhance the concentration of economic power and install the dominance of finance over economy (a statement shared by many authors). Globalization is not just what conservative profit-seekers are making of its technology.

This said, what has been achieved in order to keep São Paulo plugged-in to the global environment? The former lady mayor Marta Suplicy created an International Relations Department that activated all dormant links with local governments and international associations, enhanced the association with Mercosul cities, made agreements, and keeps close friendly contacts, mainly with the mayors of Paris, Geneva, Rome, Barcelona, and Buenos Aires (because of political affinities). Active in the support of a stronger position of cities in the United Nations, Marta Suplicy worked with other mayors in order to establish a new representative organization of local governments, recently founded (CLGU), and was elected as its first president. São Paulo also set up URBIS, a yearly international conference for the discussion of urban issues, then in its third edition. The present local government (2005–8) led for one year by elected mayor José Serra followed by his deputy mayor Gilberto Kassab, when Serra stepped down in order to be a candidate for state governor (2006), does not seem to concern itself with such global links.

Beyond these activities the new *Strategic Master Plan,* issued in 2003, thirty years after its last comprehensive design, tried to include a contemporary vision of world challenges as well as local ones. I believe its main innovations could be applied in many other large cities with similar challenges. In a nutshell: first, in our plan, strategic actions are not ideological neoliberal deviations from state planning. They are tools for ensuring that private interests and resources are funneled through public-interest solutions. They are born from two standpoints: a city is a plural construction, and to plan means to prepare a desired future. Thus one has to project, but also to indicate resources. There is no contradiction between strategic actions and master (directive) planning in the new São Paulo plan. The actions are the starting engines of transformation processes intended to build up the final aims of the plan. Similarly, urban operations, according to the plan, are not the same as the previous one mentioned by Deák. Now they have to attain four aims: solving the problem of *favelas,* increasing public space, producing a better environment, and implementing infrastructure. Developers that wish to participate in an urban operation are allowed to reach the highest floor ratio level, purchasing this additional building right.

Second, quoting Jean-Jacques Rousseau, "the public interest is not the same as the interest of all." Opposing interests in a society are legitimate. They were voiced emphatically during the 265 public hearings preceding the acceptance of the plan, with more than 10,000 participants in an intense participatory process. The local governmental role goes beyond the presentation and debate of a proposal. It makes the most of its vital asset, that is, the confrontation with private corporate interests through the treatment of zoning and ruling on floor ratio indicators. The plan established two levels of this ratio. Everybody can build for free one time the area of its lot; but to go up to 2.5 and to 4 times the lot area developers have to pay the difference. The resources go to a public fund dedicated to environmental, public housing, and infrastructural issues. Many other incentives to enhance public space are included in the plan. To preserve the environment and historical buildings it is possible to transfer building potentials from one lot to another. To value the importance of these aspects of the plan one has to understand that the building industry and real-estate interests are very active and strong in São Paulo.

Third, from the global-link point of view, we consider that if security, urban mobility, and environment-townscape are enhanced, São Paulo will be seen as a very attractive metropolis for any activity. Real-estate capital and know-how are mainly national. Market opportunities will be better if the middle class is enlarged, diminishing the crucial gap mentioned before. Although this is a national development issue, the present local government implemented a social policy of inclusion that has had quite effective results: financial support to the very poor in the city periphery, digital inclusion through telecenters, and special education and cultural facilities in the periphery. For the two main unemployment regions (east and south), we prepared urban operations that should enhance new economic activities, mainly in the service and small-industry economy typical of large cities. The solution to the three handicaps mentioned earlier will be useful to all people, going beyond the interest of foreign investors.

The present administration does not seem concerned with deeper social concepts but did not change any of the *Master Plan*'s regulations; although it does not make use of the participatory councils in order to foster urban policies, it abides by everything that was regulated by law.

I hope that the above comments will contribute to the reader's comparative analyses of the four selected metropolis.

Shanghai
Zhu Linchu

Shanghai is located at the midpoint of the eastern seaboard, where the Yangtze River—the longest river in China—merges into the sea. It boasts an eminent port and advanced railway, highway, and water transportation network. With two international airports and one container deepwater port, Shanghai has become a gateway through which overseas investors and merchants pour into the mainland market of China. At present, based on its commitment to being a modern cosmopolitan city, Shanghai has energetically implemented the strategy of invigorating the city through science, technology, and education. It thereby strives to hasten the establishment of international economy, finance, trade, and shipping centers (the four centers) and to increase the comprehensive urban competitiveness of Shanghai.

Within the next one or two decades, the municipal government of Shanghai will be dedicated to perfecting the market mechanism, promoting the urban function, increasing the level of international economic competitive power, optimizing the urban economy and population distribution, and participating in the integration of the Yangtze River Delta.

First, there are much more predominant players on the market in Shanghai due to the restructuring of state-owned enterprises and public institutions, the cultivation of factor markets such as the capital market, and other system reforms. Drawing on the experiences of foreign countries in economic development, the economy of Shanghai will move toward a new height and maintain a relatively healthy growth. It is estimated that the per capita GDP will attain 7,500 USD by 2007, basically equivalent to the middle-developed countries.

Second, Shanghai will further improve the synthesis transport system, multifunctional greening system, and waterside landscape system, so as to enhance the quality of the urban environment. With its "human-oriented" concept, Shanghai will make an effort to establish the fundamental framework of a "national garden city" and "ecological city," which is suitable for domestic citizens and overseas businesses to reside in.

Third, in accordance with the prerequisite of urban-rural integration, Shanghai will vigorously enhance the industrial distribution pattern of the Pudong Golden Triangle Accruement, implementing a modern logistics belt, modern services belt, heavy and chemical industry belt, water, entertainment, and tourism belt, and suburban industrial belt. By facilitating the establishment of a brand-new urban system, such as the central city, new cities, new communities, key towns and key villages, a number of new cities with a population of 800,000 will represent the suburban style of a cosmopolitan city. Additionally, dozens of new cities with a population of 200,000 and key towns in various styles with populations of 80,000 to 100,000 will be set up selectively.

Fourth, boosting the integrating process of the Yangtze River Delta and striving to build the Yangtze River Delta Metropolis into a global city group, Shanghai should play a vanguard role in serving the whole nation and in joining the world economic competition as well. The cooperation, concordance, and innovation of a regional transport system, ecological system, regional market, and mutually beneficial service system will be established in the Delta.

The research findings of Fulong Wu and the other two scholars have expounded the process of Shanghai urban development from different viewpoints of historic, geographic, economic, social transformation, management structure regulation, and cultural image promotion, and have grasped the key questions of Shanghai urban transition.

Fulong Wu remarks that the development of Shanghai suggests a strong dimension of local politics in the formation of a global city region. The decision-making process and organization of current developments have shifted from the central government to local municipalities, from municipalities to subordinated district governments, and further down to development corporations. This shift is called "two levels of government, three tiers of management" in Shanghai, which means that district governments have gained more administrative powers from the municipal government in economic, social, and urban planning. This has aroused the enthusiasm of district and county governments, but has also caused some side effects such as competition. For instance, the construction planning of skyscrapers is getting out of control. Hence, at the beginning of this year, there was a redistribution of power between municipality and districts through financial policy and planning mechanisms. For instance, the policy "double plus, double minus" was pushed in the central city area. Double plus means increasing green space and public open space. Double minus means decreasing total floor area and building height.

Zhongxin Sun analyzes the impact on Shanghai of globalization at the cultural and social level. Sun says that it is scarcely possible to walk down any major street without encountering at least one sign of global influence, from trendy fashions to the ubiquitous McDonald's golden arches. Shanghai is not yet, at present, an integrated, global city. At the same time, Shanghai still faces many conflicts and problems during its development, and there are shortcomings and imperfections in city governance too. In the future, Shanghai will continue to adapt to the needs of both China and the global community. It is to participate in the competition of the global city region jointly with the surrounding fourteen cities by forming a city group. Thus, Shanghai is burdened with the responsibilities of both taking part in global competition and serving the Yangtze River Delta and the whole nation. This makes Shanghai different from other global city regions.

Weiping Wu has estimated that Shanghai will become a global city region. She reaches this conclusion by studying the relationship between central and local government and the economic connections in and out of China. The achievement of the global city status depends on the extent to which China further opens up and implements various municipal policies that enlarge its base of producer services, expands global and regional linkages, ensures an adequate supply of human capital, increases the availability of housing and infrastructure services, and improves the overall quality of life. The municipality is carrying out the idea of people first and also promoting modern services and smart manufacturing. It is to be the theme of Shanghai's economic and social development that a better global city region will be constructed for a better life in the next decades.

Comparing Shanghai with three other cities (Johannesburg, Mumbai, São Paulo), I can not be presumptuous to give any comments, as I have not researched the other cities. However, I do think that as far as the study of global city regions is concerned, both the experiences and lessons of Shanghai should be studied from an international comparative standpoint, so as to share both gains and losses with those cosmopolitan cities that intend to be global city regions.

6 | Conclusion
Challenges Ahead for the Southern Contenders
Simon Raiser and Krister Volkmann

While nation-states are still key actors in international relations, it is widely accepted that the expansion of economic activities around the world is increasingly perforating their borders. Flows of capital, goods, services, people, and content do not stop at borders but move swiftly around the globe in search of the best place to augment profits. Thus we have entered a post-Westphalian era and need a new cartography of power and access (see the introduction to this book). This fundamental change in international relations would not have been possible without a change in the policy agenda of national governments. Governments have endorsed the integration of the world economy by opening up their markets to external investors and reducing state regulations. This is the case in the four countries to which the selected city regions belong. In China, liberalization began with Deng Xiaoping's 1978 reforms and the designation of fourteen open coastal cities—including Shanghai—in 1984. In South Africa, the end of the apartheid regime in 1994 set the ground for building new links with the world, which have been further intensified by the progrowth strategy of the ANC government since 1996. Deliberate liberalization and decentralization policies were also introduced in India in the early 1990s, while the Plano Real of 1994 was one of the key Brazilian policy decisions to stabilize the economy and renew the financial community's interest in Brazilian markets.

The integration of global markets and the measures taken by national governments have triggered far-reaching economic change in many countries, which has been particularly evident in urban areas. Former industrial centers have lost their role as secondary-sector production sites. Factories have moved out into the wider region as well as to countries with cheaper labor costs and less rigorous regulations. This process of industrial decline can be observed in the four presented cities as well. Located outside of the core regions of Europe and North America, they all share the impact of a colonial past, which left its specific imprint on their cityscapes and early economic patterns. In the second half of the nineteenth century all rose to be the prime industrial centers of their respective countries and the colonial economy. São Paulo turned into the economic heart of Brazil with the rapid growth of the coffee plantations in the hinterland. Bombay surpassed Calcutta as the main port of India when the cotton agriculture and subsequent textile industry were introduced in the region. Johannesburg, initially founded as a mining town, soon developed into the economic center of South Africa. And Shanghai, an old fishermen's town, became the key entry point to China after the forced opening in the wake of the Opium War. All four city regions experienced further rapid industrialization in the first half of the twentieth century, making them the industrial powerhouses of their nations.

On the Frontier of Globalization

In the past decades the economy of these prime cities has undergone intense restructuring. Much of traditional industry is in a severe state of decline. Factories are being either closed or relocated to other places in the wider region. In Gauteng, which includes Johannesburg, the share of industrial production went down from 32.0% in 1995 to 26.6% in 2000. In Greater Mumbai there was a respective fall from 37.6% in 1993 to 27.4% in 2000. In the São Paulo Metropolitan Region the share decreased from 62.2% in 1995 to 53.1% in 2000. In Shanghai, the former industrial powerhouse of China, the share of industrial production went down from 57.3% in 1995 to 47.5% in 2000. At the same time, the service sector (in particular finance, insurance, and real estate) has grown steadily. The share of the tertiary sector in the gross regional product increased from 65.7% to 71.7% in Johannesburg (figures for 1995 and 2000), from 61.1% to 71.0% in Mumbai (figures for 1994 and 2001), from 37.5% to 46.9% in São Paulo (figures for 1994 and 2000), and from 40.2% to 51.0% in Shanghai (figures for 1994 and 2000).[1] This tertiarization has ensured the ongoing national or regional dominance of the respective city regions. However, the accompanying employment structure has radically shifted from manufacturing to service-related jobs.[2]

As Sassen (1994) has pointed out, the dispersal of production sites has also increased the need to integrate and control growing resource and information flows. In global networks certain cities emerge as nodes and hubs (Taylor 2003; Castells 1996; Sassen 2002). From the central business districts of these nodes and hubs, worldwide commodity chains are being controlled through a sophisticated and flexible system of financial institutions, headquarters, and specialized producer services. Sassen calls them the "command points in the organization of the world economy" (1994, 4). These global cities are on the winning side of globalization—as financial centers, but also as key sites for the media, culture, information technology services, and politics. While many global cities have been in the upper ranks of the hierarchy of cities for a long time (most notably London, Paris, and New York), others have moved up and replaced older economic centers (see, for instance, Tokyo, Singapore, and Miami). These dynamic hierarchies and recent ambitions by other cities have led to a growing competition between cities around the world.

The city regions of this book are located in the (semi)periphery of the world economy, but due to their increasing linkages with the core economies, they can be called the "frontier of globalization" (see Fulong Wu in this volume). They are already the regional hubs of their larger region. As the prime financial and business centers, they are the sites of the leading stock exchanges, most banks, and the regional headquarters of transnational corporations. Their telecommunications facilities are the best in their countries and per capita income is exceptionally high.

Pudong New Area, with the futuristic skyline of Luijazui financial district, is now illustrated in many journals and publications as a symbol for the spectacular rise of a new global city. The central business district of São Paulo has moved in several waves toward the southwest, now featuring the glittery high-rises of Pinheiros River as the latest site for corporate headquarters. The wealthy suburb of Sandton has emerged as the prime site for businesses in Johannesburg alongside other suburban business centers in Rosebank and Fourways. This shift is less pronounced in Mumbai, although the regional authorities have built the Bandra-Kurla Complex as a financial district and other business centers were put up in Andheri and Navi Mumbai. Still, in Mumbai the historic Fort Area has retained its role as a prime site for business.[3]

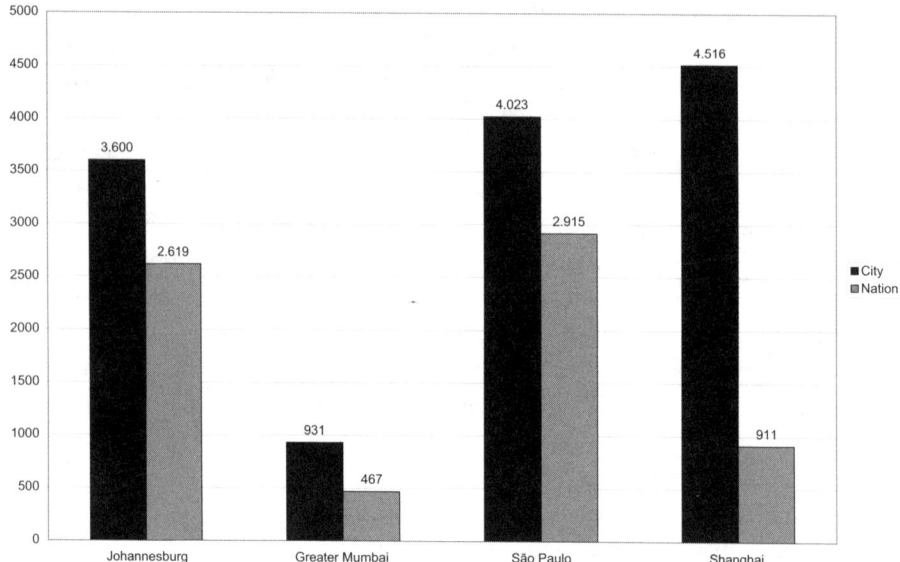

GDP per capita in comparison to nation, in millions (current USD). Note: The figure of Shanghai/China relates to average per capita annual disposable income. Source: Statistics South Africa 2001, Government of Maharashtra 2003b, SEADE 2001, Shanghai Municipal Statistics Bureau 2003, World Bank 2003.

Under Pressure: Competition between City Regions

With the rise of such substantial global areas within their regions, these cities may aptly be called the southern contenders, challenging the established centers of the north. Shanghai is the most prominent case, showing a highly dynamic development and ambition to move up the city hierarchy. However, Shanghai, too, has had to deal with important competitors for the dominating regional position. This competition is most pronounced between Shanghai and Hong Kong, and Shanghai is engaged in a fierce race to displace Hong Kong as the prime city in China.[4] In East Asia, Shanghai is further competing with Singapore, Taipei, Seoul, Osaka, and Tokyo, of which the latter is usually counted in the top trio along with New York and London (Short and Kim 1999; Sassen 2001). Mumbai/Bombay faces serious competition, particularly in the technology sector, from the emerging centers in Bangalore and Hyderabad. Economically, the capital Delhi is challenging its dominance. São Paulo's rivals in Latin America are primarily Buenos Aires, Rio de Janeiro, and Santiago de

Chile, of which, however, none seriously threatens São Paulo's leading position in the region. The prominent position of Johannesburg is nearly unrivaled in southern Africa. Cape Town, Nairobi, and Lagos are the cities south of the Sahara that follow next in terms of global connectedness, albeit with a great distance (van der Merwe 2003; see also the introduction to this volume).

In the face of such urban competition, city administrations around the world realized that they no longer can be passive if they wish to attract investments, as "in virtually all cities policy-makers have perceived their economic base as endangered by competition from other places and have strived to devise programs that would attract expanding businesses" (Fainstein and Campbell 1996, 11). This points to a general shift away from regulatory and distributive measures toward the promotion of economic growth and competitiveness (Rodriguez, Moulaert, and Swyngedouw 2003; Hall and Hubbard 1998). Despite substantial differences between the actions taken by cities, there seems to be a common trend toward more flexibility, efficiency, and urban entrepreneurship. Thus, the increasing (fear of) competition between cities around the world has provoked similar actions to improve a city's position relative to other cities. The aim is to create a positive image of the city and thereby attract visitors and investors, in part by downplaying existent problems (see Ward 1998; Short 1999). This influences the perception of strategy and weakens potential alternative representations of the city (Fincher and Jacobs 1998). The competitive attitude of selling a place—the city—is characteristic of the entrepreneurial city, which presents itself as "proactive in promoting the competitiveness of [its] respective economic space in the face of intensified international (or inter-regional) competition" (Jessop 1997, 28).

The promotion of competitiveness and economic growth supported by the creation of a positive image has become the central feature of urban planning (Swyngedouw, Moulaert, and Rodriguez 2003). In fact, it constitutes the basis for the making of a global city region. The rationale behind these initiatives is that "being globally connected will have significant future payoffs and trickle-down benefits" (Beauregard and Pierre 2000, 474). While there have been a few remarkable success stories in place marketing, like Barcelona or Atlanta (Rutheiser 1996), it is important to note that there is more often than not a huge gap between the image sold and reality. This gap is linked to problems caused by growing socioeconomic fragmentation.

In the depicted city regions, the decline of the older industries has given rise to severe unemployment.[5] The new service companies, although being highly dynamic, provide some new jobs, but not enough to absorb the growing number of job seekers. Many of the new jobs are created in small firms and lack the formal status of earlier factory work. As a result, the economy is becoming increasingly informalized.[6] Although there is always a sector of well-paid informal jobs, the majority of those employed in this sector is confronted with precarious working conditions and a shift of economic and social risks from the employer to the employees.

Ambitions to polish up historical sites and build state-of-the-art business districts are also at odds with the harsh realities in the marginalized parts of the city regions. Despite the relative wealth of the cities, income gaps are extreme in São Paulo as well as in Mumbai and Johannesburg. Residential areas are highly segregated. Wealthy globalized areas are contrasted with slums, *favelas,* and townships where unemployment is high and even basic services are inadequate. More than half of the population of Mumbai lives in crowded slums on less than 6% of Mumbai's territory (see Patel in this volume). The 3,100 informal settlements in the city of São Paulo house approximately 2.5 million people (Cymbalista and Santoro 2005). The majority of the black population in Johannesburg still lives under poor conditions in segregated townships (see Mabin in this volume). Due to the legacy of socialist rule, such extreme polarization is not to be found in Shanghai, but income and wealth differences are increasing. In Shanghai there is already a population of 3 million migrant workers without legal access to urban services.[7]

Dilemmas in Making a Global City Region

In the attempt to build and "imagineer" (Rutheiser 1996) a global city region, the discussed cities face difficult dilemmas (see Hunter in this volume). How can they become world-class cities while at the same time avoiding and reducing socioeconomic fragmentation? Should they follow a strategy of building high-tech infrastructure for global actors or focus on providing basic services to the general population? How can they reconcile the need for quick decisions with the aim of building broad consensus? And how can the influence of strong actors be balanced against new participatory practices? In sum, how can a dual city be integrated into one? These dilemmas are being faced by most cities in the world. However, the duality of a globally connected elite on the one hand and great parts of the population living on the margins and engaged in a daily struggle for survival on the other hand is particularly pronounced in the cities of the global (semi)periphery.

Caught in suspense between these two opposite worlds—wealthy global spaces and wretched local places—the making of global city regions therefore poses an enormous challenge. Priorities and strategies to address the previously mentioned dilemmas differ across diverse city regions and the different approaches can be classified in a number of ways.[8] First, one can identify redistributive programs as opposed to strategies relying on economic growth, both of which are a means to enhance the competitiveness of the city (Roberts and Sykes 2000; Hall and Hubbard 1998; Oatley 1998). Which strategy to chose is a recurring question of political choice. Balancing the contending demands of locally tied inhabitants and global elite travelers is certainly a difficult task.

A second classification addresses the number of decision makers. One approach stresses the importance of involving only a few actors who are then able to formulate a focused strategy. This approach assumes that fewer actors are able to agree on key issues easier, although this may come at the cost of a transparent and democratic decision-making process. Other approaches stress broad participation with the aim of developing a common understanding of the relevant questions to be addressed (Wilheim in this volume). To some extent the choice is between a top-down model versus bottom-up concept that naturally involves a plurality of decision makers. Closely linked to the question of the number of powerful actors is the issue of creating the capacity for flexible and quick reactions within a highly fluctuating environment. The need for quick decisions has increased along with the growing competition between cities. However, it is felt that only consensus building can ensure a long-term commitment to a chosen policy on the part of a diverse selection of actors.

Finally, the existence of a clear strategy for city region development can be distinguished from cases where a coherent strategy does not exist or a strategy is explicitly missing. The latter may be due to a lack either of the capacity to formulate a common strategy (e.g., due to the absence of communication or consensus among actors) or of will on the part of key actors. Different models of global city strategies (or even nonstrategies) can be thought of as combinations along these theoretical dimensions. Although they are located in a common context of globalization, the cases presented in the book show important variations in approach. While the practice does not follow the ideal pictures presented by theoretical analysis, the key characteristics of the four case studies will now be discussed on the basis of the findings in the previous chapters.

Similar Challenges, Different Strategies

Shanghai follows the most ambitious and coherent strategy in the "making" of a global city region (see Zhu Linchu in this volume). This strategy is jointly pursued by national and local government in a manner unknown to the other regions and countries. Shanghai is an extreme case of the activist state, which is determined to direct the resources of global enterprises into its own territory. The state retains a commanding role, but as Fulong Wu observes, the state is not a static entity. Instead, it has transformed itself by reestablishing itself at the local level. A new apparatus and new instruments have been created at the city level, which previously had been merely a "collection of production sites" under the socialist economy. At the same time, the local state has rearranged itself according to the logic of the market economy. Politics has become a matter of intelligent management, and government officials have turned into urban entrepreneurs who design projects and try to procure necessary financing on the global market. Fulong Wu calls this an "entrepreneurial gigantic City Inc."

Still, the central government has preserved its influence. It fosters the formation of the entrepreneurial city with deliberate strategies to make it the Chinese global city, as dramatic spatial changes like the development of the Pudong New Area have shown. Yet, as Weiping Wu points out, the central state retains the ultimate control in foreign relations by regulating Shanghai's contacts with foreigners, the movement into and out of the country, and Internet access. Far-reaching economic reforms have been implemented without a parallel opening-up in political and social affairs. So far, this has ensured a rather peaceful transformation, but the growth of an enormous migrant worker population with a precarious legal status that excludes it from any social insurance poses great challenges for the continued transformation of Shanghai. The authors portray initial steps to reform the social structure under the name of "community construction." Both Weiping Wu and Zhongxin Sun stress, however, that there is a need for a tolerant, creative, and cosmopolitan atmosphere. Such an atmosphere depends on reforms in the political sphere as well. In the long run, creativity and innovation will improve where a free exchange of ideas is possible. One of the key questions will be whether the extraordinary support from the central government will continue to emphasize Shanghai's transformation into a world city. As such, Shanghai's future development is closely linked to the development path that China will take as a whole.

If Shanghai is a prominent example of the influence of the "activist state," then São Paulo in some respect represents the opposite—at least at the metropolitan level. Schiffer and Deák argue that any coherent development plans at the metropolitan level have been abandoned in favor of fragmented "strategic plans" at the level of all thirty-nine municipalities or even below that. This is because the city region lacks an institutionalized administrative structure at the metropolitan level. The existing organization EMPLASA is a mere planning agency with very limited funds and no actual decision-making power. The thirty-nine municipalities in the São Paulo Metropolitan Region have conflicting interests with no or very little coordination of their policies. Destructive fiscal wars concerning tax exemptions have been the result. With this in mind, São Paulo appears to be the globalized, but uncoordinated metropolis.

In this complex setting, many urban services have been delegated to public-private partnerships. A great part of them may have good intentions, but some are formed only to pursue singular elite interests. Although the local government is supposed to regulate the privatized activities, the authors observe a lack of capacity to do so. These structural deficits are used by the established elite to deliberately weaken the state. Formally at least, of the cities presented in this book, the municipalities of Brazil enjoy the greatest autonomy from the national government. This enabled the former Partido dos Trabalhadores (PT) government to introduce a number of innovations to strengthen the participation of citizens. Participatory budgeting and the introduction of subadministrations within the city of São Paulo were among the most prominent changes in the recent years. The evaluation of these policy changes leads to differing assessments. While Sueli Schiffer and Csaba Deák regard them as too weak to overthrow the encrusted power structures of Brazilian society, Pedro Jacobi sees them in a more positive light. He also refers to encouraging examples of social entrepreneurship, which combine entrepreneurial spirit with engagement for the poor.

Regardless of the difference in assessment, the policies of the former PT city government revealed a strategy different from that in Shanghai. Citizen participation has had high priority. However, the ambition to achieve a global status is much less pronounced than in Shanghai (see Wilheim in this volume). The somewhat more relaxed global city aspirations may be due to the already long-standing economic domination of São Paulo in South America. The competition from Buenos Aires or Santiago de Chile appears less aggressive than the rivalry between Shanghai and Hong Kong.

Mumbai/Bombay shares with São Paulo a fragmented governance structure (though competition is to be observed between different levels of government rather than between municipalities at the same level). Mumbai is furthermore confronted with the impact of ethnic and linguistic diversity, vividly portrayed in Jim Masselos's and Ranjit Hoskote's contributions. Lack of imagination has led to the loss of a common identity, as Ranjit Hoskote argues. As a result, regionally defined identity politics dominates the city's political landscape. According to Sujata Patel, this fact makes Mumbai distinctly different from global city regions elsewhere. Mumbai is a city of extremes, where a globalized service economy thrives next to a "bullock-cart economy" without interlinkage. However, strong social cohesion at the community level is characteristic for Mumbai and ensures daily survival in the midst of a confusing city.

Visions for promoting Mumbai/Bombay as a global city region do not exist (see Phatak in this volume). The power to implement any political agenda is split among rivaling institutions and political parties. Similar to the São Paulo Metropolitan Region, a coherent development strategy is far out of sight. Ethnic and linguistic cleavages and blurred lines between formal and informal power structures further complicate its formulation. Rather than resembling the "City Inc." model of Shanghai, Mumbai/Bombay could be classified as a "patchwork city." If there is any integrating image, it is most likely the dreamworld created by the world's largest film industry, Bollywood.

Johannesburg probably shows the most remarkable similarities with the Shanghai model. The ambitious city government actively promotes an explicit strategy to make Johannesburg the world-class city of Africa, thereby generating an African contender. The Johannesburg approach is much more coordinated than in the previous two cases. This is certainly made possible through the dominance of one political party—the ANC—which rules at the national, the provinicial, and municipal levels. Susan Parnell stresses that much of the balancing and negotiating of interests takes place within party structures. Similar to São Paulo, new instruments for improving citizen participation have been introduced, but in her conclusion Parnell shows that this has rather obscured the locus of power. Thus, there seem to be some parallels with the observation of Csaba Deák and Sueli Schiffer.

The legacy of apartheid creates frictions for South Africa in a way that reminds us of the problems of the elite society in Brazil. Although political power has clearly shifted, economic power largely remains in the hands of the white business elite. This leads to a perpetuating pattern of geographies of exclusion, as Alan Mabin shows in his contribution. Robert Beauregard and Richard Tomlinson caution in their contribution that the present city administration shies away from addressing this apparent conflict. Consensus is assumed and political questions are treated through a purely managerial approach, neglecting the need for conflict resolution. New public forums are meant to achieve efficient government, but not to challenge governmental policy. Likewise, the initial focus on redistribution of existing wealth has made room for a growth strategy that relies on policies to make Johannesburg a prime business center and create an environment conducive to investment. While the strategy emphasizes the need to generate skills and reduce the crime rate, little attention is paid to the HIV/AIDS problem. This is even more surprising considering the fact that the city's and the country's future will largely depend on how this pandemic is dealt with.

Final Remarks

The contributions of this book show that the selected city regions are situated in a similar context of current globalization but that they nevertheless vary in the ways in which they address the making of a global city region.

The recent development of Shanghai is economically very impressive. It shows a strong determination of the key actors of the city. In the form of an "entrepreneurial gigantic City Inc.," it follows a model where a limited number of decision makers shape the rapidly changing city region. This model has been very successful in attracting enormous amounts of investment. The question is how to ensure the social integration of the city and to foster an atmosphere of creativity and openness. This will be necessary in the long run, if not only capital, but also vital human skills are to be attracted.

São Paulo, on the other hand, has been very innovative in other fields, experimenting with new instruments of participation and the inclusion of private actors in city governance. Some of the participative tools, such as participatory budgeting, have attracted international attention. However, the innovations have come at the cost of a lack of a coherent metropolitan strategy. It remains to be seen whether they are powerful enough to overthrow the old elitist system of extreme inequality.

Mumbai/Bombay is very distinct in many ways. It is a patchwork city of numerous identities that is characterized by the parallelism of communities. The complex number of actors involved at different political levels and the magnitude of pressing social problems make the formulation of a coherent strategy probably even more difficult than in São Paulo. On the other hand, there is a lot of social commitment and organization at the community level, which helps to keep everyday life manageable and crime rates significantly lower than in Johannesburg and São Paulo.

Johannesburg exhibits—in some ways similar to Shanghai—a very ambitious strategy to make a world-class city. It is led by a dynamic city administration, again resembling the model of a few key decision makers who design the policies. The managerial approach avoids open confrontation. However, the success of Johannesburg's strategy to make it an African contender relies strongly on the way in which Johannesburg also deals with pressing social problems, including the disastrous consequences of HIV/AIDS.

Many cities (not only) in the developing world face similar dilemmas. At the same time most cities are engaged in place marketing and promotion to enhance their competitiveness. The city regions presented in this book show such similarities of context. A closer look, however, reveals differences in the way they respond to these dilemmas. This remarkable diversity suggests further research: What are the reasons behind the different choices? In dealing with city development and its inherent dilemmas, which of the different strategies are most successful for the long term?[9]

This study provides some important indications for further addressing these questions as it focuses on the local context and the role of the relevant actors within each city region. The strength of this approach is that it provides a differentiated picture on the diverse dimensions and their interplay within each city. What the study did not cover are the relations between city regions and how ideas and concepts travel between them.[10]

Taking up the three classifications mentioned previously, Shanghai and Johannesburg pursue strategies that are predominantly oriented toward economic growth and competitiveness. In São Paulo the focus is more on social inclusion, while in Mumbai/Bombay a coherent development strategy is lacking. As concerns the number of relevant actors and the decision-making process, the city government in Shanghai seems able to reach decisions very quickly, while the need to reach broad consensus is strongly felt in Mumbai/Bombay and São Paulo. This correlates with only a few strong actors in the case of Shanghai, on the one hand, and the introduction of new participatory practices in São Paulo, which encourage the involvement of a broader spectrum of actors, on the other hand. The case of Johannesburg, in turn, reminds us that strong administrative actors can go hand in hand with participatory tools, although they do not automatically deliver greater power to the citizens.

None of the four city regions seems to be able to neglect the demands by global actors for high-tech infrastructure. At the same time, they all acknowledge the need to ensure the provision of basic services, but opinions and strategies in the city regions differ with respect to the ways the services can and should best be provided: through public services, private enterprises, public-private partnerships, or community organizations. Sometimes this may be a deliberate choice embedded in a clear and coherent strategy. At other times, however, a well-formulated strategy is lacking and privatization occurs in a rather chaotic way, leading to unsatisfactory results. Overall, it becomes evident that local traditions and particularities are influencing the priorities set by a given city region.

Concerning the question of a strategy's success, the following observation derives from the presented case studies: when designing strategies for making global cities, it is important to keep the "city" in mind. Only if the essence of the city is maintained and citizenship rights are guaranteed (Beauregard and Bounds 2000) can the project of making a global city region be successful in a sustainable manner. The essence of the city is urbanity, which can be translated as shared public space, where different cultures and classes meet. Under such conditions, encounters with other people can serve as sources of ideas and innovations. Shared public space provides room for the exchange and negotiation of interests.

Mario Polèse has pointed to the need of a "shared vision of the city" (2000, 330–32). Such a shared vision can create a common understanding of the basic direction for development. Quick decisions and strong actors are then ideally embedded in a shared culture. This may open opportunities to solve or at least balance the dilemmas that accompany the making of a global city region. The studies in this book have revealed the difficulties in creating a shared vision for the city. But a sustainable future of each of these city regions will depend on it.

Notes

1. Statistics South Africa 2001; SEADE 2001; Government of Maharashtra 2001; 2003a; 2003b; Shanghai Municipal Statistics Bureau 2003.

2. In Shanghai, employment in the secondary sector dropped from 58.4% to 45.9% between 1990 and 2000, with a corresponding rise in the tertiary sector from 29.3% to 42.6% (Shanghai Municipal Statistics Bureau 1991; 2001). In São Paulo, 600,000 industrial jobs were lost between 1989 and 2000, while in the same time period 1.5 million new jobs were created in the service sector (SEADE 2001). In Mumbai, employment in the finance and real-estate sector and equally in communications, social, and personal services increased by 2.5 times between 1980 and 1998 (Ghorpade 2005). Figures for Johannesburg are more ambiguous, showing a drop of employment in manufacturing from 24% in 1980 to 13% in 1996 (Beall, Crankshaw, and Parnell 2002). On the other hand, new employment has been created in the service economy, more specifically in the information technology sector, in the creative industries, and in the field of tourism: an impressive 70% of the jobs in the South African technology sector are located in Johannesburg (Rogerson 2002; Moleketi 2003).

3. For an overview on the spatial changes in the four city regions, see Raiser and Volkmann 2005.

4. So far, Hong Kong continues to be one of the most connected cities in the global networks, only being surpassed by London and New York (Taylor 2003). As most data on the global connectivity show, Shanghai still has a long way to get to the top of the global hierarchy (see the introduction to this volume). According to some observers, however, it seems only a question of time before Shanghai will take over as the leading city in China (interviews held on 9 and 10 March 2003 in Shanghai with Tina Kanagaratnam and Patrick Cranley from AsiaMedia, Bernd Reitmeier from the Delegation of German Industry and Commerce).

5. In Johannesburg, unemployment has increased from 29.2% in 1996 to 37.3% in 2001 (City of Johannesburg 2001), but due to a change in geographical demarcations in Johannesburg, no direct comparison is possible. In São Paulo (RMSP) unemployment has constantly risen from 10.3% in 1990 to 19.0% in 2001 (SEADE 2001). Unemployment in Mumbai/Bombay increased by more than two times between 1981 and 1996 (see Patel in this volume). Even in Shanghai, with relatively modest unemployment, the rate rose from 1.5% in 1990 to 4.8% in 2002 (Shanghai Municipal Statistics Bureau 2003). In the same time period, more than 1 million formal jobs were lost due to industrial restructuring.

6. Figures for the informal sector are almost by definition only estimates. In Mumbai, according to Patel in this volume, there is an increase of workers in the informal sector from 49% in 1961 to 65.6% in 1991. According to a survey in 1996, roughly 60% of new jobs in São Paulo are attributable to the informal sector (Schiffer 2002, 227). In Johannesburg, employment in the informal sector rose very rapidly between 1996 and 1999 from 9.6% to 16% of total employment (see Mabin in this volume). And also in Shanghai, the presence of approximately 3

million migrant workers without urban household registration contributes to the formation of an urban informal sector (see Weiping Wu in this volume).

7. There is an important difference in the legal status of the urban and rural population in China, restricting residence in cities.

8. The authors would like to thank Celina Souza for her valuable contribution to these thoughts. Björn Warkalla also provided useful comments on an earlier draft version of this text.

9. Note in this context that success can be defined in various ways. For example, there is an important difference between defining success solely by achieving global competitiveness or by aiming to ensure sustainable development for the entire city.

10. For such a network approach, see the work done by GaWC at Loughborough University.

References

Beall, J., O. Crankshaw, and S. Parnell. 2002. *Uniting a Divided City: Governance and Social Exclusion in Johannesburg*. London: Earthscan.

Beauregard, R., and A. Bounds. 2000. Urban Citizenship. In Engin F. Isin (ed.), *Democracy, Citizenship and the Global City*, 243–56. London: Routledge.

Beauregard, R., and J. Pierre. 2000. Disputing the Global: A Sceptical View of Locality-Based International Initiatives. *Policy & Politics* 28, no. 4: 465–78.

Castells, M. 1996. *The Rise of the Network Society*. Vol. 1. Oxford: Oxford University Press.

City of Johannesburg. 2001. *Johannesburg Census, 2001*.

Cymbalista, R., and P. Santoro. 2005. Multiple Actors, Diverse Arrangements: Infrastructure and Basic Services in São Paulo. In K. Segbers, S. Raiser, and K. Volkmann (eds.), *Public Problems—Private Solutions? Globalizing Cities in the South*, 207–28. Aldershot: Ashgate Publishing.

Fainstein, S., and S. Campbell (eds.). 1996. *Readings in Urban Theory*. Cambridge, Mass.: Blackwell.

Fincher, R., and J. Jacobs (eds.). 1998. *Cities of Difference*. New York: Guilford.

Ghorpade, K. 2005. Economic Restructuring by Default. In K. Segbers, S. Raiser, and K. Volkmann (eds.), *Public Problems—Private Solutions? Globalizing Cities in the South*, 35–50. Aldershot: Ashgate Publishing.

Government of Maharashtra. 2001. *District Domestic Product of Maharashtra, 1993/94 to 1998/99 (Base Year 1993/94)*. Mumbai: Directorate of Economics and Statistics.

———. 2003a. *District Domestic Product of Maharashtra, 1999/2000, 2000/01 and 2001/02*. Mumbai: Directorate of Economics and Statistics.

———. 2003b. Statistical Facts and Figures. http://maharashtrastat.com.

Hall, Tim, and P. Hubbard (eds.). 1998. *The Entrepreneurial City. Geographies of Politics, Regime and Representation*. Chichester: John Wiley & Sons.

Jessop, B. 1997. The Entrepreneurial City: Re-imaging Localities, Redesigning

Economic Governance or Restructuring Capital? In N. Jewson and S. MacGregor (eds.), *Transforming Cities: Contested Governance and New Spatial Divisions*, 28–41. London: Routledge.

Moleketi, J. 2003. Gauteng 2003/2004 Budget Speech. www.geda.co.za.

Oatley, N. (ed.). 1998. *Cities, Economic Competition and Urban Policy.* London: Chapman.

Polèse, M. 2000. Learning from Each Other: Policy Choices and the Social Sustainability of Cities. In M. Polèse and R. Stren (eds.), *The Social Sustainability of Cities: Diversity and Management of Change*, 308–34. Toronto: University of Toronto Press.

Raiser, S., and K. Volkmann (eds.). 2005. Emerging Patterns of the Global City Region. Spatial Changes in Johannesburg, Mumbai/Bombay, Shanghai, and São Paulo. Working Paper Series of the Osteuropa-Institut, Freie Universität Berlin, no. 53. http://userpage.fu-berlin.de/~segbers/working_papers.html.

Roberts P., and H. Sykes (eds.). 2000. *Urban Regeneration: A Handbook.* London: Sage.

Rodriguez, A., F. Moulaert, and E. Swyngedouw. 2003. Urban Restructuring, Social-Political Polarization and New Urban Policies. In F. Moulaert, A. Rodriguez, and E. Swyngedouw (eds.), *The Globalized City: Economic Restructuring and Social Polarization in European Cities*, 29–46. Oxford: Oxford University Press.

Rogerson, C. 2002. Knowledge-Based Regions in the Global Periphery: The Case of South Africa. In R. Hayter and R. Le Heron (eds.), *Knowledge, Industry and Environment: Institutions and Innovation in Territorial Perspective*, 313–35. Aldershot: Ashgate.

Rutheiser, C. 1996. *Imagineering Atlanta: The Politics of Place in the City of Dreams.* London: Verso.

Sassen, S. 1994. *Cities in a World Economy.* Thousand Oaks, Calif.: Sage.

———. 2001. *The Global City: New York, London, Tokyo.* Rev. ed. Princeton, N.J.: Princeton University Press. (Originally published 1991.)

——— (ed.). 2002. *Global Networks, Linked Cities.* New York: Routledge.

Schiffer, S. 2002. São Paulo: Articulating a Cross-Border Region. In S. Sassen (ed.), *Global Networks, Linked Cities*, 209–36. New York: Routledge.

Shanghai Municipal Statistics Bureau. 1991. *Shanghai Statistical Yearbook 1991.* Beijing: China Statistics Press.

———. 2001. *Shanghai Statistical Yearbook 2001.* Beijing: China Statistics Press.

———. 2003. *Shanghai Statistical Yearbook 2003.* Beijing: China Statistics Press.

Short, J. R. 1999. Urban Imagineers: Boosterism and the Representation of Cities. In A. Jonas and D. Wilson (eds.), *The Urban Growth Machine: Critical Perspectives Two Decades Later*, 37–54. Albany: State University of New York Press.

Short, J. R., and Y.-H. Kim. 1999. *Globalization and the City.* New York: Addison Wesley Longman.

Sistema Estadual de Analise de Dados São Paulo (SEADE). 2001–3. Economia, Demografia. www.seade.gov.br/index.html.

Statistics South Africa. 2001. *Census 2001.* www.statssa.gov.za/census2001/census 2001.htm.

Swyngedouw E., F. Moulaert, and A. Rodriguez. 2003. "The World in a Grain of Sand": Large-Scale Urban Development Projects and the Dynamics of "Glocal" Transformations. In F. Moulaert, A. Rodriguez, and E. Swyngedouw (eds.), *The Globalized City: Economic Restructuring and Social Polarization in European Cities,* 9–28. Oxford: Oxford University Press.

Taylor, P. J. 2003. *World City Network: A Global Urban Analysis.* New York: Routledge.

van der Merwe, I. J. 2003. *The Global Cities of Sub-Sahara Africa: Fact or Fiction?* Research Bulletin, no. 126. Globalization and World Cities Study Group and Network. www.lboro.ac.uk/gawc/rb/rb126.html.

Ward, S. 1998. *Selling Places: The Marketing and Promotion of Towns and Cities, 1850–2000.* New York: Routledge.

World Bank. 2003. *World Development Indicators, 2003.* Washington, D.C.: World Bank.

List of Contributors

Robert A. Beauregard is professor of urban policy at the Graduate School of Management and Public Policy, New School University (New York). His most recent books are *Voices of Decline: The Postwar Fate of U.S. Cities* (second edition, 2002) and *Emerging Johannesburg: Perspectives on the Postapartheid City* (coeditor, 2003).

Csaba Deák is professor of urban planning at the Faculty of Architecture and Urbanism, University of São Paulo. His main interests are the provision of urban infrastructure and the specific features of Brazilian society and economy. His publications include *The Crisis of Hindered Accumulation in Brazil* (1988) and *Globalisation: Yesterday and Today* (1999).

Ranjit Hoskote is currently assistant editor with the *Hindu*, Mumbai/Bombay. He is a cultural theorist, poet, and independent curator of contemporary art. The most recent of the six books he has authored or edited is *Reasons for Belonging: Fourteen Contemporary Indian Poets* (2002). A major outcome of his project on art production in postcolonial societies undergoing globalization was the collaborative trans-Asian exhibition, Under Construction (Japan Foundation, 2002–3).

Roland Hunter is currently executive director of finance and economic development in the city of Johannesburg. He has previously held a similar position at the Gauteng Provincial Government, where he ran the Department of Finance and Economic Affairs. He has also lectured at the University of the Witwatersrand in Johannesburg and has spent time with a Johannesburg-based NGO working in the field of local government and development planning.

Pedro Jacobi, economist and sociologist, is currently associate professor at the School of Education and the Graduate Program of Environmental Science at the University of São Paulo. His recently published books are *Citizens at Risk: From Urban Sanitation to Sustainable Cities* (coauthor, 2001) and *Políticas Sociais e Ampliação da Cidadania* (2000).

Zhu Linchu is the deputy director general of the Development Research Center of the Shanghai Municipal Government and deputy leader of the Asia Development Bank consulting team and holds various other directory posts of scientific institutions in Shanghai. He is experienced in a wide range of professional fields, including the directory of the EXPO 2010 Shanghai bidding office.

Alan Mabin, born in Johannesburg, has written many articles about cities and urban issues in South Africa and other countries. He is professor of Urban Management and Public Policy at the Graduate School of Public Management, University of the Witwatersrand, Johannesburg. His edited books include *La question urbaine en Afrique Australe* (1999).

Jim Masselos is honorary reader in history at the University of Sydney. In his studies he focuses on modern South Asian history, Indian art and religion, as well as the transformation of Bombay city. In 2003 he coedited with Sujata Patel *Bombay and Mumbai: The City in Transition*.

Susan Parnell is associate professor in geography at the University of Cape Town. She is a geographer with more than seventy published academic articles, many of them on Johannesburg. She coauthored *Uniting a Divided City: Governance and Social Exclusion in Johannesburg* (2002) and *Democratising Local Government: The South African Experiment* (2004).

Sujata Patel is professor of sociology and head of the Department of Sociology at the University of Pune. She has published and coedited various books on Mumbai, including *Bombay and Mumbai: The City in Transition* (2003) and *The End of Bombay: The Beginnings of Mumbai* (2003).

Vidyadhar K. Phatak is a professional planner with a long experience in a wide range of subfields of urban planning and development. As chief of the Town and Country Planning Division at the Mumbai Metropolitan Region Development Authority (MMRDA), he led a multidisciplinary team to prepare a strategic plan for the Mumbai Metropolitan Region, coordinated and monitored an urban development project, and developed environmental management and resettlement plans for a transport project, both assisted by the World Bank.

Simon Raiser is research fellow at the Institute of Political Science, Free University Berlin, and the coordinator of the Global City Regions project. His recent publications include *Public Problems—Private Solutions* (with Klaus Segbers and Krister Volkmann, 2005) and a working paper on the new world of cities, *Die neue Welt der Städte: Metropolen im Zeitalter der Globalisierung* (with Krister Volkmann, 2003).

Sueli Schiffer is titular professor at the Faculty of Architecture and Urbanism of the University of São Paulo. She has published various academic articles. Most recently she edited *Globalização e Estrutura Urbana* (2004) and coedited *O Processo de Urbanização no Brasil* (1999).

Klaus Segbers is professor of political science and international relations at the Free University Berlin. His most recent publications include *Public Problems—Private Solutions* (with Simon Raiser and Krister Volkmann, 2005), *Alternative Futures: Anarchy, Gated Communities, or Global Learning* (2003), *Explaining Post-Soviet Patchworks* (editor, 2001) in three volumes, and *The Globalization of Eastern Europe: Teaching International Relations without Borders* (with Kerstin Imbusch, 2000).

Zhongxin Sun is an associate professor in the Department of Sociology at Fudan University, Shanghai. She is the author of *A Sociological Study of School Failure* (1997) and has conducted several research works on gender, sexuality, youth, and urban community in contemporary China. Her recent articles include the coauthored paper "Extramarital Love in Shanghai" (2003).

Richard Tomlinson is professor at the Graduate School of Public and Development Management at the University of the Witwatersrand. In his research he currently focuses on urban international best practice and on local government and the delivery of shelter and services (water, sanitation, etc.) as well as HIV/AIDS care and prevention. He is coauthor of *Emerging Johannesburg: Perspectives on the Post-Apartheid City* (2003).

Krister Volkmann is research fellow at the Institute of Political Science at the Free University Berlin. His recent publications include *Public Problems—Private Solutions* (with Klaus Segbers and Simon Raiser, 2005), an article on the new role of global cities, *Die neue Rolle der Metropolen* (2001), and a book on the Local Agenda 21, *Lokale Agenda 21 in Potsdam und Osnabrück* (2002).

Jorge Wilheim is a Brazilian architect and urbanist, responsible for the master plans of São Paulo, Curitiba, Campinas, and many other Brazilian cities. He was the deputy secretary general of the UN Habitat 2 Conference (Istanbul, 1996). He is the former São Paulo State secretary of planning, secretary of the environment, and São Paulo City secretary of planning. He is author of several books on urban planning and city life.

Fulong Wu is reader at the School of Geography of the University of Southampton. He received in 2001 the Otto Koenigsberger Prize from Habitat International and published many papers on urban spatial structure in Chinese cities, urban housing, and land development. He coedited *Restructuring the Chinese City: Changing Society, Economy and Space* (2004, with Laurence Ma) and recently edited the book *Globalization and the Chinese City* (2006).

Weiping Wu is associate professor of urban studies and geography in the School of World Studies and the School of Government and Public Affairs at the Virginia Commonwealth University, Richmond (USA). She has published widely, including: *Local Dynamics in a Globalizing World* (2000) and *Facets of Globalization: International and Local Dimensions of Development* (2001).

Index

actors, 135–38, 140–41, 162, 226–28, 344–51 passim; and decision-making process, 140–41, 162, 190, 196, 287, 351; economic, 9, 10, 207, 214, 217–21, 291; formal, 136; global, 224, 263, 344, 351; global city regions as, 7, 10, 12, 23n8, 237; informal, 136; interactions between, 6, 273; interdependent, 9; key, 136, 209, 223, 339, 345, 349; local, 207, 211–12, 221–24; new, 30, 203, 207; nonstate, 5, 193, 203, 235, 291; political, 8, 207, 242; private, 135–36, 313; public, 136, 313, 350; relevant, 2, 5–6, 11, 19–21 passim, 137–38, 350–51; societal, 10; state, 5, 137; states as, 4, 12, 237, 339; strong, 344, 351; urban, 262
African contender, 348, 350
African National Congress (ANC), 29, 39, 54–58 passim, 136–38, 149, 159–61, 237–44; contradictory interests, 57–58, 161, 240; progrowth strategy, 55, 247, 339; as ruling party, 54–55, 140, 159, 239, 254, 348
African renaissance, 159
Anti-Privatisation Forum (South Africa), 149, 247–48
apartheid, 28–29, 39–41, 44, 52–53, 251, 254, 349

authority: arenas of, 170–71; central, 7, 21, 173; consensual, 263, 265; decentral, 8; elite, 92; formal, 170–71; government, 238; informal, 182, 268; lacking, 269, 327; legal, 172; local, 81, 143, 146, 148, 198; metropolitan, 40, 136, 321; ritualized, 265; social, 174, 176; state, 7, 21, 173; traditional, 174–76
Ayodhya, 179, 268

Babri Masjid. *See* Ayodhya
Bandra-Kurla Complex, 341
Bharatiya Janata Party (BJP), 78, 169, 171, 178, 181–82, 259, 264, 268, 270–71, 274, 277n8, 325
Blue IQ, 53, 250, 251
Bollywood, 74, 348
Bombay. *See* Mumbai/Bombay
Bombay First, 325–26
Brazil: coffee production, 29, 88; economic miracle, 29, 93, 96; elite society, 85, 91–102 passim, 137, 188–89, 192, 202, 349; Plano Real, 339
budget: Johannesburg, 53, 143–44, 149–49, 160, 243, 322; Mumbai/Bombay, 78; national, 5, 10, 103; participatory, 197, 285, 347, 350; São Paulo, 197, 202; Shanghai, 120, 211

capitalism: Brazil, 88; China, 216, 298; guanxi, 214; India, 64; new forms of, 70, 98–100, 107, 332; Victorian, 275
capital market, 6, 319, 335
cartography, 5, 274, 339
caste, 11, 69, 169, 173–76 passim, 268–71 passim, 275, 325, 328
central business district (CBD), 41, 224, 241, 324, 341; new, 67, 117, 128. *See also* Bandra-Kurla Complex; Fort Area (Mumbai/Bombay); Lujiazui (Financial District); Pudong (New Area); Sandton
China: command economy, 116, 209; fiscal regime, 119; market-oriented economy, 208; open-door policy, 217; postsocialism, 209; socialist regime, 209, 210, 223
citizenship, 147, 193, 207, 244, 246, 252, 271, 286, 309, 351
city: development, 2, 20, 41, 146, 302, 307–9, 350; governance, 140–42, 162–63, 302–3, 311, 337, 350; management, 146, 162, 188–89, 197, 202
city council (Johannesburg), 37, 55, 57, 147–48, 240, 242, 246, 249
"City Inc.," 19, 33, 207, 229, 346, 348–49
city manager (Johannesburg), 55, 145, 151, 240, 317
city region: metropolitan area (Johannesburg), 32–33, 39–48; metropolitan area (Mumbai/Bombay), 65–68, 168; metropolitan area (São Paulo), 85–88; metropolitan area (Shanghai), 114–17, 296–97
civic organizations, 152, 155, 235, 237
civil society: and governance, 238–39; interests, 142, 149; Johannesburg, 139, 153–55, 160–61, 163, 252; Mumbai/Bombay, 69, 261, 265; São Paulo, 186–87, 196, 199, 290–91

class: differences, 281; disempowered, 264–65; inequalities, 47, 169, 176; interests, 73, 263, 268, 328; middle, 45–46, 58, 69, 78, 87, 101, 176, 178, 180–81, 267, 286–87, 334; new global, 74, 176; political, 274; ruling, 91, 186, 188–89, 329–30; segregation, 240; struggle, 297; subaltern, 266–67; upper, 75, 77, 201–2; violence, 262–63; working, 45, 69, 73, 75, 87, 181, 264, 266–67
Cold War, 3–4, 6, 209
communicative disengagement, 261–63, 271
Communist Party: African, 39, 161; Chinese, 21, 138, 210, 297, 300, 309
community construction (Shanghai), 212–13, 304, 306, 346
competition with/between cities, 11, 49, 114, 260, 341–45
competitiveness, 20, 27, 29, 233, 343, 345, 350; Johannesburg, 144, 251, 253; Mumbai/Bombay, 325; São Paulo, 187; Shanghai, 222, 227, 311, 313, 335. *See also* global competitiveness
Congress of South African Trade Unions (COSATU), 149–50, 161, 248
Congress Party (India), 68, 171–72, 182–83, 263–64, 268, 270–71, 274
connectedness, global, 13, 343
consensus: assumed, 234, 242, 253, 349; building, 328, 344–45, 351; as a mechanism, 243
Constitution: Brazil, 98, 103, 190–91, 196–97; India, 170, 324, 326; South Africa, 52, 54, 146, 156, 164n13, 246
contradictions: of a global city, 1, 248, 272, 280, 286, 303; historical, 293; resolution and management of, 59, 322
corporatization, 54, 55, 147

crime: Johannesburg, 39, 47, 56–57, 148, 240, 249, 251, 349; Mumbai, 64, 177, 264, 266, 350; São Paulo, 281–82
culture, 7–8, 51, 128, 193, 273, 283, 296, 302–3, 341; company, 301; of deprivation, 78; Hai-Pai, 115, 295–96, 300, 308, 313; indigenous, 302; local, 131, 273; migrant, 330; new urban, 265, 296, 311; political, 58, 152; popular, 223; shared, 351; socialist spirit, 309; tolerant, 31; traditional, 38, 254, 303; urban industrial, 79, 301

dalit(s), 173, 263, 268–71, 328
decentralization, 13, 194, 203, 208, 210, 227, 339; administrative, 196–98, 222; economic, 210, 212, 221; fiscal, 120, 211–12, 219; Johannesburg, 240; Mumbai/Bombay, 70–71, 324; political, 13, 18, 324; of power, 212; São Paulo, 106–7, 196–98; Shanghai, 120, 209, 211–12, 219, 221–22
decision-making process, 136–38, 345, 351; São Paulo, 186–90 passim, 194, 196–97, 200, 202; Shanghai, 227, 336
deindustrialization, 27, 70, 72, 106–7
democracy, 92, 253; Brazil, 92; China, 306; India, 271, 328; local, 213, 238, 242; radical, 140; social, 99–100; South Africa, 139, 142–43, 162, 247
Democratic Alliance (DA) (South Africa), 57, 159, 161, 242–43, 247, 254
democratic transition, 140, 142
deprivation, 76–78, 82n20, 286, 327
developing world, 9, 12, 21, 72, 156, 350
dilemmas, urban, 21, 27, 344–46, 350–51
discourse, 5, 11, 18, 233–36, 239–40, 279–80, 295–313 passim; competing, 235, 293; dominant, 58; fragmentary, 260–63, 271; global, 4, 141, 235, 253; governance, 254, 321; government, 246, 248, 283–86, 289, 291–92; participatory, 149. *See also* "dragonhead"; "elder brother"; "indigenization"
donor agencies, 135, 322
"dragonhead," 211, 224, 297–300, 303, 313

East Rand, 40, 49
Ekurhuleni, 40, 42, 43, 45
"elder brother," 175, 297–300, 313
"entreguismo," 100, 101
entrepreneurial city, 207, 216, 222, 343, 346
ethnic diversity, 70, 282
ethnic segregation, 235, 265
exclusion: geographies of, 47–48; social, 48, 156, 282–83, 286
Executive Mayor (Johannesburg), 52, 240–41, 321

favelas, 47, 87, 196, 198, 200, 333, 344
fiscal balance, 210, 245
fiscal crisis, 54, 143–44, 147, 151, 156, 247
flows, global, 4–16 passim, 27, 207, 279, 292, 297, 339, 341
foreign direct investment (FDI), 13, 23n13; Mumbai, 81n7, 323; Shanghai, 217, 217–20, 314n3
Fort Area (Mumbai/Bombay), 172, 341
fragmentation: administrative, 106, 190; of the decision-making process, 136, 198; industrial, 130; social, 37, 184, 234, 327; socioeconomic, 21, 27, 343–44; spatial, 30, 48, 92–94, 98; urban, 53, 275, 283; of urban policy, 192–95

gated communities, 47, 57, 280
Gauteng (province), 28, 32, 40, 42, 53, 251, 340

GDP. *See* gross domestic product
gentrification, 199, 234, 264
geography. *See* city region
global cities: comparison with others, 308–9; debatable status, 2, 13, 22, 85, 123, 331; hierarchy, 312, 331; as key sites, 341; making of, 251; and mega-cities, 331; production of mega-projects, 215, 292
global city region. *See* city region
global competitiveness, 27, 251, 253, 353n9
global connectivity, 331–32, 352n4
global economy, 9–10, 12–13, 18; Mumbai/Bombay, 29, 36, 65, 73, 79; São Paulo, 282; Shanghai, 208, 211, 214, 291
globalization: definition of, 4–5; dynamics of, 7–8; effects of, 4, 7, 279; frontier of, 209, 340–41
Globalization and World Cities Research Group (GaWC), 23n11
global market, 27, 72, 79–80, 142, 226, 247, 339, 346
global network connectivity, 14–15, 23n14
global politics, 4–10
governance: actors, 5–6; capability, 6; formal, 171–72; good, 245–47, 250, 253–54, 321–22; urban, 54, 59, 136, 141, 210–15 passim, 221–22, 239, 304–5
government: central (*see* national); central (China), 30, 116–23, 128–29, 137, 209–12, 297–300, 346–47; central (India), 77, 136, 170–72, 324, 326; de-politicization of, 242–43; essence of, 322; local, 12, 346–47; local (Johannesburg), 33–41 passim, 52–59, 142–48 passim, 237–41; local (Mumbai/Bombay), 69, 324 [*see also* Municipal Corporation of Greater Mumbai (MCGM)]; local (São Paulo), 195–97, 331–34; local (Shanghai), 116–19, 209–12 passim, 217–19 passim, 221–23, 335–37; metropolitan (Johannesburg), 40, 140, 247; municipal (*see* government: local; national), 4, 10, 339–40 [*see also* central (China), central (India)]; national (South Africa), 58, 141, 146–148, 156, 239, 241; performance, 238, 241–45
gross domestic product (GDP), 342; Brazil, 93, 101; Johannesburg, 342; Mumbai/Bombay, 342; São Paulo, 97; Shanghai, 16, 116, 118, 120, 123, 217, 335, 342
gross geographic product (GGP), 49
Growth, Employment and Redistribution (GEAR), 147, 161, 241, 247

Hai-pai culture. *See under* culture
hindered accumulation, 30, 91–92, 96–100 passim, 186–92 passim, 203, 329
history: Johannesburg, 37–39; Mumbai/Bombay, 68–70; São Paulo, 88–91; Shanghai, 114–16, 295–96
Hong Kong, 13–14, 16–17, 208, 229n1, 323; competition with, 113, 120–23, 342, 348, 352n4; foreign direct investment from, 217–19, 298
household registration (China), 125–26, 210, 353n6
housing, 107; improvement, 66, 78, 108, 123–25, 131, 287, 305–6, 325; migrants, 69, 126; neighborhood, 173, 176, 269; poor, 47, 76–78, 88, 240–41, 244, 267, 280, 284, 323, 334; private, 126, 130, 216; public, 43, 54, 126, 333; slums, 70, 79, 289; social, 196, 199, 223, 246, 288, 304; wealthy, 76–78, 88, 128, 214, 267, 299. See also *favelas*; gated communities; informal settlements; slums; townships
hub, 8–13 passim, 16, 21, 27, 121, 341; Johannesburg, 159; Mumbai/

Bombay, 74; São Paulo, 235, 281; Shanghai, 120–21, 131
human development, 253, 287, 332

identitarian politics, 263, 270
identity, 259, 348; of the city (urban), 11, 73, 136, 170, 261–62, 275, 309, 313; cultural, 259; global vs. local, 258; movements, 79, 181; politics, 29, 65, 260–61, 348; post-apartheid, 143; religious, 79, 174–75; separatist, 178; social, 174–75
iGoli 2002, 54, 143–45, 147–50, 156, 160, 320–22; as city discourse, 247–48
iGoli 2010, 55, 143–45, 153–55, 157, 160; as city discourse, 248–49
image(s), 233–36; creation, 222, 233, 336, 343; distinct, 19–20; Johannesburg, 237, 240, 248, 252; Mumbai/Bombay, 258–61, 265, 269, 275–75, 348; negative, 64, 240, 299, 308; new, 5, 11, 299; São Paulo, 279–84, 331; second reversed, 6; Shanghai, 295, 299, 307, 310, 336
inclusion, social, 5, 234, 259, 271, 284, 334, 350
income distribution, 101, 103–4, 298
India, regionalism, 65
"indigenization," 236, 300–303, 314n4
inequality, 35, 59, 194, 281, 284, 292–93, 350
informal activities, 45
informal economy, 50
informal employment, 29
informal sector, 27, 352n6; Johannesburg, 39, 50, 151, 155; Mumbai/Bombay, 72, 75, 266, 269; Shanghai, 126
informal settlements, 288, 344
institutions: financial, 115, 129, 156, 218, 220, 229n1, 324, 341; formal and informal, 136–37, 170; governance, 8; government, 57, 135, 137, 222, 252; international, 3, 286, 317; market, 123–24; metropolitan, 18, 54–55, 290; political, 65, 348; post-independence, 88; public, 195, 335; societal, 289, 305; welfare, 22
Integrated Development Plan (IDP), 148, 243, 248, 251, 253, 320
international relations, 2, 4, 7, 286, 332, 339

Joburg 2010. See *iGoli 2010*
Joburg 2030, 36, 56, 143–45, 152–64 passim, 320; as city discourse, 234, 238, 243, 248–53
Johannesburg: fiscal crisis, 54, 143–44, 147, 151, 156; literature, 34–36

languages: Johannesburg, 28, 32–33; Mumbai/Bombay, 73, 169, 174, 234, 261–62, 325; São Paulo, 332; Shanghai, 296, 301
Latin America(n), 30, 202, 282–83, 332, 342
local autonomy, 113, 123, 147
local politics, 161, 207–8, 214–15, 227–28, 287, 320–21, 336
Lujiazui (Financial District), 30, 124, 129, 307, 341

Maharashtra State, 65–66, 68–69, 81n7, 136, 170–71, 258–60, 325–26
marginal population, 45, 272
market logic, 207
Master Plan, Strategic (São Paulo), 92, 196–99, 234–35, 333–34; debate on, 286–292
Mercosul, 86, 109–10, 282, 332
middle-income country, 139, 156
migrant workers (Shanghai), 131, 344, 346, 353n6

migration, 29; circular, 42, 45; Johannesburg, 38–39, 42; Mumbai, 68–69; São Paulo, 93, 97; Shanghai, 125–26, 131, 297; temporary, 125
modernity, 73, 265–67, 283–84
multinational corporations. *See* transnational corporations
Mumbai/Bombay: naming, 168, 258–61, 327; organized crime, 177, 266; textile industry, 68–72, 75, 263–64, 323–24, 326, 328
Mumbai Metropolitan Region (MMR), 65–67, 72, 81n5–7, 168–69
Mumbai Metropolitan Region Development Authority (MMRDA), 66, 81n5–6, 170, 324–25
Municipal Corporation of Greater Mumbai (MCGM), 66–67
Muslim(s), 169, 173–79, 263, 268–71, 328

National Congress Party (NCP) (India), 171, 182, 270–71, 274
national context, 1, 10, 12; Shanghai, 117, 120
national government, 4, 10, 141, 339, 347; India, 172, 263, 241; South Africa, 39, 58, 146–48, 156, 239, 241
national politics: China, 118; India, 68
nation state. *See* state
Navi Mumbai/New Bombay, 70, 72, 171, 176, 341
negotiation, sites of, 143
neo-apartheid, 46
neoliberal city, 228
neoliberal discourse, 189
neoliberal framework, 196
neoliberalism, 98–100, 189, 228, 237, 254
neoliberal policies, 85, 99–100, 108, 188, 200, 239, 332
New Bombay. *See* Navi Mumbai/New Bombay

OECD, 12–13, 16, 21–22, 27, 111n5
open cities, 120, 298, 339
operação urbana. *See* urban operations
outsourcing, 242, 247, 328

participation, 135, 138, 143, 290–91, 345; business, 74, 152; citizen, 250, 306, 347–48; civil society, 142, 187, 190, 197–99, 203; community, 262, 273; contradictions, 155, 162; marginalized groups, 136, 187; mass, 179, new instruments, 349; planning, 104, 106; public (popular), 148–50, 155, 194, 226, 286; quality of, 153–54; women, 45
participatory process, 136, 143, 145, 153–54, 192, 203, 333
Partido dos Trabalhadores (PT), 108, 137, 196, 283–86 passim, 292, 347
"patchwork city," 348, 350
patchwork politics, 9
Pearl River Delta, 116, 121, 208
periphery: global, 135, 139, 141, 162, 209, 228, 279; Johannesburg, 48; São Paulo, 87, 94–96, 189, 200, 287–88, 291–92, 334; semiperiphery, 13, 228, 341, 345; urban, 126, 280, 334
planning, 48, 107–8, 212; comprehensive, 30, 103, 160, 186–89, 209–10; decentralized, 336–37; development, 30, 103; economic, 240, 250, 324; fragmented, 190, 195, 198, 291; medium-term, 141, 143, 148, 170; new, 106, 146–49 passim, 202–3, 286–87, 324; participatory, 197, 286; sectoral, 103, 189; strategic, 30, 99, 104, 141, 186–90, 287–88, 333; symbolic, 251; town, 44, 72, 147; urban, 186, 197, 248, 285, 324, 336, 343
Plano Real. *See under* Brazil
polarization, class, 176; ideological, 259; labor market, 280; social, 35, 279, 281; socioeconomic, 29, 285, 344

post-apartheid, 19, 42, 48, 136, 139, 140, 142, 143, 144, 148, 156, 160, 237, 239, 240
post-etatist global configuration, 8
post-Fordist city, 222
post-Fordist industries, 207
postmodern, 64, 139, 168, 176, 184, 267, 327
postmodernity, 266–67
post-socialism. *See under* China
post-Westphalian: era, 339; world, 11
poverty reduction, 148, 159
power: formal and informal, 19, 136, 168–69, 196, 225, 347–48; forums of, 136–38, 140–43, 146, 162–63; patterns of, 136, 162, 170, 180; structures, 19, 136–37, 177–78, 183, 186–88, 195–96, 208–9
privatization, 351; infrastructure, 102, 108, 127, 192; Johannesburg, 144, 150–51, 160–61; Mumbai/Bombay, 80; of public space, 58; resistance to, 242, 247–49; São Paulo, 100; services, 108, 213; Shanghai, 113, 210
property rights, 126, 192, 215, 221
public participation. *See* participation; participation: public (popular)
public sector, 66, 80, 136, 190, 193, 201–2, 226, 287
public services. *See* services, public
public space, 268, 287; abandonment, 281; creation of, 199, 252; increasing of, 333; privatization of, 58; restoration of, 273; shared, 351
public sphere, 260, 262, 267
Pudong (New Area), 30, 119, 122, 128, 130, 210, 213, 217, 219, 220, 221, 223, 224, 297, 299, 302, 336, 341, 346

quality of life, 233; Johannesburg, 246, 249, 250, 254, 283, 285, 287; Mumbai/Bombay, 273; Shanghai, 131, 307, 337

Reconstruction and Development Programme (RDP), 161, 241
religion, 173–74, 179, 234, 261, 325
resettlement (Shanghai), 126
residents' committee (Shanghai), 213–14, 304–6, 314n5

Sandton, 32, 34, 44–45, 54, 151, 341
São Paulo: *bandeiras*, 88–89; Metro, 94–96, 102, 108; subprefectures (São Paulo), 105–6, 196–97, 203, 285
São Paulo Metropolitan Region (RMSP), 97, 102, 105–6, 186, 195, 340, 347–48
security, 8; Johannesburg, 47, 57–58, 152; Mumbai/Bombay, 181; private, 201, 204; São Paulo, 281–82, 334; Shanghai, 226; social, 304–5; of tenure, 76
segregation, 37, 43–45, 53, 94, 235, 240–41, 281, 291–93
Semana de '22, 90
services: banking, 74, 114, 263, 264, 272; basic, 8, 146–48, 234, 244, 344, 351; financial, 50, 74, 87, 264, 272, 324; global, 23n14, 123; IT, 74, 263, 272, 324, 341; media, 65, 341; privatized, 54, 189, 191, 247; producer, 73, 75, 114, 123, 221, 337, 341; public, 108, 191–94 passim, 238–39, 245, 253, 351; urban, 47, 53, 216, 285, 290, 344
Shanghai: city district(s), 137, 304; city spirit, 306, 308, 313
Shanghai Metropolitan Area, 117, 118, 125
Shiv Sena, 78–79, 169–72 passim, 178–83, 235, 259–74 passim, 325
skills development, 56, 152, 158, 160, 249, 253; Johannesburg, 36, 245, 349; São Paulo, 267, 290; Shanghai, 30, 113, 117, 125, 131, 301, 349

slums, 29, 64, 70, 76–79, 179–81, 267, 325–27, 344
"small government, big society," 213, 304, 313
socialist city, 210, 235, 299
South Africa: Anglo-Boer War, 37; Group Areas Act, 151; transition period, 44
South America, 15–17, 29, 85, 110, 235, 348
"Southern contenders," 22, 339, 342
sovereignty, 2, 4
Soweto, 39, 43, 48, 151
space: civil, 269, 271; green, 308, 337; urban, 30, 94, 128, 225, 280–84 passim, 292. *See also* public space
spatial reorganization, 29, 72, 208
Special Economic Zones (SEZs), 298, 323
state: devolution of, 1, 148, 221; postmodern, 139; reterritorialization of, 137, 214, 226; role of, 208, 228
state-work unit(s), 209–10, 212–13, 224, 226
Statute of the City (São Paulo), 105–6, 137, 192, 196, 198, 288–91
Steering Committee (Johannesburg), 145, 149–54 passim, 157
stock exchange, 16, 341; Johannesburg, 45; Mumbai/Bombay, 69, 74, 80, 324; São Paulo, 282; Shanghai, 119, 124, 129, 216–17, 224
strategies: city marketing, 233–34; development, 254; different, 345–46, 350–51; in the economic periphery, 286; for inclusion, 234; in reaction to globalization, 1, 5–6, 10–11, 345–46. *See also* City Development Strategy; *iGoli 2002*; *iGoli 2010*; Johannesburg
street office (Shanghai), 212–14, 222, 225, 304–6
sustainability, 156, 158, 351

tertiarization, 106–7, 340
tourism, 50–51, 72, 74, 251, 283, 332, 336
townships, 28, 40–47 passim, 53–55, 58, 237, 344; development, 158
trade unions, 39, 73, 75, 235, 242, 264, 323, 327–28
transdisciplinary approach, 18
Transformation *Lekgotla* (Johannesburg), 143, 147, 149–50, 156, 159, 163n11
transnational corporations, 5, 194, 266, 279, 281, 283, 298, 341

unemployment, 27, 34; Johannesburg, 43, 49, 240–41, 251, 352n5; Mumbai/Bombay, 75, 80, 352n5; São Paulo, 107, 212, 280–84 passim, 334, 352n5
unit of analysis, 4, 66
urban economy, 30, 50, 124, 335
urbanization, 13, 64, 86, 93, 96–98, 141, 169, 286–88, 331
urban management, 141, 149, 156, 187, 203, 291, 304
urban operations (São Paulo), 104–6, 193, 196–201 passim, 285, 333
urban politics, 58, 140, 163, 171–72, 207
urban renewal, 37, 201, 285

violence: Johannesburg, 47, 56, 57; Mumbai/Bombay, 175, 177, 179, 260, 262; São Paulo, 200, 204, 281, 282, 290
vision, 19, 233–36; Johannesburg, 56, 141, 148, 157, 238, 243, 248–54, 319; Mumbai/Bombay, 259–61, 325; São Paulo, 108, 282–87, 290–91, 333; Shanghai, 129–30, 226, 295, 308–14; shared, 236, 351
Vision 2030. See *Joburg 2030*

Witwatersrand, 40, 151
Workers Party (Brazil). See Partido dos Trabalhadores (PT)

World Bank, 3, 78, 81n6, 144–45, 156, 322
world-class city: discourse, 234, 237, 242, 248–50, 254; Johannesburg, 19, 21, 55, 141, 234, 319, 348–50; Shanghai, 309, 313, 350
world politics. *See* global politics

Yangtze River Delta, 208, 211, 221, 335–37

zoning: Johannesburg, 44, 147; Mumbai/Bombay, 326; São Paulo, 188, 193, 285, 289, 333; Shanghai, 225, 298